Marginal People in Deviant Places

MARGINAL PEOPLE
IN DEVIANT PLACES

*Ethnography, Difference,
and the Challenge
to Scientific Racism*

Janice M. Irvine

University of Michigan Press
Ann Arbor

Copyright © 2022 by Janice M. Irvine
Some rights reserved

[CC BY-NC-ND]

This work is licensed under a Creative Commons Attribution-NoDerivatives 4.0 International License. *Note to users*: A Creative Commons license is only valid when it is applied by the person or entity that holds rights to the licensed work. Works may contain components (e.g., photographs, illustrations, or quotations) to which the rightsholder in the work cannot apply the license. It is ultimately your responsibility to independently evaluate the copyright status of any work or component part of a work you use, in light of your intended use. To view a copy of this license, visit http://creativecommons.org/licenses/by-nc-nd/4.0/

For questions or permissions, please contact um.press.perms@umich.edu

Published in the United States of America by the
University of Michigan Press
Manufactured in the United States of America
Printed on acid-free paper
First published July 2022

A CIP catalog record for this book is available from the British Library.

Library of Congress Cataloging-in-Publication data has been applied for.
ISBN 978-0-472-05538-8 (paper : alk. paper)
ISBN 978-0-472-90265-1 (OA)

DOI: https://doi.org/10.3998/mpub.11519906

*To Marsha Burke, my sister, and co-traveler through a marginal past.
And to my Portland friends, who welcomed a stranger.*

Contents

List of Illustrations	ix
Acknowledgments	xix
Preface	xxiii
ONE Introduction	1
TWO Making Up Hobos: Nels Anderson and Other Tramp Tales	26
THREE *The Taxi-Dance Hall*: Paul Cressey's Ambivalence	70
FOUR Zora's Florida: Ethnographic Explorations of Zora Neale Hurston	102
FIVE Asylum Stories	141
SIX *Tearoom Trade*: Tales of Public Sex	169
SEVEN District for Deviants: Sherri Cavan's *Hippies of the Haight*	204
EIGHT Conclusion	252
Notes	267
Index	303

Digital materials related to this title can be found on the Fulcrum platform via the following citable URL: https://doi.org/10.3998/mpub.11519906

Illustrations

Note: Figures not identified with a page number can be found on the Fulcrum platform at https://doi.org/10.3998/mpub.11519906

Preface

Figure 1. Howard Becker, piano, performing at the 504 Club in Chicago, circa 1950. xxiv
Figure 2. *Mad* magazine cover, December, 1971. Available on Fulcrum.
Figure 3. Zora Neale Hurston collecting folklore, late 1930s. Available on Fulcrum.
Figure 4. Early gay pride march, Mattachine Society of New York. Available on Fulcrum.
Figure 5. Columbia University sociologist C. Wright Mills. Available on Fulcrum.
Figure 6. Center Building, St. Elizabeths Hospital in Washington, D.C., circa 1900. xxx
Figure 7. Lobby card for the 1927 film *The Taxi Dancer*. Available on Fulcrum.

Chapter 1

Figure 8. Book cover, *Must You Conform?* by Robert Lindner, 1956. Available on Fulcrum.

Figure 9. Ernest Burgess course notes for Social Pathology, October 4, 1927. Available on Fulcrum.

Figure 10. Cesare Lombroso, six figures illustrating types of criminals, 1888. Available on Fulcrum.

Figure 11. W. E. B. Du Bois in his office, circa 1948. Available on Fulcrum.

Figure 12. Georg Simmel, circa 1901. Available on Fulcrum.

Figure 13. Industrial Workers of the World (IWW) demonstration, New York City. Available on Fulcrum.

Figure 14. Federal Bureau of Investigation, American Sociological Association, September 14, 1965. Washington, DC: FBI Freedom of Information—Privacy Acts Section. 14

Figure 15. Street signs marking the intersection of Haight and Ashbury Streets in San Francisco. Available on Fulcrum.

Figure 16. "Urban Areas," map illustrating the growth of cities. 18

Figure 17. The sleeping porch in the Allison Building at St. Elizabeths Hospital, Washington, DC. Available on Fulcrum.

Figure 18. Israel Levin Senior Center, December 2018. Available on Fulcrum.

Figure 19 *Marginal People in Deviant Places*. Map by Janice M. Irvine ©. Artist, Molly Brown, South Portland, Maine. 25

Chapter 2

Figure 20. The National Hobo Museum, at the former Chief Movie Theatre on Main Street, Britt, Iowa. Available on Fulcrum.

Figure 21. *The Hobo*, by Nels Anderson. 28

Figure 22. More than twenty-five years a bindle stiff. Photograph by Dorothea Lange, 1938. 31

Figure 23. Advertisement for the book, *The Hobo*, from the University of Chicago Press. Available on Fulcrum.

Figure 24. Lou Ambers with a large bag mounting a train. Photograph by Alan Fisher, 1935. Available on Fulcrum.

Figure 25. Front page of *The Adventures of a Female Tramp*, 1914, by hobo writer A-No. 1. Available on Fulcrum.

Figure 26. Downtown Chicago intersection in the late
   nineteenth century, congested with horses, carts, carriages,
   and train cars. Available on Fulcrum.
Figure 27. Chicago Gangland, 1927. Created by University of
   Chicago sociologist Frederic Milton Thrasher for his book
   The Gang: A Study of 1,313 Gangs in Chicago. 47
Figure 28. Nels Anderson included samples of menus from
   restaurants in hobohemian. From *The Hobo: The Sociology of
   the Homeless Man*, 1923. Available on Fulcrum.
Figure 29. Century-old hobo graffiti found by anthropologist
   Susan Phillips under a concrete bridge of the L.A. River. 48
Figure 30. Lou Ambers cooking over a campfire, using a
   tin can on a stick. Available on Fulcrum.
Figure 31. A squatter in Chicago, named Blackie, reading
   a newspaper in the type of living area Nels Anderson referred
   to as a hobo jungle. Available on Fulcrum.
Figure 32. A boxcar located at the hobo jungle on Diagonal,
   one block off Main Street in Britt, Iowa. Available on Fulcrum.
Figure 33. Russel-Morgan print of a tramp smoking cigar with
   cane over his arm, 1899. Available on Fulcrum.
Figure 34. Charlie Chaplin as the Tramp. Available on Fulcrum.
Figure 35. Physician and occasional hobo, Ben Reitman. From
   The Hobo: The Sociology of the Homeless Man, 1923. Available
   on Fulcrum.
Figure 36. A poster by the International Brotherhood Welfare
   Association advertising a hobo rally and lecture entitled
   "The Hobo and His Welfare," with Dr. Ben Reitman and
   James Eads How. Available on Fulcrum.
Figure 37. Industrial Workers of the World, "The Little Red Song
   Book," 1918. Available on Fulcrum.
Figure 38. Publicity photograph of Charlie Chaplin for the
   film *Modern Times*, 1936. Available on Fulcrum.
Figure 39. Toward Los Angeles, 1937. 57
Figure 40. Century-old hobo graffiti under a concrete bridge of
   the L.A. River. Available on Fulcrum.

Chapter 3

Figure 41. Film poster for 1931 Lionel Barrymore production,
   Ten Cents a Dance, starring Barbara Stanwyck. Available
   on Fulcrum.

Figure 42. Chicago sex work establishments during the Prohibition era, 1920–1933. 72

Figure 43. A photograph of Jane Addams, cofounder of Hull House, in Chicago, was included in a gallery of Keepers of the Faith. Available on Fulcrum.

Figure 44. Book cover of Hull House associate Louise DeKoven Bowen, *The Public Dance Halls of Chicago*. Available on Fulcrum.

Figure 45. Cover of antidance treatise, *From the Ball-room to Hell*, 1892. Available on Fulcrum.

Figure 46. Road map of Chicago and vicinity, produced by Cities Service Oil Company, 1937. Available on Fulcrum.

Figure 47. This Knights Templar postcard, of the 31st Triennial Conclave "Welcome" sign, held in Chicago, August, 1910. 78

Figure 48. System of Chicago Surface Lines, 1929. Available on Fulcrum.

Figure 49. On the dance floor, 1938. Available on Fulcrum.

Figure 50. The Migration of Negroes, 1890, *The Georgia Negro*. Available on Fulcrum.

Figure 51. Nationalities Map No. 1—Polk Street to Twelfth, Halsted Street to Jefferson, Chicago. Available on Fulcrum.

Figure 52. Paul Cressey's map for *The Taxi-Dance Hall* text, "From Where They Come in the City." Available on Fulcrum.

Figure 53. Paul Cressey's base map of Chicago, marking the locations of taxi-dance halls licensed in 1927. Available on Fulcrum.

Figure 54. Moral crusades against taxi-dance halls in Chicago and other regions of the United States were widely reported in newspapers. Available on Fulcrum.

Figure 55. *The Social Dance* book cover, 1921. An antidance treatise by Dr. R. A. Adams that argues that dancing is both immoral and physically unhealthy. Available on Fulcrum.

Figure 56. Paul Cressey's book on taxi-dance halls received widespread coverage in the Chicago newspapers. Available on Fulcrum.

Figure 57. A taxi dancer responded to the flurry of news coverage about Paul Cressey's book, *The Taxi-Dance Hall*. Available on Fulcrum.

Figure 58. Book cover, *Taxi Dancers*, by Eve Linkletter, 1958. Available on Fulcrum.

Illustrations   xiii

Figure 59. Excerpt from Paul Cressey's field notes in which he discussed seeing the book (which he misspelled) *The Well of Loneliness*. Available on Fulcrum.

Figure 60. Book cover, *The Well of Loneliness*, by Radclyffe Hall. Available on Fulcrum.

Chapter 4

Figure 61. Road map of Florida, 1938. Available on Fulcrum.

Figure 62. Zora Neale Hurston and an unidentified man, probably at a recording site in Belle Glade, Florida, 1935. Available on Fulcrum.

Figure 63. Commemorative plaque celebrating Hurston as "Eatonville's Daughter," at the Zora Neale Hurston National Museum. Available on Fulcrum.

Figure 64. Zora Neale Hurston as a student at Howard University, 1919–23.   106

Figure 65. Zora Neale Hurston and three boys, in Eatonville, Florida, 1935. Available on Fulcrum.

Figure 66. Zora Neale Hurston, half-length portrait, at the Florida Writers' Project exhibit, at the *New York Times* Book Fair, 1938. Available on Fulcrum.

Figure 67. *Florida: A Guide to the Southernmost State*. Compiled and written by the Federal Writers' Project of the Work Projects Administration for the State of Florida, 1940. Available on Fulcrum.

Figure 68. Segregation at the bus station in Durham, North Carolina, 1940. Photographer, Jack Delano. Available on Fulcrum.

Figure 69. Notes taken by Stetson Kennedy on dialogue between Zora Neale Hurston and Dr. Carita Coree, director of the Florida Writers Project about reporting of the Ocoee Incident. Available on Fulcrum.

Figure 70. Zora Neale Hurston, with Rochelle French and Gabriel Brown, in Eatonville, Florida, 1935. Available on Fulcrum.

Figure 71. Phosphate mine in the Bone Valley Formation region. Available on Fulcrum.

Figure 72. Gulf, Florida & Alabama Railway Company turpentine camp, circa 1900.   115

xiv *Illustrations*

Figure 73. Zora Neale Hurston, smoking a cigarette, at the Aycock and Lindsay turpentine camp, Cross City, Florida, 1939. Available on Fulcrum.

Figure 74. Zora Hurston's manuscript, "Cross City: Turpentine Camp," written after her visit to the Aycock & Lindsay turpentine camp, 1939. Available on Fulcrum.

Figure 75. Burned, typewritten title page of Hurston's article, "Florida's Migrant Farm Labor." 119

Figure 76. Newspaper advertisement for Negro dolls and the Negro Doll Company. Available on Fulcrum.

Figure 77. Cover of anthropologist Melville Herskovits's 1930 text, *The Anthropometry of the American Negro*. Available on Fulcrum.

Figure 78. Eugenics Society exhibit, 1930s, advising visitors to "Marry Wisely." Available on Fulcrum.

Figure 79. Flag, announcing lynching, flown from the window of the NAACP in New York City, 1936. Available on Fulcrum.

Figure 80. Florida and the Railroad Barons map shows the expansion of rail lines in Florida, which bolstered industrial expansion in areas such as phosphate mining, sugar production, and myriad fruit and vegetable products. Available on Fulcrum.

Figure 81. Trainman signaling from a Jim Crow coach, St. Augustine, Florida, 1943. Available on Fulcrum.

Figure 82. Zora Neale Hurston and her car, Cherry. Available on Fulcrum.

Figure 83. Cover of the *Negro Motorist Green Book*, by Victor Hugo Green, 1940 edition. Available on Fulcrum.

Figure 84. Dell's Café, Eatonville, Florida. Available on Fulcrum.

Figure 85. People dancing, probably from the Georgia, Florida, and Bahamas expedition, 1935. Available on Fulcrum.

Figure 86. Migratory laborers playing checkers in front of jook joint during slack season for vegetable pickers, Belle Glade, Florida, 1941.

Figure 87. Burned fragment from Hurston's papers expressing her frustration with Southern racism. Available on Fulcrum.

Figure 88. Letter from Zora Neale Hurston to W. E. B. Du Bois, June 11, 1965. Available on Fulcrum.

Figure 89. Zora Neale Hurston moved to this single-story, stucco house in Fort Pierce in 1957. Available on Fulcrum.

Figure 90. Zora Neale Hurston's weathered cemetery marker at

the Garden of Heavenly Rest Cemetery in Fort Pierce.
Available on Fulcrum.

Chapter 5

Figure 91. Hospital for the Insane of the Army and Navy and
the District of Columbia, 1860.   142
Figure 92. https://arcg.is/1KvXfG0. ArcGIS map.
Figure 93. Surveillance dog in action by the Department of
Homeland Security. Available on Fulcrum.
Figure 94. Erving Goffman's text, *Asylums*, 1961. Available
on Fulcrum.
Figure 95. St. Elizabeths Hospital, Washington, DC,
between 1909 and 1932.   145
Figure 96. Maps of St. Elizabeths Hospital, Washington, DC,
circa 1860. Available on Fulcrum.
Figure 97. The former Recreational Therapy Branch building
on the St. Elizabeths campus. Available on Fulcrum.
Figure 98. Two editions of the *Diagnostic and Statistical Manual*.
Available on Fulcrum.
Figure 99. David Rosenhan. Available on Fulcrum.
Figure 100. Original blueprint showing rendering of the Male
Receiving Building at St. Elizabeths Hospital in Washington, DC,
circa 1934. Available on Fulcrum.
Figure 101. African American patients eating in a segregated
dining hall in Building Q circa 1915. Available on Fulcrum.
Figure 102. Indian Asylum, Canton, South Dakota. Available
on Fulcrum.
Figure 103. Historical highway sign in South Dakota marking the
Hiawatha Asylum for Insane Indians. Available on Fulcrum.
Figure 104. The Burroughs Cottage on St. Elizabeths campus,
March, 2017. Available on Fulcrum.
Figure 105. Marion Chace launched dance therapy at St. Elizabeths
in 1942 and taught for several decades.   155
Figure 106. Ken Kesey in 1974. Available on Fulcrum.
Figure 107. The 1946 novel, *The Snake Pit*. Available on Fulcrum.
Figure 108. St. Elizabeths woman patient in a rocking chair.
Available on Fulcrum.

Figure 109. Advertisement for Haldol, the antipsychotic drug released in 1967. Available on Fulcrum.

Figure 110. Book cover of a reader compiling articles from *Madness Network News*. Available on Fulcrum.

Figure 111. Buildings remain closed and shuttered at St. Elizabeths Hospital, 2018. Available on Fulcrum.

Figure 112. Aerial view of St. Elizabeths Hospital, west campus. Available on Fulcrum.

Chapter 6

Figure 113. Sociologist Laud Humphreys. Available on Fulcrum.

Figure 114. Draft cover page of Laud Humphreys's dissertation. Available on Fulcrum.

Figure 115. Book cover of a 1975 enlarged edition of *Tearoom Trade: Impersonal Sex in Public Places*. 170

Figure 116. New York State Historic Site plaque at the Stonewall Inn on Christopher Street, New York City, marking the uprisings in June, 1969. Available on Fulcrum.

Figure 117. Laud Humphreys 1968 diary. Available on Fulcrum.

Figure 118. Systematic Observation Sheet developed and employed by Laud Humphreys in recording tearoom encounters. Available on Fulcrum.

Figure 119. Map of Forest Park indicating some of the restrooms that served as popular tearooms. Available on Fulcrum.

Figure 120. Map of the World's Fair in St. Louis, 1904, also known as the Louisiana Purchase Exposition. 178

Figure 121. One of the outdoor restrooms in Forest Park. 179

Figure 122. Men's restroom in the Minneapolis–St. Paul International Airport, where US Senator Larry Craig (R-Idaho) was arrested for lewd conduct. Available on Fulcrum.

Figure 123. Advertisement by Guild Book Service for the report, "Homosexuality and Citizenship in Florida." Available on Fulcrum.

Figure 124. Photograph of an apparent tearoom sexual encounter. Available on Fulcrum.

Figure 125. Book cover of the fiftieth-anniversary edition of *City of Night*, by John Rechy, originally published in 1963. Available on Fulcrum.

Figure 126. Laud Humphreys autographed a first edition of *Tearoom Trade* to his friend and colleague, sociologist Carol Warren. Available on Fulcrum.

Figure 127. The physical altercation between Laud Humphreys and Alvin Gouldner was covered by the *New York Times*, headlined, "Sociology Professor Accused of Beating Student." June 9, 1968. Available on Fulcrum.

Figure 128. Laud Humphreys's diary entries from May 20–21, 1968. Available on Fulcrum.

Figure 129. Sociologist and activist Mary McIntosh. Available on Fulcrum.

Figure 130. Photograph of a glory hole published in a gay magazine. Available on Fulcrum.

Chapter 7

Figure 131. Traffic heading toward the Woodstock Music & Art Fair, August 16, 1969. Available on Fulcrum.

Figure 132. Book cover, Sherri Cavan's *Hippies of the Haight*. Available on Fulcrum.

Figure 133. Cover of the first issue of the men's magazine *Playboy*, December 1953. Available on Fulcrum.

Figure 134. Cover of the *Saturday Evening Post*, September 23, 1967, which ran writer Joan Didion's famous article, "Slouching Towards Bethlehem." 212

Figure 135. The Death of Hippie funeral notice, scheduled in Haight Ashbury for October 6, 1967, attributed the hippie's death to mass media. Available on Fulcrum.

Figure 136. Sociologist Sherri Cavan at her home in Haight Ashbury stands in front of some of her sculptures, 2014. 215

Figure 137. Street signs mark the famous intersection of Haight Street and Ashbury Street in San Francisco. Available on Fulcrum.

Figure 138. 1967 Screen print of San Francisco represents the city's art and music scene. Available on Fulcrum.

Figure 139. Sherri Cavan's house on Page Street in 2014. Available on Fulcrum.

Figure 140. Hippie is a Straight Theater Celebration, 1967. Available on Fulcrum.

Figure 141. Hippie is making mandalas, 1967. Available on Fulcrum.

Figure 142. Tourists peer out a bus window on the Gray Line bus company's "Hippie Tour," 1967. Available on Fulcrum.
Figure 143. Hippies with marijuana stash in an apartment, 1969. Available on Fulcrum.
Figure 144. The Jimi Hendrix Red House, Haight Ashbury. Available on Fulcrum.
Figure 145. Janis Joplin performing in 1969. Available on Fulcrum.
Figure 146. Hippie is salesmanship, 1967. Available on Fulcrum.
Figure 147. Hippie is getting busted. Available on Fulcrum.
Figure 148. Newspaper article reporting the Death of Hippies ceremony at Buena Vista Park, 1967. *San Francisco Chronicle*. Available on Fulcrum.
Figure 149. Haight Ashbury continues to attract tourists to shops commercializing the region's hippie history. Available on Fulcrum.
Figure 150. *Life Magazine* cover depiction of the new youth communes as a confrontation with the United States. 237

Conclusion

Figure 151. *Number Our Days* book cover. Available on Fulcrum.
Figure 152. Barbara Myerhoff, with members of the Israel Levin Senior Adult Center. 253
Figure 153. Israel Levin Senior Adult Center. Available on Fulcrum.
Figure 154. Colorful murals on Israel Levin Senior Adult Center. Available on Fulcrum.
Figure 155. Gathering Place on the Bench. Available on Fulcrum.
Figure 156. Life Not Death in Venice protest. Available on Fulcrum.
Figure 157. K.O.S. protest. 256
Figure 158. Act Up members engage in street protest, circa late 1980s. Available on Fulcrum.
Figure 159. Queer and Queer Nation. Available on Fulcrum.
Figure 160. Senior Center demolition. Available on Fulcrum.
Figure 161. Bench outside Israel Levin Senior Adult Center, December, 2018.

Acknowledgments

Writing about deviants is exciting. Until it isn't. On the one hand, this has been the most fun I've ever had doing research. It involved my favorite activities: travel, exploring archives, and talking to people. This project deepened my recognition of how my life has been so profoundly constructed by knowledge, art, and politics by, and about, those of us on the social margins. On the other hand, this book brought more than its share of heartache. For one thing, people died. The news, by email or word of mouth, that one of my interviewees had died brought a lingering sadness. This was a historical project, and poring over obituaries and reports of memorial services for an earlier generation of scholars kindled a new poignancy about their lives and work. This bittersweet reminder that I, too, am simply a small part of a longer tradition of rethinking difference led me to locate myself on the map of scholars and our research places that I designed for this book. Additionally, it is an understatement to note that immersion in histories of relentless racism, sexism, and homophobia was painful. The persistence of bias, injustice, and stigma toward unconventional ways of living and unconventional forms of knowledge is dispiriting and enraging.

This project would not have become a book without Sara Cohen. It was an easy decision to follow her to the University of Michigan Press after our several years of rich collaboration at Temple University Press. I'm grateful for her unwavering faith in this book and my writing process, for her incisive comments on multiple drafts, and for generally putting up with me. Many thanks to University of Michigan Press for producing a beautiful book. Likewise, I was lucky to have two anonymous reviewers whose very smart comments made this a better book.

It has always amazed me how generous people are with their time and memories when they agree to do interviews! Many thanks to the numerous scholars, artists, and activists who agreed to talk with me, and to those who participated in video interviews. Your insights and stories lent depth and nuance to my thinking about the texts, places, and time periods I've explored in this book. Every interview was a powerful reminder of the interconnectedness of personal and historical dimensions in the production of knowledge about social difference.

I received crucial institutional support for this project from several sources. Many thanks to the American Sociological Association for a grant from their Fund for the Advancement of the Discipline, and to the University of Massachusetts for a Social and Behavior Sciences Faculty Research Grant. A stipend and digital support from the University of Massachusetts's Innovate program supported a very early pilot chapter, "Asylum Stories," built as an Open Educational Resource on the Scalar platform. I'm deeply grateful to Michele Turre, our uber-competent senior instructional technologist, for her "assistance" on that project, which basically consisted of her building everything while I sat next to her, watching. Likewise, I received crucial digital support from UMass Amherst IT, Instructional Innovation. The UMass SOAR Fund and the College of Social and Behavior Sciences offset the subvention cost necessary for publication. In our year-long seminar in the Institute for Social Science Research Scholars Program, faculty members, particularly cofacilitators Naomi Gerstel and Laurel Smith-Doerr, provided helpful feedback on tender, early drafts. Laurel's enduring enthusiasm for my work helped me think this deviant project was viable. Finally, the Conti Fellowship from UMass was an unexpected and welcome gift of release time for a year-long focus on research and writing.

The cover image, *Untitled* 1987, is by the Australian artist, poet, and mental health advocate Graeme Doyle (1947–2021). Doyle's art is held in The Cunningham Dax Collection, Melbourne, Australia, which notes that Doyle, who experienced a long-term struggle with mental illness, "identified himself as an 'outsider artist,' intentionally acknowledging his position on the margins." Doyle's outsider art, which depicts complexity and stigma related to mental illness, resonates powerfully with this book's themes of outsiders, marginality, and difference. Many thanks to Julia Young at the Dax Centre, who facilitated permission to feature Doyle's painting on the cover.

A huge shout-out to archivists and librarians! The interlibrary loan staff at UMass delivered at warp-speed the vast range of sometimes-obscure materials I requested over the years. I worked in several special collections, and I'm grateful for the friendly efficiency of the many archivists there: the University of Chicago, the London School of Economics, Northeastern University, the University of Southern California, the New York City Public Library, the University of Florida, the University of Massachusetts, and ONE National Gay & Lesbian Archives. Thanks also to Sarah Leavitt, curator at the National Building Museum, for helpful conversations about St. Elizabeths and comments on an early draft chapter. My last research trip unfolded, and unraveled, in Florida during the week of March 9, 2020. When it became clear I would have to change my flight and go home early, I rushed to the University of Florida special collections a day ahead of schedule. Many thanks to Flo Turcotte, literary manuscripts archivist, for rearranging her schedule to come to the library to chat about Zora Neale Hurston and facilitate my collection of digital images. It was the day the World Health Organization declared the COVID-19 outbreak a pandemic, and Flo was the last archivist I spoke with in person for a very long time.

Finishing a book in a pandemic was, well, basically like doing anything else in a pandemic—scary and hard. Several months into lockdown, with pretty much everywhere, including UMass, closed, I left Northampton, Massachusetts, and moved to Portland, Maine. For many months I was lost, in every sense of that word. I mourned the sudden absence of local friends and colleagues, and was untethered from institutional resources. I'm grateful to fellow sociologist Wendy Chapkis at the University of Southern Maine for academic collegiality, friendship, and for directing me to the phenomenal Osher Map Library at USM. Executive Director Libby Bischof and Osher Professor Matthew Edney were welcoming and generous on my first pandemic-era visit back to an academic space. Libby and Matthew, along with Bob Spencer and Louis Miller, located and then produced high-resolution scans of several fabulous maps in this book. Thank you all for your kindness to a displaced scholar!

Portland offered additional supports, in ways unexpected and moving. For one, soon after arriving there, I decided to create a graphic representation of all my research sites. Although I brainstormed ideas for this conceptual map, I had no idea how to artistically render such a thing. Unexpectedly, I found an artist who is also a geographer! I'm exceedingly grateful to Molly Brown, of MollyMaps in South Portland, for her collaboration in turning my fantasy map into reality. Colleen Bedard also gave me helpful artistic advice during my early mapmaking foray. Additionally, after a chance conversation on a freezing, masked, January Meetup beach walk, Barbara Cray generously volunteered to edit my videos for me (Sara Cohen heroically picked up the ball at the end.) Finally, my new Portland friends regularly asked how the book was going, fed me, patiently explained my new city and state to me, and invited me to that classic Maine cultural experience, "camp."

Then there are the other all-important people. Like many academics, my intellectual webs traverse state and national borders. Without naming them all, I newly appreciate, in their abrupt dislocation during the pandemic, how ambient connections to broader intellectual conversations shape our work. Zoom and Skype helped them endure. In different ways, my closer circle of scholars has strengthened this work and kept me sane-ish: Kathy Davis, Arlene Stein, Regina Kunzel, Katie Young, Jackie Urla, Sarah Babb, Jen Lundquist, and Jon Wynn. Finally, Barbara Cruikshank, along with everything else, helps me remember myself as a scholar. You have all talked me through this project's broader frameworks and finer points of analysis, the roller-coaster of thinking and writing, and life's pleasures and vicissitudes during ten years of research. Just knowing you are out there has made all the difference.

Preface

> We tell ourselves stories in order to live. We interpret what we see, select the most workable of the multiple choices.[1]
>
> Joan Didion

In mid-twentieth-century publishing, "the outsider" arrived. Four books—all similarly entitled "outsider"—highlighted a robust cultural visibility of, and curiosity about, those who defied social convention. During the McCarthy-era Red Scare, the Harlem Renaissance writer Richard Wright explored themes of racism, segregation, and the American Communist Party in his 1953 novel *The Outsider*. The 1956 book by working-class English writer Colin Wilson, *The Outsider*, surprised everyone, including the author, by becoming an instant bestseller. Heralded as capturing "a representative theme of our time . . . of our deepest predicament," the book explored writers who fled a "cow-like" herd mentality to seek a deeper existential truth.[2] S. E. Hinton's novel a decade later, *The Outsiders*, about marginalized, working-class teenage "greasers," inspired a film adaption by Francis Ford Coppola. Recently, actor and writer Lena Dunham wrote that "over 50 years later" *The Outsiders* "has never felt more relevant—or true."[3] Finally, sociologist Howard Becker's 1963 essays featuring dance musicians, *Outsiders*, helped turn the social science of difference on its head.[4] It was the century of the outsider.

These authors wrote against the grain of Cold War, midcentury conformity. They all described themselves as outsiders, and their characters struck similar chords in their critique of social conventionality. Richard

Howard Becker, piano, performing at the 504 Club in Chicago, circa 1950. Courtesy of Howard Becker.

Wright's outsider, Cross Damon, represented "a black man's attempted escape from stable, essentialist forms of identity, including race."[5] Colin Wilson celebrated the alienation of his artistic outsiders, Hinton's gentle juvenile delinquents overcame the stigma of poverty to become heroes, and Becker indicted those who made and enforced social rules, thereby creating "outsiders" of his then-edgy marijuana-smoking musicians. And yet, as suggested by the almost simultaneous publication of these books, the outsider theme already had an enduring cultural presence. From the turn of the twentieth century, social marginality had been growing increasingly visible, whether through hierarchies of racial, national, gender, or economic inequality, or as the margins chosen by bohemians and political radicals. Paradoxically, outsiders were also, well, popular! At least, some of them were. And discovering which outsiders could be marketed and sold would become central to what I call "outsider capitalism."

Together, sociology, popular culture, political activism, and even the process of commodification all reflected and produced this zeitgeist of the outsider. As literary critic Carla Cappetti has argued, urban sociologists and novelists "intellectually rubbed elbows" and served as reference points for each other.⁶ University of Chicago sociologists had a direct impact on the novels of key early-twentieth-century writers such as Richard Wright, James T. Farrell, and Nelson Algren. Conversely, Roger Salerno dubs the work of Chicago School scholars "sociology noir" for its overlapping sensibilities with noir popular culture.⁷ In addition, emerging forms of technology enabled innovative cultural production such as television, film, and photography. For example, mid-twentieth-century photographer Diane Arbus notoriously challenged positivist and eugenic theories of knowledge and scientific categorization within documentary photography and celebrity portraits, with her conceptual reversals of the freakish and the normal.⁸ *Mad* magazine, founded in 1952, fostered a new deviant aesthetic of quirky, outsider critique. Alfred E. Neuman (the E stands for Enigma) helped a generation of young people develop a posture of snarky wit. These myriad outsider stories intertwined to make visible the perils, pleasures, and politics of difference.

This, too, is a book about outsiders. It explores cultural ideas about strangers, marginality, deviance, and differences. The social-scientific knowledge production about difference is its central theme. I explore different stories we tell about differences, and how those have changed, and not changed, over time. When this book begins, in the early twentieth century, race science produced the dominant narratives about human variations. Biological theories of difference produced a narrative othering that produced and reinforced caste hierarchies of race, ethnicity, gender, sexuality, social class, mental status, age, and other variations. Discourses on nature and biology framed otherwise benign human differences as unnatural, deficient, and even dangerous.

In contrast, during this same period, some social scientists reconceptualized scientific knowledge, theoretical frameworks, and languages of human differences. They honed ethnographic practices to capture the diverse worlds of differences and outsiders, and of the places they inhabited. They rewrote social knowledge about differences, against the individualizing pathologies of scientific racism. Instead, these scholars told complex stories about social worlds of marginality, inequality, exclusion, and stigma, as well as vibrancy, creativity, and rebellion. They uncovered cultural logics in the social worlds of those who were nonconformist and different, and developed new ideas that blurred the boundaries between normalcy and deviance.

This book examines those early- to mid-twentieth-century redefinitions of difference. Each chapter is a time capsule, following a classic or little-known ethnographic text published between 1923 to 1978, or, in the case of anthropologist Zora Neale Hurston, a body of her ethnographic research in Florida. The book explores hobos and taxi dancers and their immigrant dance partners of early Chicago. It traverses the social worlds of rural, southern African Americans brought to life by Hurston. It journeys through the asylums inhabited by midcentury mental patients, the "tearooms" of men having public sex, and the Haight Ashbury hippie district. We end with elderly Eastern European Jewish immigrants at a Venice Beach senior center.

These snapshots of ethnographic knowledge production illuminate ways of knowing about difference in specific historical moments. In this book, I braid together the stories told by the ethnographic text with the metastory of how the story was crafted. These stories about the story explore the where, how, and when of the authors' projects, such as their methods, theoretical frameworks, and intellectual networks (or absence of them), as well as the challenges and support they encountered in their research. The historical, cultural, and political contexts—the experiences of researchers—influenced what stories could be told and who could tell them.

The chapters tell multifarious stories about modern outsiders, weaving the ethnographers' tales together with other sources of journalistic, artistic, and political evidence. As such, I tell my own stories of outsiders and outsider scholarship through the lens of these ethnographic texts. These tales depict textured, nuanced social worlds, with some common themes, such as norm defiance, boundary-crossing, hierarchies of bias and social worth, and stigma. They show how difference was lived in a daily way, including, in some cases, the differences of the scholars themselves.

Three interlaced themes weave throughout and organize the chapters. The central theme is a critical history of the making of social knowledge about difference, in which social researchers challenged the dominant narrative of scientific racism. A disparate cohort of early- to mid-twentieth-century scholars engaged with new social worlds, human differences, and emerging social types emblematic of modernity. Early social theorists and ethnographers, culminating with later sociologists of deviance, rewrote the stories of strangers and outsiders. The second major theme is a social history of certain American outsiders. I explore the types of stories social researchers told about overlapping domains of difference. These differences include intersections of race, class, gender, sexualities, and age. However, my conceptualization of difference is more capacious. It features a wide swath of social outsiders and marginal figures who arose in early to mid-twentieth-century modernity, such as hobos, taxi dancers, and hippies.

The third theme unites the first two by considering how specific places shaped the emergence of modern outsiders and the ethnographic writing about them.

Several subplots emerge within these central stories. One focuses on how social changes associated with modernity and capitalism gave rise to new forms of difference. A second explores a long-standing American paradox by which social differences are both despised and desired, and conformity is disdained yet enforced (I use the term "American paradox" because my focus in this book is largely on the United States, not because I am making an argument that this dynamic is uniquely American). A third explores the rise of an outsider capitalism that packaged and marketed social difference. Finally, we see how ethnographic stories of difference were entangled with those of artists, popular writers, and the political activism of outsiders themselves. These subplots appear when pertinent, and not all of them feature in every chapter.

There is a lot going on here. However, the multiple themes and threads underscore one of my key points. These ethnographic approaches to studying the social worlds of others opened up new questions and avenues for exploration—in this case, my own—rather than foreclosing curiosity with determinist explanations. In 1959, sociologist C. Wright Mills argued that we can only understand individuals, and this would certainly include strangers, outsiders, and deviants, by locating them within their specific social and cultural circumstances. Mills called this capacity to grasp the intersections of biography and history "the sociological imagination," a term we instantly embraced.[9] I have allowed myself the freedom to follow my own sociological imagination down the various paths that beckoned.

This book tells stories about stories that echo through the decades. Several overarching claims interconnect chapters. First, I argue that early social scientists—certain sociologists and cultural anthropologists—were crucial to an epistemic departure from the ideas of race science. Ethnography, and later sociological deviance studies, didn't change the master narrative of scientific racism. However, they represented a critical rupture to the cultural authority of scientific racism, producing new forms of social knowledge. By "critical rupture" I mean an interruption or a break from the past, in this case from the dominant knowledge production of race science.[10] Despite early ethnography's shortcomings—for example, its partial essentialism and exoticism—it introduced other stories of difference into mainstream culture. The ethnographic texts of early sociologists were generally characterized by attempts (not always successful) at moral neutrality and a benign, and increasingly respectful, stance toward social differences.

Second, I show how, by midcentury, sociologists developed key concepts by which to analyze difference differently. The sociology of deviance, as it came to be known, built on earlier sociology of strangeness and marginality. While deviance studies suffered conceptual limitations now apparent from our contemporary historical context, the field nonetheless posed an epistemic challenge to race science through its anti-essentialist approach to differences. I argue that these theoretical advances served as bridge ideas between early ethnographic departures from race science, and later poststructuralist, feminist, and queer approaches to difference. Their work resonates with ongoing cultural and political battles over social differences, nonconformity, privilege, and exclusion. Sociologists Scott Frickel and Neil Gross argue that the emergence of scientific/intellectual movements is generated by high-status actors in prestigious positions.[11] However, the pioneering sociologists of deviance were arguably the first generation of scholars who were able to study marginality from positions as marginal women and men themselves, sometimes openly as outsiders. As such, some were beset by the same stigma as the marginal communities they studied.

Third, I suggest to readers that social knowledge has emotional valences. This book is about knowledge production, not knowledge reception. I can only posit to the reader that different intellectual questions and ways of knowing can shift the affective register of difference knowledge. Cognition and emotion are intertwined. The ideas, vocabularies, and symbols of discourses represent, as cultural theorist Raymond Williams said, "not feeling against thought, but thought as felt and feeling as thought."[12] This is particularly evident in knowledge about difference. There is a deep affective component to our cultural ambivalence toward difference. Nonconformists are suspect and demonized, while also charismatic and seductive. The outsider is both hated and cool, in a dense affective mix. I suggest that the divergent narratives of race science and ethnography spoke to opposites poles of this paradox. Knowledge can support and produce feelings of fear, anger, and hatred. Or it can support and produce curiosity, acceptance, and appreciation. I believe our long history of political culture wars evinces this dynamic.

I suggest that this new social knowledge and methods, such as the texts that I'm clustering under the term "ethnography," represent different stories, better stories, about human differences. Better stories, a concept extrapolated by cultural theorist Dian Georgis, are emotional resources for understanding our past, present, and future existences.[13] A "better" story, she suggests, helps us imagine what is possible. Better stories are queer forms of knowledge, in the sense of being characterized by ambivalence, ambiguity, paradox, and the destabilization of what we assume we know. As sociologist Kathy Davis argues, the term "better stories" does not imply moral superiority.[14] There are always better stories that can surprise, move, and open us to future possibilities.

Ethnographies, I argue, are better stories about difference. They are open-ended, rather than foreclosing curiosity. They capture complexity, messiness, affect, and contradictions in the myriad forms of difference in the social world. They generate more questions and even more stories. As we will see in the texts I have chosen, better stories are not perfect, nor do they need to be.

Finally, these chapters travel through deviant places. I argue that places, actual research-site locations, shaped the making of social knowledge and ethnographic stories. I locate the scholars examined here in their geographic location, sketching some of the intersections of place, research, and stories. Most of the sites of these classic texts have changed radically over time, some no longer exist, and some—like *The Hobo*—are multiple and transient. Yet even these changes tell a story. In the next chapter, I examine the analytic possibilities afforded by the study of research locations in the making of social knowledge.

Government professor Charles King tells a triumphalist tale about some of the figures who appear in my book, such as Franz Boas, Ruth Benedict, Margaret Mead, and Zora Neale Hurston (King largely overlooks the important sociological work during this period). King argues that this "circle of renegade anthropologists reinvented race, sex, and gender in the twentieth century."[15] He claims we can thank Boas and his "contrarian researchers" for bringing about an outlook King calls "modern and open-minded." It is a worldview, he suggests, that rejects racism as "morally bankrupt and self-evidently stupid," and instead embraces social differences and diverse cultural expressions. It is an outlook, for example, that now makes it "unremarkable for a gay couple to kiss goodbye on a train platform." In his telling, cultural anthropologists freed difference from cultural and political demonization.

But did they? My own story in this book is different. And darker. It complicates the idea of an arc of cultural progress. Major changes in culture, laws, and forms of knowledge over the last century are indisputable. But it would be a mistake to see those advances as settled. The landscape of difference, outsiders, and marginality is still hotly contested, not reinvented and resolved. I argue that the work of this loose cohort of early- to mid-twentieth-century social researchers, in particular sociologists, pro-

Center Building, St. Elizabeths Hospital in Washington, DC, circa 1900, a key place featured in Chapter 5. Dr. Charles Nichols, the hospital's first superintendent, and architect Thomas Walter designed the building. Courtesy of the National Archives and Records Administration.

duced social knowledge about types of difference that were, and remain, at the center of the volatile battles that in the 1980s became known as the culture wars. They did not vanquish biological determinism, which we see achieving broad popularity again in the twenty-first century. Nor did they quell a bitter emotional politics over difference. It is possible, in fact, that this social science contributed to culture wars as a result of the heightened visibility it brought to modern differences. Finally, many of these scholars were stigmatized for studying stigmatized outsiders, and the field of deviance studies was itself beset by discrediting dynamics that undercut its legacy.

Caveats and guideposts are in order. Like all stories, this one is partial. I selected texts, authors, and topics in keeping with a certain methodological logic that would support a meaningful and diverse story about the social-knowledge production of difference. The texts I have chosen allow me to explore familiar, and less-familiar, categories and types of difference: race, gender, class, age, and sexualities; places of marginality and deviance; forms of transgression such as impersonal public sex, and choosing to live outside of conventional nuclear family structures.

The chapters tell stories over time as well as place. The early texts—*The*

Hobo, *The Taxi-Dance Hall*, and the field research of Zora Neale Hurston—suggest an early ethnographic rupture of the determinist narratives of race science. They depict field researchers shaped by new social ideas about difference while also grappling, variously, with ambivalence, moralism, bias and stigma, and structural inequalities. Midbook we reach midcentury, and Erving Goffman's canonical text, *Asylums: Essays on the Condition of the Social Situation of Mental Patients and Other Inmates*. The remaining chapters highlight the epistemic transformation in the study of social differences brought about by these midcentury sociologists and their students. Goffman, Laud Humphreys, and Sherri Cavan unapologetically featured mental patients, hippies, and men having impersonal public sex as savvy social actors fashioning their own normative communities. Old age and death weave through the conclusion, in anthropologist Barbara Myerhoff's classic ethnography, *Number Our Days*. By this point, as aging was increasingly medicalized, and the sociology of deviance was suffering criticism from emergent disciplinary approaches to difference, Myerhoff's portrait of the dailiness of immigrant Jews underscored that old age—itself a form of strangeness—was more cultural than biomedical, reinforcing the power of ethnographic rather than biomedical stories.

Most of the authors I examine in this book are sociologists. This is for reasons beyond my own disciplinary affiliation. The book tells US histories, and the cohort of early- to midcentury social scientists studying marginality and deviance in local neighborhoods were largely sociologists. As anthropologist Esther Newton told me, until the latter part of the century, there was pressure for anthropologists to work in foreign, seemingly exotic places: "They were all running off to New Guinea. That was the real anthropologist—with the helmet and the beard."[16] The anthropologists I include here, Zora Neale Hurston, Barbara Myerhoff, and Esther Newton, felt compelled to explain why they were studying US localities (Erving Goffman crossed between the disciplines but is generally referred to as a sociologist). Not all the scholars I discuss would have described their work as ethnographic—the term was not widely used by early-century sociologists, for example. But the work I profile shares the methodological approaches of deep, extended cultural observation, along with "thick descriptions"[17] of, and a new epistemic approach to, different social worlds.

There are expansive literatures on all the different social types explored in these chapters, as well as numerous histories of the social sciences, sociology, the Chicago School, anthropology, and ethnography. My book does not aspire to fully incorporate or review that scholarship. Rather, I stick closely to my own stories, using these texts to show how certain early and midcentury social scientists, particularly sociologists, embraced themes of strangeness, marginality, and outsiders, and rewrote deviance. It is a less-told tale of how this strain of social science introduced new and different ways of thinking and feeling about human difference. While new social knowledge and ways of knowing about difference center this book, the chapters are not a linear movement through theory-building, nor a fine-grained exposition of theoretical debates across the decades. I've chosen texts that feature historically diverse outsiders—along with outsider institutions, buildings, scholars, businesses, and places—and that showcase the narrative possibilities of the broad ethnographic imagination in telling their stories. Cumulatively, the texts explore the worlds of marginal people in deviant places. Likewise, I keep my focus on the ethnographers and their texts, rather than giving equal time to the historical views of race science toward the marginalized people in these chapters. Readers can find those stories elsewhere.

A number of tensions, paradoxes, and discontinuities weave through this book. For example, the American paradox of cultural rejection and embrace of difference; the swagger and stigma of deviance; the exploitations and appreciations in the ethnographic gaze; the conflicts and conciliations generated by the cultural visibility of outsiders. There are the paradoxes of capitalism. As historian John D'Emilio has argued, the expansion of wage labor and capital profoundly transformed "the nuclear family, the ideology of family life, and the meaning of heterosexual relations."[18] Capitalism, then, helped support the possibilities for new types of social difference, at the same time that outsider capitalism commodified, exoticized, and in some cases normalized difference. I have identified, rather than resolved, these paradoxes, which by their very definition are unresolvable.

I use the terms "ethnography" and "difference" in this book both broadly and narrowly, another paradox. For one, I use "ethnography" to refer to a social-science methodology of deep cultural observation, as I explain in the next chapter. As sociologists Patricia and Peter Adler note, the scholarship on ethnography has become "a huge industry,"[19] and I do not review that literature or generalize my claims to all ethnographies. Rather, I suggest an ethnographic potential. My ethnographic optimism is not a refutation of the many thoughtful criticisms of it, many of them from anthropologists. Some of these criticisms are exposed in these chapters, in particular certain early scholars' connection to moralistic social reformers. However, I remain appreciative of ethnography's history of, and possibilities for, producing the better stories that capture the pluralities and complexities of differences.

In addition, I use the term "ethnography" as shorthand for the fusion of method and epistemology. Since this book focuses on the epistemology of social difference, I use "ethnography" as an umbrella term to denote new ways of knowing, thinking, feeling, asking questions, and writing about outsiders, deviants, and difference. It is, to adapt Mills's term, an ethnographic imagination. By this I mean an epistemic stance characterized by curiosity, not about the origins, treatment, and eradication of human variation, but about the cultures, worldviews, and ways of living of those who are different.[20] In other words, better and different stories about difference. I connect early explorations of outsiders, strangeness, and urban marginality (and in Hurston's case, rural differences) to midcentury theoretical ruptures with biological determinist narratives of difference, culminating in a sociology of deviance. This shorthand departs from narrower, conventional definitions of ethnographic method, but makes it possible to write a manageable story.

Likewise, there are different ways of being different, of being marginal and outside. I use the term "difference" both broadly and specifically. Familiar forms of difference figure prominently in these chapters—the expected "menu," such as race, class, and gender, as anthropologists Carol Greenhouse and Davydd Greenwood call these "official discourses of difference" operationalized by state bureaucracies.[21] We see how some early social scientists prefigured later critical-race scholars, feminist theorists, and queer-studies scholars who documented how allegedly essential categories such as race, gender, and sexuality are invented and reproduced through structural, cultural, and interactional dynamics. However, a central theme of this book is the emergence of new kinds of people in modernity—new social differences—and how some social scientists studied and ascribed meaning to these differences. Therefore, many of the marginal people who appear in these pages are those defying norms, such as living outside of nuclear families or following unconventional career trajectories. These chapters move through different forms of difference.

The title of this book—*Marginal People in Deviant Places*—employs the terms "marginal" and "deviant" in their critical, even oppositional, sociological spirit. Outsiders have gone by different names in different historical eras: degenerates, deviants, outcasts, misfits, reprobates. More specific pejoratives refer to race, mental status, gender, sexuality, and other variations. The vocabulary of difference has changed over time, and the stories in this book delineate some of those historical shifts. I use the language specific to each text and its historical period, and avoid the use of scare quotes and qualifiers, such as "alleged deviance." Notably, the sociological term "deviance" is today often misread as negative and judgmental. However, sociologists flipped this vernacular meaning into a critique of how rule-makers create what we consider to be deviance. Deviants are, as sociologist Howard Becker put it in 1963, "sufficiently bizarre and unconventional for them to be labeled as outsiders by more conventional members of the community."[22] This sociological reframing, universalizing, and respect for marginality, deviance, strangeness, outsiders, and difference is a central theme of this book.

Marginal People in Deviant Places tells a critical history of knowledge production and a social history of myriad American outsiders and their places. These chapters do not cumulatively represent a tidy, comprehensive story about social science, ethnography, or difference. Rather, they historicize an interruption of the dominant race-science stories of the era, and suggest the narrative power of ethnographic stories to confound essentialist categories and hierarchical meanings of difference. While I use the terms "marginal" and "deviant" to evoke this historical rupture, the possibility that they retain emotional traces of shame signifies that this rupture is partial and ongoing.

The stories, people, and places examined in this book show that we are not one, or even two Americas, but that there are potentially endless variations on how to be a person in the modern world. This multiplicity of American difference has been foundational to the country's artistic creativity, economic vibrancy, technological innovation, and much more. Yet there is a shadow over these stories of marginal people in deviant places. In this book, we see social condemnation and political opposition to differences—and to the scholars who wrote about them. It is timely, then, to investigate our history of social-science knowledge production about difference, and how we know what we think we know about those who diverge from conventional norms. Dian Georgis argues that "we are not obligated to live by the stories that no longer help us live well."[23] We can tell different stories about difference. Culture wars over issues such as race, immigration, gender, trans identities, and other variations, highlight how debates about social inclusion and social marginality, about normalcy and nonconformity, and about who matters in American democracy and culture are not in our historical past, they linger in our ongoing, unsettled present.

Methods, and Such

I, too, am a storyteller of outsiders, writing in a specific historical moment, with my own intellectual and political passions. Some of this book's topics—hobos, taxi dancers, older Jewish immigrants, asylums—were new to me and exciting to explore. Yet I have been writing about these overarching themes—the history of knowledge production, marginality, stigma, social hierarchies, outsider scholarship, art, activism, and the commodification of difference—throughout my career. This mix of familiarity and unfamiliarity made it the perfect project. There was also a personal-political dimension. My own social locations, and activism, as an outsider made me a fellow traveler with the marginality, strangeness, and deviance I examine in this book.

I began this project in 2012, focused specifically on the midcentury sociology of deviance. Like so many books, it started out as one thing and ended up being, well, different. As the focus expanded to the sociological prehistory on difference—strangers and marginality—my time period moved earlier in the twentieth century to include two classic Chicago School texts (chapters 2 and 3). The digital format, available online at https://doi.org/10.3998/mpub.11519906, allowed me to veer toward subplots that enrich the main story, so I had the freedom to follow paths that were interesting and fun. I have told my own stories around and through these ethnographic stories. In the digital edition, the chapters have hyperlinks to stories connected to the main themes, including archival and interview material, as well as commentary by contemporary scholars working on these topics and in these places. Textual hyperlinks appear at the end of chapters in the print edition, but for the fully enhanced experience of the book, readers should consult the online edition.

I further expanded the book to examine ethnographic places after my visit to Laud Humphreys's tearoom sites in St. Louis. There is a magical dimension to walking in the footsteps of a long-ago ethnographer of an iconic or favorite text. It is, perhaps, for social researchers, the equivalent of visiting battlefields. Fortunately, before the pandemic shut down travel, I was able to wander the research locations of all the ethnographic work in these chapters. In the case of Zora Neale Hurston, my Florida road trip took place during the week in mid-March, 2020, when the world began shutting down. I visited Hurston's hometown, Eatonville, worked in her collected papers at the University of Florida, and then drove to Fort Pierce, where she died, all during the period when conservative radio hosts were decrying the novel coronavirus as a hoax. At other research sites, I took historical walking tours and architectural tours, combed historical museums, and explored streets and neighborhoods with knowledgeable colleagues. I went to the annual Hobo Convention in Britt, Iowa. These explorations offered glimpses of sites as they had existed during the earlier moment of ethnographic study, and of how they have changed. They also yielded insight into how places might matter in research (see chapter 1). During these trips, I took many of the photographs in this book.

This critical history is based on qualitative interviews, archival research, and primary sources. I conducted approximately fifty interviews in the United States, the UK, and Israel with pioneering sociologists, scholar-activists, public intellectuals, and artists. Regarding the criteria for my interview choices, I chose those who (1) had done pioneering research in the sociology of deviance; (2) were familiar with the field during the time period under study; or (3) were public intellectuals and activists with connections to disciplinary debates and public conversations about difference and deviance. I conducted archival research at several collections: the University of Chicago, the London School of Economics, Northeastern University, the University of Southern California, the New York City Public Library, the University of Florida, and One National Gay & Lesbian Archives. The interview material largely shows up in the later chapters, since the authors of key texts on those chapters' topics, or some of their contemporaries, were still alive. The early chapters are based on the original texts and archival material, supported by video interviews with scholars.

A word about the digital platform. This project essentially required that I visually curate my own ideas, an endeavor that social scientists are not typically trained to do. In choosing the photographs and designing the book map, I had to shift from a textual to a visual orientation for presenting ideas. This process changed me, in a good way, as a writer, and also a reader. There were quirks and nuances. For one thing, copyright restrictions limited my choices. In addition, the pandemic travel shutdown prevented my final set of research trips for gathering historical and contemporary images, and, importantly, for shooting video interviews in person and on-site. Zoom allowed me to keep interviewing, but it wasn't the same. While the loss during lockdown of UMass digital support for editing lends these videos more of a DIY quality than I had originally anticipated, they strike me as sort of heroic, given all the constraints. Video editing is also a form of knowledge production and revision. Most videos were only tweaked, but stories in a few of them were shortened to fit constraints on time and file size. In those cases, I made choices based on which stories most closely hewed to the book's key themes.

The interviewing and archival research largely took place during what now, in retrospect, seem like the relatively calm Obama years. The project felt lighthearted at that point, at least in my imagination. Much of the writing, however, took place during the four years of the Trump administration. Even prior to the 2016 election, Donald Trump had stoked anger and hatred toward many types of social differences—particularly immigrants, African Americans, women, and trans people—as a way to mobilize his base. At the same time, Trump, a White, male, elite billionaire, touted his supposed outsider status. Cultural polarization, even violence, related to social differences spiked, while the cultural meanings of "outsider" were confounded. Soon into his administration, historians had warned that the United States was drifting toward fascist politics, what philosopher Jason Stanley calls "a permanent temptation,"[24] with its intensification of hierarchical discourses of "us versus them."[25] This shifting context underscored the importance of research and stories about social differences. There are many themes in this book, yet the central one is a story about scientific knowledge production that either supports or challenges us-them thinking.

ONE

Introduction

"Must you conform?" is the question that haunts all men living in this time of crisis and decision.[1]

Robert Lindner

In 1956, psychoanalyst Robert Lindner, author of the 1944 classic *Rebel Without a Cause*, published his quirky text, *Must You Conform?* suggesting that the answer could be, no, you need not. Lindner's question, provocative in a climate of racial intolerance and cultural anxieties about nonconformity, also hinted at a zeitgeist of modern outsiders. New types of social differences were being brought into being by a pivotal half-century of unprecedented modern change. Some of these key developments of modernity included urbanization, rapid scientific and technological advances, social fragmentation, the rise of liberal individualism, and the burgeoning of industrial capitalism. These fostered new opportunities to be an outsider, while outsiders themselves became more socially visible. Social differences—and stories about them—proliferated in these early decades, continuing throughout the twentieth century.

American Studies scholar Anna Creadick argues that the idea of "normality" gained cultural currency in the post–World War II years, 1943–1963.[2] Scientific medicine and psychiatry produced discourses, circulated through popular media, promoting the widespread embrace of normality. Yet much earlier, sociologists were troubled by, and at the same time troubled, questions of difference, conformity, and outsiders. In 1927, University of Chicago sociologist Ernest Burgess scrawled at the top of his Social Pathology course notes—"What is the normal?"[3] A modern social science of difference began viewing "social pathology," which would later become "deviance," as an often-creative adaptation to modern urban life. By midcentury, sociologist Edwin Lemert argued for the abandonment of the "archaic and medicinal" idea that human beings could be classified into categories of normalcy and deviance.[4] It was a radical articulation of ideas that would be dubbed the sociology of deviance, or deviance studies. Easy assumptions about deviance and pathology, the normal and abnormal, conformity and deviance, began to crumble.

Fast forward to 1990. Pioneering literary and queer theorist Eve Sedgwick famously claimed, "People are different from each other. It is astonishing how few respectable conceptual tools we have for dealing with this self-evident fact."[5] In fact, we did have the cultural tools, with a new language of difference. They were, rather, unknown, forgotten, or ignored, even by humanities scholars sympathetic to outsiders. Time passed, and innovative ideas had faded or were lost in disciplinary silos. However, this book argues that in the early to mid-twentieth century, certain social scientists developed new conceptual and methodological tools for radical exploration of differences.

The intellectual and social landscape of difference changed throughout the twentieth century. This chapter introduces that story. The first two sections sketch a historical background useful for thinking through the ethnographic ruptures to race science. I examine two different approaches to studying, theorizing, and storytelling about human variation of individuals and social groups. Race science saw variations as largely biological in origin, manifest in inferior physiological traits such as cranial size, bone density, skin color, ear shape, and the like. They framed social identities, such as race and gender, as well as nonconforming behaviors such as criminality and sexual difference, as embodied and fixed. By contrast, social scientists rewrote difference, depicting deviant worlds as ordinary. They developed research methods and introduced conceptual frameworks that produced different stories in which outsiders and strangers were constructed by, and navigated their way through, particular historical, social, economic, and political circumstances. Ethnographers' thick descriptions represented individuals as constructing meaning and living within coherent cultural systems and worldviews. These studies of the rich social worlds of others enabled later scholars to argue that difference is socially constructed, its social meanings invented.

The final section of this introduction examines the pivotal role of ethnographic places in storytelling about difference. Ethnographers often invented pseudonyms for the villages, hospitals, bars, nudist colonies, and other sites they studied, omitting location entirely or burying the specific place in a footnote or preface. Yet this book argues that ethnographic locations, spaces, and places represent a significant aspect of how ethnographic knowledge production ruptured race science narratives.

Ethnographic stories carry traces of their locations. Extending geographer David Livingstone's call for a "geography of science,"[6] I suggest that knowledge of research places helps us differently understand these social science texts, the scholars themselves, the processes of social research, and the interweaving of research setting and the makings of social knowledge. At the end of this introduction, I suggest numerous ways that ethnographic places matter in social research and analysis. Overall, in this introduction I do not undertake the impossible task of a thorough literature review of modernity, scientific racism, the histories of ethnography and deviance studies, or the sociology of place.

Modern Social Differences and Race Science

Cultural anxieties about difference, a fear of the "abnormal," as philosopher Michel Foucault noted, "haunts the end of the nineteenth century."[7] The "monsters" Foucault discussed from this period were figures such as the masturbator and the incorrigible, yet this time saw a turbulent mix of racial, ethnic, gender, and other differences. In the United States in the post-Reconstruction era, racial hatred fueled segregationist laws and escalating violence against African Americans. Immigrants were the target of increasingly exclusionary policies. Women were still denied suffrage. Social transgression was punished by law or community sanction. Yet change, in certain respects, was in the air. Social researchers worked against the backdrop of two countervailing dynamics: social changes that enabled new ways of living and new types of differences, and the dominant discourse of scientific racism dedicated to explaining and eliminating them.

Different Differences

Modern life brought changes that allowed, forced, or encouraged new forms of difference. Steven Smith refers to modernity as the site of a "unique human being"—the bourgeois.[8] Yet modernity did not just produce the bourgeoisie, it opened up space for social transgressions of many kinds, both cultural and individual, whether by choice or circumstance. The new mobility enabled by transportation technologies introduced strangers and difference into cities and previously homogeneous villages. A wide range of nonconforming social types achieved new visibility on the streets. Later communication technologies such as radio and television, along with changes in print culture, brought strange new characters and different subcultures into mainstream homes.

These material changes helped produce a "social imaginary" of modernity—its collective background or cultural understanding that enables social life.[9] Cultural sensibilities—social imaginaries—of strangeness, ambiguity, and marginality resonated widely, as bohemia emerged in US cities early in the century, and dissident types burgeoned. These deviant types intrigued new social researchers, such as those discussed in this book, whose scholarship was surely a force in generating what historian Christine Stansell describes as "a milieu that brought outsiders and their energies into the very heart of the American intelligentsia."[10] By the mid-twentieth century, modern social changes enabled Robert Lindner and others to posit nonconformity as a decision, a choice. In time, strangeness would be embraced by some, for example hippies, while social marginality became a creative choice for others.

Capitalism played its part in this story. Economic and social changes associated with capitalism supported possibilities for new types of social difference. Individuals moved from the constraints of small village life, with its religious and familial regulations, into urban ways of living and working. This might mean living solo or in an unconventional arrangement. As historian John D'Emilio has argued, the expansion of wage labor and capital profoundly transformed "the nuclear family, the ideology of family life, and the meaning of heterosexual relations."[11] Transforming, too, were the meanings of gender, work, leisure, marriage, public places, and much more.

Capitalism celebrated difference, yet flattened it. As historian Thomas Frank argues, "liberation and continual transgression" were foundational to consumer capitalism. Unfettered desire fueled consumption. By the sixties, he notes, "hip became central to the way American capitalism understood itself and explained itself to the public."[12] Rebellion became an advertising trope. However, capitalism's role goes beyond the marketing of "hip." Broad domains of social marginality, strangeness, and difference became commodities to be bought and sold. As new forms of difference and strangeness became possible and visible, capitalism would become adept at recognizing, packaging, and marketing them.

The dynamics of what I call "outsider capitalism" emerged. In being mass marketed, some outsiders and ways of being an outsider became more visible, with paradoxical effects. Outsider capitalism could blunt the edges of difference. Widely available for consumption, difference easily morphed into conformity. Still, the packing and selling of outsider difference required making it attractive, a move arguably preferable to knowledge practices that fostered social hostility.

This necessarily brief sketch argues that early- and mid-twentieth-century dynamics fostered new possibilities to be different and new kinds of people. I extend philosopher Ian Hacking's useful concept, "making up people."[13] Hacking claims that throughout the twentieth century, scientific and medical expertise, including psychiatry and psychology, generated new, typically biomedical, frameworks and languages for people to understand themselves, their behavior, and their social interactions. Hacking identifies what he calls "engines of discovery," such as counting, scientific classification, and the generation of expert knowledge, which produced new identities across a wide spectrum of behaviors. Sociologists call this process the medicalization of everyday life.[14] I argue throughout these chapters that it was not just medicine and psychiatry that produced new types of people, with new languages, social networks, and ways of being a person. Other engines of social change were also crucial in making up people, including modernity, capitalism, political activism, cultural production, and ethnographic inquiry and storytelling. However, Hacking's focus on biomedicine and the psychiatric disciplines, and this book's historical backdrop of scientific racism, underscores these factors' long-standing discursive power in defining and regulating social difference.

Essentialized Differences

The social complexities of modernity generated a reliance on expertise. A central project of science has been to produce stories about difference, entailing efforts to explain and classify human variation. Spurred by late-nineteenth-century concerns about recent immigrants, African Americans, and native-born Whites,[15] race had become a central classification system.[16] Scientific racism became one of the dominant institutions producing social knowledge—particular narratives and stories—about human variations. Race occupied the center of intellectual attention to difference. Scientific racism, which contained several ideological and theoretical strands regarding heredity and biology, posited that innate biological differences accounted for essential hierarchies of superiority and inferiority, conformity and deviance.

As cultural authorities regarding normalcy, racial scientists at the turn of the twentieth century viewed inferior biology and deviant bodies as the sources of difference. As critical scholars Jacqueline Urla and Jennifer Terry note, the "somatic territorializing of deviance" was central to modern scientific medicine's demarcations of normalcy versus abnormalcy.[17] While this early scientific classification of individuals and the categorization of human populations centered on racial differences, evolutionary biology also scrutinized (and invented) other allegedly undesirable variations—for example, imbeciles, paupers, the promiscuous, and others deemed unfit.[18] Scientific stories of human differences mattered; they were widely deployed in inventing racial and gender categories, and were also used to classify others living outside of conventional social norms.

Race scientists drew on a discourse of nature and biology to define otherwise benign human differences as unnatural, deficient, even dangerous. These biological investigations of difference supported social hierarchies of inequality—the structures, rankings, and boundaries that make up what Isabel Wilkerson calls "caste."[19] While race occupies the center of caste in the United States, Wilkerson argues that caste is also "the basis of every other *ism*."[20] Scientific racism constructed narratives that produced social hierarchies about a wide range of differences, including race, ethnicity, sexualities, nationality, social class, cognitive abilities, and more.

Race science, including what Nikolas Rose calls "the psy disciplines," gave rise to a new form of racism—a neoracism different from "ethnic racism," directed against these abnormal figures emerging in the modern world.[21] As Science and Technology Studies scholars Ramya Rajogopalan and her colleagues put it, "Racist science constructed biological research outcomes that underscored the very differences they were looking for, and these alleged biological differences were in turn mobilized as 'explanations' for still other alleged differences across race, for example, in ability, intellect, and health."[22] Race scientists cast biology as fixed, rather than malleable, so that these supposedly physical differences were construed as innate and immutable categories of normalcy and deviance.

These narratives were entangled with myriad social policies and practices intended to eliminate supposedly inferior and deviant individuals and social groups, including colonial expansion, eugenic strategies, and intelligence-testing programs positing the heritability of genius. Biological determinism was deployed to seemingly justify Jim Crow segregation laws. Those considered inferior in mental status or behavior were readily institutionalized in asylums. Stories about the biological inferiority of others—touted as science—drove the Johnson-Reed Act, which drastically limited the number of so-called undesirable immigrants from eastern and southern Europe between 1924 and 1965. Later, Nazi Germany would praise this Immigration Act as a model, drawing on the work of US scientific racists and eugenicists as they moved toward the massive genocide of Jews, homosexuals, gypsies, dissidents, and those considered intellectually or physically disabled.[23]

Rewriting Marginal People

From its earliest years, the social sciences, in particular the disciplines of sociology and cultural anthropology, also studied questions of human differences.[24] Albeit unevenly, some scholars challenged the determinist logic of difference, troubling the rigid biological binary of normalcy and abnormality. At the turn of the century, German sociologist Georg Simmel crafted his enduring article on the promises of the stranger. Pioneering cultural anthropologist Franz Boas, famous for his comprehensive research on cranial measurements, repudiated the biological determinism of race. Sociologist W. E. B. Du Bois's work on dual consciousness and hybridity, and Hull House and University of Chicago sociology's emphasis on communities, social interactions, cultural practices, networks, and urban places, cumulatively represented a departure from dominant race science. By the mid-twentieth century, scholars of the sociology of deviance had developed an influential conceptual tool kit and produced canonical texts on marginal social figures such as hustlers, homosexuals, delinquents, and drug dealers, among others. They viewed difference not as innate and unchanging, but as a fluid process shaped by culture, situations, and interactions. These emergent theories and methods countered biological determinist narratives of difference through telling stories about the intricate social worlds of outsiders, marginal people, strangers, and deviants.

Early Departures

Most historiographers of the social sciences now recognize that the repudiation of scientific racism transpired over a lengthy process throughout the first half of the century. Racism, colonialism, and gender and sexual bias still inflected the early social sciences.[25] There was no decisive socialscientific break with essentialism, but rather a mashup of nature and nurture, culture and biology. Anthropology and sociology—the disciplines of ethnographers profiled in this book—took circuitous paths away from scientific racism. In anthropology, there was a "waxing and waning of hereditarian, biologically deterministic, and essentialist views" between 1900 and 1970.[26] Historian Joanne Meyerowitz describes how the "epistemic shift in social thought" effected by anthropology's "culture and personality" school was nonetheless only partial.[27] Psychoanalysis underwent conflicts between scholars committed to its medico-biological materialism, and those, like Erich Fromm, who advocated theoretical grounding in culture and identity.[28] Likewise, sociology was shaped by its historical and cultural moment. For example, biological determinist ideas were present in some scholarship that otherwise reflected an early social constructionist approach. More importantly, the research could be inattentive to intersections of race, gender, class, and sexuality. Those theoretical and empirical advances would all come later in the social sciences and humanities.

Still, this new social science of difference was radical. It broke with the biological race science of the early twentieth century as well as with positivist systems of classification of human diversity and social types. As Barbara Lal noted, these early sociologists valued "differences" represented by immigrants and racial minorities at a time of explicit racism and a push for Americanization and conformity.[29] They focused on racial and ethnic communities, immigrant narratives, social diversity, the contrast between life in small villages and urban centers, and the broader dislocations of modernity. They explored the myriad ways—beyond racial and ethnic differences—in which humans could be different. Some scholars began to recognize, and appreciate, how modern life fostered new ways of living, new social worlds, and new types of outsiders.

Sociologists revolutionized studies of difference partly through the attention they brought to these modern people. Further, they innovated concepts by which to understand them, their social worlds, and their ways of living. They complicated and later abandoned the framework of "social pathology," positing that nonconformity and conformity might not be so different. Chicago sociologist W. I. Thomas suggested that "the call of the wild" and "the call of duty" represented the same research problem.[30] This relativized seemingly abnormal behavior into that which could only be understood in the context of broader social stresses, cultural meanings, places and spaces, and how individuals constructed "the definition of the situation."[31]

Marginality and strangeness were potentially everywhere, within everyone. If the city is "a state of mind,"[32] as University of Chicago sociologists Robert Park and Ernest Burgess wrote in 1925, then strangeness and marginality were two important qualities of the modern mind. Two early articles captured these features of modern life: Georg Simmel's "The Stranger" (1908) and Robert Park's later adaptation, "Human Migration and the Marginal Man" (1928).[33] Simmel, an activist scholar who influenced the feminist and homosexual-rights movements in Germany, was "an iconoclastic spokesman for a new antibourgeois world," an academic outsider himself.[34] Park, a student of Simmel's, worked with Booker T. Washington at the Tuskegee Institute and later helped establish urban sociology and fieldwork at the University of Chicago.

Their ideas prefigured later social constructionism, poststructuralism, and queer theory. Simmel penned his ambiguous and paradoxical portrait of the stranger early in a century that would end with a queer theoretical embrace of fluidity and ambiguity. The stranger represented an ambivalent figure, both near and far, an insider and outsider simultaneously.[35] Simmel viewed the stranger as positive, even courageous, suggesting that we are all potential strangers through mobility and boundary-shifting. Modern mobility and cosmopolitanism were also central to Robert Park's elaboration of Simmel's ideas in "Human Migration and Marginal Man." Like the stranger, the marginal man was a cultural hybrid, a "divided self" between the old and the new.[36] For Park, the "emancipated Jew" was the iconic marginal man, the first cosmopolitan and world citizen produced by dynamics of modernity.

Simmel and Park posited strangeness and marginality as qualities of modern life rather than of a specific kind of person. The stranger, for Simmel, was not an innately strange social type, but *became* a stranger in a strange relationship. The stranger was produced through strange interactions, which, he argued, could permeate like a "shadow" or "mist" into any human relationships. He noted that a "trace of strangeness" easily entered interactions, and could "crowd in like shadows between men, like a mist eluding every designation." Similarly, Park noted that, while marginality could constitute a personality type in modernity, the quality of marginality was one that "most of us" could experience in transition and crisis. Strangeness and marginality were qualities of interaction, ways one might be a person in certain modern situations.

Other groundbreaking scholars of social difference, like Frank Tannenbaum, are less well remembered. Tannenbaum matters because his book, *Crime and Community* (1938), was an early and striking interruption of biological determinist theories of crime made popular by nineteenth- and early-twentieth-century criminologists such as Cesare Lombroso, who viewed criminality as being inherent in anomalies of the physical body.[37] Tannenbaum's life also exemplified the overlap of scholarship and activism becoming common among sociologists. He was an Austrian immigrant and member of the Industrial Workers of the World (Wobblies), who was jailed for a year on Blackwell's Island in New York for his role in political protest. Dubbed the "convict criminologist," Tannenbaum argued that searching for the roots of criminality in individual biological or psychological factors would be like looking for organic causes of religious beliefs, for example, joining the Catholic Church, or lifestyle choices such as vegetarianism. In other words, crime, in his view, was situational and socially produced rather than biological or personality-based. Law-and-order approaches only reinforced it: "The way out is through a refusal to dramatize the evil. The less said about it the better."[38] It was a thorough-going refutation of Lombroso's enduring idea of inherent criminality. He concluded that "the person becomes the thing he is described as being."

In key ways, this early sociology eschewed fixed, binary identities, and instead posited duality, ambiguity, fluidity, and fragmentation. The stranger and the marginal man became enduring scholarly tropes. Everett Hughes later expanded on Park's idea to suggest that marginality is part of the story of America.[39] And in the fifties, Helen Mayer Hacker extended the concept to women, in an early sociological argument for women as a "minority group."[40] While the iconic strangers and marginal people in the earliest scholarship were the immigrant, the Negro, and the Jew, sociologists would later apply the ideas to a wide range of new social types, such as delinquents, gamblers, and more. Simmel's ambiguity—and the way that the concept of the stranger struck a cultural nerve—enabled an extensive and ongoing literature on who and what the stranger and strangeness are.[41]

The Deviant Turn

Foreshadowed by this earlier sociology, the sociology of deviance emerged, incrementally. Edwin Lemert's 1951 text, *Social Pathology*, was the first full articulation of societal reaction theory, which highlighted cultural labeling of difference.[42] Lemert, who examined deviations such as stuttering, prostitution, drinking, and mental illness, fully broke with biological determinist and psychiatric approaches to difference. He pointed out that violations of contemporaneous ways of living were considered pathological. Yet these norms—"residential stability, property ownership, sobriety, thrift, habituation to work, small business enterprise, sexual discretion, family solidarity, neighborliness, and discipline of the will"—were actually features of "rural, small-town, and middle-class America, translated into public policy," and he urged social scientists to avoid this sort of bias and moralism.[43] The very idea of deviance, he argued, was constructed by social responses to differences—labeling an individual as a rule-breaker.

The labeling approach rested on earlier ethnographic case studies depicting outsiders such as hobos, taxi dancers, and the like as complicated, even heroic, characters forging their way in an unsettled world. Some sociologists were beginning to discourage the view that social difference was simply an individual characteristic of a small minority. Rather, everyone was likely to be deviant in some fashion, and almost anyone could be deviant, including sociologists themselves. In an exuberant critique of psychiatric theories positing criminal psychopathology, Lemert exclaimed, "Rare, indeed, is the person who at one time or another has not committed a felony."[44] If felonious behavior were ascribed to mental pathology, he mocked, most of us would be labeled "episodic psychopaths."[45] Deviance, arguably, was not even deviant, it was ordinary difference.

In retrospect, we can identify the roots of modern deviance studies of the 1960s in the publication of canonical texts such as Erving Goffman's *Asylums* (1961) and *Stigma* (1963), as well as Howard Becker's *Outsiders* (1963).[46] Howard Becker recently told me, "I certainly never intended to create a field of deviance, and I'm certain Erving [Goffman] didn't either, but you can't stop the world from careening in the direction it goes."[47] It careened in the direction of an emergent subfield that critically interrogated the meanings of, and boundaries between, allegedly fixed categories of deviance and conformity, normalcy and abnormality. The field was only later labeled "sociology of deviance" after early work had been accomplished by this eclectic group of scholars.

The sociology of deviance flipped the difference narrative. "The central fact about deviance," Becker asserted, is that "it is created by society."[48] Deviance did not reside in the individual body, it was constructed by the social body. Social rules produced deviance, rather than characteristics inherent in certain behaviors or the individuals who engaged in them. Deviance studies of the sixties focused on *becoming* deviant rather than on monolithic identities or a core (deviant) self. Outsiders and deviants were produced by the rule-making practices of moral entrepreneurs, such as laws outlawing drugs and minority sexualities. Sociologists also wrote new stories about the experiences of difference, showing how outsiders felt the sting of stigma while also building marginal but vibrant communities. Researchers moved beyond an early focus on racial and ethnic differences, also exploring what sociologist Edward Sagarin in 1971 described as "the other minorities": mental patients, prostitutes and hustlers, nudists, skid row alcoholics, and others.[49] The field acquired the nickname "nuts, sluts, and perverts." (**See section Hyperlink 1.1:** New Social Knowledge of Difference.)

This new social science of difference radically broke with positivist systems of classification of human diversity and social types. One early scholar recently recalled, "There was shock value to the idea that primary deviance characterized everybody and secondary deviance was a different matter. That everybody is a deviant. It was very exciting, arguably, the biggest revolution in sociology."[50] These ideas were very much "in the air," as another scholar put it. At the same time, they represented a striking rupture from race science and biomedical theories, arguing that deviance was produced by policing of social norms, not by characteristics inherent to certain behaviors or individuals. While Howard Becker preferred calling labeling a "perspective" rather than a "theory,"[51] labeling was, as one sociologist recently told me, "the insurgent theory."[52]

It was a Cold War social science.[53] As such, these scholars negotiated the paradoxical social and political climate of that era toward conformity and difference. On the one hand, McCarthyism fueled anxieties about deviant others, forcing suspected communists, lesbians, gay men, and others out of the federal government as alleged threats to national security. Cultural and political pressures toward conformity shaped all levels of life from national politics to domestic life. On the other hand, myriad social critics worried about the pernicious effects of excessive conformity. Haunted by the horrors of Nazi Germany and the Holocaust, postwar social scientists such as Stanley Milgram explored the social-psychological roots of obedience to authority.[54] Psychoanalytic scholars were critical of what Erich Fromm called "automation conformity," and its tendencies toward conspiratorial groupthink. The Freudian-inflected Frankfurt School formulated critical theory about the rise of an authoritarian personality. Sociologists such as David Riesman and C. Wright Mills criticized social pressures toward conformity, corporate culture, and mass consumption while disrupting earlier views of biological determinism in areas such as crime and addiction.[55] In this paradox of difference, conformity was both demanded and feared; rebels and deviants were reviled but also admired.

Meanwhile, these social researchers told stories not just with different ideas. Their work suggested a different emotional politics of difference. By the mid-twentieth century, sociologists grappled with the question of power and politics. In *Outsiders*, Howard Becker argued that labeling, or to use the term he preferred, "interactionist theories," "look (and are) rather Left."[56] Later, in "Whose Side Are We On?," he famously claimed that research was impossible without taking a point of view, and noted that sociologists generally took the perspective of the underdog. He pointed out, however, that while critics assailed sociologists for sympathy with the underdog, mainstream researchers more often took the perspective of dominant groups while nonetheless claiming objectivity (what feminist theorist Donna Haraway would later call "the god trick"[57]). Becker's conclusion about the inevitability of taking sides would resonate with a generation of sociologists: "We take sides as our personal and political commitments dictate, use our theoretical and technical resources to avoid the distortions that might introduce into our work, limit our conclusions carefully, recognize the hierarchy of credibility for what it is, and field as best we can the accusations and doubts that will surely be our fate."[58] Taking the side of the underdog implied an emotional politics supportive of a social vision of greater equality and acknowledgment of differences. As sociologist Jack Douglas put it, "While it is only a coincidence that our scientific interests correspond with this emotional interest in deviants, it is a happy coincidence and, I believe, one that should be encouraged."[59] As part of their "fate" in taking the side of outsiders and deviants, a number of these sociologists attracted the suspicion of, and surveillance by, the Federal Bureau of Investigation.[60] J. Edgar Hoover and allies viewed democratic stories of cultural pluralism as a social and political threat. (**See section Hyperlink 1.2:** FBI Surveillance.)

This challenge to systems of power and oppression in sociological deviance scholarship found political publics among the "nuts, sluts, and perverts" who comprised some of their research subjects. Some outsiders mobilized to contest the pathologizing gaze of science, and likewise resist—or embrace—social marginality. In the fifties and sixties, the political activities of civil rights, the antipsychiatry movement, the lesbian and gay movement, Black Power, and feminism all helped problematize the very notion of deviance. Some found deviance frameworks to be productive in their activism on behalf of marginalized subcultures, offering arguments to resist stigma and deviant labeling. For example, in her historiography of sexual difference, anthropologist Gayle Rubin argued that, in contrast to how anthropological ethnographies displayed "common prejudice and psychiatric hegemony as late as 1971," the challenges to dominant biomedicine through "ethnographic studies of contemporary sexual populations . . . was mostly accomplished by sociologists."[61] By the 1960s, social researchers had shifted the conversation on difference through a combination of innovative theoretical perspectives, such as labeling theory and symbolic interactionism, and earlier fieldwork methods of inquiry. Outsid-

Figure 1.2

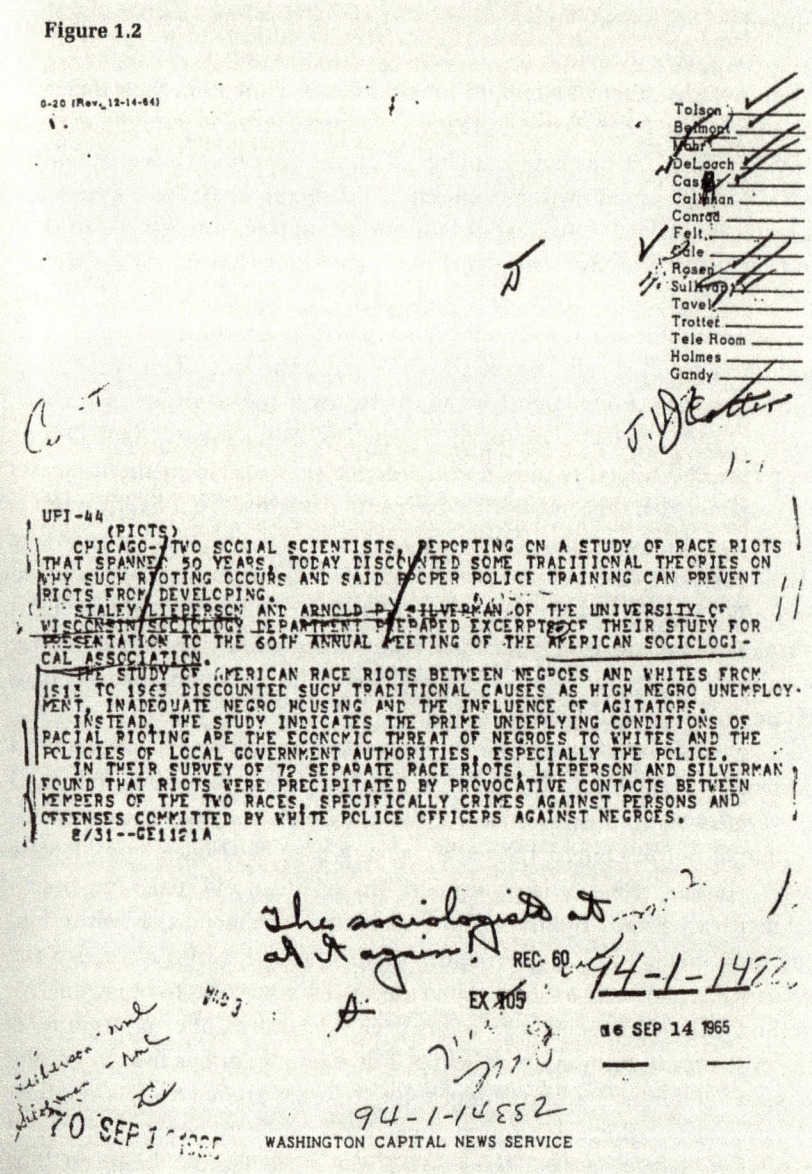

Federal Bureau of Investigation, American Sociological Association, September 14, 1965. Washington, DC: FBI Freedom of Information—Privacy Acts Section. Courtesy of Mike Keen.

ers, strangers, marginality, and deviance became enduring—and for some, endearing—subjects of study.

As this book unfolds, we catch glimpses of new ways of knowing, and telling stories about, communities and individuals considered different, marginal, and deviant. It was a gradual and partial change. Still, these chapters bring to life key differences in knowledge production by ethnographers as compared to race scientists. For one, race science depicted the central characters of this book—immigrants, hobos, African Americans, women, those with different sexualities or mental status, and even young and old individuals—as either biologically inferior or as essentially shaped and defined by their biology. By contrast, ethnographers such as Nels Anderson, Paul Goalby Cressey, Zora Neale Hurston, Erving Goffman, and others explored the ingenuity of individuals who were marginalized by differences as they created social places and cultures for themselves. While race science cast differences as immutable and fixed, ethnographers such as Laud Humphreys depicted the power of place, situation, and norms in producing fluid sexual differences. Race science reinforced social hierarchies of difference, while ethnographers such as Erving Goffman wrote appreciatively of how mental patients found dark corners in the asylum where they skillfully interacted with each other, and even with the staff, as equals. Moreover, a place itself—the total institution of the asylum—could produce the very differences that rule-makers viewed as problematic. Zora Neale Hurston—a modern outsider herself—captured the folklore of African American workers, a powerful body of stories, songs, poetry, sermons, and ways of talking that she considered a superior form of cultural expression. While race science classified differences into discrete categories, ethnographers blurred the boundaries between the strange and the familiar, normalcy and deviance. Sociologist Sherri Cavan described an emerging youth counterculture as one that, despite its embrace of strangeness and rebellion, nevertheless had a set of norms and cultural logics. Ethnographer Barbara Myerhoff's study of elderly Jewish immigrants depicted their specific cultural world, at the same time underscoring that meanings of difference and strangeness, even differences wrought by age, change over time and place. Indeed, places played a central role in these new stories.

Writing Deviant Places

Social figures who did not conform to dominant social norms achieved new visibility on the streets of the city, and ethnographic practices (fieldwork or field research) were a way to know about them. The clinical gaze of biological medicine located difference in the individual body, making it visible through scientific techniques of measurement, sorting, and classification. Ethnographic looking was a radical departure, focusing on cultural logics from the insider's point of view. Anthropologist Barbara Myerhoff said fieldwork was like "being inside and outside at the same time."[62] The method, which relies on detailed field notes of interactions, keen observation, and both formal and informal interviews, is nonetheless unstructured and inductive. Ethnographers' "deep hanging out" constituted an extended experience of living, observing, and participating in different social worlds and cultures.[63] Only by getting inside the milieu of deviant groups, sociologist Jack Douglas argued, "can we ever come to see how deviants really view the world."[64] Ethnography, Erving Goffman insisted, required physically subjecting oneself to the "demands placed routinely on members of the groups being studied."[65] And so ethnographers hung out in deviant places.

Deviant places help us understand marginal people, and those who studied and wrote about them. "Outsider," after all, signifies a place, as does marginality. Places both reflect and produce norms, as suggested in expressions such as "in place," "out of place," "proper place," and the like. Social geographer Tim Cresswell notes that deviance is "shot through with geographical assumptions concerning what and who belong where."[66] Again, I use the term "deviant" in its sociological sense, connoting people, places, or practices that have been framed as deviant through laws, policies, or social norms. Deviant places are socially constructed. They are places in which subcultures flourish. This book travels through places as varied as the jook joints of the rural South, freight train cars bearing hobos on top, the Sanctified Church, Chicago's taxi-dance halls and black-and-tan clubs, the back rooms of asylums, tearooms for public sex, the sidewalks of Haight Ashbury, and the outdoor benches of Venice Beach. They are places where outsiders are insiders, places that allow the making up of new kinds of people and of the cultures that support them.

Place characterized ethnography. Ethnographers went out to the field to produce new social knowledge, new types of stories. While most anthropologists traveled to study cultures in far-flung locales, sociologists explored local sites. University of Chicago sociologists—later dubbed the Chicago School—who pioneered US field studies in the early decades of the twentieth century equated modernity with the city, and famously used it as a laboratory. Chicago luminaries Robert Park and Ernest Burgess argued for the value of local, urban fieldwork: "The same patient methods of observation which anthropologists like Boas and Lowie have expended on the study of the life and manners of the North American Indian might be even more fruitfully employed in the investigation of the customs, beliefs, social practices, and general conceptions of life prevalent in Little Italy on the lower North Side in Chicago, or in recording the more sophisticated folkways of the inhabitants of Greenwich Village and the neighborhood of Washington Square, New York."[67] Some Chicago-trained sociologists, such as Everett C. Hughes, later continued the fieldwork tradition at Brandeis University in Waltham, Massachusetts. Faculty there sent their graduate students out to nearby communities—Dorchester, Cambridge, Watertown—with the simple instruction, as one student put it, to take "copious field notes."[68] Another noted, "We didn't read books. We went out and collected information."[69] Ethnography was a "place-making process" in the gathering and writing of outsider stories.[70]

University of Chicago sociologists had famously drawn maps of urban areas, including "vice" zones. As it turned out, vice in the modern city had no borders—sometimes it was right across the street. As we will see, some of the ethnographers in the forthcoming chapters were graduate students conducting their research for theses or dissertations. They sometimes lived in deviant neighborhoods, or simply walked from their university into unorthodox sites such as skid row bars. Before writing his classic text, *The Hobo*, Nels Anderson traveled as a hobo and lived in Chicago's hobohemia. Paul Goalby Cressey studied Chicago's taxi-dance halls, the commercial establishments where women were hired for a dime a dance. He noted, "I had to choose dancing activities relatively near the University of Chicago."[71] Zora Neale Hurston studied rural African Americans in her Southern homeland. Sheri Cavan lived in Haight Ashbury, growing intrigued by the influx of hippies into her neighborhood. Laud Humphreys studied impersonal sex among men in public restrooms for what would later become his canonical text, *Tearoom Trade*.[72] His tearooms were in Forest Park, across the street from Washington University in St. Louis, where he was a graduate student in the Department of Sociology. Like the people they studied, these sociologists were sometimes marginal people living in deviant places.

The texts featured in the upcoming chapters predate yet anticipate the spatial turn across disciplines, which has recently brought welcome focus to places and spaces. Contemporary research in cultural geography, the sociology of space and place, and urban studies highlights the centrality of places, spaces, sites, locations, and built environments to everyday social relations and our understandings of them. Still, there is significant

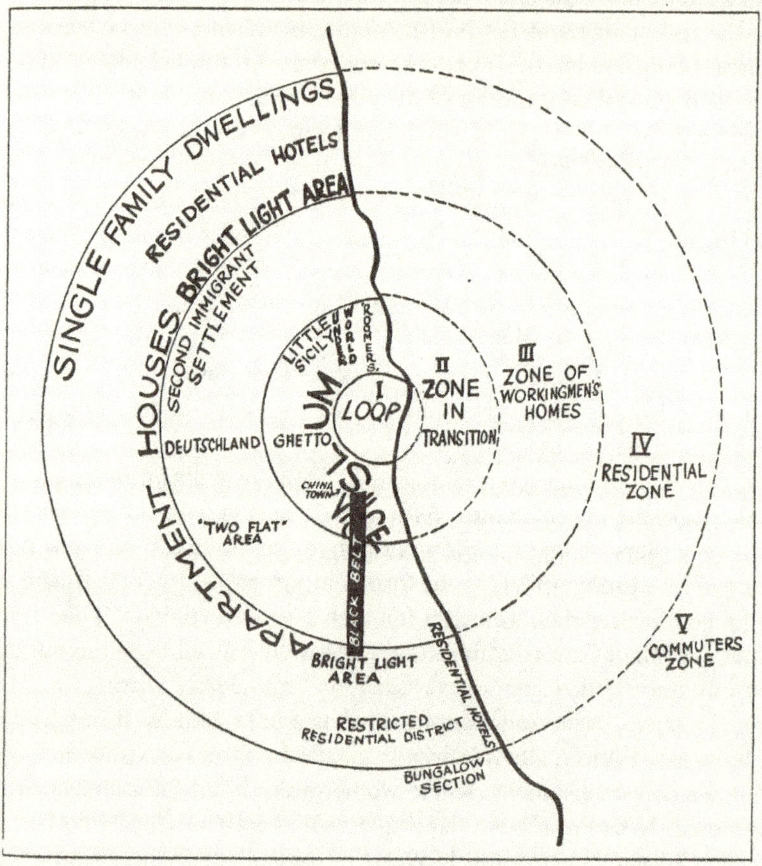

CHART II. Urban Areas

"Urban Areas," map illustrating the growth of cities, from *The City: Suggestions for Investigation of Human Behavior in the Urban Environment*, edited by Robert E. Park and Ernest W. Burgess, 1925. Courtesy of the Hanna Holborn Gray Special Collections Research Center, the University of Chicago Library.

disagreement over definitions and terms. I follow social geographer Tim Cresswell's and sociologist Thomas Gieryn's[73] definitions, wherein places consist of a geographic location, material form, and social meanings.[74] Places are "space filled up by people, practices, objects, and representations," dense with social norms.[75] These normative aspects of place are not neutral but imbued with power, reflecting and reproducing social hierarchies and inequalities.

My focus on ethnographic places in deviance studies came about after a visit to the tearooms Laud Humphreys studied in St. Louis. I began to recognize places as central characters in ethnographic stories of deviance. Below I conclude this introduction by outlining key ways that place matters in social life and social difference. Some readers will want to continue this conceptual exploration of deviant places, while others may prefer to skip to the next chapters for place-based stories about these researchers and their scholarship, controversies, and legacies.

- *Atmosphere*. Ethnographies are place stories. As the radio host of a popular storytelling show put it, "the spirit of the place always seeps into the story."[76] Yet what are spirit and atmosphere? Obviously, they are intangible qualities. What is it about particular places that prompts, for example, pilgrimages or tourism? Livingstone suggests that different "sights, sounds, and smells" are features of atmosphere, and that these site-specific conditions shape knowledge-making.[77] While the components of a place's atmosphere clearly vary, I would add that a strong affective response is undoubtedly a key component of atmosphere. The subfield of emotional geographies highlights how feelings are fluid and situated—produced by places and changing over time.[78] Places conjure feelings.
- *Places as social agents*. Foregrounding specific ethnographic locations reminds us that places are not simply blank-slate backdrops to a story set in motion by human actors. For example, if "deviance" is constructed by situations, then specific places are pivotal to such constructions. The different meanings and norms operating in a place help produce and reveal who conforms and who deviates.
- *Historicity*. Historicity is partially a matter of context, but more broadly represents the intersection of place and time. Place, as geographer Allan Pred notes, is "historically-contingent process."[79] If the ethnographer translates materiality and activities within places into stories, these specifics change over time. Analysis of ethnographic locality allows knowledge to be situated, questioned, and engaged, and these multiple stories can be retold. If, as scholars have argued, ethnographers themselves create the field of which they write, then histories of places shape the field at any given time.

  Geographer Doreen Massey described space as a simultaneity of stories, while place is a collection of those stories.[80] These place stories are multiple and antagonistic. Historical analysis of place helps reveal these layers. Erving Goffman's *Asylums* is illustrative. Having made only one early mention that his field research took place at St. Elizabeths Hospital [sic] in Washington, DC, Goffman devoted the entire text to stories supporting his argument that mental hospitals are "total institutions" that mortify the self. Yet knowledge of St. Elizabeths' history allowed other stories, questions, and place interpretations. For example, Michael Gambino argued that, contrary to Goffman's stark depiction, St. Elizabeths boasted innovative art- and dance-therapy programs in the mid-twentieth century. Gambino suggested that these therapeutic stories undermine Goffman's stories of the total institution. Another interpretation is that these two contrasting stories—therapeutic versus mortification— can not only coexist, but that the therapeutic story strengthens Goffman's argument. Ultimately, however, historical knowledge of the research sites—in this case, the specific mental hospital—can enhance analytic richness, complicate the ethnographic narrative, and make possible different questions and new retellings of asylum stories.

Likewise, the controversies over Laud Humphreys's *Tearoom Trade* acquire a new dimension when we consider that his field research was largely conducted in Forest Park, St. Louis. According to a colleague at Washington University, which is near the park, many male faculty members frequented the tearooms for sex. This confidant reported that these faculty were incensed by the book because it called attention to these activities. While this place story cannot be verified so many decades after Humphreys's book publication, it suggests the potential roles of stigma and shame in fueling furious campus controversies over the book.

- *Situational practices*. Ethnographers transform abstract spaces into places filled with normative and transgressive practices. Places themselves, as Cresswell argues, are practiced.[81] And, ethnographic places are filled with people carrying out their everyday activities. A fundamental tenet of early- and mid-twentieth-century sociology, especially deviance studies, is that situations produce human behavior and interactions. Do specific localities where ethnographers study produce particular practices? Is there something specific to the location, site, or region? How do located situations shape and produce ethnographic practice and interpretation? A geography of ethnography encourages analysis of the tension in

how places are constituted by individual practices, while simultaneously, places produce particular normative ways of being.
- *The ethnographic imaginary.* An exploration of the sites of actual classic research can help make apparent an ethnographic imaginary. Ethnographers pen their own stories, but do not ultimately control engaged readers, who develop their own imaginary about places, spaces, kinds of people, and myriad environmental details.

  Both the ethnographer and the reader are constructing place stories; one is not more real than the other. But the ethnographer extrapolates from research at the specific place, while the reader produces the imaginary. This imaginary is not random, however, but is a social product constructed of a (sometimes preconscious) brew of normative assumptions, transgressive expectations, cultural stereotypes and biases, hopes, fears, and other social fragments. A reader may or may not be fully aware of the ethnographic imaginary produced.

  My research on this book suggests to me that knowing an actual research location of an ethnography has potential outcomes. For one, it allows for a different kind of place knowledge and different place questions. For example, in visiting St. Elizabeths Hospital, I learned there were both men's and women's cottages. Had Erving Goffman studied both? It occurred to me that when I read *Asylums*, I imagined all male patients in the facility. I then asked a colleague who he imagined in Goffman's asylum—men or women? "Women," he instantly replied. Knowledge of an ethnographic places can sometimes make visible these normative assumptions the reader has made.
- *The social dimensions of buildings.* The built environment is a crucial feature of many ethnographic places. Buildings are not static structures. Rather, their meanings, norms, and functions are fluid and malleable. As William Whyte notes, architecture is not simply a text to be read, but its multiple meanings must be interpreted or translated.[82] Buildings are interactive, with ongoing exchanges between the architect's intentions and their myriad users. They act on and in turn are acted on by the individuals who occupy them. Buildings are often shaped by dynamics of the cultural and political context. Features of a building, such as style, layout, and the positions of built-in elements all communicate norms and meanings. These meanings are not transparent, and, as Whyte notes, can be challenging to interpret.

Buildings in this project reflect these dynamics. Asylums, for example, were purpose-built structures based on a vision that specific features of places and buildings would facilitate emotional health. In addition, the public restroom shows how a building's meaning can vary temporally and across varied cohorts. The same structure holds different norms for a park visitor making a quick visit than for a man interested in sex who notices glory holes and cubicle positioning. In this sense, aspects of the building communicate meanings and potential. The tearoom is a particularly productive example because, while architectural historians tend to focus on the role of the architect in expressing meaning, the public restroom is proof that individuals actively repurpose buildings for their own uses. Moreover, the repair and disrepair of stalls and windows in tearooms offer material evidence of ongoing social regulation, and transgression, of sexual norms. Buildings may also exude atmosphere—sensations and feelings intended or unintended by the architect. As Laud Humphreys wryly noted, some men were more attached to the tearoom buildings than to the men with whom they had sex there. While architectural scholars disagree about how buildings operate as social texts,[83] buildings are undeniably crucial analytic features of the stories that ethnographers tell.

- *Spatial metaphors.* "Outsiders" is, of course, the classic deviance spatial metaphor. Those who are different are on the margins. Ethnographers of difference frequently use spatial metaphors—for example, "damp corners," "interaction membrane," "territories of the self," "the other side," "driving deviance underground," and the like. These spatial metaphors evoke the marginal physicality of actual places. They show the centrality of places and spaces not only in telling stories about difference, but in the production of deviance itself. Normalcy and deviance are emplaced, difference is out of place.
- *Third places and ambient places.* Certain places represent what sociologist Ray Oldenburg calls "third places,"[84] the cafés, bars, general stores, and other public hangout spots outside of home and work. They are the places that foster interaction and public engagement. They fortify us. Ambient places are different and sometimes more generic than specific geographic locations, regions, or third places, but they can play a major supporting role in ethnographic stories. Ambient places are as varied as ethnographic stories, but are spots

of important social action in the research site. They are sometimes overlooked altogether as analytic places. Ambient places produce particular forms of activities and interactions. The benches outside the senior center or the corner of an asylum room, for example, allow for intimate exchanges, gossip, secretive negotiations, and other social dynamics that require discretion. They can foster privacy in public. While they may be conflated with spatial metaphors, they are actual places within specific research locations.

Hyperlink 1.1: New Social Knowledge of Difference

During the early- to mid-twentieth century, sociologists developed new ideas that challenged biological, psychiatric, and personality-based notions of social difference. They suggested that social marginality is a potentially universal condition, they criticized moral entrepreneurs for creating deviance, and they fostered research on differences that was not conceptualized in terms of fixed identities. Below are some of these core epistemic contributions to the social science of difference.

- *Strangeness, marginality, and outsiders.* Exemplified by the early work of W. E. B. Du Bois, Georg Simmel, Robert Park, and others, sociologists embraced the strange, marginal, different, and stigmatized. These conceptual approaches shifted emphasis from individual difference to a focus on the generalizability of strangeness, deviance, and marginality.
- *Societal reaction and labeling.* This perspective cast deviance as the outcome of a "transaction" between rule-makers and rule-breakers, or more specifically, between rule-makers and an individual *perceived* to be breaking the rules. The analytic shift from those on the margins—the deviants—to the rule-making strategies of social institutions and "moral entrepreneurs" unsettled previously stable categories of "normal" and "deviant," making it necessary to ask new questions, such as "whose rules?" This challenged midcentury essentialist assumptions that deviance inheres in the individual.
- *Becoming deviant.* Sociologists adopted the "career" metaphor to examine how individuals "become" deviant or "drift" into deviance. As part of the moral leveling implicit in the new deviance paradigm, studies of deviant "careers" traced the paths by which

alleged deviants such as nudists or street prostitutes learned, organized, and negotiated their worlds. The "career" metaphor enabled sociologists to examine how social factors elicited and sustained deviance in different ways.
- *Instability of categories.* Deviance studies of the 1960s blurred notions of fixed categories and identities and destabilized concepts of a core self. This relativized deviance, since allegedly abnormal behavior could only be understood in the context of broader social stresses, cultural meanings, location and place, and situational definitions. Modern deviance theorists also challenged the stability of deviance itself and the assumption that social categories were homogeneous. An important feature of deviance studies was this early embrace of multiplicity and heterogeneity.
- *Stigma.* Sociologists conceptualized stigma as the social control of difference. Erving Goffman famously defined stigma as "spoiled identity." In *Stigma: Notes on the Management of Spoiled Identity*, he argued that, like deviance itself, stigma was not inherent but contingent. In his famous conclusion that our inevitable failures to live up to social norms "cast some kind of shadow" on our everyday encounters, Goffman universalized the experience of difference.
- *Place and space.* Ethnographers explored specific locations and observed so-called deviant practices over time, for example in mental hospitals, pornographic bookstores, and hippie communes. While deviance scholars explored the roles of institutions, communities, and interactions in producing social difference, they also showed how deviance is constructed by, and lived out within, specific places in specific historical moments.

Hyperlink 1.2: FBI Surveillance & Keen Video Interview

Sociological ideas and some sociologists themselves were the targets of government investigation and sometimes harassment. During the McCarthy years, sociologists criticized social pressures toward conformity, while challenging positivist conceptions of categories and norms in areas such as crime. As a result, a number were placed under surveillance by J. Edgar Hoover's Federal Bureau of Investigation. These included some who feature in this book, for example W. E. B. Du Bois (author of the canonical text, *The Souls of Black Folk*, and cofounder of the National Association for the Advancement of Colored People), Herbert Blumer (whose sym-

Marginal People in Deviant Places. Map by Janice M. Irvine ©. Artist, Molly Brown, South Portland, Maine.

bolic interactionism shaped the deviance tool kit), Ernest Burgess (a critic of social Darwinism and major figure in the Chicago School), and Erving Goffman (considered by some to be a cofounder of deviance studies). Hoover was suspicious of the critical nature of sociological research, and at the bottom of one internal FBI report, about a talk on race rioting presented at an American Sociological Association conference, he penned, "The sociologists are at it again!"[85]

TWO

Making Up Hobos

Nels Anderson and Other Tramp Tales

Every hobo is a commentary on capitalism.[1]
Jeff MacGregor

Once hobos are on your mind, they seem to be everywhere. There are real and fictional hobos; famous and unknown hobos. There is a long-standing hobo convention with hobo kings and queens, a National Hobo Museum, a hobo cemetery, hobo newspapers, hobo autobiographies, a hobo vocabulary and symbol system. Hobo novels, films, songs, and poetry abound. Hobo graffiti still marks public places—some recently found at the Los Angeles River—tracing hobo wanderings in the early twentieth century. Contemporary handbooks advise hobo wannabees on how to be one. The hobo was extinct, it once seemed, yet the hobo lives on.

In the aftermath of the American Civil War, and with the rise of modern industrial capitalism, thousands of men and women traveled in search of work. Transient workers had wandered the US since its earliest days, as evident from early court records about so-called vagabonds. Yet this population swelled after 1873, prompting the invention of the term "tramp" and with it the subsequent construction of a tramp crisis. Critics cast tramps as invasive, predatory, and pathological. Popular culture later began to rebrand the tramp as a more sympathetic, feisty figure, a characterization that ultimately outlasted that of the menacing tramp. The stories told to us, and sold to us, about hobos constructed this paradoxical figure.

Hobos are an early example of modern outsiders, transgressing conventionality in significant ways. Moving from place to place, they undermined the American ideal of rootedness in a stable home. They typically moved alone, outside of the traditional nuclear family structure. They eschewed stable employment, and the obligations of child-rearing. Many adopted fluid sexualities rather than a domesticated, marital heterosexuality. Finally, they avoided material accumulation, traveling with little money and few possessions. This located them outside of a growing culture of consumer capitalism and aspirational affluence. Their rejection of middle-class domesticity in exchange for mobility, adventure, and freedom made hobos both idealized and reviled, consistent with the American attraction to, and fear of, difference.

There were multiple ways of knowing about hobos. Journalists, popular culture, medical scientists, social scientists, political activists, and hobos themselves all narrated hobo lives and ways. Different stories emerged. They were dangerous degenerates or hapless, harmless cartoon characters. Social reformers saw them as indigents in need of rehabilitation. A romantic hobo—the scruffy but beloved rebel—gradually emerged as an American icon. Ironically, the anti-acquisitive hobo figure could be packaged and sold as an edgy commodity. These myriad stories changed the emotional tenor of the hobo figure.

This chapter also tells hobo stories. It centers on Nels Anderson, a young sociology graduate student, a hobo himself, who wrote *The Hobo: The Sociology of the Homeless Man*, (1923). Hobos, and *The Hobo*, provide a useful entry into our journey through the stories of marginal people in deviant places. The book is an early departure from the pathologizing narratives of race science, yet reveals tensions in this emergent sociology as it only gradually broke from moral reform groups. Competing stories about hobos highlight different discourses on outsiders and nonconformity during a period of dynamic social change. The hobo, as a new social figure, illustrates how differences such as race, gender, sexuality, and economic status shaped possibilities for transgressing social norms.

The separate and overlapping literatures on both hobos and homelessness are as boundless as the open road. This chapter is not a comprehensive review of that material, nor an exhaustive account of hobos themselves. I do not address the broader issue of homelessness. I take the knowledge-making in sociologist Nels Anderson's text as my main theme, while exploring how multiple narrators, then and now, have told hobo stories. My timeline is largely that of his research, circa 1920–1923, and I focus on the pre-Depression hobo at the center of his study. Along the way, I

The Hobo, by Nels Anderson.

meander down paths that deepen my own story about the diverse stories that constructed hobos as modern outsiders.

What Is a Hobo, Anyway?

Key social, economic, and technological changes linked to modernity produced the hobo as a specific social type. The rise and expansion of a national railroad system allowed for freight-hopping in search of work (or adventure). Sociologist Georg Simmel's stranger, the wanderer who either leaves or lingers, might well have ridden in on a boxcar. In addition, the volatility of industrial capitalism produced unstable working conditions and transient labor markets. Communication and publishing technologies such as newspapers, magazines, silent films, and documentary photography afforded visibility to wandering workers, constructing them as tramps or hobos.

Homeless and jobless individuals often wandered by necessity, not choice. Yet it is clear from personal accounts that some individuals chose to live as hobos. They sought freedom from myriad social constraints, such as family life and a workaday world. They wanted adventure and travel. They lacked interest in stable employment and consumerism. A subculture emerged to support an "ethical code" of social defiance and pride in the hobo identity.[2] Writer and hobo Jack London gave this ebullient account of tramping:

> Every once in a while, in newspapers, magazines, and biographical dictionaries, I run upon sketches of my life, wherein, delicately phrased, I learn that it was in order to study sociology that I became a tramp. That is very nice and thoughtful of the biographers, but it is inaccurate. I became a tramp—well . . . because of the life that was in me, of the wanderlust in my blood that would not let me rest. Sociology was merely incidental; it came afterward, in the same manner that a wet skin follows a ducking. I went on 'The Road' because I couldn't keep away from it.[3]

In profound ways, it was this hobo—the one who chose a different way of living and being—who posed the real tramp menace by defying social norms.

A precise definition of "hobo" is elusive. Hobos were men—the very icon of "aggrieved National Manhood"[4]—yet there were women hobos.

Hobos were White, yet there is convincing evidence of racial diversity among hobos. Hobos were lazy drifters, yet they nonetheless built the American West. They were impoverished failures and romantic adventurers. The hobo is a symbol and myth, yet real people considered themselves hobos. The slipperiness of the term allows the hobo to be in the eye of the observer and the pen of the storyteller.

The term "hobo" has fallen out of mainstream contemporary usage, except as a historical referent. "Hobo" conjures up images of the disheveled, shuffling male figure, bindle (a sack on a stick) slung over his shoulder. Or is that the tramp? The terms "tramp," "bum," and "hobo" are often conflated and used imprecisely to refer to (stereotypically) men who are "homeless" or unhoused and unattached. Millionaire James Eads How, who founded the school known as the Hobo College in 1913, defined wanderers as follows: "The bum drinks and wanders; the tramp dreams and wanders, but the hobo, often with the same temperament as the pioneer, works and wanders."[5] Subsequent writers and historians, such as sociologist Nels Anderson, adopted and tweaked this typology: a hobo wanders and works; a tramp wanders and does not work; a bum neither wanders nor works. Historian Todd DePastino argues that hobos themselves developed this classificatory system to put themselves at the top.[6] As Anderson pointed out, these distinctions, while important, were not "hard and fast,"[7] and he at times used them interchangeably in his book.

Historian DePastino argues that the differing terminology actually represents three chronological stages of American homelessness. The tramp emerged first, in the 1870s. An economic depression in 1873 launched thousands of jobless men onto the rails in search of work. By the 1890s, the particular geographic places, social worlds, culture, and politics produced by tramping had also produced the hobo. DePastino quips that the hobo is a "tramp on steroids," since hobo culture was more organized and politically militant than trampdom. The bum appeared in the 1940s and '50s, marking an end to the romantic hobo subculture.[8] Also in the 1940s, traveling workers became known as migrants and migrant workers. This periodization does not completely hold up (hobo writer A-No. 1 wrote in 1914 that the twin of the hobo was "the City Bum"[9]), but it highlights, as does its fuzziness, that these were not distinct categories of different social types. The individuals, their social worlds and practices, and the various terms for them were overlapping and unstable.

The vocabularies, subcultures, and popular representations of unattached transients shift historically. The term "hobo" became popular dur-

More than twenty-five years a bindle stiff. Photograph by Dorothea Lange, 1938. Courtesy of Farm Security Administration, Office of War Information Photograph Collection, the Library of Congress.

ing the depression of 1893, and it has various origin stories. Many suggest that "hobo" stems from "hoe-boy," or farm hand, reflecting an agricultural derivation. Others argue that "hobo" comes from the Latin "Homo Bonus" (good man), or a common hobo greeting, "Ho, boy."[10] Both the terms "hobo" and "tramp" have been romanticized at different historical moments. Likewise, all terms for homeless wanderers have been stigmatized, their subjects associated with danger, disease, laziness, assault, even murder. Nels Anderson viewed the hobo as a migratory worker, one pivotal to developing the American frontier, and he believed that this particular figure was disappearing by 1920.

A Hobo Writes *The Hobo*

Sociologist Nels Anderson's 1923 text, *The Hobo*, represented an early sociological and ethnographic approach to studying social differences. He came to the graduate program at the University of Chicago in 1921, having been a hobo for many years. His father had been a hobo; his family had been extremely mobile, relocating ten times; and then he himself became a "hobo worker" starting in 1906. He worked as a field hand, miner, lumberjack, and more, later catching up on his education at Brigham Young University from 1912 to 1920. On advice from mentors, he enrolled in the University of Chicago's sociology department, riding a freight train to get there.

Chicago sociology embraced, and in key respects pioneered, the study of marginality and outsiders. Many courses required field research, and Anderson was surprised to discover that his professors permitted him to write about the hobo world. Given his firsthand experiences as a hobo, he found this a "practical" solution to the "unexpected demand on [his] time"[11] that field research represented. Anderson met Ben Reitman, a physician who worked with Chicago's indigent and homeless population. Reitman later helped him secure grants and funding for his research from social services such as the Chicago Council of Social Agencies and United Charities. This support, and the intervention of his Chicago mentors, such as Ernest Burgess, shaped his research in significant ways.

Although subsequent scholars have described *The Hobo* as ethnography or participant observation,[12] Anderson himself later wrote that he did not think of his methods in this way at the time (and indeed, participant-observation had not yet emerged as a methodological term in sociology). Anderson, who had lived as a child near this area, rented a room on Halsted Street in the area known as Hobohemia, and began compiling documents and taking notes for his thesis and the reports his funders would expect. He regularly interacted with the residents there, also conducting relatively informal interviews. He collected sixty life histories for his funders. This immersion in the field, extensive documentation, and abundant gathering of life histories are consistent with the ethnographic method.

Anderson compiled these documents and interviews into a report that he could submit to his funding agencies, and he submitted it to mentors Robert Park and Ernest Burgess with some anxiety. The "report" ultimately became his master's thesis, and the first monograph published in the sociological series of the University of Chicago Press.[13] His professors were reportedly delighted with the manuscript, Park telling Anderson, over his protestations, "They will publish it as soon as we can get it ready."[14] Today's students would be unlikely to have a master's thesis rushed into publication, but Anderson's advisors' robust support for his hobo report underscores the department's support for the study of outsiders and perhaps an early recognition that such research might generate a profitable buzz. According to Anderson, Park heavily edited the manuscript and suggested that Anderson use the term "hobohemia," hobo jargon for low-rent areas frequented by bohemians and hobos. Park was also apparently responsible for changing the title—Anderson later reported not knowing the book was entitled *The Hobo* until it was published; his title had been *The Homeless Man in Chicago*. Park's title reflects his preferring "the standpoint of the bohemian to that of the philistine."[15] Park, Burgess, and Anderson worked nonstop together to revise and submit the book to the press.

There is an uneasy tension in *The Hobo* between disparate constructions of the hobo: the romantic wanderer who hops trains and sometimes finds migrant jobs; a heroic modern figure who built the railroads and frontier, and was vanishing in the twenties; and the impoverished, homeless worker. The book's title tried to resolve some of this tension by including all types: *The Hobo: The Sociology of the Homeless Man*. Anderson later recalled that his successful term papers on the hobo opened up funding opportunities with reformers engaged with the problem of homelessness. "I had never thought of the hobo in this way, but in Hobohemia, his Chicago habitat, he was indeed among the homeless. I began reading articles, reports, and books about the homeless and the vagrancy problem. None touched the hobo as I knew him."[16] He referred, derisively, to "the homeless man" as "a social work term."[17]

Anderson later noted that from his former hobo perspective, he saw the compilation of the book as a way of earning a living, or "getting by" in his new sociological world.[18] In this sense, the book paid off for him. He later pointed out that *The Hobo* served more as an "asset" for Robert Park, who had been trying unsuccessfully to launch his series with the press. Anderson recalled that when he turned in his MA thesis, Park smiled enigmatically.[19] Park, this suggests, had found a new social type and social knowledge about difference that he could package and sell. It was the first of many canonical sociological texts to examine marginal social figures such as taxi dancers, delinquents, gangs, and others.

Becoming a Hobo

In the early twentieth century, race science designated social differences as innate biological characteristics.[20] Although focused on racial differences, evolutionary biologists also classified other alleged undesirables they deemed unfit.[21] One of these was the tramp.

Race scientists viewed tramps as genetic deviants. Historian Jeffrey Brown notes that tramps were depicted as biological degenerates, with "beady eyes and sloping foreheads."[22] Scientists argued that tramps had a genetic disposition to wander rather than settle. They diagnosed tramps with various allegedly congenital pathologies, such as wanderlust, roving disposition, railroad fever, or dromomania, a type of ambulatory automatism. Likewise, American eugenicist Charles Davenport cast "nomadism" as a genetically based racial or tribal characteristic. Tramps, therefore, became targets of late-nineteenth-century eugenicist strategies designed to eliminate them. For example, W. H. Brewer argued that tramps were "like a tribe of savages" and needed to be confined and segregated to prevent their reproduction.[23] Incarceration, institutionalization, and sterilization were some of the solutions proposed to address the dangerous and diseased tramp. Journalists amplified these stories, generating widespread cultural anxieties about tramps.

Anderson's hobo project at the University of Chicago was, in part, a repudiation of these dominant pathological and essentialist constructions of wanderers. He wrote a different story about the hobo by describing the practices by which hobos, in specific historical contexts, were made, not born. In retrospect, we can see *The Hobo* as following in the sociological footsteps of W. E. B. Du Bois, Hull House scholars, and the University of Chicago with its early emphasis on historical context, communities, and urban places. Like others of his era, Anderson ignored women hobos.

The Historicized Hobo (Male)

Anderson historicized the hobo. He emphasized that the hobo, as a wandering laborer, was produced by the needs of industrial and agricultural society. In the wake of the depression of 1893, hobos built the railroads, and later the automobile roads. They worked in mines, logged the forests, built bridges and factories, and worked in farm fields. The "true hobo," for Anderson, was one "willing to go anywhere to take a job and equally willing to move on later."[24] But the true hobo learned it as a set of practices. Anderson challenged essentialist conceptions, pointing out that the terms "wanderlust" and "dromomania" pathologized hobo workers and assume "an inborn urge to be mobile, an inability to resist the pull of the road."[25] Rather, he stressed, "on the American scene mobility was imperative, else the frontier would still be wilderness."[26] Hobo labor, then, essentially built a society that then derided hobos as savage menaces. As such, it was an early form of what Chicago sociologist Everett Hughes would later call "dirty work,"[27] jobs that were simultaneously necessary yet stigmatized.

In addition, *The Hobo* helped effect an early conceptual shift from viewing difference not as innate and unchanging, but as a fluid process of *becoming*, shaped by culture, situations, and interactions. One became a hobo by going to certain places and learning and performing specific practices to organize and negotiate hobo social worlds. *The Hobo* was the first major sociological glimpse into these places, practices, and performances.

In his autobiography, Anderson recalled his first hobo venture. First, he paid for train tickets, then, after running out of money, walked fifty miles over twenty-four hours: "Not less than a dozen long freight trains passed me but I knew naught about using them."[28] Trains were places, but they were also a set of practices. Riding the rails—free—was a basic hobo practice that had to be learned. Over time, others taught him the train schedules, the best positions on the trains, and how to minimize his shadow so that the railroad police didn't notice him on top of boxcars. To avoid being caught, hobos jumped onto trains while they were moving, so they also needed to learn ways to hop on and off safely.

Train tickets were expensive, and as Nels Anderson recounted about his hobo years, he could not afford to buy them. Freight-hopping (or train-hopping) was therefore a necessary hobo practice. It was both illegal and dangerous, heavily policed by the railway bulls, or police. Early hobo autobiographies, such as the one by Jack London,[29] described the practices. Hobos rode on top of boxcars, in between cars, or inside boxcars, sometimes tearing up floor boards to make fires. Jumping onto a rolling boxcar required strength and nerve. In addition, "riding the rods" referred to riding on the truss rods located about eighteen inches under the train. Hobos would squeeze into the space, sometimes positioning a board across to lie on. Glen Mullin told of harrowing danger in his 1925 memoir, *Adventures of a Scholar Tramp*: "With sickening vividness my imagination focused upon my own mangled body in the twisted and smoking wreckage. I saw my severed head wedged in the tracks, the ghastly eyes staring at the beholder through blood-flecked spectacles. . . . I had heard an engineer tell once of finding a gory human head with foam in its mouth riding on a truck."[30] Every year, many hobos were mutilated or killed from freight-hopping.

And there was more to learn: how to "hit back doors"[31] to panhandle; the proper etiquette in hobo jungles: and hobo slang. Jack London discussed learning hobo lingo: "A new world was calling to me in every word that was spoken—a world of rods and gunnels, blind baggages and 'side-door Pullmans,' 'bulls' and 'shacks,' 'floppings' and 'chewin's,' 'pinches' and 'get-aways,' 'strong arms' and 'bindle-stiffs,' 'punks' and 'profesh.' And it all spelled Adventure." The ability to tell a good story was also crucial in what Jack London called "a story-telling debauch" frequently held in jungles or boxcars. Hobos took new names, reinventing themselves. Often, they based these names on the places with which they identified (Pittsburg Jack), race (Chi Whitey), or ethnicity (New York Irish). Anderson later wrote a "how-to" manual under the pseudonym Dean Stiff. This "handbook for hobos" covered a range of essential hobo practices, such as "mooching," what the "well-dressed hobo should wear," hobo health tips, how to avoid social workers, enjoying hobo leisure, and hobo sexuality.[32] Although primarily a humorous book, the handbook underscored the sociological argument that one became a hobo through social practices, not biological predisposition.

Likewise, being a hobo was a transient identity, not a fixed one. A hobo might acquire a "wish to settle," or, conversely, a domesticated individual might, as Anderson said of his father, have "lost for a time his wish to settle."[33] One became a hobo, or one could stop wandering to hobo places and cease practicing a hobo existence. Anderson's description of these fluid identities anticipated later queer ideas.

Finally, *The Hobo* accomplished much more than challenging biological determinism and championing hobo workers. It was a fundamental critique of what we would now call heteronormative consumerism. Anderson was critical of hobo literature that depicted them from the standpoint of "middle-class conventional values."[34] In Anderson's text, the hobo represented more than a laborer building the American frontier. He was a modern figure living outside the traditional nuclear family structure and on the margins of capitalist society. Anderson later wrote about the hobo, "Their homelessness was seen as pathological in a society which assumes as axiomatic that every individual must belong somewhere, must have family, must have economic roots."[35] Hobos, he noted, did not belong "to a world of appointment keeping."³⁶ Hobos were outsiders, yet also insiders within their own social world of hobohemia.

While Anderson and later scholars complained about the romanticization of the hobo in popular culture, this idealized depiction also illustrates the strong mainstream appeal of rebellion—the fantasy of independence, detachment from traditional social constraints, and freedom from an increasing emphasis on consumption. The hobo embodied this new outsider possibility. In some of these respects, the hobo prefigured later countercultural figures such as the Beats and the early hippies.

Women Hobos

Anderson and other scholar-pundits of the era, however, got it wrong when it came to women. Anderson wrote, "Tramping is a man's game. Few women are ever found on the road. The inconveniences and hazards of tramping prevent it."³⁷ This was a common misconception in the late nineteenth and early twentieth centuries. A "tramp census" of over 1,000 homeless men conducted by Trinity College sociologist J. J. McCook in 1893 claimed there were no women tramps, while Ben Reitman, writing as the fictional woman hobo, "Boxcar Bertha," said hobo women were so rare at the turn of the century that encountering one would "cause a little stir."³⁸ (**See Hyperlink 2.1:** Citing Bertha, on Queer Evidence.)

Several years after Anderson published *The Hobo*, hobo writer Clifford Maxwell wrote that despite the myriad tales of women hobos, he had never met one, since women did not hit the roads out of "incurable wanderlust" as hobo men did.³⁹ The invisibility of women hobos was even codified—in most states, tramps were, by legal definition, men.⁴⁰

Yet thousands of women hobos hitchhiked or rode the rails across the United States when Anderson wrote in the 1920s, and even more in the 1930s during the Great Depression.⁴¹ Estimates are difficult for the pre-Depression era, before wandering women caught the attention of social reformers. Many female hobos dressed as men, which is perhaps why Anderson and others did not recognize them. Hobo writer A-No. 1, who wrote about Hobo Nell in *The Adventures of a Female Tramp*, in 1914, included a front page claiming that 10,000 women and girls took to the road every year, with 2,500 of them becoming vagabonds. The source of these figures, however, is unclear. Studies during the 1930s indicated that one in ten transients was a woman.⁴² In his 1934 study, Thomas Minehan collected the life histories of 1,465 young tramps, of whom 88 were girls.⁴³

Riding the Rails, a 1997 documentary on young people hopping freight trains during the Great Depression, offers some contemporary evidence.[44] Based on 3,000 letters from hobo veterans of the 1930s, the film includes interviews with a woman who became a hobo with her girlfriend after running away from home. Another woman wrote to the filmmakers about how shameful it had been to be a hobo. Hobo men recalled that they had seen numerous women and girls on the rails, most of them passing. Passing women—women who dressed and lived as men—did so for numerous reasons, including economic imperatives, the need for safety, and the wish for freedom from gender discrimination and the constraints of traditional femininity. Undoubtedly for some hobo women, riding the rails was a flight from the suffocating cult of domesticity. Others were probably not "passing women," but rather might have identified as what we would now call trans, a category that, as Ian Hacking might say, was not then a way to be a person in the way it is today.[45]

Transient women wandered for myriad reasons. They included single mothers with children, women fleeing domestic violence, older women, and poor women. Like hobo men, economic demands drove many women to wander looking for work in the transient labor market of the early twentieth century. And like hobo men, some women hobos sought adventure and freedom. Similar to men, the tramp identity was often fluid for women, who might move in and out of hobo life based on economic and other factors.

If the male hobo represented a modern outsider repudiating social constraints, the woman hobo signified an even more radical departure from the deeply policed demands of femininity, conventional domesticity, marriage, and motherhood. Becoming a woman hobo, then, required different social practices than for men. Appearance was key to the safety and agility of transient women. They dressed as men, wearing overalls, khakis, flannel shirts, and sturdy shoes. Cross-dressing was illegal in this era, and hobo women could be criminally charged if discovered (these laws also ensnared what we now term gay, lesbian, and trans people as well). Women hobos often adopted short haircuts and the slouching "typical hobo gait."[46] Historian Lynn Weiner notes that while women hobos did ride the rails, they also tended to hitchhike because they could be more successful soliciting rides.[47] Finally, women hobos transgressed deeply gendered social norms barring them from the new public places of modernity. Women wanderers, whether passing or not, transgressed normative prohibitions against inhabiting public places like the street, which were culturally framed as male and unsafe for women. In an era when some women were newly entering gender-segregated workplaces and commercial leisure sites, women hobos probably inhabited male-dominated hobo places, such as jungles.

Scientific racism was entwined with scientific sexism in Anderson's era of research, defining women by their bodies. Biological determinism naturalized gendered inequality, while sociologists were gradually beginning to tell different stories. Anderson ignored women hobos, but he did challenge gender stereotyping—for example, the assumption that only women possessed skills such as cooking and mending. He pointed out that in the jungles, hobo men themselves were quite adept at establishing "domesticity" outside of the nuclear family structure. Sociologist Walter Reckless, in his 1934 article about why women became hobos, more explicitly challenged biological determinist views. He noted that men had an easier time being hobos, not because of biology or psychology, but because of "sociological conditions."[48] Reckless observed—accurately, it turns out—that there was no reason to assume that transient women "will not invade Hobohemia and the jungles just as women generally have encroached upon all the other original provinces of men. The indications are that women are making pretty good hoboes as hoboes go."[49] Women, it turned out, continued to encroach on male provinces, including the academy, gradually shifting how gender stories were told.

Hobosexuality

Whether it was sex with women or sex with men (or boys), Nels Anderson's overall depiction of it was grim. Gone, and apparently undeserving of sexual pleasure, was the plucky hobo who wandered for work, motivated by some combination of economic need and wish for independence. In his place was a dirty ("unpresentable appearance"), unhoused social outcast ("unattractive personality") doomed to soliciting prostitutes, who themselves were "forlorn and bedraggled creatures."[50] Anderson characterized hobo sexuality variously as isolated, fleeting, unhealthy, and "perverted." His brief chapter reveals unresolved tensions between his focus on the romantic hobo and the unhappy homeless man; between sexual essentialism and an early social constructionism; between emphasis on sexual danger versus sexual pleasure; and between appreciation versus the derogation of hobo life. Defying the book's overall defense of the detached man seeking work and freedom, he barely allowed his hobo a decent sex life.

This moralistic spin was not inevitable. Stories about hobo sexuality—whether by hobo authors themselves or by their ethnographic observers such as Nels Anderson—would have been shaped by countervailing cultural discourses in the early twentieth century. On the one hand, sex is easy to condemn. Religious dictates, social policies, social reformers, and other institutions upheld a traditional morality of heterosexual marriage, monogamy, and prohibitions against nonreproductive sexuality. Homosexuality was prohibited, regulated, and stigmatized. On the other hand, sex had become a topic of public discourse and a subject of scientific research. The sexual revolution of the 1920s was beginning as Nels Anderson wrote his thesis. Public dance halls, speakeasys, taxi dances, black-and-tan cabarets, and other forms of sexualized urban leisure places burgeoned in cities such as Chicago. Homosexual advocacy arose among diverse cohorts such as urban bohemians, political activists, artists, and some sexologists and social scientists. Meanwhile, hobos themselves presented a challenge to traditional, domesticated sexuality. The sexual culture, and the production of sexual knowledge, were changing.

Sexologists and social scientists were inventing new ideas about sex, and they disagreed with each other. In the late nineteenth century, sexologists began establishing cultural authority over sex. Researchers such as Richard von Krafft-Ebing (Germany-Austria), Magnus Hirschfeld (Germany), and Havelock Ellis (England) were key figures in this new scientific study of sex. Cumulatively, they developed taxonomies and classifications of sex, inventing new ways of thinking, talking, and feeling about sexuality. These early sexologists differed among themselves in their methods, theories, and ideological approaches concerning sex. Braided through this early medicalization of sex, however, were determinist ideas that defined both sex and race as located in the physical body. As Siobhan Somerville notes, these new experts "assumed enormous cultural power to organize and pathologize those marked as sexually deviant or racially 'other.'"[51] As Anderson was studying in the 1920s, European sexologists had already established research institutes and academic journals, and had published canonical texts.

Essentialist and eugenic discourses of scientific racism pervaded sexual science. As early sexology traveled to the United States, Chicago physicians such as James Kiernan and G. Frank Lydston figured prominently. They collaborated with European sexologists on studies of sex perverts, and established Chicago as a center for sex research. Lydston pursued the practice of physiognomy to determine whether sex criminals could be identified by their photographs. Other physicians promoted methods such as anthropometry to measure differences, along with castration, clitoridectomy, and institutionalization to treat sex deviants.[52]

Research on sexuality was newer among social scientists in the United States at that time. Immediately prior to Anderson's graduate work, University of Chicago scholar W. I. Thomas had been dismissed from the university because of a sex scandal, possibly creating a chilling effect. Still, by the 1920s, commercialized sex, marriage, homosexuality, and related topics occupied sociologists and other social reformers. Several University of Chicago sociologists served on the city's Vice Commission. Formed to investigate prostitution, the commission expanded its purview to investigate the increase in "sexual perversions."[53] Chicago School sociologists Robert Park and Ernest Burgess are known for having assigned students to explore the city, including its sexual undergrounds.

These new and competing forms of knowledge circulated as Anderson crafted his own sexual story. Anderson's analysis reads as only marginally shaped by this intellectual climate, as opposed to his immediate material influences. His social-reformer funders considered unconventional, non-heteronormative sexuality to be a social problem (Anderson placed his chapter, "The Sex Life of the Homeless Man," in the book section entitled "The Hobo Problem"). As historian Chad Heap notes, student researchers paid by urban reform and antivice organizations were put in the position of policing the very groups they studied.[54] Finally, physician Ben Reitman mentored Anderson, and Reitman's dedication to treating venereal disease among hobos undoubtedly focused his student on sexual disease and danger.

Hobos, Anderson argued, have few "ideal" sexual relationships with women, and, since most were unmarried, their sex lives were "naturally illicit." Heterosexuality as a term for social identity signifying desire between women and men had only emerged in the early twentieth century. The word first appeared in Merriam-Webster's *New International Dictionary* in 1923 (the year *The Hobo* was published), but its definition as "normal sexuality" would not appear until the dictionary's second edition in 1934.[55] Not surprisingly, then, Anderson referred to "associations with women" rather than heterosexuality. These associations took two forms in the book: relations with prostitutes; and noncommercial short-term relationships. Anderson painted a gloomy picture of both.

Since commercialized sex concerned Anderson's funders, he largely focused on prostitution. Some younger hobos could "put on a front" and frequent Chicago's cheap burlesque theaters on West Madison Street or State Street, which Anderson described as "vulgar and inexpensive" (perhaps they also went to taxi-dance halls, which were popular when Anderson studied). Most, however, had to settle for the "second-rate prostitute," who might rob a hobo, infect him with venereal disease, or both. Anderson conceded that relationships like these could be positive: "These attachments between homeless men and prostitutes are often quite real."[56] Those were, however, according to him, rare. Anderson acknowledged that "tramps" entered into "transient free unions" with women when possible.[57] However, Anderson said almost nothing about these transient relationships, possibly because this was not commercialized sex.

Homosexuality claimed most of Anderson's attention, which he called "perversion among the tramps."[58] The term "homosexuality," to refer to behaviors and social identity, was invented in the 1860s, much earlier than "heterosexuality." Anderson used this term, although he often referred to "perversion" and to the men as "perverts." Sexologists disagreed about the precise nature and definition of homosexuality, but Anderson cited the work of German physician Iwan Bloch, who was considered the founder of *Sexualwissenschaft* (sexology), and British scholar and social reformer Havelock Ellis.

Ellis, the first sexual modernist,[59] challenged traditional institutions such as marriage, and contested conventional sexual beliefs of the era, such as those prohibiting masturbation. His influential text, *Sexual Inversion*, argued against nineteenth-century notions that homosexuality was acquired through "perversions" such as frequent masturbation.[60] (The text was censored in England, but published in Germany in 1896 and soon after in the United States.) Instead, he argued that homosexuality was a congenital and natural condition, and should be decriminalized and destigmatized. Unlike other sexologists, such as Richard von Krafft-Ebing, who viewed inversion as both congenital and acquired, Ellis insisted that it was congenital.

In *Sexual Inversion*, Ellis included an appendix by author and occasional hobo Josiah Flynt (whose full name was Josiah Flynt Willard), "Homosexuality among Tramps." Flynt, who lived among tramps in disguise, supported Ellis's idea that male homosexuality could result from the absence of women. Flynt saw these older men as a threat to boys, whom he likened to slaves. He depicted hobos as dangerous predators and boys as innocent victims (Flynt died, perhaps fittingly for his transient life, in a hotel in 1907). This sentiment was consistent with tramp anxieties of this era, and accounts of tramp rapists in the late nineteenth century prompted public talk of lynching them. These accounts of predatory homosexuality exacerbated tramp stigmatization.

Although Anderson referred to the arguments of Havelock Ellis, he may not have actually read or understood Ellis's text. Anderson quoted

Ellis as saying that certain men have a "congenital predisposition" to homosexuality. But Anderson went on to say that these men are feminine in traits and tastes, a view that Ellis disputed. Anderson claimed there was a "second group" who "temporarily substituted homosexual for heterosexual behavior."[61] In this depiction, homosexuality could be acquired, another stereotype from that era that Ellis had disputed, although Ellis acknowledged the prevalence of same-sex behavior in certain situations, such as prisons. Anderson called these hobos "perverts by conversion," arguing that homosexuality mainly arises because of the transience and isolation of homeless men. Anderson's disparaging approach to sex between hobo men was more consistent with the condemnation of such behavior by social reformers, rather than reflecting the influence of new theoretical perspectives and debates among sexologists.

Cultural expressions from that era—such as slang, memoirs, and song—do point to exploitation of boys by men. Hobos had a language of predation: "jockers" or "wolves" were older hobos who took young "punks" in a sexualized relationship in exchange for protection or other material goods. Historian Regina Kunzel notes that prisoners also used the slang of "jockers," "punks," and "wolves," and incorporated these dynamics in prison sexual culture.[62] This similarity is not surprising, since hobos and prisoners were not infrequently an overlapping population. (*The Hobo* was also the site of one of the first appearances of the term "fag," which Anderson included in his "types of hobos" as "men or boys who exploit sex for profit."[63] Some scholars have suggested that the hobo term "gay-cats" was an early example of the slang term "gay" for homosexual, but hobos defined it as a tramp who is new to the road, or a "tenderfoot" in hobohemia[64]).

A number of hobo memoirs mention seduction, such as ones by Jack London (who also vividly described boys, or "road-kids," preying on older men), and Carl Sandburg. The popular hobo folk song, "Big Rock Candy Mountain," had the jocker-punk dynamic as its theme. Harry McClintock, the song's author, cited the final verse in a later copyright dispute, expurgated from its many mainstream versions: "I've hiked and hiked till my feet are sore / And I'll be damned if I hike any more / To be buggered sore like a hobo's whore / In the Big Rock Candy Mountains."[65] The gendered rendition of a masculinized jocker and a feminized punk reflects a familiar dynamic in that era.

Traces of cultural anxieties shadow Anderson's account of hobo "sexual perversion," especially concerning men and boys. He perpetuated Flynt's ideas that hobos were dangerous predators. Still, Anderson disputed the common notion that boys were held in "slavery," and instead acknowledged that there could be genuine intimacy between a man and a boy, although he quickly qualified that claim. Such intimacy, in his view, would be as transient as hobos themselves. Overall, Anderson saw men as a threat to boys, and sex between them as an outcome of their "habits and their isolation."[66] Unlike heterosexual men, who were the inevitable victims of women prostitutes, he cast homosexual men as the inevitable victimizers. In this, Anderson echoed the popular perspective of various antivice organizations.

Since Anderson claimed that women hobos were virtually nonexistent, they were absent from his account of hobo sexuality. In *The Hobo*, women appeared only as dangerous prostitutes, not wanderers themselves. Yet although women did live as hobos, there is scant evidence about their sexuality, aside from claims that they exchanged sex for needed goods, and that they endured sexual assault. Indeed, most accounts of hobo women construct her as essentially sexual in nature. The woman hobo was so strongly equated with sexual immorality that the word "tramp" came to prefigure "slut" as a slang term for promiscuity.

Similarly, lesbians were completely absent in *The Hobo*, and largely invisible in the broader culture. Anderson had relied on the work of Havelock Ellis to explain homosexuality, and Ellis himself barely discussed lesbians, giving them "weak treatment" and upholding stereotypes.[67] So Anderson's omission is perhaps not surprising. Yet the lesbian hobo may most fully realize the idealized romanticized hobo image of a modern outsider defying social conventions of family structures and consumerism. Like hobo men, lesbian hobos typically had economic motivations for hitting the road, yet they were additionally sexual and gender outlaws.

Anderson's final analysis was one likely to appeal to his reform-oriented funders, who viewed hobo lives as social problems. His bleak view of hobo sexuality belied how he otherwise appreciated the hobo for purposefully transgressing the conventional norms of the nuclear family. He concluded, "A social outcast, he still wants the companionship which his mode of life denies him. Debarred from family life, he hungers for intimate associations and affection."[68] In his later autobiography, Anderson seemed to break with the Juvenile Protective Association and with his own analysis in *The Hobo*. The JPA, he said, feared that boys were being sexually victimized by hobo men. Anderson later recounted, "What I did learn, which I had not mentioned in *The Hobo*, boys were much more exposed to homosexual contact in downtown movies and along the lakefront park than in Hobohemia."[69] In *The Hobo*, however, Anderson mounted only a tepid defense of hobo homosexuality, while mainly condemning it.

Places and Traces

Nels Anderson's text represented a quintessentially Chicago School approach to how places within the modern city constructed new ways of being a person. He did not fully challenge determinist and moralistic stories about sexuality. Yet Anderson's close examination of place emphasized *how*, not *why*, one became a hobo. New social theories and methods shifted ways of knowing about differences, and prompted new questions.

Places—and movement through them—defined the hobo. Their transience and mobility distinguished hobo social worlds from traditional, settled family life. Unless they became part of the "home guard" who no longer wandered, hobos lived and navigated through many places. This section considers Anderson's explorations of hobo places and their hobos. These include Chicago's Hobohemia and main stem (a section of West Madison Street from the Chicago River to Halsted Street), hobo jungles, railroad boxcars, and the sites of hobo graffiti by which hobos sometimes communicated their locations and destinations.

Hobos moved through many places, but Chicago's distinct location and history led to its reputation as the hobo capital of the world. The city built its first rail connection in 1848, and by the end of the nineteenth century had more rail lines, with tracks radiating in more directions, than any other North American city. At the time Nels Anderson wrote *The Hobo*, Chicago had thirty-nine different railways and 2,840 miles of steam railway tracks inside the city itself.[70] Trains and tracks dominated the downtown, killing pedestrians, blocking intersections, belching smoke, and roaring furiously. Locals said a pig could travel straight through Chicago by train, but not a person—all ongoing travelers had to change trains there.[71] Such abundant opportunities for hopping trains made it a good place to be a hobo.

The hobo was produced by broad economic factors, such as the volatility of industrial capitalism. Yet on the local level, hobos were a product of where they lived. *The Hobo* began with several chapters on hobo places—hobohemias, the main stem, jungles. Robert Park's preface to the book represents an early theorization of place. Human nature, Park argued, was the product of environment; places shaped people, and places produced insiders and outsiders. Anderson's study, Park continued, would examine "the 'homeless man'" in "his own habitat; the social milieu which he has created for himself within the limits of the larger community by which he is surrounded, but from which he is, in large part, an outcast."[72] This articulation of the social role of places is not only emblematic of the Chicago School's urban sociology, but it prefigured a cross-disciplinary turn to theorizing place by many decades. (Park used scare quotes for "homeless man," a hint that he may indeed have viewed the book in the way he pitched it to the University of Chicago Press, as one about the romantic hobo rather than the disadvantaged homeless.)

If, as anthropologist Susan Phillips suggests, hobos carried their places with them,[73] it is also the case that they established places, both transient and stable, where they could be insiders on the outside. As historian Todd DePastino put it, on the main stem, hobos "were relatively free to flaunt their countercultural way of life."[74] Hobohemia was where hobos congregated in cities. These places, while in the city, were also separate from residential and business districts. Because of Chicago's location at the intersection of railroad lines, Anderson noted, it was the largest hobohemia. West Madison had once been a wealthy residential area where, as one observer noted, marble-fronted houses lined the streets and horse-chestnut trees bloomed in large yards. It declined after the Great Chicago Fire of 1871, becoming an area where "grimy" and "dilapidated" tenant houses, hotels, and rooming houses provided dingy lodging for a largely male, immigrant population of jobless men.[75] During his field research, Anderson lived in a working-class hotel on Halstead Street, near the Madison Street main stem, close to where his family had lived in 1899. It was home territory for him.

Anderson's careful delineation of hobo places is one of the earliest exemplars of how Chicago sociologists narrated the complex social worlds of outsiders. Hobohemia was not just an urban area, it was a rich environment filled with cultural institutions such as restaurants, missions, flophouses, employment agencies (in hobo argot, "slave markets"), pawnshops, radical bookstores, and saloons. Anderson described the various streets and parks—the drunks who slept in Jefferson Park ("Bum Park"), the racially segregated streets and hotels (the Douglas Hotel "is a colored man's lodging-house"), and the hobo intellectuals who congregated in Bughouse Square, reading poetry and orating from soapboxes. He included details of material culture, including restaurant menus. Like hobos themselves, hobohemias can be transient, so in Anderson's introduction to a later edition of *The Hobo*, he specified that his descriptions were for the period of 1921–1922: "At that time Hobohemia was brighter and livelier."[76] His nostalgia for his vanished heroic hobo was apparent. One hundred years later, this section of *The Hobo* conjures a colorful, bygone world.

In Hobohemia, Nels Anderson noted, hobos all found others of their kind, anonymity, and "the freedom and security that only the crowded city offers."[77] These particular qualities of place attracted other outsiders as well. As DePastino notes, Chicago's Hobohemia area overlapped with the

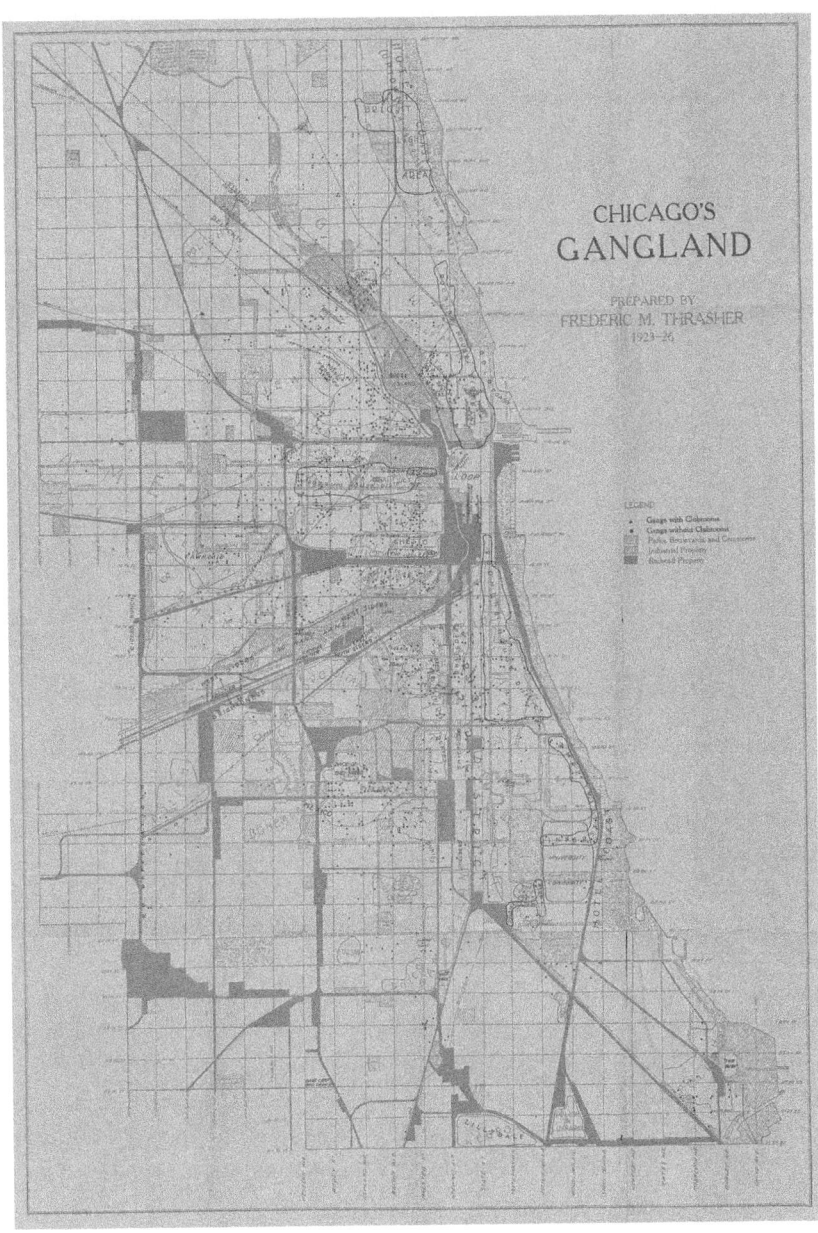

Chicago gangland, 1927. Created by University of Chicago sociologist Frederic Milton Thrasher for his book The Gang: A Study of 1,313 Gangs in Chicago. Courtesy of Osher Map Library, University of Southern Maine; https://oshermaps.org/map/49234.0001

Century-old hobo graffiti found by anthropologist Susan Phillips under a concrete bridge of the L.A. River. Photograph by the author.

urban gay world burgeoning in certain cities in the early twentieth century.[78] Privacy and mobility in these places fostered diverse erotic possibilities such as prostitution and same-sex interactions.

Yet hobohemia was deeply racialized and gendered. It was a domain of masculinized, working-class whiteness.[79] The fact that most hobo women passed as men implied the danger of hobohemia for them. Nels Anderson gendered this place—"It is quite definitely a man's street"[80]—although it may be that he did not recognize the women hobos who passed as men. African American men who had come to Chicago in the Great Migration were excluded from its main stem, and instead found segregated housing on the Near South Side or as boarders with Black families. Homeless Asian workers were similarly excluded. Todd DePastino notes that Southern and Eastern European immigrants found jobs through their own internal networks, not through the "slave markets" in hobohemia.[81] Jack London, Nels Anderson, and others describe (sometimes using the offensive racialized language of the era) racial differences and interactions on the rails and in boxcars, but largely the hobo identity and his places were White and male.

Hobos needed camps, and these were the "jungles" near railroads on the outskirts of cities. Jungles were social centers where hobos congregated to cook, bathe, wash and mend clothes, sleep, and tend to other everyday needs. Ideally, they were located in a dry and shady place. Anderson claimed jungles were the "melting pot of trampdom," welcoming all races and having "absolute democracy."[82] In jungles, hobos sang and told stories, passed along news and advice, talked politics, and held meetings. As they moved from place to place, they sometimes left drawings or markings—graffiti—to communicate with each other. (**See Hyperlink 2.2:** Finding Hobo Graffiti.)

Jungles taught wanderers to be hobos. The places depended on a set of practices and norms that visitors needed to learn. As noted above, Anderson pointed out that men were perfectly capable of completing these traditionally gendered domestic activities (a point that sociologists would continue to make well into the twenty-first century). For example, hobos (whom he imagined as men) not only cooked, they invented their own dishes—"mulligan" stew, made from whatever ingredients were available. Jungles had domesticity without women and housewives without wives: "The hobo who lives in the jungles has proved that he can become domesticated without the aid of women. . . . The hobo learns here the housewife's art of keeping pots clean and the camp in order."[83] Jungle norms (a "code of etiquette") consisted of maintaining the area: cleaning all pots and utensils, storing them properly, observing proper fire procedures, not wasting food, and the like. The older residents—"jungle buzzards"—typically enforced these norms.

Finally, trains and boxcars were crucial places, enabling hobo mobility, sleep, and community. (Jack London wrote: "I rode into Niagara Falls in a 'side-door Pullman,' or, in common parlance, a box-car. A flat-car, by the way, is known amongst the fraternity as a 'gondola,' with the second syllable emphasized and pronounced long."[84]) The invention of the train allowed movement across the country in the decades before the automobile, thereby facilitating the hobo as a new kind of social identity and practice. Although early railcars evolved from English models, the boxcar was uniquely American.

Harsher weather conditions in the US and the threat of fires from wood-burning locomotives prompted the development of the enclosed freight car in the 1830s. An early, doorless "covered gondola," at a scant twelve feet with a round roof, "resembled a gypsy wagon," an apt metaphor for a vehicle that enabled hobo life.[85] By the late nineteenth century, the design had evolved to a much larger car body with side doors. The boxcar became the quintessential railcar, and the moniker for many a hobo, such as musician Boxcar Willie and the fictional Boxcar Bertha. Cultural critic John Lennon argues that trains and boxcars are inextricably intertwined with hobo agency. It was "in the hidden, dark recesses of boxcars" that hobos came together in social and political mobilization.[86] Trains were paradoxical places—the railroads helped produce corporate capitalism, yet through hobo practices they became "politicized spaces of resistance."[87]

Rebranding: Hobo Art and Politics

The period we now characterize as the tramp scare lasted from the 1870s until the 1940s.[88] The scare drew on scientific determinist theories of pathological tramps to create widespread fear and anger toward wandering workers. It was launched by social reformers, amplified by law enforcement, and fueled by newspapers and media. Journalists reinforced stories about unemployed drifters as dangerous, lazy, depraved, and criminal. Hobos allegedly spread diseases such as syphilis. Disparaging media accounts, such as by the *Chicago Tribune* of 1877, advised readers to "put a little arsenic in the meat" given to tramps: "This produces death within a comparatively short period of time, is a warning to other tramps to keep out of the neighborhood, keeps the coroner in good humor, and saves one's chickens and other portable property from constant destruction."[89] Reinforcing gender assumptions, journalists depicted tramps as male predators and thieves who posed a particular threat to women.

The tramp scare spread to Great Britain. The *London Times* in 1876 took note of this new problem arriving from the United States, the tramp, and described him as a "low-browed, blear-eyed, dirty fellow."[90] Later, in the 1960s, UK sociologist Stanley Cohen coined the term "moral panic" to describe these kinds of cycles wherein expert discourse, fueled by media dissemination, created scapegoats and repressive measures to eliminate them. (**See** Chapter 7.) The concept of moral panic was one by which sixties sociologists shifted the discourse on difference away from allegedly pathological individuals to instead focus on how the rule-making practices of moral entrepreneurs created deviance.

Then tramp stories changed. Artistic representations, popular culture, and political activists all told tramp and hobo stories, as did hobos themselves. As the twentieth century unfolded, the hobo story became largely the preserve of popular culture. Films, novels, and songs rebranded hobo mythology from the early era of the tramp scare. Hobo stories were stripped of pathology, poverty, fear, aggression. Instead, the hobo came to signify the allure of adventure and a brave, if quixotic, defiance of social conventions. The hobo figure was that of a harmless, nonconforming outsider, a rebel without a cause, by personal choice. They came to be seen as generally harmless, sometimes enviable, and eventually comic. These myriad stories highlight the malleability of the hobo identity, the many different ways of telling their stories, and the emerging possibilities for marketing those stories.

Tramp entertainment emerged in the late nineteenth century. During that period, Anderson's father emigrated to the United States from Sweden, becoming a hobo for some years circa 1882. The tramp comic of that era performed on stage in concert saloons, and succeeded through a mix of shock and outrage that nonetheless upheld mainstream conventionality.[91] Early actors performed the tramp character in the blackface used in minstrelsy, later switching to grayface (a simulation of dirtiness mimicked still at Halloween and other hobo-impersonation events[92]). A controversial 1885 stage show with actor Lew Bloom, who claimed to be the first stage tramp, pleased the audience, outraged the manager, and ended in Bloom's arrest.[93]

The late-nineteenth- and early-twentieth-century tramp comic was generally vulgar, aggressive, transgressive, and, to social reformers' dismay, irrepressibly free from social conventions. Feisty, defiant tramps starred in cartoons as well as on stage. Tramps were no longer just coming to homes to beg at the back door; they came in through the front door via newspaper and magazine comics. The outsider vaudeville tramp was becoming, as one critic put it, "a national symbol," wildly popular with audiences.[94] Earlier tramp entertainment, which had relied on racialized tropes and critiques of class oppression, shifted at the turn of the century to become, as DePastino put it, "one of the era's most remarkable emblems of modernity."[95] The romantic tramp was emerging—an icon of freedom, mobility, and urban pleasures.

In 1914, Nels Anderson had just graduated from a Utah high school at the age of twenty-five, having stopped his wandering. That year saw the debut of British actor Charlie Chaplin's famous tramp character, in the film *Kid Auto Races at Venice*. The Little Tramp embodied the paradoxes of hobo mythology. Chaplin himself described these tensions: "You know this fellow is many-sided, a tramp, a gentleman, a poet, a dreamer, a lonely fellow, always hopeful of romance and adventure. He would have you believe he is a scientist, a musician, a duke, a polo player. However, he is not above picking up cigarette butts or robbing a baby of its candy."[96] The Tramp became internationally popular, with the public apparently willing to overlook both the tramp's flaws and Chaplin's controversial political views and relationships with women. Chaplin helped consolidate the romantic hobo mythology as representing male freedom from the oppressions of consumer capitalism, and the obligations of domestic home life and settled ownership.

Other artists in the 1920s constructed the hobo as a romantic icon. In particular, illustrator and artist Norman Rockwell produced several hobo-themed covers for the mainstream magazine the *Saturday Evening Post*. Like the Little Tramp, Rockwell's hobo was a bumbling but benevolent scamp. *Hobo and Dog*, from October 18, 1924, was the quintessential hobo with a stem pipe, shabby clothing, and abundant facial hair, cooking hotdogs over a tin-can fire. *Dog Biting Man in Seat of Pants*, published August 18, 1928, depicted a tramp fleeing from a dog whose teeth were affixed to his rear. Rockwell may have been drawn to hobos because he described himself as isolated, ungrounded in place or community, without ties to family or friends.[97] Critic Richard Halpern argues that Rockwell's paintings represent "all those disturbing social and psychic forces that the innocence industry tried to keep locked up and under control."[98] Undeniably, Rockwell's hobo paintings on magazine covers and advertisements brought the hobo into millions of American households, and Rockwell's reputation for painting sentimentalized, innocent Americana helped transform the hobo into a figure of pathos rather than danger. The romantic hobo had become more firmly established in mass culture.

Meanwhile, hobos told their own stories. Hobos had organized politically in workers' unions since the early twentieth century. In this political context, they produced their own knowledge, art, and music, their own versions of hobo identity. Hobo artistic expression and political activism were braided together. Hobos wrote autobiographies, essays, novels, poetry, and songs. They had a strong oral tradition of storytelling in the jungles and boxcars, and with the soapbox orators in hobohemia. They published their work in papers such as *Hobo News* ("of the hoboes, by the hoboes, and for the hoboes"[99]) or *Solidarity*. They might speak or attend lectures at the Hobo College. Physician Ben Reitman founded the local branch in Chicago. They patronized the Dill Pickle Club, a Chicago establishment that attracted artists, intellectuals, and hobo activists. Protest was a common theme in their cultural production.

Nels Anderson documented this political culture in a section likely titled with his reformist funders in mind: "How the Hobo Meets His Problem." Here he vacillated again between depicting hobos as social and political agents and presenting them as a social problem to be solved. On the one hand, he constructed hobos as prolific producers of vibrant art and cultural expression. On the other hand, he depicted these "soap-boxers" as victims: "His speeches and his poetry are filled with protests against the social order which refuses to make a place for him; against the system that makes him an outcast."[100] Still, the poems and songs of protest, Anderson claimed, emerged from, and created, hobo community and political solidarity. Hobos engaged with numerous political organizations, including the Industrial Workers of the World (IWW, whose members were known as Wobblies), the International Brotherhood Welfare Association, the Migratory Workers' Union, the United Brotherhood of American Laborers, and the Ramblers.

The IWW—through its political agitation, social services, and cultural production—played a crucial role in hobo representation. Founded in Chicago in 1905 by activists such as Mary Harris "Mother" Jones, Eugene Debs, "Big Bill" Haywood, and others, the IWW fought hard for migratory workers in those early decades. The early twentieth century saw many groups of transient workers (this was particularly true later during the Great Depression). Both men and women immigrants came to the US for work, from Southern and Eastern Europe and the Asian and Pacific Islands, especially before the Immigration Act of 1924 established national-origins quotas. Migrant laborers came north from Mexico. African Americans began moving north and west in search of work in the Great Migration that began around 1915. However, the IWW focused on class struggle and solidarity, subordinating differences by race or gender. Physician Ben Reitman said that because of the IWW, "the hobo has evolved from a despised shiftless creature to a powerful, useful man."[101]

The IWW harnessed the power of art and culture to promote political mobilization in hobohemia, on farms, and elsewhere. Hobo songs, poetry, speeches, and humor burgeoned, and with the growth of print media and record labels, spread to other main stems and to the mainstream. The IWW published its *Little Red Songbook* in 1909, including songs such as "Hallelujah, I'm a Bum," and the songbook endures as "hobohemia's most important cultural artifact."[102] Record labels with ties to wandering musicians emerged in the 1920s and released hobo recordings on 78 rpm records to a wider public. During this era, Harry McClintock first recorded (an expurgated version of) "Big Rock Candy Mountain" (1928), which was then covered by many later musicians, such as Burl Ives, and reached number 1 on *Billboard*'s country music charts. The sanitized version (minus the buggering stanza) helped repackage the hobo into a more wholesome figure.

By 1920, the IWW was collapsing. One legacy of its political strategy was fostering the hobo "frontier myth,"[103] the narrative of the hobo as a masculine, proletarian hero building the industrial West. Nels Anderson had reinforced this heroic hobo theme in *The Hobo*, while also underscoring the challenges of hobo life. Charlie Chaplin's later film, *Modern Times*, pointed an accusing finger at industrial capitalism. In its shrewd depiction of class struggle, the Tramp struggled in a large, assembly-line factory, participated in labor battles, and was suspected to be a communist. It remains one of Chaplin's most enduring films, having indeed captured important dynamics of modern times.

As time passed, Anderson grew frustrated by his inability to control the narrative about hobos. His critiques of them aside, he had depicted his hobos as resembling his hobo father and his hobo self—industrious, ingenious, and male. Yet hobos increasingly became a punchline. In his 1975 autobiography, he lamented that his heroic hobo had been rendered into a caricature: "He is a comic character in television, or the weary willie tramp in cartoons, one who scrounges for food, an amiable, parasitic fellow. Perhaps he is portrayed by newsmen as the habitué in the 'jungles,' those legendary, hidden camp sites by some stream where men cook, eat, sing jolly songs and have their rude shelters. Much whiskey must also be there. And they are said to have a language of their own."[104] Popular culture became more powerful than scientific experts, social scientists, reformers, and law enforcement in telling the story of the hobo.

Cultural producers tapped into the exoticism associated with newly visible social figures who transgressed tradition and social norms. This was especially powerful in an early-twentieth-century moment when traditional meanings of home, nuclear family structure, gender expectations, and other social domains were shifting. The packaging, visibility, and marketing of social deviants like hobos showed a cultural openness to antinormativity and likely opened new possibilities for transgression. One hobo recently reflected back on the Depression-era film *Wild Boys of the Road* (1933), in which several teens become hobos: "Well, I think, *Wild Boys of the Road*, kids loved that movie. If you see a movie like that, with kids travelling on trains, well, that put the idea in your head—well, I could do that too."[105] While conformity was socially rewarded, rebellion seemed increasingly possible.

The potential pleasures of nonconformity had a market, and the hobo figure, along with *The Hobo*—Robert Park's first sociology-series publication—can be seen as early examples of outsider capitalism. Not all types of social difference were marketable, however. The cultural hobo was White and male. This whiteness and male privilege probably enabled his successful repackaging as a loveable figure. The transgressive edge, and class politics, receded in the rebranded mythic, romantic hobo. That hobo, at one point an icon of class struggle, became a product to be sold and consumed.

Two twenty-first-century stories show contemporary hobo permutations. In a scene from the 2014 film *Wild*, a reporter from the *Hobo Times* screeched to a halt as he drove past a hitchhiking Reese Witherspoon, portraying writer Cheryl Strayed's experience hiking the Pacific Crest Trail in 1995. In his eagerness to interview a woman hobo, he ignored her increasingly irritated denials: "I'm not a hobo. . . . Just taking a little time out. This is not a hobo life." He wanted to publish an article on women hobos in *Harper's*. "I gotta tell you," he insists, "lady hobos—hard to find." Finally, still convinced she's a hobo, he takes her picture, tosses her a "hobo care package" (popcorn and a soda), and speeds off, without offering her a ride. Film director Jean-Marc Vallee later called this "the funniest scene in *Wild*."[106] It is funny—the mansplaining, for one—but wrong, reinscribing through this humorous device the trope of hobos as mainly male wanderers. And a 2011 hobo handbook, "a field guide to living by your own rules," uses male pronouns throughout its modern hobo story: "Adaptive modern-day hobos are just as likely to find a job on Craigslist while sipping a soy latte they put on a debit card as they are to brew a pot of cowboy coffee over a small campfire by the tracks as they wait for word to arrive on where the jobs are."[107] To the extent that hobos are remembered today, there is no dominant hobo narrative, but these examples show the tendency to depict them as men, untethered from discernable class politics.

Expert authority, medical and psychiatric science, journalists, and eugenicists all played a role in representing the hobo. Yet they are not always the most powerful forces in constructing difference and deviance. Although Ian Hacking identified the human sciences as central to the classification process he called "making up people,"[108] it is also the case that popular culture in the twentieth century sometimes trumped science, making up alternative versions of new people living in new ways. Films, songs, memoirs, newspapers, novels—all proved instrumental in rebranding the hobo into a sympathetic nonconformist.

Once a Hobo . . . Nels Anderson's Career

Studying outsiders might put one on the stigmatized outside. Some Chicago School scholars, whose focus on marginality has been characterized as "sociology noir,"[109] found that they could not easily shake the grit of noir. Those building a discipline on the study of outsiders and social difference could find themselves similarly marginalized by a conservative academy that never viewed them as insiders. Nels Anderson was one of those scholars. He reported a keen sense of alienation from his fellow graduate students, humiliations in class discussions, and his conviction that other students could never understand his study of hobos or their social world (a social world that had once been his and his father's). He cast himself, even years later, as a "stranger at the gate" of Chicago sociology.[110] He wrote, "It bothered me that word had passed around that I was making a study of hobos."[111] Decades after publication of *The Hobo*, Anderson's painful description of his oral examination on the thesis suggests a student still on the outside of academia: "I was not able to answer most of the questions put to me." His committee chair, Albion Small, "pointed to the street. 'You know your sociology out there better than we do, but you don't know it in here. We have decided to take a chance and approve you for your Master's degree.'"[112] He still had not escaped his place on the outside.

Nels Anderson never secured a full-time tenure-track position in the United States. The stigma associated with his study of hobos followed him. In his autobiography, he described the paradoxical legacy of *The Hobo*: on the one hand, its success afforded him some sociological recognition; on the other hand, it "continued to mark me as something less than a fully accepted sociologist." After a job interview for a teaching position, "I learned indirectly that some professors objected to me because of my identity with hobos. They thought it meant equal familiarity with 'other underworld characters.'"[113] His next job, it turned out, was with underworld characters. The Juvenile Protective Association hired him for a series of vice investigations. He examined homosexuality in hobohemia, and assisted a JPA social worker in a study on brothels and night clubs. His long-standing mentor, Ben Reitman, warned him against participating in these vice investigations: "Your sociology friends will not be proud of acquaintance with one who is an expert in vice problems. It is safer to be an expert on poverty, if you don't get too close to the poor."[114] Yet Anderson found that, unlike their response to his hobo research, his fellow students considered his new jobs adventurous and enviable: "It was near enough to vice to be naughty but not tabu [sic], as knowing the hobo was."[115] Hobos, unlike prostitutes, were apparently uniquely stigmatized in the eyes of his colleagues. Later researchers who studied marginalized groups also found that stigma was contagious in ways that affected their careers.[116]

Toward Los Angeles, 1937. Photographed by Dorothea Lange. Courtesy of Library of Congress Prints and Photographs Division.

Conclusion

Our ongoing fascination with the romantic hobo is probably a factor in *The Hobo's* longevity, confirming Robert Park's marketing impulse to rush to publication the master's thesis of a young graduate student. Nels Anderson would probably have been surprised had he known that, a century after its publication, *The Hobo* would still be part of historical conversations. Yet the text is instructive in several ways. For one thing, Anderson's detailed descriptions of the lives, art, and politics in hobohemia continue to be cited as authentic hobo history. His analyses of social class and capitalism resonate today. His hobo stories highlighted how new social identities emerging in modernity could elude a singular interpretation. Fixed definitions were elusive—were these new kinds of people bums, tramps, or hobos? Were they dangerous or sympathetic? Should they be cured or emulated? As biological and medical science increasingly categorized, classified, and counted types of individuals, the slipperiness of seemingly fixed identity categories was becoming apparent. Different questions and different stories about them were necessary. Nels Anderson's *The Hobo* offers a glimpse into how early-twentieth-century ways of knowing about difference began to shift.

In this respect, *The Hobo* illustrates ways that the early social science of difference contrasted with medical and biological determinist approaches. He championed, criticized, and sometimes romanticized the hobo underdog, while helping effect conceptual ruptures in race science's study of social difference. Rather than seeking cures, elimination, or improvement of hobos, Anderson explored their social worlds with curiosity about their cultural logics. His delineation of *becoming* a hobo, and emphasis on the crucial role of places in producing hobo norms and practices, refuted theories of inborn degeneracy. Hobos, Anderson showed, were social creatures, and there were multiple ways of knowing and telling stories about them.

The Hobo is also illustrative because of its weaknesses. From our contemporary perspective, the text can seem quaint, or compromised by moralism and rudimentary social concepts and methods. This is particularly the case regarding his biases, judgmentalism, and omissions on the subjects of gender and sexualities. These analytic stumbles can be partially, but not completely, explained by the intellectual climate of the early 1920s, and by the moral expectations of Anderson's reformist funders. They also suggest how myopias compromise research practices. Theoretical, methodological, and normative assumptions sometimes induce a tunnel vision that blinkers researchers for what does not fit neatly into their preexisting frameworks.[117] Sexual stigma and gender inequality are social problems that continue to manifest on the level of individual research (and in the lives of individual researchers).

Still, as we saw in the preface, better stories do not have to be perfect stories. Indeed, ambivalence and uncertainty can permeate a better story. Anderson's hobo narratives, despite their disappointments, destabilized biological determinist stories of hobo degeneracy. In the end, Nels Anderson concluded about the hobo, "Whatever his weaknesses, and I knew them full well, I present him as one of the heroic figures of the frontier."[118] His respect for them ultimately outweighed his moralism. His better stories brought to life a social world of outsiders, enabling us to ask new questions about them, and him, one hundred years later.

Modern Times was the final screen appearance of Charlie Chaplin's Tramp. It was 1936. Prohibition had recently ended. Chicago had been a landscape of speakeasys, brothels, hobohemia, criminal haunts, black-and-tan clubs, and taxi-dance halls. Students in the sociology department at the University of Chicago were out in the city exploring the perils, pleasures, and social dynamics of these deviant new places. The city would inevitably change. In *Modern Times*'s finale, the Little Tramp walked down a highway toward the horizon, leaving the future ambiguous.

Hyperlink 2.1: Citing Bertha, on Queer Evidence

Accounts of women hobos typically cite Bertha Thompson, aka Boxcar Bertha, as source material. The book, *Sister of the Road: The Autobiography of Boxcar Bertha*, was first published in 1937. It has been reprinted several times, and inspired the Hollywood motion picture, *Boxcar Bertha* (1972), directed by Martin Scorsese. Advertising copy for the fourth book edition reads, in part, "Another raging slab of real American history you're not likely to find in the textbooks."[119]

Actually, *Sister of the Road* is exactly what you find in the textbooks. It is a commonly cited source of evidence in the scholarly literature on hobos, and the obligatory footnote in scholarship on hobo women. Many scholars consider Bertha an authentic woman's voice, and it is typically the primary source in the scant literature on lesbian hobos. Numerous historians have quoted Bertha Thompson in scholarship on working-class women, early lesbian subcultures, furnished-room districts in Chicago, women offenders, and biographies of various contemporaneous figures. Bertha also earned biographical entries in at least two collections on women travelers, and a source guide to the American Left.[120]

Sister of the Road established its authenticity from its subtitle—*The Autobiography of Boxcar Bertha*—and the title page statement: "As told to Dr. Ben L. Reitman." A reader easily imagines the colorful Bertha being too busy, or simply lacking the resources, to write her own memoir. It then follows that Bertha might have met Reitman at any of the marginal places he frequented, such as the Chicago branch of the Hobo College, which he founded in 1907 as a venue to foster education, activism, and social services for transient workers. Somehow (the reader perhaps does not ponder this), Bertha narrates this incredibly rich description of her life and experiences with hundreds of hobos, political activists, and other lively and eccentric figures.

Sister of the Road was reissued in 2002 by Nabat Books, a series dedicated to "reprinting forgotten memoirs by various misfits, outsiders, and rebels." Reprinting *Bertha*—the quintessential misfit—seems an obvious choice for them. An afterword written by Barry Pateman, curator of the Emma Goldman Archive at the University of California, Berkeley, noted, "In this, the fourth time that Boxcar Bertha has been reissued, we feel obliged for the first time to make it plain that this is in fact a work of fiction."[121] Pateman insists that this revelation "takes nothing away from the book," but one can imagine a small crowd of scholars collectively screaming, "Wait. What?!"

So, who was Bertha, or, perhaps more precisely, how was she made up? Ben Reitman, the flamboyant hobo physician who invented Bertha, grew up in Chicago, became a hobo at a young age, then finished medical school in 1904. Yet his medical practice, political activism, and social circle centered around outsiders, whom he often referred to as social outcasts. His medical practice focused on treating and preventing venereal diseases, a specialty that took him to Lawndale Hospital. Reitman was deeply involved with the radical politics of the era, such as anarchism, worker's rights, and free-speech activism. He performed abortions—illegal at that time—and served time in prison for violating the Comstock Laws prohibiting public birth-control advocacy. Reitman married three times, and had a long-term relationship with the anarchist Emma Goldman. He was both enamored with, and critical of, University of Chicago sociology, and became a mentor to the young sociology graduate student Nels Anderson.

Bertha emerged partially from early-twentieth-century trends in both commercial publishing and sociology. The rise of tabloid journalism and noir fiction fostered what Roger Salerno calls "sociology noir."[122] University of Chicago sociologists studied the sort of outsiders who were central to Reitman's world; they valued students and scholars with authentic outsider experience, and urged students to write compelling narratives. Synergies among sociological knowledge production, political activism, and forms of art and popular culture were evident in the entanglements of sociological texts such as *The Hobo* and novels by key early-twentieth-century writers such as Richard Wright, James T. Farrell, and Nelson Algren.[123] Reitman, who viewed himself as an amateur sociologist and writer, had a number of unpublished manuscripts on social outsiders, including a book of prose poems (*Outcast Narratives*). He published a book on pimps and prostitution, *The Second Oldest Profession*, and was struggling to complete a second book, *Wandering Women*. Finally, his editor, J. B. Lippincott, encouraged Reitman to write the book "in novel form,"[124] thereby launching Bertha during this moment of blurred boundaries between fiction and scholarship.

Bertha herself contains multitudes. She is a composite figure based on many stories, real and not. An exhaustively researched, unpublished dissertation by Martha Lynn Reis traces the many sources of Ben Reitman's writing of Boxcar Bertha. First, Reis argues that Reitman based Bertha on three "real-life individuals:" Lizzie Davis (a hobo and bohemian who had written her own memoir, now lost); Retta Toble (hobo, and Reitman's former lover), and, as Reitman's correspondence and other archival materials show, himself. "Both of my books," Reitman writes, "*Sister of the* Road and the *Second Oldest Profession*, are largely autobiographical."[125] In addition to this heavy reliance on two women's stories, Reitman mined his voluminous correspondence and medical-case records for material. He asked a number of women he knew to submit fictional stories that he could add to the book, including Emma Goldman, who repeatedly ignored or denied him, at one exasperated point writing him: "I have written you that I know nothing of the subject, you are a much better authority on women hobos."[126] He made up anecdotes, and Reis notes that he "played fast and loose with facts." Finally, a number of writers and editorial assistants heavily revised the final manuscript—Reitman complained that these were aimed at "respectabilizing" Bertha—further layering, and fictionalizing, the storytelling.

Bertha coined the term "lady lovers" for lesbian hobos, a benign term adopted and requoted by many later historians. Yet she was strikingly homophobic, which some recent scholars note with surprise. Bertha expressed outright hostility toward lesbians: "They are typically anti-social, selfish, and willing to exploit others. So few of them show a desire to earn an honest living. . . . I don't know any group which has so many chiselers, racketeers, and petty larceny grafters. Their sins are cheap sins."[127] Martha Reis attributes this antipathy to Reitman. She describes Reitman's virulence about homosexuality, and shows how some of Bertha's dialogue was lifted straight from his own letters. He believed homosexuals were obsessed with sex, lacked a social conscience, were a "menace to society," lazy, and cowardly.[128] He urged Eve Adams, a lesbian activist now recognized for having written the first ethnography of lesbians in the US,[129] to "live as near a normal life as is possible . . . it is necessary to 'fall in line.'"[130] He used the terms "cheap homos" and "fagots" [*sic*]. Reis documents Reitman's "violent swings between sympathy for and condemnation of" homosexuality, and she argues that he suffered from internalized homophobia—his papers show that he engaged in sexual activity with other men.[131] Whether or not that was true, his homophobia is indeed curious, given his other progressive views. Reitman was a proponent of free love, the early utopian belief that love, not marriage, should serve as the basis for sex. He was also a man who championed outcasts of all other stripes.

Reis concludes that *Sister of the Road* cannot be taken at "face value." What, then, does the saga of Bertha's invention suggest in terms of citing her as historical evidence? *Sister of the Road* has a colorful history of invention, but is it less "real" than sociological texts such as *The Hobo*? The texts are similar in key ways: both employed a sort of magpie approach to evidence collection, drawing on correspondence, case files from hospitals or reform agencies, and on personal experience, conversations, and anecdotes. Both drew on the authors' own lived experiences as hobos. Moreover, we cannot necessarily clearly argue that Anderson's interviews represent more authentic and objective evidence than Reitman's fictional narratives. There were different standards and practices for interviews conducted by sociology graduate students like Nels Anderson (and, as we see in chapter 3, Paul G. Cressey). In his autobiography, Anderson described his early interviews as "informal"—he would be "sitting with a man on the curb, sitting in the lobby of a hotel or flop house, going with someone for a cup of coffee with doughnuts or rolls."[132] Later, possibly, they became more structured. Still, since they were collected before the invention of portable recording devices, they would have been remembered and reconstructed, and probably embellished and perhaps (even inadvertently) invented when converted to transcripts. In what ways does this embellishment or fictionalization differ from how Reitman asked his non-hobo friends to write sections of his book?

The question nags—can we cite Bertha as scholarly evidence about historical people in a historical time? Prompting other questions—what counts as evidence? How do we know what we think we know about hobos? About women and lesbian hobos? Hobos were full of their own stories, often embellished. In *The Road*, Jack London described a "set-down" with two "maiden ladies" in Harrisburg, Pennsylvania. They had not just given him food at the back door. They invited him in for a "set-down" with them at their table, where he regaled them with stories, "thrilling them, not alone with my own adventures, but with the adventures of all the other fellows with whom I had rubbed shoulders and exchanged confidences. I appropriated them all, the adventures of the other fellows, I mean; and if those maiden ladies had been less trustful and guileless, they could have tangled me up beautifully in my chronology. Well, well, and what of it? It was fair exchange."[133] Contemporary scholars have complicated the concepts of evidence, authenticity, objectivity, and experience. Still, Reitman's penchant for fabrication and his transparent solicitation of others to pen fictional accounts, might today give a scholar pause about quoting Bertha as an authoritative source, or, indeed, as a real person.

Sister of the Road poses a queer dilemma. Indeed, it is a queer text—queer in the analytic sense of unsettling fixed categories and binaries, and confronting us with ambiguity. As an autobiography of a woman written by a man, it blurs the gender binary. It destabilizes numerous other boundaries: between fact and fiction, sociology and literature, evidence and anecdotes, authenticity and inauthenticity. Almost one hundred years after *Sister of the Road*, genres such as literature, social sciences, and journalism have been significantly blurred. We describe writing the lives of ourselves and others in new ways, such as autoethnography, evidence novels, historical novels, creative nonfiction, documentary fiction, and fiction as autobiography. We are now more accustomed to hybrid narrative forms, especially in the social sciences.

Queer method—a set of practices that encourages our "openness to the unexpected, the uncertain, and the unknowable."[134]—invites us to examine knowledge production such as that in *Sister of the Road*. It allows us to explore the making of this queer text and some of the conditions under which Bertha's voice was constructed. It encourages new ways of interrogating our assumed knowledge about hobos, and disrupts what we thought we knew about hobo gender dynamics and sexuality when we were citing Bertha. Queerness as method troubles Bertha's narrative, which may leave us with without clear answers to the questions here, but opens up new ways of thinking and asking questions about wandering women and men in the early twentieth century.

Hyperlink 2.2: Finding Hobo Graffiti

One sunny December morning found me up to my ankles in the cold water of the Los Angeles River with anthropologist Susan Phillips. A professor at Pitzer College, Phillips had recently garnered international media attention for noticing century-old hobo graffiti on a bridge underside at the L.A. River and Arroyo Seco, an area Phillips describes as "a landscape of marginality."[135] She had agreed to take me there. We met in front of the outdoor plant section at a nearby Home Depot. In heavy work boots, Susan was prepared for the slog, and she had thoughtfully brought me plastic bags to fasten over my sneakers. Foolishly, I declined, and paid the price of frigid feet and a mild skin rash.

We sprinted across a busy intersection, then down the concrete path to the river. We passed a woman furiously sweeping the path with a broom, and I worried that she might have mental health issues. Susan called out a friendly greeting to her. Clearly familiar turf for them both. On wading in, the cold water shocked, but I quickly acclimated to my cold, sodden sneakers. Sun glimmered on the water, and there was an old pickup truck parked mysteriously in the middle of the river. It was like being in a beautifully weird concrete canyon, the many overpasses appearing almost sculptural. We rounded a slight bend in the river and there it was—a wall of markings dating back to the era in which Nels Anderson was studying hobos far away in Chicago. Perhaps some of them had wandered through Los Angeles.

Hobos left traces of themselves in the places they wandered. They carved messages or painted with grease pencil, charcoal, railroad tar, or shoeshine. This communication system, early graffiti, signaled to other wanderers their presence, direction of travel, and other pertinent information. Jack London noted that water tanks were "tramp directories." Often hobos carved their moniker wherever they could. (Hobos referred to "monikers" as "monicas.") A-No. 1, the well-known hobo Leon Ray Livingston, who wrote a dozen books on hobo living, described this practice of carving "into which, with their pocket knives, more or less artistically, according to length of previous practice, each one carved his 'name-de-road' and beneath it the date and an arrow pointing westward, the direction of their journey."[136] This ability to communicate through monicas suggests the potential significance of hobo community—they sought to stay connected.

Phillips argues that hobos created "the foundational graffiti genre" in the United States.[137] Both London and Livingston claimed that hobos often searched for the markings of others, using them as vehicles for gossip among themselves, while many searched for carvings so they could find their friends. Livingston called the practice of marking, "the most sacred duty of the road."[138] The existence of hobo graffiti suggests how much hobos might mean to each other, and the significance of places to their social worlds and interactions.

In a city like Los Angeles, hobos gathered at the riverbank to camp and sleep. There, in 2000, Susan Phillips was walking in the riverbed with friends, looking for historical graffiti. They happened upon some surprising markings high on the wall under the San Fernando Road Bridge, which was completed in 1913. A mix of grease pencil, rock, and charcoal drawings, symbols, and letters, they were "as understated as the bridge,"[139] she later wrote. It would have been easy to miss it. Phillips had found hobo markings from 1914 to 1922, largely preserved, because the L.A. River paving project of the 1930s and '40s had put them out of reach. Serendipitously, they were so high up that the city's attempts to cover urban artwork with gray antigraffiti spray had left them untouched.

Over time, Phillips deciphered some of the markings. Some were hobo monikers, and there were drawings by the hobos Tucson Kid and Oakland Red. Some were symbols indicating hobo travels. Phillips clarified to journalists that those looking like "little heart things" were actually directional arrows. She noted, "Putting those arrows that way means 'I'm going upriver. I was here on this date and I'm going upriver.'"[140] Phillips thinks the location would have been on the pathway toward a hobo jungle called Jackson's Park, located in nearby Griffith Park. A true highlight, however, was finding monikers bearing the name A-No. 1, who was infamous for his prolific use of graffiti and was once even arrested for it in San Francisco. While their authenticity cannot be absolutely confirmed, Phillips found two monikers for A-No. 1 under the bridge.

Researching graffiti is not for the timid. Phillips describes a range of fieldwork perils. She has climbed into long-abandoned places, for example a bridge abutment, and then found herself locked in by workers. She has been denied access to key sites by city officials, and has then snuck in anyway (as any dedicated researcher would). Perhaps scarier are the scholarly misses and near misses. She tells of getting home from one productive site visit only to discover that she had forgotten to photograph crucial early-twentieth-century drawings. On returning, she found that the historical markings had been covered by modern graffiti, and spray paint cans littered the ground. Of her noteworthy uncovering of markings perhaps by America's most famous hobo, she writes that not only did she almost overlook them, but "A-No. 1 almost slipped by me. I had looked at his name many times without grasping its significance. I even had read Spanish into it: *año*, for year. Over a decade after first seeing it under the San Fernando Road Bridge, I realized what it was: A-No. 1. The A-No. 1."[141] The thrill of discovery is easily accompanied by shivers of dread—what if I hadn't figured this out?

Phillips has written compelling stories about the wanderers who camped at the L.A. River and left their traces on its walls. She has also photographed the graffiti, preserving it in digital form. Still, she attempts to reconcile herself to its ephemerality. Eventually it will be lost. "It's contrary to conservation best practices to want to remove a piece of history from its in-situ location. But keeping this graffiti where it sits means that it will die eventually. It will be destroyed by water, weather, or people. It will be vulnerable to river revitalization around Confluence Park. I imagine chipping the whole thing off and sending it up the river to the Autry Museum of the American West. I imagine coating the writing with a substance that will protect it."[142] As a result of her efforts, the hobo wall is now listed as a Vintage Art Mural in Los Angeles. She notes, however, that this designation offers it no protection. "That is just the way of graffiti," she said, sounding more sanguine than I think she feels. (**See Hyperlink 2.3:** A Conversation with Anthropologist Susan Phillips.)

Hyperlink 2.3: A Conversation with Anthropologist Susan Phillips

Janice Irvine (JI): You mention in your book that you almost "missed" realizing some of the graffiti was (possibly—you are very careful to qualify many of your claims) A-No. 1's moniker. Can you talk a little about your process of analyzing and interpreting the markings?

Susan Phillips (SP): In general, I like to be very cautious about drawing conclusions about graffiti. Before the "conclusion" stage comes some combination of selective vision and creative abandon. These are pitted against each other in my brain like heavyweight prizefighters. Graffiti interpretation asks you to resist pre-existing biases (what your mind is patterned to see) and instead to see things in a different way, from a variety of angles. Graffiti literally changes your thinking. I love that process. Some people, like A-No. 1, are or were addicted to writing graffiti. But I'm addicted to the rapid-fire, on-the-ground connecting of dots that for me is graffiti interpretation. Your understanding can change in a heartbeat, because your mind made a new connection. It's exhilarating. In the case of A-No. 1, I thought it had said "year" in Spanish (*año*.) It took a friend saying simply, "That says *A-No. 1*," that allowed me to piece the story together. A-No. 1 had many imitators. He visited Los Angeles many times beginning when he was a child hobo, but there's no definitive proof that he was in L.A. in 1914. Whoever the author is, though, A-No. 1's name on the wall allowed me to tell his story, which is what I value the most.

JI: When and how did you first garner media attention for the hobo graffiti? What were some of the media outlets and countries that contacted you, and what was it like to have your work be the subject of so much attention?

SP: It all started in 2016 with a presentation I gave at the Autry Museum of the American West as part of the Huntington-USC Metro Studies group. In the audience were Kim Cooper and Richard Schave, who run an amazing alternative touring agency of the city. They are also dedicated to the preservation of older buildings that are in danger of being torn down. When I mentioned that I was concerned that the hobo graffiti marks were in danger due to exposure or river restructuring, they showed immediate interest. I eventually took them to the site. Kim Cooper wrote about the visit on their blog, where it was picked up by reporter John Rogers from the Associated Press. It was a syndicated AP article, so I didn't get contacted by any international news sources directly. But the article was reprinted everywhere from the *New York Times* to the *Korea Times*. My family in Alaska actually contacted me, because it had been in print there as well in the local paper. And then the story was reconfigured and reprinted in other venues. Websites, blogs, and radio or additional news agencies circulated new stories, and some did interviews, but many did so without any contact from me. Also, a few dozen people contacted me from around the United States. Most of them wanted to simply remember stories or places involving hobos, and tell me about their family members that had been on the road, or graffiti marks they remembered seeing as kids. These were lovely connections. And in a few cases, the connections brought me to other researchers, or to people and places or collections that later became the basis for future work. It was a little overwhelming and absolutely remarkable.

JI: Why do you think there was so much media attention?

SP: Hobos are like a touch point for American society. The idea of the hobo rekindles people's fascination with a simpler time, with the American West. The hobo takes all the magic of the North American railroad, combines it with freedom-seeking and the notion of making your own way in the world, and then mashes that up with the human fallout of capitalism. It's American independence and pathology all wrapped up in a little railroad bindle and carried on a stick. People love that. So many of the notions surrounding hobos are false, of course, but the mystique remains. Hobo living was brutal, but the romance of it—even at the time—was undeniable. Today, hobos are 90 percent myth. Writing about them poses certain challenges for that reason. And the same is true for graffiti. Both are good reminders of the tenuous nature of knowledge production in general. The ambiguity surrounding hobo lives can be self-referencing and often furthers the unsubstantiated mythologizing that they've always been subject to. But the ambiguity around them can also help us to ask more informed questions, and to create more reliable narratives surrounding hobo experiences.

I've taken a wide range of people to visit the hobo graffiti at that site. Some people get it right away, and others just don't. The odd thing is how infectious my co-viewers' experiences are to me. When people get it, we just bask in the wonder of it (that was the case with you, by the way). It becomes kind of a bonding experience. In other cases, people just look at it, kind of like, "That's it?" And then I get the feeling that maybe I am just a bit off my rocker and these little writings on the wall are just insignificant scrawlings, and why do I think they're so important? I am forced to see my work through their eyes. That feeling is always short-lived, but useful in terms of my own grounding in the material.

JI: You have been careful not to use the word "discovery" in your work, as in, for example, "Susan Phillips discovered hobo graffiti." Can you talk about that?

SP: Yes, I dislike the word "discovery"—primarily due to its colonial implications. I prefer to use and think about the word "uncovering," which is more archaeological in its orientation, like removing layers of stratigraphy to reveal something unseen or forgotten. Discovery has to do with conquest and claiming; uncovering has to do with seeing and learning. The other thing about discovery is that it implies a solo venture. And while most of my graffiti work has indeed been just my camera and me, some of the best stuff—including the hobo graffiti—was found during collaborative adventures, or somebody tipped me off to a cool spot, or brought me in to see some graffiti for whatever reason. In other words, I may be the first person to write about or interpret any given piece of writing, but I'm not the first person to see it or know about it. No discovery. That said, I am pretty sure I am the first scholar to write about hobo graffiti by interpreting materials that hobos wrote or carved themselves, which is pretty cool. Similarly, nobody's ever written about the graffiti of Hollywood grips and electricians, or the long-standing written tradition of containership sailors in harbors. But I will never lay claim to them. That is for the workers who do the writing themselves. It's been a privilege for me to be able to write about these lesser-known graffiti genres and share them with the public.

JI: What have been some of the most exciting, rewarding, scariest, challenging moments for you as a researcher of graffiti?

SP: Doing graffiti research in the built environment of Los Angeles has changed my perspective on the city permanently. It has also changed me, inside and out. I feel an intimate connection to the L.A. River and other urban waterways, to storm drain tunnels, or to the areas under bridges. I've been lucky enough to be able to access places people don't normally go—Hollywood sound stages, old military bunkers. I've snuck into many of these places, and also have gone with occasional permission. I love to see old writing, still up after eighty or ninety years. You think of the person who wrote it, standing right where you are standing, and you have a sense of connection to them. I also love it when I find graffiti from any era that I can't read. The lack of my ability to interpret something means there's a whole world out there to learn about. Getting to find and fit together all these puzzle pieces that are intertwined with the landscape of the city itself is the most rewarding thing to me. The excitement, scariness, and challenge are all bound up in it due to the marginality of some of the places I visit—which are often the places I love the most.

THREE

The Taxi-Dance Hall

Paul Cressey's Ambivalence

> Even minor characteristics of a person's behavior and manner may become, to the dance-hall world, the means for identifying him as either an "insider" or an "outsider."[1]
>
> Paul Goalby Cressey

Popular culture loved the taxi dancer. The life of a woman who rented her time to dance in public places with strange men proved an irresistible plotline, with its potent, if fictional, mix of sex, sassiness, seduction, and danger. Taxi-dance halls, commercial establishments where men paid women for a short dance, served as dramatic fictional settings over several decades, arising in the dance madness of the twenties. Songs, movies, musical theater, pulp novels, and short stories all took taxi-dance halls as their theme, making the taxi dancer visible as a modern social character both navigating and producing a revolution of gender and sexuality. Her melodramas, real or fictionalized, provided fodder for the burgeoning film industry, the new, mass-market paperbacks, and other genres of popular culture. (**See Hyperlink 3.1: "Life's Gutters:"** Popular Culture Represents the Taxi-Dance Hall.)

Taxi-dance halls were a microcosm of modern social change. They emerged at the same time as the automat.[2] In other words, for ten cents, men could purchase the time and companionship of women as efficiently as they could get lunch from a machine. Dances were ninety seconds, the length of a song, and women dancers earned half the proceeds from their accumulated tickets. Unlike large public dance halls and palaces, they were known as closed dance halls, since single women could not attend as paying customers, only as "hostesses" for hire. The dancers were the commodity for men, a mix of Filipino, Japanese, Chinese, and Mexican immigrants, traveling businessmen, men with disabilities, and the occasional skilled dancer.

Their place on the social margins made taxi-dance halls, and their dancers, appealing to University of Chicago sociologists. Paul Goalby Cressey, a graduate student, was one of them. He studied Chicago's taxi-dance halls between 1925 and 1928, a period marked by Prohibition, a plethora of sex-work establishments scattered throughout the city, and the rise of commercialized leisure places such as amusement parks and dance halls. Cressey depicted an outsider world largely invisible to the mainstream. He documented the cultural logics of marginality, showing how the dancers negotiated complex places of work and leisure.

It was the Jazz Age. Bohemians, hobos, intellectuals, and immigrants all mingled in the modernizing city. It was also a period of hatred and bias. Chicago had been one of the large US cities to see major protests against White supremacy and racial oppression during the 1919 Red Summer.[3] A virulent race-science and eugenics movement succeeded in radically restricting immigration to the United States by the mid-1920s. Women had only recently won suffrage, and while the sexual culture was changing, it was predominantly heteronormative.

Like *The Hobo*, Paul Cressey's book, *The Taxi-Dance Hall: A Sociological Study in Commercialized Recreation and City Life* (1932), represents a transitional text in the making of new social knowledge of difference. Cressey, like other graduate students in his department, received funding from Chicago's social-reform organizations. His book manifests early tensions between sociological research and social reform. His portraits of the dance halls read as bleak, even judgmental. Subsequent critics have rightly called out Cressey for his biases, and some of those critiques braid through this chapter. Yet he wrote in the context, and against the grain, of a dominant cultural discourse of race science and eugenic practices to eliminate outsiders and differences.

Paul Cressey spun his stories about women, immigrants, maleness, sexuality, and nonconformity in an era of pervasive biological determinist narratives, and these topics would become among the most central in twentieth-century sociology. This chapter explores ways that his early sociological focus on places, mapping social worlds, and the loneliness of

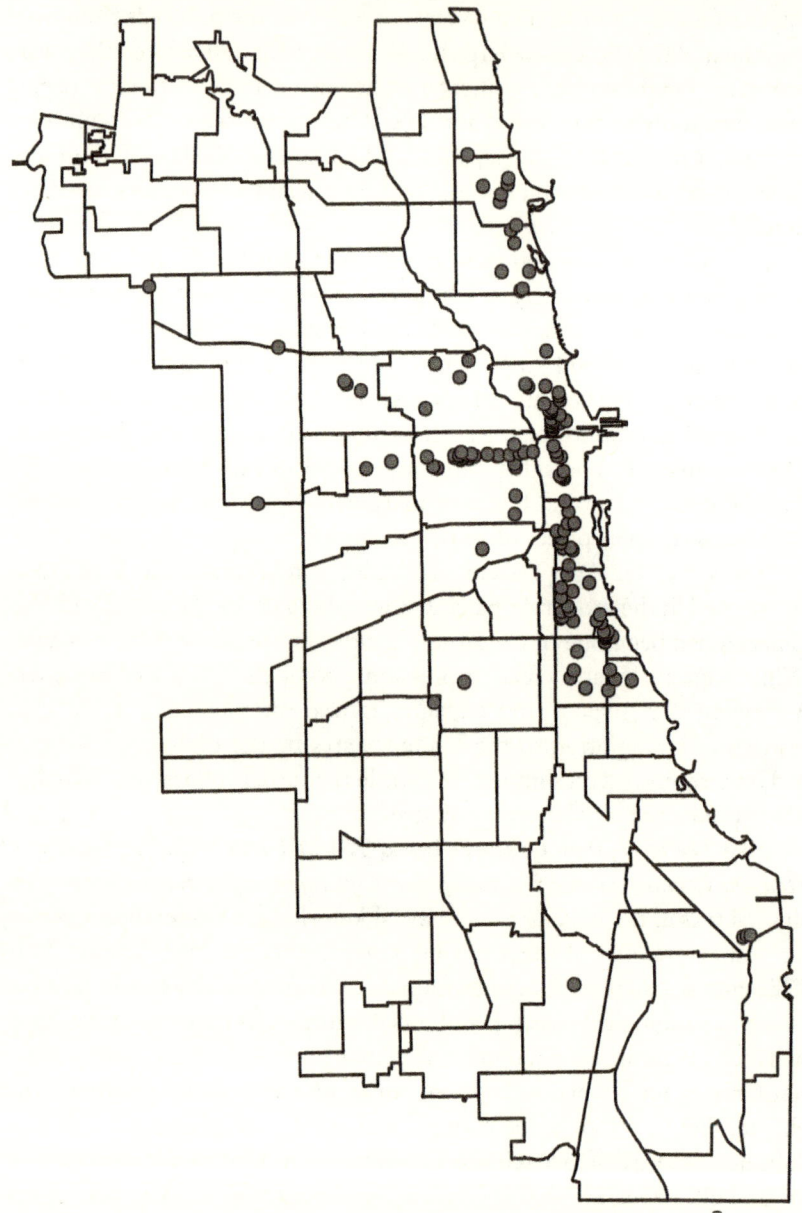

Chicago sex-work establishments during the Prohibition era, 1920–1933. Map produced by sociologist Chris Smith. Courtesy of Chris Smith.

immigrant men conceptually challenged essentialist narratives of early-century scientific racism. I examine his research practices and challenges in a modernizing Chicago, his analysis of the dance hall as an outsider place characterized by its own norms and languages, the mixed responses to his work, and the stigma of studying the stigmatized. Like *The Hobo*, Paul Cressey's text endures as one historical snapshot of a now-vanished deviant place.

Studying the Dance Hall

Taxi-dance halls highlighted the triumphs and challenges of modern working-class women seeking independence, and the men who paid to dance with them. From the post–Civil War era into the early twentieth century, large numbers of women in the United States moved to urban centers like Chicago. They established work lives, and lived—often together—outside the traditional roles of marriage and motherhood. Dubbed "women adrift," they were a heterogeneous mix by race, age, and other social backgrounds.[4] Many were immigrants, like their male patrons. They were, as historian Catherine Simpson put it, "a robust, gritty crew."[5] Social reformers viewed them as redeemable, unlike the women tramps who rode the rails for adventure. But like the hobo, they too wandered for work, seeking employment in cities as a transient labor force in factories, restaurants, stores, and various service industries. Some of these women adrift—"pioneers of social space"[6]—found taxi-dance halls.

Both Chicago sociologists and the city's social reformers also found the dance halls. Paul Cressey's adviser, Ernest Burgess, secured Cressey a position as caseworker and investigator for Chicago's Juvenile Protective Association (JPA). The JPA provided Cressey not only with financial backing, but with case files and background information. The University of Chicago sociology department and various Chicago social agencies shared overlapping interests and collaborations. Graduate students often worked for these organizations while conducting their research. As we saw with Nels Anderson's research on hobos, these connections to reform agencies raise questions about whether and how their research might have been affected. Their analyses reflect their sometimes-unsuccessful attempts to balance the moralistic wishes of their funders with an emergent sociological analysis of different social worlds. In a number of research projects, like the *Taxi-Dance Hall*, the sociological methods, the explicit or implicit agendas of the funders, and the subsequent textual analyses were deeply entangled.

The Reformers

A place seen as fostering loose sexual behavior, the taxi-dance hall was the site of fierce reformist attention, including by the JPA. Urban reformers in the late nineteenth and early twentieth centuries targeted alleged social problems such as drinking, gambling, public smoking, pornography, and sexual immorality related to new public places and the activities they seemingly fostered. Women's sexuality was a particular focus, crystalized in fears about prostitution and promiscuity. Like other large cities, Chicago had anti-vice groups, women reformers, and moral crusaders—all with diverse and sometimes competing political agendas—dedicated to the elimination of urban dilemmas.[7] The differences among these groups, and the history of this era's women reformers, have been extensively documented, along with two long-standing traditions in feminist approaches to women's sexuality, which we currently describe as the tensions between a focus on pleasure versus fears of danger.[8]

JPA reformers, along with their associates at Hull House, defy easy political characterization. Hull House, a settlement on the Near West Side, was cofounded by Jane Addams and Ellen Gates Starr to help working-class and poor European immigrants. It also functioned as a progressive intellectual center to address urban problems, although by Paul Cressey's era in the 1920s, the research academy had diminished Hull House social science as being applied social work rather than scholarship. Incorporated in 1909, the antivice organization the JPA was particularly concerned about eliminating prostitution. It was led by social reformers Louise DeKoven Bowen and Jessie F. Binford, both associates of Addams.

They were progressive in many ways. Both Addams and Bowen of the JPA were leaders in the women's suffrage movement. Jane Addams served as vice president of the National American Woman Suffrage Association, and also cofounded the American Civil Liberties Union. As historian Joanne Meyerowitz notes, this type of community activism "foreshadowed the female social welfare policymakers of the New Deal."[9] Moreover, like other sociologists who came under the surveillance of the Federal Bureau of Investigation starting in the 1920s, Addams was surveilled by the Department of Justice as a result of her connections with protests against repressive government policies.

While undeniably antiprostitution, the JPA nonetheless advocated for women "more dispassionately" than some other reformers.[10] Jane Addams, who referred to the taxi-dance halls as a "canker,"[11] also wrote appreciatively of the independent working woman (the very type who might have been a taxi dancer): "thru [*sic*] the huge hat, with its wilderness of bedraggled feathers, the [working] girl announces to the world that she is here. She demands attention to the fact of her existence, she states that she is ready to live, to take her place in the world."[12] Moreover, Hull House reformers were musical progressives. They used music as a "reform tool" to promote robust public culture, civic engagement, and democratic places, particularly among ethnic and immigrant working communities (although, as Derek Vaillant stresses, these initiatives excluded African Americans.)[13]

Still, the JPA worked to close taxi-dance halls and celebrated their success at helping accomplish this. Clearly, in their view, not all music (or places) were conducive to democracy-building. The JPA opposed, as Louise DeKoven Bowen put it, the "sensuous music" of jazz that played in Chicago's many types of cabarets, leading couples to "unbridled license and indecency."[14] Taxi-dance halls were, likewise, deeply suspect. The organization hired investigators to document, and urged law enforcement to crack down on, the alleged immoral and dangerous conditions of Chicago's dance halls, cabarets, and soda parlors.[15] Paul Cressey began his project studying dance halls in 1925, occupying dual roles of graduate student and JPA fundee. He worked in the field during 1927 and 1928.

The Funded Sociologist

Paul Cressey launched his taxi-dance research in the immediate aftermath of the Immigration Restriction Act of 1924. Opponents to the law called it the "carnival of exclusion."[16] Biological determinist theories of alleged inborn inferiority were used to justify the exclusion of immigrants, reinforce bias against women, and enforce eugenic policies against deviants. At that same time, sociologists were studying their social worlds.

It was a turbulent era for a young man to be studying outsiders and their places on the social margins. Cressey, whose family relocated several times to accommodate his father's pastoral assignments, attended Oberlin College and then moved on to the University of Chicago sociology department in 1920. His advisor, Ernest Burgess, had urged Cressey to research the taxi-dance halls. It must have been emotionally complicated. Gender and sexual ideologies transformed over the decade he worked, as Victorian sociosexual boundaries of separate spheres blurred. In the "marginalized spaces"[17] of taxi-dance halls, dancers actively transgressed, reconfigured, and sometimes reinforced, traditional dynamics of gender, race, sexuality, and class. Cressey's conservative religious childhood was clearly in tension with the cosmopolitanism he encountered in a new city of vibrant and chaotic differences. In an unpublished manuscript, he described his earlier belief that dancing was "inherently evil," and revealed his anxieties that his own sexual arousal would affect his analysis: "Then, there has been a personal difficulty in that this study has been for me 'stimulation'—a reaction to material which satisfied the wishes. There is danger that one's interpretations may be colored by one's own unconscious desires to achieve what may be only possible through behavior such as observed in this study."[18] Finally, the agency funding him was mobilizing to shutter the halls. These countervailing influences all played out on the floors of taxi-dance halls. They also played out in his text.

Cressey immersed himself in the taxi-dance halls, in field research characteristic of the University of Chicago. He personally attended taxi dances and other public dancing establishments, along with other graduate-student observers solicited by Burgess and Cressey. All of them kept field notes. He danced, talked informally with dancers, patrons, and proprietors (after deciding, like Nels Anderson had, that formal interviews were impractical), and visited the residences of participants. Chicago mentors such as Robert Park and Ernest Burgess encouraged graduate students to "use every opportunity" to collect evidence and personal documents.[19]

This mix of fieldwork, informal interviews, and use of documents is consistent with what sociologists would later call ethnography or participant observation. However, it was not yet a refined sociological research method, there was scant training, and ethical guidelines can seem rudimentary or absent from today's vantage. For example, a contemporary reader in the archive cringes when finding Cressey's report that a social worker with the Morals Court had given him access to obtain and read the mail of four dancers while they were then committed to Lawndale Hospital.[20] In addition, sociologist Roger Salerno points out that, before the advent of portable recording devices, Cressey would have engaged in "creative reinvention" and "imaginative embellishment" of interviews and conversations.[21] How aware, Salerno wonders, were University of Chicago mentors Robert Park and Ernest Burgess that "much of their students' research was but a creative rendering of the existing social world?"[22] Yet given Park's wish that students render the social world with the narrative force of contemporaneous fiction, one suspects he might have been fine with it.

Cressey's research strategies, however problematic today, would probably not have troubled his mentors. Sociologist Jennifer Platt notes that participant observation only emerged as such in the 1940s, significantly later than Cressey's research.[23] Moreover, personal documents such as diaries and letters were a popular form of evidence in the 1920s. Paul Cressey, the young graduate student, would have scavenged for such data however possible. Finally, as Platt points out, agencies like the JPA regularly conducted this type of research, and indeed, *The Taxi-Dance Hall* made heavy use of their extensive histories. Platt notes that the methods "which were characteristic of the 'Chicago School' were equally characteristic of social workers and voluntary activists who were in the field somewhat earlier."[24] In other words, it was a different time with different standards.

Modern Chicago: Bright Lights, Big City

Cressey's enduring contribution was his methodological and conceptual focus on place. His rich depiction of the halls as historically unique sites in the modern city exemplified the Chicago School's signature conceptual departure from race-science narratives. He approached the taxi-dance hall as a social place "with its own ways of acting, talking, and thinking."[25] Cressey wondered, "This strange structure of iron and steel, brick and mortar, of skyscrapers and traffic lights, has potentialities for weal or woe. Now that man has built the city, can he thrive in it?"[26] His answer seems to have been, "Maybe."

Chicago itself played a starring role in Cressey's story of dancers and urban dance halls. New types of places, and their prominent roles in public life, helped make the city modern. In the twenties, urbanization, new forms of mobility, immigration waves, the movement of women into the public domain, and a burgeoning consumer society all fostered the rise of commercialized places of leisure (and, for the dancers, workplaces) like the dance halls. In Chicago, dancers might have been women adrift, while many were young daughters of working-class immigrants, particularly Polish. In the absence of a cohesive village life, Ernest Burgess wrote in his introduction to Cressey's book, the "fundamental human craving for stimulation appears often to be dissociated from the normal routine of family and neighborhood life."[27] Instead, the city offered "bright-light areas" of commercial recreation. Both Burgess and Cressey used "bright-light areas" as a spatial metaphor for this new commercialized entertainment.

Taxi-dance halls, and these bright lights, relied on various modern technological advances. Indeed, electricity—a fairly new technology—was, as Sandy Isenstadt notes, "modernity's medium." The invention of spectacular neon signage transformed the night with warmth and promise, while at the same time neon came to symbolize the seediness of film noir. In the early decades of the twentieth century, so-called "spectacular signs" transformed urban places with their "electric scream."[28] Times Square, of course, is iconic of this transformation, but dazzling electric signs also lit Chicago's Loop area. These bright-light areas not only changed the nighttime social world; new forms of electric lighting changed "the character, use, and certainly the understanding of space."[29] Bright lights symbolized myriad new possibilities, pleasure being foremost among them.

The urban soundscape also underwent dramatic transformation into a modern acoustical era. As historian Emily Thompson notes, by 1933, "the nature of sound and the culture of listening were unlike anything that had come before."[30] The commodification of sound, accomplished through new technologies—radio, sound motion pictures, amplified phonographs, microphones and loudspeakers, and public address systems—produced modern ways of listening. Taxi-dance halls, probably not the most acoustically sophisticated, were nonetheless a public venue for the consumption of this new aural culture.

Finally, modern transportation systems were necessary to the success of the taxi-dance hall. Paul Cressey argued that the most successful venues were located on busy public transport routes. In addition, the railroads were as essential to independent women as they were to hobos. As historian Catherine Simpson noted, women started their journey to the city on the vehicle that was "the symbol of a technological, mobile society . . . the train station became the gateway into a new life."[31] Not only was Chicago a central railroad hub by the mid-nineteenth century, the elevated railroad system (the "L") opened in 1892 and expanded rapidly.[32] Along with streetcars, these transportation lines moved dancers and their patrons to the dance halls.

Modernity was not simply the transformations wrought by "machines, speed, electricity" and other innovations—it was, as Christine Stansell notes, a "new temper of mind."[33] Modernity produced new types of people, living lives with new possibilities, different precarities, and new ways of thinking and feeling. In Chicago, some of these modern types were bohemians, independent working women, hobos, lesbians and gay men, and gangsters, among others. The transformations of modernity were inextricable with where they went and how they got there; the music they listened to and how they experienced the sounds; the way they moved their bodies, danced, chose dance partners, became sexual or not; and the kinds of places they danced in.

Pleasures of all kinds were newly available in a range of modern public places. Young women and men could intermingle unsupervised in venues such as factories, offices, streetcars, restaurants, skating rinks, and parks.

This Knights Templar postcard, of the 31st Triennial Conclave "Welcome" sign, held in Chicago, August 1910, boasts that the sign is the tallest, most spectacular electric sign in the world.

Perhaps most importantly, dance halls were emblematic of a new discourse of sexual liberalism marking that decade. Contemporary historians view the period in the twenties when Cressey conducted his research as "a critical turning point" toward sexual liberalism—the spread of modern norms whereby sex became increasingly detached from marriage and reproduction, and sexual pleasure became a valued goal.[34] Sexuality became more publicly visible, sexual regulation moved outside of the family, procreation was no longer the only justification for sex, and heterosexual pleasure attained new cultural value.[35] This period of the 1920s represented one of the most significant transformations of sexual meanings and practices of the twentieth century—a "sexual revolution."[36]

The dance craze that swept the nation during Cressey's research reflected this new sexual liberalism. As Joanne Meyerowitz notes, although these transformations in the sexual culture are often portrayed as moving from the middle to the working class, it is more likely that "middle-class pleasure seekers" copied new sexual possibilities while slumming in dance halls, or from popular-culture portrayals of the sexual lives of independent working women. In this sense, she argues, women lodgers—some of whom worked as taxi dancers—"helped chart the modern American sexual terrain."[37]

On the Dance Floor

It's late when we arrive. A neon sign is "dully lighted," a wall panel "crudely painted." The room is narrow and claustrophobic, the orchestra performing for dancers who are "musically unappreciative" and "oblivious." The halls, which attracted European and Filipino immigrants, were a "polyglot aggregation" of "uncouth" and "motley" patrons. The girls "seem much alike," at least superficially. Some are "loud" and "profane," others "decorous." The saxophone "squawks." The hall pulses with the energy of a sinister, commercialized, leisure. Yet "no one speaks. No one laughs. It is a strangely silent crowd." Still, the dance platform is "a mass of seething, gesticulating figures." When a taxi dancer receives tickets from her patrons, she tears them in half and tucks them into a hem of her stocking, where they accumulate to resemble a "large and oddly placed tumor." By the last waltz, dancer and patron alike are fatigued and "drooping." There might be a fight between men of "swarthy complexion," but eventually everyone goes home, either alone or in couples. This is the portrait Paul Cressey painted of a spin through an allegedly typical night at his composite site, the Eureka Dancing Academy. The taxi-dance hall was, he concluded, "a mercenary and silent world."[38]

Chicago, like other modern cities, featured myriad types of public dance venues. Dances were sponsored by cities themselves, by social agencies and fraternal orders, by dance academies, and by hotels, restaurants, nightclubs, and roadhouses. African Americans—excluded from the taxi-dance halls—hosted public dances known as rent parties in private homes. Compared with other northern cities, Chicago also had the most black-and-tan cabarets, the racially mixed clubs that featured interracial and same-sex dancing.[39] Taxi-dance halls represented a specific type of these new commercialized leisure places.

The taxi-dance social world featured specific interior places and spaces, specific social characters, and acceptable practices and behaviors. Like hobo jungles and other marginal places, it was governed by rules and riven by transgressions of them. As such, insiders and outsiders were legible based on their cultural competency in these specialized ways of talking, dancing, and negotiating the space. Taking Robert Park's advice to craft compelling sociological narratives that read like novels, Cressey created vivid stories about these places within the taxi-dance hall.

Place produced the taxi-dance self. Cressey's sociological eye keenly captured how the dance floor—the hall's most crucial space—transformed into a social place of norms and negotiations. The dancer herself commanded the floor, earning Cressey's recognition: "the most distinguishing aspect of the taxi-dance hall is the position of prominence and prestige occupied by the successful taxi-dancer." The taxi dancers established "certain codes and techniques of control," which they communicated both to patrons and newer dancers. Social guidelines were transmitted (and violated) in places such as restrooms, dressing rooms, and dark corners. Cressey quoted one dancer describing her first night: "During the intermission I went back to the restroom and found the girls powdering, painting, using lipstick, swearing, smoking, and drinking. . . . I didn't go back to the restroom for almost a week. . . . But it didn't take long to get used to things. I gradually got to using their talk and now when I get back there I talk just like the rest of them." Restrooms, like other ambient places such as park benches, facilitated gossip and networks crucial to the dissemination of place-based social norms. Likewise, dressing rooms served as women-only places where dancers prepared, rested, bonded, and probably argued. As the evening's dancing began, the women would emerge together from the segregation of the dressing room, often dancing with each other before the patrons approached them.

The taxi-dance hall was an affective place. The dance floor, restrooms, dimly lit corners, the lobby itself, could all generate a dynamic mix of emotions—hope, excitement, happiness, fear, boredom, pleasures of all kinds, and more. Taxi-dance-hall emotional possibilities drew on broader affective cultures, such as those related to sexuality, city life, and new ways of being a modern person.

Power and place intersected on the dance floor and in the dancing. One JPA investigator reported that taxi-dancers performed a "violent twisting of the hips when two girls dance together." Reformers lamented that "muscle dances" in same-gender pairs or individually conveyed a strong sense of women's empowerment.[40] Dance floors were places of inclusion and exclusion, sites on which gender, sexuality, and race were actively negotiated and reconfigured. The taxi-dance hall can be viewed as a type of sexual service industry, and yet historians suggest that these muscular and same-gender dances also challenged male dominance and helped redefine ideas about women's bodies and sexuality. Historian Randy McBee argues that during this era, dance "offered women opportunities to claim ownership of public spaces."[41] In addition, taxi-dance halls burgeoned during an era of racial segregation, antimiscegenation, and anti-immigrant sentiment. Dancers sometimes reinforced racial hierarchies on the dance floor. Yet anthropologist Rhacel Parreñas contends that the taxi-dance interactions between working-class White women and Filipino men potentially encouraged "intimate relationships, cohabitation, marriages, and love to blossom for the heterosexual patrons and employees of the dance halls."[42] Taxi-dance halls, even as transient and marginal places, facilitated some of the early century's cultural changes.

Dance styles also varied by region and social class, and dance halls even within the same neighborhood might favor different dances. Cressey, who taught himself to dance after his early family prohibition of it, took a dim view of taxi-dancing. He complained that, although taxi-dance halls postured as dance academies, no real instruction took place. Consistent with his overall view of taxi-dancers as gold diggers, he claimed that dancers employed suggestive dancing to make more money: "Schooled in the practices of exploitation, the seasoned taxi-dancer uses the techniques of the 'sex game' for all the returns which they will net her." Overall, he dismissed the dancing as "anything but uniform": some couples "gallop" over the floor, others do a "curious angular strut and a double shuffle or a stamp and a glide." Dance historians are more specific. For example, Chicago taxi dancers preferred a dance called the South Side (a recent YouTube video where a woman recorded her mother demonstrating the South Side in her kitchen suggests that this might be the "violent twisting of the hips" derided by reformers). Randy McBee notes that in the early twentieth century, when working-class couples danced, they were derided as vulgar[43]—yet another way that social practices reinforced inequalities.

Cressey, despite his ambivalence about the exuberant, loud, sensual, exploitive taxi-dance world, interrupted dominant gender and immigrant narratives with more textured narratives of different places and lives. He was sometimes sympathetic, often critical. *The Taxi-Dance Hall* represented the halls as seedy and degrading. He depicted the dancers as opportunists exploiting men. Yet he noted that independent women in other occupations of "transient associates," such as waitresses and salesgirls, also find "the sex game" to be advantageous. The taxi-dance hall, in his analysis, was not uniquely victimizing. Further, he argued that the halls could provide deep satisfactions to the dancers, in particular women who resisted conventionally domestic lives. He used these women's own words—somewhat ironically, from case records collected by JPA investigators—to show the pressures of their lives, but also the pleasures. This was a step away from his funders' fulsome condemnation of the halls and their desire to redeem its fallen women.

Against pervasive stories of racial and gender biological inferiority, Cressey told a social story—one about loneliness. He historicized the taxi-dance hall, identifying conditions that he believed produced them. In particular, he saw taxi-dance halls as places haunted by women and men made lonely by the changes wrought by modern life. Immigrant men in particular, he argued, were beset by the strange new loneliness of the modern city. Cressey viewed the taxi-dance halls as arising to meet the needs of "homeless and lonesome men" unable to establish traditional nuclear families.[44] He much preferred the noncommercial Lonesome Club, Inc.—a social project of weekly dances for strangers in Chicago (its motto: A Bright Spot in a Blue World)—to the potentially sexualized taxi-dance hall. But the taxi-dance hall, although less wholesome in Cressey's view, offered social ties to these modern men and women who shared a modern loneliness. *The Taxi-Dance Hall* anticipated later twentieth century loneliness studies. As the century progressed, other sociologists, such as David Riesman (1950) and Robert Putnam (2000), would famously (but differently) pursue this theme of modern loneliness, depicting individuals in a lonely crowd beset by commercialization and pressures to conform.[45] **(See Hyperlink 3.2: The Well of Loneliness: A Queer Note?)**

Paul Cressey viewed the taxi-dance hall as both a problem of the modern city and as one solution to problems of the modern city. In the end, he recommended not closing or policing the halls, given what he saw as their positive functions for immigrants, the disabled, and various types of strangers. Indeed, one headline in the *Chicago Daily Times* read "Taxi Dance Halls Win Prof's O.K.: Necessary for Masculine 'Misfits.'"[46] The articles cited Cressey's argument that the halls could ameliorate the loneliness of cities. The Juvenile Protective Association had probably hoped for a more robust condemnation by Cressey of the taxi-dance halls. In the foreword of Cressey's book, Jessie Binford delicately noted that "our interpretation of the dance-hall problem may not coincide entirely with Mr. Cressey's."[47]

"From Where They Come in the City": Mapping the Taxi-Dance World

The mapping of social differences within neighborhoods was one innovation by which social science departed from race science's location of difference within bodies. Mapping told a visual story about places and geographies of social differences. At the time of Cressey's research, sociology already had a history of mapping neighborhoods and social worlds. In the late nineteenth century, W. E. B. Du Bois produced maps, graphs, and charts to visually document African American educational attainment, occupational achievements, income levels, and much more in *The Georgia Negro: A Social Study*.[48] These visualizations represented Du Bois's dedication to "establishing the Black South's place within and claim to global modernity."[49] The maps were first displayed in Paris at the *Exposition des Nègres d'Amérique* in 1900.

In Chicago, social mapping had been pioneered by Jane Addams, Florence Kelly, and other women activists of Hull House. Published in 1895, *Hull-House Maps and Papers* mapped spatial patterns of settlements, living conditions, ethnicities, wages, and poverty in a district of Chicago; it served as a "stinging indictment of industrial capitalism."[50] Historian Kathryn Kish Sklar called *Hull-House Maps and Papers* "the single most important work by American women social scientists before 1900."[51] Sociologist Mary Jo Deegan argues that the book had "a monumental influence on Chicago sociology and, in turn, American sociology."[52] And yet, given entrenched gender bias and the exclusion of women from social-science faculty positions, this earlier Hull House history was ignored, even erased. Their work, however, fostered a methodological climate for mapping the social dynamics of space and place. Chicago School men adopted mapping later, famously producing mapping schemes of social organization in urban areas whose significance endures to this day.⁵³

Mapping exercises were a required feature of some Chicago sociology courses. Consequently, maps featured prominently in *The Taxi-Dance Hall*, as literal schemas of the taxi-dance world. Cressey constructed actual maps of the neighborhoods of taxi-dance halls, their dancers, and their patrons. *The Taxi-Dance Hall* included two maps of taxi dancers' neighborhoods and one map of their male patrons' residences. Ideally, these maps would have illustrated how places in the city were shaped by social dynamics such as class, ethnicity, and race. Yet Cressey himself acknowledged the weaknesses in his mapping methodology, citing difficulties in securing addresses ("taken casually") and the nonrepresentativeness of his samples (insufficient "for any scientific finality").⁵⁴ His map of the male patrons excluded Filipinos, a significant customer base at Chicago taxi-dance halls. Despite these shortcomings, Cressey employed these maps to support his portraits of taxi dancers and their patrons.

Using his maps, Cressey argued that taxi dancers came from varied backgrounds. Some, as depicted in films and novels, came to the city from small towns and villages, the women adrift. Cressey argued that most had "parental families . . . somewhere in Chicago," often immigrant families. In particular, he noted "the apparent ease with which the girl of Polish parents may be absorbed into the life of the taxi-dance hall." Even local girls, he argued, were alienated from their early neighborhood ties. Instead, these young women tended to lodge in the furnished-room districts of Chicago, where, contemporary historians argue, they established formative social and sexual networks.⁵⁵ Angela Fritz, for example, argues that taxi-dancing was an obvious occupation for Polish American daughters, who grew up happily dancing in the back rooms of local Polish saloons, and for whom dance was a crucial form of cultural expression.⁵⁶ Cressey, however, saw social problems. Based on his mapping of the residential areas of women dancers, he argued that few of them came from "'normal families' in which both parents were still living and maintaining the family." He saw the dancers as fleeing family conflict and demoralization.⁵⁷

Cressey was equally blunt in his descriptive mapping of the male patrons. He described them as a varied group: suave but shady businessmen; young men unable to "assimilate"; hobos passing through the city; Eastern European and Filipino immigrants; old and middle-aged men; and men "handicapped by physical disabilities," whom he described as "dwarfed, maimed, and pock-marked." He said that many patrons were "denied social acceptance elsewhere because they bear an invidious racial mark." The "globe-trotter and the slummer" were the only types of patrons who escaped Cressey's damning evaluations. His map supported his argument about what made a taxi-dance hall successful: it ideally would be located in the rooming-house districts where its patrons lived, and would afford easy access to late-night public transportation.

More historically significant are Cressey's maps of actual locations of Chicago taxi-dance halls. Although his book was based on the "composite" site, the Eureka Dancing Academy, he identified and mapped actual Chicago taxi-dance halls toward the end of his book. His sociohistorical analysis of these city places shines in this final section. Cressey's tale of the "natural history of the taxi-dance hall" depicted the entrepreneurial spirit of immigrant proprietors, the not-infrequent political corruption, city crime, and contests over morality. These maps are perhaps the most significant legacy of *The Taxi-Dance Hall*, representing an important historical record of Chicago taxi-dance halls in the 1920s.

Although very popular, taxi-dance halls were transient places, frequently moving or closing. They were often tucked into attic space, situated off the street or in other inconspicuous locations. One observer noted that "everywhere they are found in some half-secluded region of the building."[58] Cressey identified the Athenian Dancing Academy, at 1321 North Clark Street, as the city's first successful taxi-dance hall. It was originally located in a small room of the Haymarket Burlesque Theater Building, the hobo's "main stem" (main street for hobo activity) along West Madison Street. Others included the Apolon Dancing Club, Paradise Ballroom, and Colonial Dancing Academy. (**See Hyperlink 3.3:** Chicago's Taxi-Dance Halls.)

Cressey mapped successful and unsuccessful dance halls, and noted that flourishing halls had specific requirements, including being accessible to unmarried and immigrant male boarders and with nearby inexpensive late-night transportation to get them home. Taxi-dance halls clustered, he argued, in the "rooming-house area" within the Loop. He noted that those "interstitial areas" were most likely to "tolerate" the taxi-dance halls, rather than the bright-light areas. By 1923, competition among taxi-dance halls became robust. However, halls failed because of intense competition or were forced to close due to allegations of immoral conditions.

By the time *The Taxi-Dance Hall* was published, Chicago was closing them down through a combination of police crackdowns and new licensing laws. In 1932, the JPA's executive director, Jessie Binford, boasted to Ernest Burgess—who had originally urged Paul Cressey and other students to study the taxi-dance halls—that nearly all of them had been shut down. The taxi-dance hall largely became extinct. (Los Angeles, however, saw a revival of the halls in the seventies, with seven of them clustered around the Convention Center by 1990. At that point, tickets went for thirty-five cents per minute, twenty-one dollars per hour.[59] Some of the conditions that had fostered the early taxi-dance halls—a freer sexual culture and lonely immigrant men—gave rise to them.)

Paul Cressey's Dirty Work

In 1918 (after his dismissal from the University of Chicago in a sex scandal), Chicago School luminary W. I. Thomas told a reporter for the *Chicago Tribune* that sex was a "dangerous subject of study because it is the only remaining subject which has not been opened up freely to scientific investigation . . . it possesses unsuspected possibilities of danger to the reputation of those concerned."[60] Sex, however, was a central plot of taxi-dance stories. Sexual activity—real or imagined—was feared by social reformers, and desired, or not, by dancers and patrons. Cressey was conflicted about writing sex into his stories of *The Taxi-Dance Hall*—a book otherwise about work, immigration, gender, marginality, and loneliness in a modernizing city.

Paul Cressey's research and writing reflect tensions in US sexual culture in that period. On the one hand, the taxi-dance hall's very existence was at least partly due to the sexual revolution of the 1920s, which had enabled the rise of new sexual places and possibilities. On the other hand, sexual taboos and silences persisted. Cressey experienced ambivalence about his own sexual feelings, his career, and what could—and could not—be said about sex in his book. The stories of *The Taxi-Dance Hall*, then, are about sexual pleasure, but also about sexual stigma, both for the dancers and the scholar.

Scholars who studied sexuality (and other deviant topics) encountered various career constraints, such as limited funding sources and job prospects, censorship, public controversy, and even death threats. In 1921, the National Research Council established the Committee for Research in Problems of Sex, which sought to establish scientific legitimacy for a subject that had—as Thomas had earlier pointed out—remained in relative disrepute. European sexuality scholars were well established in the 1920s, with sexuality journals, institutes, and service organizations. However, in 1933, the year after the publication of *The Taxi-Dance Hall*, the books and archives of the Institute of Sex Research, founded by Magnus Hirschfeld in 1919, were publicly burned in Berlin's streets by the Nazis. Internationally, sexuality research continued to be misunderstood, attacked, or considered disreputable, with later scholars describing it as "dirty work," sociologist Everett Hughes's term for an occupation that is socially important but also stigmatized.[61] Back in Chicago, in the twenties and thirties, Paul Cressey wrote about a stigmatized place and then felt stigmatized for doing so.

The taxi-dance hall was a marginalized place and type of employment, discredited (among some) as a place of sexual service and immorality. Dancers and patrons alike were vulnerable to what sociologist Erving Goffman, decades later, would call the "spoiled identity" of stigma. Goffman's typology of stigma offers a useful lens through which to consider Cressey's ambivalence. Goffman identified three types of stigma: tribal, "abominations of the body," and character "blemishes" such as alcoholism or homosexuality.[62] Cressey's analysis of the taxi-dance denizens reflected all three of these types of stigma—the "tribal" stigma of racial bias, particularly his condescension toward Filipino patrons; his disdain toward the "abominations of the body" of older and physically disabled patrons; and his overall dim view of the dancers' personal morality, particularly the women's.

Yet Cressey himself felt discredited by his association with a stigmatized place of research (Goffman would later note that stigma could be contagious). Cressey feared that *The Taxi-Dance Hall* was a book that would taint him. He specifically worried about sexual content in the book, writing to his editor, "I have spent considerable time going over the manuscript, trying to delete and change everything which may give the material an aspect of being too 'sexy.' You will notice that I have even altered the documents in some instances in order to prevent people getting this type of reaction.... I am very anxious that nothing be retained in the manuscript which will given [sic] even the more prurient a strong reaction."[63] And so, Cressey set about sanitizing the book.

A comparison of Cressey's 1929 master's thesis and his 1932 book, *The Taxi-Dance Hall*, shows he virtually scrubbed the manuscript clean. He did this by changing his vocabulary and by eliminating terms, descriptions, and sections of the thesis. Consistent with his goal of deleting "prurient" content, he eliminated terms that referred to sexuality. For example, he frequently changed "sexual" to "sensual," or simply omitted it. He dropped even inoffensive words that referred to sex, such as "vulgarity." He became more reticent in the book about describing dances, for example the popular Shimmy and Shake.

Taxi-dance halls had their own vocabulary. Both the MA thesis and the book contained glossaries, in which Cressey listed common terms with their definitions. The terms included on both lists, as Chad Heap notes, reflect cultural anxieties about sexuality and interracial sexuality, for example *bata*, a Filipino term for a "white sweetheart."[64] However, Cressey radically edited the glossary for the book. In the MA thesis he wrote, "To a considerable extent, the vocabulary is constructed from common slang and vulgarity, and from the West Side dialect."[65] This appeared in the book as, "To a considerable extent, the vocabulary is constructed from common slang and from the West Side dialect." Cressey deleted many more sexual references in the book manuscript. In his anxious manuscript revisions, we can see the challenges scholars faced in rewriting sexuality against the dominant narratives of essentialism, condemnation, and stigma. (**See Hyperlink 3.4:** Paul Cressey's Self-Censorship.)

Cressey's anxieties mounted as his manuscript moved through production. He regularly communicated with his editor at the University of Chicago Press, Gordon Laing, about the book's cover, title, and the potential publication of names and visual material. His fears of stigmatization led him to worry that "the public is all too eager" to view the book negatively, even without reading it.[66] Likewise, the press had its own legal concerns. Press representatives urged Cressey to ensure that he had used pseudonyms in the book, worried about naming actual dance halls, and vetoed the use of photographs.

Both the press and Cressey knew the book, as an outsider commodity, could profit from sexual sensationalism or suffer from stigmatization. They were torn. In April 1931, Rollin Hemens from the press suggested changing the book title from *The Taxi-Dance Hall*, because he feared that most people did not know what a taxi-dancer was. Around this time, however, a number of movies and songs took the taxi dance as their theme, including the Ruth Etting song, "Ten Cents a Dance." Hemens wrote, "Explained in terms of Ruth Elting's [*sic*] 'Ten Cents a Dance' the subject clicks immediately. Why not change the title to *Ten Cents a Dance?*"[67] While a press editor agreed that the public might not know about taxi dancers, he ventured that this could be a virtue of the title: "Curiosity is aroused and that is a good preliminary to a sale. 'Ten Cents a Dance' is a little bit undignified."[68] This concern with dignity reemerged after publication.

Cressey tried to assert control over his book. He was disappointed with book sales, and that the press did not "in some way take advantage of the unique human interest material that the book includes."[69] He proposed a new cover, and submitted a sketch made by one of his students of a "typical dance hall" with various dancers, including "a typical young American fellow," "an Oriental," and "a slickly-dressed young fellow of the gangster type."[70] Balancing competing wishes for commercial success and sexual propriety, Cressey noted that a more explicit cover "would be very profitable," but it could be removed from library books, and thus would not "lessen the dignity of the book as part of a permanent collection."[71] His editor responded that the legal advisors found it too dangerous, and the book was "stronger and more dignified" without it.[72]

Cressey's career hit other troubles. Shortly before his anxious prepublication correspondence with the University of Chicago Press, controversy unfolded over his appointment to a research team on movies and youth sexuality, sponsored by the Payne Fund. In 1929, Reverend William Short, who had deep connections to University of Chicago sociology, proposed a study to examine boys' "sex attitudes" toward the movies.[73] Sexuality research was already taboo and academically perilous, and as Short wrote to his colleague, W. W. Charters, there had been "disastrous results to an inquiry, and incidentally to the professor connected with it, at the University of Missouri, because some rather innocent sex questions were included." When they decided to proceed regardless, Chicago sociologists touted Cressey because of his taxi-dance research. Yet there was a cloud over his candidacy—the JPA's Jessica Binford had charged Cressey with "sexual misconduct," and there were rumors about his dubious research practices. There are few details about these allegations, but according to communication scholar Garth Jowett and colleagues, Binford charged that "the unmarried Cressey had acted with impropriety" in collecting taxi-dancers' stories. He had allegedly instructed his assistants to interact with dancers in myriad ways "to loosen their defenses and extract more of their stories."[74] Charters wrote to Short, "We ought to be able to find a reputable scientist capable of doing good work who does not have something wrong with him sexually, in connection with a sex study."[75] Still, Paul Cressey joined the research group in 1931. It is unclear whether he ever knew about the controversy surrounding his appointment or addressed the allegations of impropriety.

In the end, Paul Cressey's efforts to avoid sexual stigma appear to have been unsuccessful. Before *The Taxi-Dance Hall*'s publication, Cressey had a teaching position at Evansville College in Indiana. In a letter to his editor on August 17, 1931, he discussed his own career: "From my own interest, professionally, I fear that even at best the book will be more of a handicap than a help.... During my years at Evansville College I have been under some embarrassment because of the nature of my research work at Chicago. While the president there has not had his faith shaken in me personally he has had the feeling that, with the popular prejudices as they exist, such a book published by one of his faculty would be a liability rather than a help."[76]

Cressey's career difficulties may or may not have been wholly or partly the result of sexual stigma. Yet his challenges securing tenure-stream employment, along with the Payne Fund controversy, suggest that possibility. Over time, he took a series of adjunct positions and social-service jobs. Eventually, in 1950, Cressey landed a full-time faculty position at Ohio Wesleyan University. He was fifty years old, and would live five more years. Like Nels Anderson, he never had the successful academic career for which he had hoped.

Conclusion: Taxi-Dance Legacies

The Taxi-Dance Hall has endured, at least in part, because Paul Cressey explored the social dynamics of a transient, marginal place and the people who worked and played there. It is the only scholarly monograph from its era about the early-twentieth-century taxi-dance hall, and it is still cited as a historical source. The book was, and remains, a flashpoint for disagreement about his analysis and methods, and about the dance halls themselves.[77] It has been criticized for its shortcomings and praised for its contributions.

The book was immediately controversial. If Cressey was not critical enough of taxi-dance halls for the Juvenile Protective Association, he was too critical in the view of taxi-dancers themselves. Dance halls garnered enormous public attention when *The Taxi-Dance Hall* was published in 1932, partly because of the Chicago police crackdown and partly because of the publicity blitz for Cressey's book. The University of Chicago Press published ads and press releases, while the *Chicago Daily Times* published a series of excerpts from the book as a prepublication strategy. Taxi-dancers responded—with fury.

There was an outpouring of critical letters to the *Chicago Daily Times* in what one dancer called "the taxi dance war."[78] One writer slammed social reformers: "The moralists who closed these places down certainly should sit back and feel satisfied that again they have done their worst." Others blamed gender bias and the failures of capitalism. One young woman wrote, "If you and other critics are against taxi dancing, how about getting some of us young girls a decent job, and, believe me, we won't have to dance with old grouches."[79] Another said, "I've been trying to get a job at a department store or factory for over a year, and I haven't succeeded yet."[80] One letter writer, who signed as "Another Taxi Dancer," explained that she had been a dancer, then got a job at what some would call "a decent living," but when it didn't work out she went back to taxi dancing. She continued, "It was work too, the way some men made us jump around the hall. Otherwise it was pleasure with pay."[81] As contemporary historian Angela Fritz argues, taxi dancers were "early urban sex workers," and "Cressey's book would have done little to stop their vulnerability."[82] This outcry by taxi dancers makes clear that the book had a public impact ("Paul G. Cressey certainly has started something,"[83] one writer complained). These critiques by taxi dancers highlight how social outsiders mobilized on their own behalf, a manifestation of political resistance that would escalate among other marginal groups in later decades.

Scholarly reviewers also found flaws with his research. Sociologist Winifred Raushenbush found the book "disappointing" and "unsatisfactory," arguing that Cressey "did not compare the sexual practices of the taxi dancer with the contemporary sexual practices of girls of a higher economic and social level."[84] This suggests her recognition of the profound sexual changes underway in Chicago in that era, and Cressey's inattention to them. And in the *American Journal of Sociology*, Evelyn Buchman Crook, in an otherwise favorable review, expressed skepticism about Cressey's findings, and wished for "a more thorough analysis of the cultural mixture of the areas represented by girl dancers."[85] Despite these early critiques, many later sociologists saw Cressey as representative of the early Chicago School's pioneering methodological advances.[86]

The taxi-dance hall was a workplace where gender, sexuality, race, and social class were reinforced and redefined. These topics have only grown in cultural, political, and academic significance, keeping *The Taxi-Dance Hall* relevant. Some contemporary scholars have taken issue with Cressey's analysis of dance-hall dynamics (while, curiously, sometimes also using his evidence to make their own arguments), and some disagree with each other. In her early work, historian Joanne Meyerowitz, for example, criticized Cressey and other sociologists of that era for depicting "self-supporting women," including taxi-dancers, as hedonistic and "opportunistic," while downplaying their vulnerability to poverty and sexual harassment.[87] She viewed this portrait as emblematic of the larger shift in cultural discourses from the late nineteenth century to the early twentieth century, in which representations of independent working women changed: "In the late nineteenth century, women lodgers, alone in the city, epitomized the purity of endangered womanhood; in the early twentieth century, the same women were the among the first 'respectable' women broadcast as happy sexual objects."[88] While this argument characterizes Cressey's depictions as more monolithic than they were, it also recognizes the entanglements of sociology and popular culture in reshaping the era's images of women into agents rather than victims (even if that agency was cast as opportunistic).

In a more recent critique, historian Angela Fritz indicted Cressey on multiple fronts: his "paternalistic attitude" toward the girls and women; his reliance on disguises and impersonations; his use of secondhand information, such as gossip and eavesdropping; and his use of gifts and "treating" in exchange for information.[89] Ultimately, she argues that his race, class, and gender biases deeply undermined his empirical investigation and interpretations, all in service of telling dramatic stories about the taxi-dance hall.

Scholars are still debating each other about the taxi-dance halls themselves. Historian Kevin Mumford argues that the halls were complicit in sexual racism, for the ways in which they excluded women of color, and offered the sexualized services of Caucasian women to men of color (although not African Americans).[90] In response, communication scholar Derek Vaillant argues that Mumford "oversimplifies the power dynamics between employers and employees at the dance, and it mistakes the visible signifiers of the dancing environment ('white' and 'black' skin) for the parodic manipulation of these supposed racial essences by the mechanics of the dance and by male and female participants."[91] Vaillant argues, instead, that gendered and racialized norms were performative, and thereby mocked, in the taxi-dance hall. The taxi-dance was an "unprecedented public performance" that undermined, rather than reinforced, essentialized binaries of race and gender.[92] This analysis basically queers the taxi dance, in the sense that it challenges conventional notions of stable identity categories. While early interpretivist sociology anticipated and helped lay the foundation for this type of queer critique, it could not have been accomplished by scholars of the 1920s, Paul Cressey included.

Almost a century later, with sophisticated critical and queer theories, advances in ethnographic research practices, and the rise of Institutional Review Boards (IRBs), *The Taxi-Dance Hall* lends itself to many criticisms. Extensive discussion of topics such as consent, privacy, vulnerability, accountability to communities being studied, and the use of deception and disguises would all come later in the century, along with the regulatory regime of IRBs. The theoretical complexities introduced by decades of women's and gender studies, critical race studies, and queer studies all fostered ways of thinking and writing that were simply unknown in 1932.

Ultimately, Cressey encouraged acceptance, albeit reluctantly, of what he saw as the outsiders and misfits. The text's key limitations—his disparagement of women and ethnic minorities, for example—leap from the page in a contemporary reading. They underscore the intersectional dimensions of racism, sexism, and classism in early social science and mainstream culture.[93] Yet Cressey's ambivalent stories also recognized the vitality and satisfactions in complex, new social places. Like *The Hobo*, his book is a glimpse of modern individuals making bold choices against the grain of contemporary conventionality. It depicted a marginal social institution during a moment of cultural change. The text—with its promise of being able to tell different kinds of stories about overlooked corners and margins of society—captured the imaginations of young social scientists who came after him.

The Taxi-Dance Hall remains a classic text of the early Chicago School. It reflects the University of Chicago's curiosity about modern urban life and its new outsiders. Cressey's immersion in the field prefigured the emergence of a more sophisticated and ethically astute ethnography. His focus on places, communities, and interactions characterized the Chicago School's rupture from biological determinism in an era of determinist scientific racism. As a young graduate student, he grappled with enormous and intransigent social dilemmas—poverty, immigration, workplace gender bias, racism, sexuality, emotional labor, loneliness. Later sociologists would hone sharper conceptual tools in order to think differently and tell new stories about these topics.

Hyperlink 3.1: "Life's Gutters": Popular Culture Represents the Taxi-Dance Hall

The taxi-dance hall highlights the entangled interests of social researchers and cultural producers. Paul Cressey's research about, and writing of, *The Taxi-Dance Hall* unfolded in an era when music and dance, film and fiction all played crucial roles in fostering rapid changes in gender, sexual, and racial norms and practices. Sociologist Roger Salerno described Paul Cressey's participatory research as "the stuff of pulp fiction."[94] Historian Joanne Meyerowitz argued that popular culture, like noir fiction, influenced sociological research on "women adrift."[95] In fact, taxi-dance-hall narratives featured prominently in popular culture well before Cressey's book came to popular attention. While readers of a University of Chicago monograph may not have patronized a taxi-dance hall, a broad range of films and fiction had made the dancers and dance halls visible to a broader public. The period between 1925, when Cressey began his research, and 1932, when his book appeared, saw three dance-hall films: Charlie Chaplin's *The Gold Rush* (1925), *The Taxi Dancer* (1927) with Joan Crawford, and *Ten Cents a Dance* (1931) with Barbara Stanwyck. That film was inspired by the popular Rogers and Hart song of the same name, sung by Ruth Etting and charting at number 5 on *Billboard* in 1930 (later sung by Doris Day, Ella Fitzgerald, and Anita O'Day).

Taxi-dance-hall fiction capitalized on cultural tensions between conventionality and transgression. The dance hall itself was a deviant place, representing the paradoxes of empowerment and vulnerability, pleasure and punishment. The halls boasted names like "The Palace"; by contrast, the cover of a pulp novel described them as "life's gutters." Likewise, the taxi dancers teetered between agency and victimization. Cressey found that in Chicago, many taxi dancers were Eastern European immigrants or their daughters, and their male customers were frequently Filipinos. Their fictionalized counterparts, however, were typically US-born Whites. In those stories, dancers had defied domesticity, left small towns, and moved to the city to seek careers. Yet they faced hardship, danger, and stigma, and allegedly yearned for traditional, yet elusive, heterosexual marriages. In *Ten Cents a Dance*, Etting sang, "Sometimes I think, I've found my hero. But it's a queer romance. All that you need is a ticket. Come on big boy, ten cents a dance."[96] Typical dance hall plots featured hardship, struggle, and at least the hope of rescue. Historian Joanne Meyerowitz noted that by the mid-1920s, popular culture represented women adrift, such as the taxi dancer, less as victims than as gold diggers preying on men.[97]

Charlie Chaplin's *Gold Rush* united two of the era's notable marginal figures—the hobo/Tramp and the dance-hall girl. Chaplin's Tramp character traveled to the Yukon, becoming a gold prospector (a tramp who travels for work fits Nels Anderson's definition of "hobo"). Although living in a wilderness cabin, the "lone prospector" met and fell in love with Georgia (played by Georgia Hale), a local dance-hall worker. Georgia—with her mink coat and fancy dresses—represented the bawdy "archetype of femininity" crucial to Chaplin's working-class popularity.[98] Both characters, despite her glamour and his dishevelment, inhabited working-class culture. In this powerfully gendered redemption narrative, the Tramp—in his ill-fitting clothes—promises to save the well-groomed Georgia when he comes back from seeking his fortune in gold: "I love you. I'm going to take you away from this life. I am going away. And when I return, I shall come back!"[99] And, indeed, he returned a rich man, rescuing Georgia to (presumably) live happily ever after. Whatever the aspirations of actual taxi dancers, marriage represented the obligatory happy ending for fictionalized popular culture.

The mid-1920s, the period of Paul Cressey's field research, marked a shift in cultural representation of women's sexuality. Meyerowitz argues that by 1925, readers and audiences did not expect women to be punished for sexual transgressions. However, dance-hall pulp, which emphasized sex and alcohol, continued to feature violence against dancers. For example, the taxi dancer figured prominently in the noir writer Cornell Woolrich's fiction, such as *The Dancing Detective* (penned under the pseudonym William Irish). In this story, a serial killer murdered taxi dancers and then danced with their corpses, placing dimes on their bodies.

The paperback revolution of the early twentieth century coincided with the taxi-dance heyday. These small, cheap, and immensely popular books were easily purchased in drugstores, kiosks, or bus depots. They were "the transitory and transportable artifacts of an increasingly mobile and uprooted society."[100] Pulp novels, in particular, were populated with various marginal characters of modern life, who thereby gained greater cultural visibility in these fictional representations. *Taxi Dancers*, by Eve Linkletter (born in Britain as Eva Irene Linkletter), was one of these. *Taxi Dancers* featured a young White woman, Linda, who moved to New York to be an actress but quickly found herself in a dance hall instead. The novel showed the pluck of dancers. Linda, for example, arrived at the Dance Palace for her first night. As the bright neon light blinked "Dance Palace—100 Beautiful Girls," Linda "walked up the stairs, and her heart was full of adventure as she entered the hall, this time with her permit, ready to be for the first time, A TAXI DANCER"[101] (capitalization in the original). On the up side, Linda found freedom, autonomy, friends, and thrilling, illicit sex. The final page finds Linda planning her wedding with her true love, Tom. On the down side, a stranger stalked and murdered other taxi dancers, until captured at the end.

No clear historical evidence exists about the extent of prostitution or sexual activity in the taxi-dance halls. However, Meyerowitz refers to taxi-dancing as "sexual service work,"[102] and the taxi-dance halls of fiction underscored the danger and the disrepute attached to sex and sex work. Yet they also showed glimpses of what autonomy, adventure, and freedom, including sexual freedom, could look (and feel) like for women. As women increasingly entered public places in the early twentieth century, these films, novels, songs, and other stories showed them doing so, regardless of vulnerability. Meyerowitz notes that the cultural visibility of women outside the family probably inspired others to seek urban adventure, while also warning them of potential dangers for women venturing alone to the city.

Paradoxes of gender conformity and transgression, sexual pleasure and danger, remain enduring themes in popular culture. Dance-hall plots anchored film and fiction from their heyday in the 1920s, and continue into the twenty-first century. Early examples include *Let's Dance* (1933), which featured Gracie Allen and George Burns at the Roseland Dance Hall in Los Angeles, while *Dime-A-Dance* (1937) starred Imogene Coca. A modern outsider, the taxi dancer prefigured more recent fictional sex workers, such as Iris Steensma (Jodie Foster) in *Taxi Driver* (1976) and Vivian Ward (Julia Roberts) in *Pretty Woman* (1990). The protagonists of twenty-first-century novels *Ten Cents a Dance* (2008) and *A Girl Like You* (2016), are both young Chicago women who work as taxi dancers after falling on hard times.[103] Actual taxi dancers of the 1930s and '40s were young, and therefore some are still alive or have close living relatives. Author Christine Fletcher wrote *Ten Cents a Dance* after discovering that her mysterious Aunt Sofia had been a taxi dancer in Manhattan.

Eve Linkletter, the author of *Taxi Dancers*, also penned *The Gay Ones* ("Were they pranks of nature? Or were they the third sex—the gay ones?")[104] When both were published, in 1958, the taxi dancer had receded and "the gay ones" were coming into their own, yet these new social types shared the thrill and taint of sexual transgression, intriguing both sociologists and popular culture producers.

Hyperlink 3.2: *The Well of Loneliness*: A Queer Note?

Almost a century after Paul Goalby Cressey's graduate research, a sociologist exploring his papers at the University of Chicago makes a queer finding—Cressey's mention of the now-iconic lesbian novel, *The Well of Loneliness* (1928), in his early paper, "A Study of Gaelic Park." While still a graduate student, Cressey visited the Chicago public dance pavilion, and afterwards visited the apartment of one of the patrons. Cressey described leaving the dance and taking a taxi to a private party on Jackson Boulevard with a group of young people he had just met. It was "Uncle's" apartment, "a modern, three-room suite of nicely furnished rooms." He spied the novel on a coffee table. As drinking and dancing ensued, he wrote, "Blondy stretched herself in full possession of the davenport. As she lay down she picked up 'The Wells of Lonliness' [*sic*] that lay opened on the coffee table. She became engrossed in the book and answered disinterestedly to 'Uncle' who sat at her feet."[105] Why, the contemporary sociologist wonders, did Paul Cressey notice this novel, and why did he mention it in his field notes? Was it an insider's nod to the bohemian crowd in which he found himself? Or simply part of a field researcher's thick description of the scene?

The Well of Loneliness was the first lesbian novel published in the United States. Historian Chad Heap notes that Chicago sociologists were indeed aware of new novels challenging conventional sexual practices, and several students during this time studied the book-borrowing patterns in almost 100 Chicago libraries to assess their cultural impact. They found that overall, the sexual novels were so popular they were "worn out" by readers.[106] However, based on the publication dates of the novels they studied, two of which appeared in 1932, this study came out after Paul Cressey's Gaelic Park paper of the late 1920s. It seems unlikely that Cressey recognized the book and its subject, despite its notoriety. For one, he mistakenly called it *The Wells of Lonliness*. Moreover, since Cressey viewed taxi-dance halls as lonely places, he was predisposed to view the novel's title through that prism.

However, *The Well of Loneliness* was a very different kind of book about misfits and outsiders, one foregrounding sexual and gender difference. Upon publication in England on July 27, 1928, British author Radclyffe Hall's candid book about lesbian desire, with its gender-nonconforming protagonist, generated fierce debates. Hall used the work of early sexologists Richard von Krafft-Ebing and Havelock Ellis to lend scientific credibility to her plea for social acceptance of sexual difference. Her novel helped popularize sexology and the modernization of sex, while fostering a lesbian public consciousness.[107] By November, 1928, the British courts had declared it obscene, a ban that lasted until 1948.

Regardless, the book became widely available in the United States in the fall of 1928. It was already into its seventh printing when in February, 1929, its publishers appeared in a New York court to face obscenity charges.[108] In April, the book had been cleared of all charges by the Court of Special Sessions, which allowed for broader circulation. The publishers took out a full-page advertisement in the *New York Times Book Review*, saying, "The Most Controversial Book of the Century—Suppressed in England and Vindicated by an American Court." The enhanced circulation of the book, along with an expansion in the publication of lesbian novels in the 1930s, surely would not have happened had the verdict been otherwise. It might well not have been on the table at Jackson Boulevard for a young graduate student to notice.

The woman absorbed in reading a lesbian-themed novel at a robustly heterosexual party hints at the cultural practice of slumming common in cities like Chicago in the early twentieth century. Slumming took various forms, typically boundary-crossing exploration of marginal urban places by affluent Whites. Chad Heap argues that slumming was more than thrill-seeking. It fostered the establishment of commercialized leisure places that supported diverse sexual and racial identities, thereby reshaping "the sexual and racial landscape of American urban culture and space."[109] The pansy and lesbian craze was one iteration of these "great slumming vogues."[110] During the years of Cressey's research and on through the 1930s, slummers sought thrills by visiting lesbian and gay cabarets, speakeasys, and nightclubs. Their knowledge of these urban places reflected the broader cultural visibility of homosexuality in film, theater, and fiction. *The Well of Loneliness*, although perhaps unfamiliar to Paul Cressey, was part of this cultural conversation. One Chicago woman reported that she and a friend "decided to go on a sluming [*sic*] party to one of the places" after they "had read of homosexual life in books," such as *The Well*.[111]

Cressey's "Gaelic Park" was never published. Its reference to the pioneering lesbian novel of the era sits hidden in the university archive as an artifact of queerness, evidence of that era's destabilization of traditional sexual, gender, and racial identity boundaries and reconfiguration of such dynamics in urban places. It signals an increasingly visible queer culture in early Chicago and elsewhere, in the most expansive sense of that term. We will never know why Paul Cressey noticed the book and how he understood it. And, the contemporary sociologist concludes, this kind of indeterminacy is one of the pleasurable vexations of archival research.

Hyperlink 3.3: Chicago's Taxi-Dance Halls

Although Paul Cressey used the Eureka Dance Academy as a pseudonym, at the end of his book he identified numerous actual taxi-dance halls in an analysis of successful and unsuccessful businesses. His was probably not an exhaustive list, yet it nevertheless captures the extensive taxi-dance culture in that historical era.

- Athenian Dancing Academy 1321 N. Clark Street. The Athenian was first located in a small room of the Haymarket Burlesque Theater Building, located on the hobo's "main stem" along West Madison Street.
- The Palace d'Arts Dancing Academy and the Apollo Dancing School were a few blocks to the south of the Athenian and in the heart of Chicago's North Side underworld.
- The Majestic Dancing School in the bright-lights area of the Polish Northwest Side, near the American Dancing School. Later rechristened the New Majestic Dancing School.

- The Plaza Dancing Academy, on North Clark Street, near Division Street.
- The Moonlight Dancing School, near the intersection of Chicago and Western Avenues.
- The Haymarket Burlesque Building, on West Madison Street.
- The Apolon Dancing Club, near Jane Addams's Hull House, on the Near West Side.
- The New England Dancing Studio, midway between Hull House and the Athenian, on Madison Street.
- The La Marseilles Dancing Academy, on the third floor of a building on Randolph Street.
- The New American Dancing School No. 1, at the intersection of Madison Street and Western Avenue.
- The American Dancing School No. 2, on the corner of Robey Street and North Avenue.
- The Vista Dance Hall, on East Forty-Seventh Street.
- The Colonial Dancing Academy, in the Masonic Temple Building in the Loop.
- The Royal Dancing School, on the northwestern margin of the Lower North community.
- The Up in the Clouds Club, on the twenty-first floor of the City Hall Square Building.
- The Park Dancing School, on North Clark Street.

Briefly mentioned taxi-dance halls: Victoria Hall, the Paradise Ballroom, the Dreamland Ballroom, the Colonial Dancing Academy, the Madison Dancing School, the Lane, the Starry, the Grand, the Belvedere, the Paulina-Madison, the Lakeview, the Washington Boulevard, the Oakland.

Hyperlink 3.4: Paul Cressey's Censorship

Below are terms and definitions excerpted from Cressey's MA thesis. They do not appear in his book.[112]

> Breakfast, "She cooks his breakfast"—she grants him overnight dates.
> Bum—a low-grade promiscuous girl. 'A bum out on territory'—a prostitute giving earnings to a cadet.
> Dry stuff—sexual gratification in the dance.
> Good time—sexual intercourse.

Hustler—a soliciting prostitute.

It—"Can you get it?" "Did you get it?," i.e., sexual intercourse.

Lady lovers—lesbian lovers.

Monkey business—sexual intercourse.

Never miss yan—term used by Filipinos to describe a girl from whom sexual cooperation is easily secured.

P.O.—a promiscuous girl.

P.T.—a taxi dancer who practices sex stimulation in the dance hall, from whom no other late-night privileges can be expected.

S.A.—sex appeal.

Shake-up, or "to shake"—sensual dancing.

Shimmy—sensual dancing.

Smart girl—a taxi dancer who encourages attention from men by giving impression that she will grant sex favors, but who later proves to be sparing of these favors.

Socking—sensual dancing.

FOUR

Zora's Florida

Ethnographic Explorations of Zora Neale Hurston

Research is formalized curiosity.[1]
Zora Neale Hurston

Zora Neale Hurston: novelist, folklorist, poet, filmmaker, and raconteur. Best known for her literary genius, Hurston was also an accomplished cultural anthropologist and ethnographer. She earned a bachelor's degree in anthropology at Barnard College, studied for her PhD at Columbia University, and received a Guggenheim Award for her research. Her ethnographic essays were widely published in academic journals. Both Hurston and her work were celebrated and criticized during her lifetime. She struggled financially, working as a maid near the end of her life, and was buried in an unmarked grave. The writer Alice Walker located and placed a headstone on a spot she believed to be Hurston's Fort Pierce grave in the early 1970s.

Often associated with the Harlem Renaissance, Zora's true place was Florida. Hurston grew up in Eatonville, one of the first all-African American, self-governing municipalities in the United States. Eatonville was her artistic and scholarly muse. She would later return periodically to live there as resident-scholar, collecting community folklore and writing. Hurston recalled her childhood days as a budding anthropologist, as she observed White outsiders who passed through her town on their way in and out of Orlando. The front porch was her "gallery seat," from which she waved and called out friendly greetings to the passing White people. She was, she noted, an ersatz Chamber of Commerce welcoming committee. Nonetheless, the White people "rode through town and never lived there";[2] they were strangers and outsiders. The *New York Times* once referred to Eatonville as "a place apart."[3]

I can see why Zora loved her Florida towns. Eatonville, although a place apart, retains the intimate feel of a thriving insider community. Street signs sport markers that say, "The town that freedom built." Spanish moss hangs from the trees along the main thoroughfare, E. Kennedy Boulevard, and around the Old Florida–style houses on surrounding streets. Residents work in their yards, sit on front porches, or chat amiably on the sidewalks. Evidence of Hurston abounds. The library bears her name, as does the Zora Neale Hurston National Museum of Fine Arts.

Seeking traces of Zora's most important places, I drove from the Orlando airport to Eatonville one March day in a small, black rental car. Unable to find the museum, I drove up and down E. Kennedy several times before finally stopping at the library to ask directions. The museum, it turned out, was right down the street. Inside its one room, I told the older African American museum manager that I had been lost. The museum, she told me, had just moved, and its sign had not yet been put up. "Do you have a black car?" she asked. "I saw you driving up and down." Her friendly comment welcomed me yet underscored that I had been noticed because I was an outsider. I was the White stranger passing through.

Alice Walker's powerful essay—"In Search of Zora Neale Hurston"[4]—swept Hurston back into the literary canon. Yet Hurston was, as one journalist puts it, "a cultural anthropologist first."[5] Over the course of an adventurous, challenging, brilliant, and idiosyncratic career, she conducted research across the Jim Crow South, and specifically in Florida regions such as Eatonville, the turpentine and sawmill camps in Polk County and Cross City, and myriad other places. She lived in Eatonville, Jacksonville, Belle Glade, Sanford, Eau Gallie, and Miami, she sailed Florida rivers and lived in houseboats on the coast, and she died in Fort Pierce. Her mobility, boundary crossings, genre defiance, race and gender transgressions, and love of cars all cast her as a modern outsider.

Anthropologist Zora Neale Hurston shows that early social scientists took divergent paths to tell different stories about difference. She is not in the typical pantheon of Chicago School–style scholars who prefigured the conceptual advances of midcentury deviance theories. Yet there are important similarities in the stories she told. Hurston was an ethnographer of difference, marginality, and outsiders. Her scholarship encompassed race, gender, sexuality, color, religion, and much more. She highlighted how and why places mattered in creating cultures, communities, and identities. She challenged racism, and, importantly, troubled scientific ideas of fixed, biological racial categories. Hurston viewed race, in particular blackness, as a distinctive cultural system, with "ways of thinking and acting, of commonplace expectations, humor, language, and style."[6]

Hurston's stories about difference fused the literary and the ethnographic. Other early sociologists, such as W. E. B. Du Bois, had written fiction in addition to scholarship. Hurston created "hybrid texts"[7] that reached broad audiences by blurring the boundaries between the two, and between the academy and mainstream public. Her anthropological imagination brought alive the cultural richness of outsider communities. Hurston wrote about the White Florida "cracker," but her focus was on showcasing the complex vibrancy of Black communities. She studied "black people on their own terms."[8] While insisting that "Negroes are no better nor no worse, and at times just as boring as everybody else,"[9] she conversely celebrated the superiority of Black culture. Zora Neale Hurston's ethnographic folklore gave us different ways of knowing and feeling about race and gender. This chapter explores her ethnographic life in Florida.

The Anthropologist

Zora Neale Hurston was a pioneering cultural anthropologist and ethnographer, although she is not typically remembered that way. Like almost every ethnographer in this book, Hurston studied her own people and their places. She made visible, through her fusion of fictional and ethnographic writings, the complex and animated social worlds and cultural lives of African Americans in the South. Since her rediscovery in the early 1970s, Hurston has become firmly established in the national literary canon. Yet, as anthropologist Helen Robbins argues, Hurston's "ethnography is obscure and is rarely read by anthropologists."[10] Nevertheless, her prodigious body of work represents an early example of what contemporary literary scholar Saidiya Hartman calls "an exorbitant archive,"[11] allowing different storytelling of different lives.

Hurston was a Black woman in the academy at a time when most scholars were White men. She wrote stories about what we would now call the intersectionalities of race and gender. Meanwhile, racism and sexism undermined her career at every step. She entered high school at the late age of twenty-six (reportedly at least one of the reasons she typically knocked a decade off her stated age was to qualify for free high school, she claimed to be younger than she actually was). She moved on to the historically Black university, Howard, and then in 1925 enrolled at Barnard College with a scholarship. She became the first Black student at Barnard. By doing so, Hurston joined a "miniscule circle"; of approximately 13,000 African American college students in the 1920s, fewer than 300 attended White schools.[12] Yet at the height of the Harlem Renaissance, she felt accepted at Barnard. Alert to the potential for racialized microaggressions, Hurston had written to a friend: "I suppose you want to know how this little piece of darkish meat feels at Barnard. I am received quite well. In fact I am received so well that if someone would come along and try to turn me white I'd be quite peevish at them."[13] Poet Arna Bontemps wrote that in mid-1920s Harlem, it was "fun to be a Negro," while at the same time, social historians note, Harlem was becoming "a slum."[14]

At Barnard, Hurston's childhood curiosity grew into an expansive anthropological imagination. She discovered what she called the "spy-glass of anthropology."[15] She was mentored by Franz Boas, considered the father of American anthropology, and also worked with well-known scholars Ruth Benedict and Melville Herskovits. These social scientists launched ethnography. Both Franz Boas and his contemporary, sociologist Robert Park, were noted pioneers in field research, sending their students out to conduct ethnographic studies in other countries or on the streets of US cities. Hurston's first exploration was in New York City, where she measured the heads of pedestrians on the streets of Harlem with an anthropometric caliper. Boas, the founder of the Columbia University anthropology department, was Hurston's primary mentor. Known for his cultural relativism and emphasis on rigorous fieldwork, Boas later sent her to the South to study the folk cultures of rural Negroes. She first went to Eatonville.

In an era when the stereotypic White male anthropologist traveled in a pith helmet to unfamiliar and seemingly exotic locales, Hurston's return to her own town of Eatonville troubled the binary of the familiar and the strange in ethnography. She was both an insider and outsider there. Hurston reported being glad to conduct research in her "native village first" because it was bursting with folk material that she could collect "without hurt, harm, or danger,"[16] a crucial consideration for a young Black woman anthropologist in the Jim Crow South. Yet she had been away, studying in the North, had "dwelt in marble halls"[17] of Barnard, learning new ways of being and talking: "And then I realized that I was new myself, so it looked sensible for me to choose familiar ground."[18] Although her newly acquired Northern sensibility undermined that first research trip by alienating

Zora Neale Hurston as a student at Howard University, 1919–1923. Courtesy of Zora Neale Hurston Papers, Special and Area Studies Collections, George A. Smathers Libraries, University of Florida, Gainesville, Florida. Acquired from Stetson Kennedy in 1990.

Eatonville residents, she would fruitfully return there many times in later years, eventually weaving her ethnographic material through her stories, essays, concerts, and novels.

Hurston was exceedingly productive in ethnographic projects and publication between 1927, when she made her first disappointing research trip to Eatonville, and the late 1930s, when she joined the Federal Writers' Project (discussed below). Her 1928 formative field research in Polk County was where "anthropology had won out over literature," as Hurston's biographer Valerie Boyd put it.[19] Her rich folklore archive would enduringly shape her literary arts. In addition to her successful novels, such as *Their Eyes Were Watching God* (published in 1937, and based on field experiences in Florida, including the hurricane of 1928), Hurston published numerous essays in venues such as the *Journal of American Folklore* and the *Journal of Negro History*. A public intellectual, she published in venues such as the *Washington Tribune*, the *Messenger*, the *Saturday Review*, and the *Saturday Evening Post*. *Mules and Men*, her ethnographic memoir of gathering Florida folklore during her research of 1927 to 1932, came out in 1935. Worried that anthropologists like Boas might view her style in *Mules and Men* as unscientific, she described wanting to represent "folk tales with background so that they are in atmosphere and not just stuck out into cold space. I want the reader to see why Negroes tell such glorious tales."[20] Hurston was a member of the American Folklore Society, the American Ethnological Society, and the American Anthropological Society. Anthropologist Irma McClaurin describes her as a "progenitor of Black Studies," and a pioneer for scholars seeking to blur genres and disciplinary boundaries.[21]

Hurston's own career was beset with intersecting oppressions based on race and gender, as well as social class and region. Never financially secure, Hurston cobbled together funds from odd jobs, a wealthy White patron, intermittent fellowships, relief employment from the Federal Writers' Project, and small royalty payments in order to finance her research. Despite these obstacles, she published prolifically, although it was never easy or taken for granted. She described having to borrow the $1.83 postage to submit the manuscript for what would become her first novel, *Jonah's Gourd Vine*, to J. B. Lippincott Company. She was elated when they accepted it: "I never expect to have a greater thrill than that wire gave me. You know the feeling when you found your first pubic hair. Greater than that."[22] Lippincott gave her a $200 advance; the largest royalty payment she ever earned in her lifetime was $943.75.[23]

Zora Neale Hurston was an anthropologist in an era when social scientists began reinventing dominant frameworks about human differences. Scientific knowledge in the early twentieth century located racial and other human differences in biology, viewing them as innate characteristics, and thereby supporting eugenic practices. Anthropologists such as Franz Boas and sociologists such as W. E. B. Du Bois and Robert Park broke with the race science of that era, instead highlighting social and cultural factors as key to understanding human variation. They stressed the significance of communities, cultural practices, and urban and rural places in understanding difference. They were a diverse group, with sometimes differing ideas and arguments. Some of these scholars, like anthropologists Edward Sapir and Margaret Mead, and psychiatrists such as Erich Fromm and Karen Horney, comprised the "culture and personality" school, which sought to understand the generational transmission of cultural knowledge.[24] Hurston was part of the cohort that Charles King dubs "renegade anthropologists."[25]

Still, ever the iconoclast, Hurston parted ways with her anthropological mentors as well as major contemporaneous political figures and some of her literary associates. Charles King describes how, despite anthropology's radical emphasis on cultural relativity rather than the rigid determinism of biological theories of race, the field nonetheless minimized the cultural value of Blacks in the United States. Boas and his associates "felt, when it came to the idea of black culture, it was hard to see anything except a degraded form of whiteness. . . . Cultural inferiority now stood in for . . . biological inferiority."[26] Hurston's literary ethnography resisted that notion. She celebrated cultural differences between the races. Likewise, her emphasis on the everyday triumphs, heroism, ingenuity, and originality of rural Southern Blacks earned her the derision of Black Left intellectuals, in particular Richard Wright, who insisted that the work of scholars and artists must stress the damaging impact of racial oppression inflicted by White society.

Hurston steadfastly represented Black culture on its own terms, which she viewed as distinct, creative, and valuable. She resisted the directive to use art for propaganda, as sociologist W. E. B. Du Bois demanded of Black artists, and she derided what she called the "best foot forward Negroes" who sought assimilation.[27] She deplored any propensity for Blacks to emulate Whites, calling it "intellectual lynching" that lands African Americans "right back where we were when they filed our iron collar off."[28] She frequently argued against what she called "Race Leaders" who sought racial solidarity, instead insisting that there was no singular Black identity: "Our lives are so diversified, internal attitudes so varied, appearances and capabilities so different, that there is no possible classification so catholic that it will cover us all, except My people! My people!"[29] This contrarian gaze generated controversies during her career, and probably contributed to her fall into obscurity.

The Works Progress Administration Projects

During the Great Depression of the 1930s, Hurston was joined in her financially precarious life by a quarter of people in the United States who were unemployed in early 1933. Jobs vanished, stores and factories closed, breadlines flourished, homelessness escalated. Men, and some women, took to riding the rails as hobos in search of transient employment opportunities. (**See** chapter 2.) President Franklin D. Roosevelt created the Works Progress Administration (WPA) in 1935, by executive order, as a way to provide jobs to Americans. During its eight years, it employed 8.5 million people on 1.4 million public projects, Zora Neale Hurston among them.

Even in its day, the WPA (and the broader New Deal) was attacked by Congressional conservatives. Republican critics cast it as a boondoggle for lazy dissidents. The House Un-American Activities Committee (HUAC), formed in 1938 to investigate potential communist infiltration of the United States, institutionalized the attacks. One of its first investigations was of the Federal Theatre Project, which it charged was subversive. The investigators made unsubstantiated claims—broadcast by the media— that writers and theater workers were known communists. Although some WPA officials opposed these attacks during HUAC hearings, the agency fired the artists named. By the late 1960s, HUAC had destroyed the lives and careers of many Americans, including university professors and students (**see Hyperlink 6.1:** Women and the Early Gay Canon) before it was finally discredited for its intimidating, unethical, and destructive tactics. Yet it succeeded in damaging the WPA's public image.[30]

Despite these attacks, WPA workers built much of the nation's modern infrastructure, including highways, airports, bridges, and schools. Strikingly, the WPA also put artists and writers to work in initiatives such as the Federal Theatre Project, the Music Project, and the Federal Writers' Project (FWP). The FWP was notable for its embrace of African American writers such as Richard Wright, Margaret Walker, and Ralph Ellison.[31] As Ellison noted about Black artists, "writers and would-be writers, newspaper people, dancers, actors—they all got their chance."[32] The WPA ended in 1943, but before that, it had given Zora Neale Hurston meaningful research opportunities, as well as much-needed income.

Zora Neale Hurston was, as Alice Walker memorialized her, "A genius of the South," in particular of that "southernmost state," Florida. Her extensive Florida fieldwork informed her fiction and drew the attention of officials who decided to hire her for the FWP. She worked on various WPA initiatives organizing folklore concerts and theater, but her research and writing projects—in particular the Florida *Guide*, and fieldwork in the turpentine, sawmill, and citrus camps—drew from, and deepened, her ethnographic studies throughout Florida. Hurston's WPA work constitutes a monumental anthropological contribution to understanding the culture of rural, Southern Blacks of that era.

The State Guidebooks

The American Guides series endures as one of the FWP's most expansive and influential projects. Building on a nascent penchant for travel, at least among more affluent citizens, the FWP launched an ambitious project to create guidebooks for every state (including Alaska and Puerto Rico), as well as one chronicling the Maine-to-Florida highway, US 1. They hired photographers, librarians, mapmakers, and historians to compile travel guides that would be creative, useful, and allow Americans "to see America anew."[33] Guide staff drove the lengths and widths of the states, mapping routes along what we now, in the superhighway era, consider back roads. These texts varied widely by state, but they now stand as expansive compendiums of state history, folklore, geography, flora and fauna, and local cultural mores. Who better than the folk anthropologist Zora Neale Hurston to write about her beloved home state, Florida? Hurston, who had been part of the Negro Unit of the New York Federal Theatre Project in 1935, joined the Florida Writers' Project in April 1938.

Florida: A Guide to the Southernmost State, published in 1939, captured the wild diversity of the state, its "many Floridas."[34] In the book's foreword, John Tigert, president of the University of Florida, wrote that Florida was often considered "the last American frontier."[35] Likewise, Florida residents had an outsider reputation. The *Guide* described how, in 1755, a Territorial Assembly member, Edmund Grey, accused of "seditious utterances," fled Georgia and across the border "founded a colony of outlaws and malcontents."[36] The *Guide* writers braided together the voices of formerly enslaved people, later Free Negroes, sightseeing Northern tourists, vibrant indigenous communities, and the White Florida cracker to capture Florida as a state "replete with contrasts, paradoxes, confusions, and inconsistencies."[37] In other words, Florida and its people were different. Florida writer Cathy Salustri, who recently traveled the Florida *Guide's* twenty-two travel routes, quipped that even today, "Florida is America's Australia."[38]

Racial dynamics and racism suffused the Florida FWP, and its subsequent *Guide*. On the one hand, the project was racially inclusive. Both Black and White writers comprised the staff. This was not true of the *Guides* for certain other states. Georgia, for example, had no African Americans on its staff. A wealth of information on Black Florida lives appeared in the *Guide to the Southernmost State*. Moreover, the Florida FWP begat the Florida Negro Unit, an ambitious writers' initiative to collect and preserve the African American Florida legacy. Florida was one of only three states, along with Virginia and Louisiana, to establish these so-called Negro Units.[39] This staff collected thousands of pages of documents, seventy-two interviews with formerly enslaved individuals, and abundant folklore materials.

On the other hand, Hurston suffered biases of racism and sexism. She was one of the most acclaimed writers on the Florida staff. She had two Guggenheim awards and three published books, including *Their Eyes Were Watching God*. Yet she was hired as a writer, not an editor. Her supervisor, Stetson Kennedy, was a tender twenty-one years old. She was seriously underpaid, especially compared to the White, male staff. The Black writers were never included in editorial meetings and were excluded from the main office. At the time, African Americans could not work in the public libraries or county records offices, only the libraries of Black colleges such as Florida A&M College.[40] Additionally, much of Hurston's ethnographic production went unpublished. Numerous essays and interviews lay unnoticed in "far-flung state and national repositories" until collected in an edited volume in 1999.[41] Likewise, the manuscript of the *Guide's* companion volume, *The Florida Negro*, languished. It was rejected for publication, consigned to the archives, and only appeared in print more than fifty years later, in 1993.[42] Its two original editors—Stetson Kennedy and Robert Cornwall—had deleted all of Hurston's writing from the final manuscript.[43]

Hurston joined the Florida *Southernmost State* project during its final rewrite, after state editors had deemed the earlier versions to be "dull and lifeless."[44] Hurston put her inimitable stamp on the *Guide*. Although she seemingly disappeared intermittently from the project, she would then send rich troves of folklore materials that the editors wove through the *Guide*. Historian Pamela Bordelon argues that, given the timeline, it is likely that Hurston did not conduct new fieldwork for the *Guide*, but rather "dipped into her files"[45] from her extensive earlier field research, in particular her Polk County work. Some sections were pulled from *Mules and Men*. The *Guide's* section on her hometown, Eatonville, comes from the folksy beginning of Hurston's book, *Their Eyes Were Watching God*: "Maitland is Maitland until it gets to Hurst's Corner, and then it is Eatonville."[46]

The state guides were envisioned for tourist boosterism, inviting adventurers to wander off the beaten path. The automobile was a relatively new technology—the Ford Model T, introduced in 1908, became the first mass-produced car in 1913—as was automobile leisure travel. Most roads were made of packed dirt or, in some coastal locations, oyster shells. The Interstate Highway System was in the far-away future of 1956, created by President Dwight Eisenhower in the interest of national security. There were twenty-two driving guides in the Florida *Guide*. Each guide began with warnings about road conditions (usually unpaved), availability of fuel and lodging, and possible wildlife encounters along the way, such as alligators and snakes. African American tourists encountered another travel danger ignored by the *Guide*—Jim Crow laws and racist culture.

Hurston brought small towns to life—their churches, screened porches, back streets "full of little houses squatting under hovering oaks," and the heart of small towns, the local store. Yet she also explored Florida's dark side. She penned a town history of Goldsborough, another self-governing African American town near Eatonville. Goldsborough, however, ceased to exist in 1911, absorbed by the contiguous White town, Sanford. Hurston described Goldsborough's founding, its store, churches, post office, and the legislative machinations by which White Sanford politicians revoked its charter: "Thus ended the existence of the second incorporated Negro town in Florida."[47] The essay was not included in the Florida *Guide*, and remained unpublished during Hurston's lifetime. Editor Pamela Bordelon, who collected many of Hurston's unpublished WPA manuscripts, proposes that Hurston may have written of Goldsborough's demise as a cautionary tale to protect Eatonville.[48]

Yet *Guide* editors did include some of Hurston's documentation of Florida's racist underside. For example, Hurston's account of 1920 racial violence in the central Florida town of Ocoee in the aftermath of an election differed radically from the version told by the town's White residents (the *Guide* published the two conflicting versions, although only part of Hurston's essay). Hurston wrote about how Whites resented the "Ocoee Negroes swarming to the polls," and described the subsequent mob violence and massacre: "Mobs had surrounded the Negro section of the town and fired it, burning 30 houses and two churches, forcing men, women, and children back into flames. In all, some 35 negroes perished."[49] White children stood jeering as Black people were burned alive. At least one man had been castrated.[50] (Hurston wrote to a friend about the openness of

Southern racism: "The South, having been perfectly frank all along, was unembarrassed."[51]) Bordelon notes that Hurston's Black version of the massacre was only included in the *Guide* because Hurston had been called to the national WPA office in Washington—which employed a more liberal set of editors than in Florida—to help with the final editing. Had the Florida editors completed their *Guide*, it would have included solely the White version of the violence.[52] The deadly Ocoee massacre predated the racial genocide soon to come in nearby Rosewood, Florida, in 1923.

Hurston lived in Eatonville while on the Florida Writers' Project, in a little house by a lake. Like other FWP writers, she also did her own writing, including on *Moses: Man of the Mountain*, her fifth novel. In a 2005 National Public Radio interview with Stetson Kennedy, he was asked about being Hurston's boss on the project, and replied, "I was only nominally her boss. She was her own boss."[53]

Field Research: The Worker Camps

In addition to the state guidebooks, the FWP sought to compile exhaustive collections of multiethnic cultural expression. The FWP hired Hurston on a statewide recording expedition to capture audio of diverse songs and stories of Florida. As described below, she had earlier conducted productive field research in work camps in the late twenties, folklore experience that appealed to the Florida FWP officials. Hurston, along with folklorists Stetson Kennedy and Alan Lomax, traveled in Florida with a large disc recorder to capture folktales, songs, and life histories in turpentine, phosphate, and sawmill camps.

Florida's natural resources were a ready target for exploitation by Northern industrialists, European businessmen, and local developers.[54] Phosphate mining, big timber industries, and turpentine extraction all moved Florida into the modern industrial era in the late nineteenth century. Turpentine was a key ingredient in paint, varnish, soap, and certain pharmaceuticals. With approximately twenty million acres of virgin long-leaf pine, as well as abundant cypress stands, the turpentine industry flourished in Florida from the late nineteenth century until its decline in the '40s. The Florida camps produced nearly 20 percent of the world's turpentine, while devastating natural habitat and pine forests. The development of artificial paint-thinning solvents eventually collapsed the turpentine industry.

In the post–Civil War Jim Crow era, private owners of turpentine camps relied on two forms of labor: convict leasing and debt peonage. Prisons leased convicts as a way to pay expenses, rather than taxing Florida residents. In addition, free laborers shunned turpentine work because it was physically exhausting and dangerous. One owner said, "Natives of Florida's piney woods would quickly abandon the work when any other type of livelihood became available."[55] Likewise, debt peonage kept workers in virtual slavery. Most of the turpentine debt peonage workers were Black men, whom camp owners still treated as if they were enslaved. The peonage system basically enslaved workers to White employers based on real or fabricated debts. Both convict leasing and debt peonage were controversial, and eventually outlawed.

Turpentining proceeded year-round in Florida, and camp conditions were typically brutal. The camps themselves were usually enclosed by a stockyard or high fence to prevent escapes. Workers were housed in crudely built pine bunkhouses. Food was minimal, repetitious, and subpar. Workers were chained together by leg irons in the forests as well as in their bunkhouses to prevent escapes. They worked from dawn to dusk. Some camp guards forced workers to run miles in bare feet to the work site. They not infrequently beat workers, sometimes killing them. Convict leasing was prohibited by Florida law in 1923, yet debt peonage continued.[56]

Hurston had honed her ethnographic skills in Polk County before the FWP project. In 1928, she conducted field research in the Loughman sawmill and turpentine camps, owned by the Everglades Cypress Company. She wrote to a friend, "A hasty good-bye to Eatonville's oaks and oleanders and the wheels of the Chevvie split Orlando wide open—headed southwest for corn (likker) and song."[57] Conditions in the Loughman camp were harsh and discriminatory. The industry destroyed both forest and laborers. When historian Tiffany Patterson visited one in 1999, she found a barren clearing of "chalk-white dirt" where locals believed the bodies of workers were buried.[58] Patterson reminds us that in 1928, when Hurston conducted research in the Loughman camp, the bodies would have been recently dead.

Hurston hit her stride there as an ethnographer, finding an influential gatekeeper who helped her overcome her outsider position and earn trust from the diverse Black community. Big Sweet was a powerful insider who was "Bessie Smith, Ma Rainey, and all the bad and brazen women they sang about rolled into one."[59] In Loughman, Hurston learned to recognize evasiveness, or what she called "feather-bed resistance,"[60] among the Black laborers and camp members. Nonetheless, she learned to successfully collect their stories, work songs, spirituals, colloquialisms, sermons, and jokes. Hurston decided to leave Loughman after Big Sweet saved her from a knife-wielding woman, but the anthropologist in Hurston rejoiced

Gulf, Florida & Alabama Railway Company turpentine camp, circa 1900. Courtesy of Florida Memory, State Library and Archives of Florida, http://www.floridamemory.com/items/show/17685

over her ethnographic success: "I shivered at the thought of dying with a knife in my back, or having my face mutilated. At any rate, I had made a very fine and full collection on the Saw-Mill Camp, so I felt no regrets at shoving off."[61] The Everglades Cypress Company closed soon after she arrived there. As Patterson notes, Hurston's fiction and essays are the only historical record that remains of that world.[62]

By the time Hurston and the FWP crew arrived in Cross City at the Aycock and Lindsay turpentine camp in 1939, the industry was declining overall but still operating. Florida's myriad work camps for the production of lumber, citrus, and turpentine were rich sources of the folklore of indigenous Black culture. As Bordelon notes, the turpentiners were uneducated, did not leave written records, and "their folklore was one of the few barometers of their attitudes and feelings about themselves."[63] Jim Crow laws prohibited Hurston from traveling with the White crew, so she was sent ahead to prepare for the recording crew, collect songs and stories, and interview workers. Kennedy later recalled that when he arrived, he found Hurston "sitting on the porch of a turpentiner's shack, rocking and smoking. I couldn't resist taking a candid shot."[64]

While most Florida camps refused entrance to outsiders like the WPA crew, Aycock and Lindsay admitted them. Bordelon attributes this to the confidence of Catherine Lindsay, the widow of the company's cofounder, who firmly dominated the sprawling fifteen-camp operation and its hundreds of workers. Known as "Miss Catherine," Lindsay seemed to have impressed the FWP crew. William Duncan, the state editor, wrote that Miss Catherine, who slept with revolvers and shotguns nearby, ran "the largest turpentine plant in Florida in America's last frontier, West Florida, an area largely populated by escaped felons and fugitives from justice during its early days. Even today it is untouched."[65] Yet apparently any felons or misfits who worked at Aycock and Lindsay would have needed as much protection against Miss Catherine and her camp guards as she did from the workers.

Hurston found both poetry and danger in Polk County. She later wrote of "Those poets of the swinging blade! . . . Polk County. Black men laughing and singing . . . Polk County. Black men from tree to tree among the lordly pines, a swift, slanting stroke to bleed the trees for gum."[66] She wrote copious field notes, and a short essay, "Turpentine," about her ride through a turpentine camp with Foreman McFarlin. The essay is purely descriptive and uncritical. With no mention of the brutality with which a foreman typically forced workers through the forests, Hurston described how McFarlin started at 5:30 a.m. and got the men to work by 6: "Every man took his tools, went to his task—whatever he was doing when he knocked off at five-thirty that afternoon before, he got right on it in the morning."[67] She asked whether the workers made up songs. McFarlin told her no, "'Taint like sawmills and such like that. Turpentine woods is kind of lonesome."[68] Yet Hurston did hear songs of hardship, debt, and brutality. One song about an escape ended with: "The Woodsrider caught me and brought me back; He said, 'If you don't work, I'll beat your back!'"[69]

Eventually, workers confided to Hurston the many abuses in the camp, the beatings, sexual abuse, and even murders. The bodies of Blacks were weighed down and dumped in the Gulf of Mexico, they told her. Hurston compiled notes about the absence of schooling for children, the Klan parades, and the workers' tales of violence. Hurston, Stetson, and other FWP crew reportedly attempted to alert authorities to these atrocities, to no avail. Hurston wrote to Miss Catherine but received no reply. In his later book of Florida folklore, *Palmetto Country* (1942), Stetson Kennedy wrote that a "Negro collecting folklore in a West Florida turpentine camp"—presumably Zora Neale Hurston—"feared to fill her notes out in greater detail."[70] She was, Stetson implies, fearful of repercussions. Hurston herself, as a Black woman, was not invulnerable, and her biographer, Valerie Boyd, notes that "Hurston might have counted herself lucky to get out of town unharmed."[71] Polk County was where Hurston had been almost killed in a jook joint. She later recounted that she was only saved "because a friend [Big Sweet] got in there and staved off old club-footed Death."[72] Hurston learned to pack a pistol.

Hurston's ethnographies, often underappreciated, represent vital historical stories. Her "Turpentine" essay was unpublished by the FWP, although the *Guide* contained snippets about the turpentine industry. Hurston later integrated the songs and sayings from her turpentine fieldwork into her fiction, in particular the novel *Seraph on the Suwanee*, and the memoir, *Dust Tracks on a Road*. In those years of the Great Migration of African Americans to Northern cities, Hurston had interviewed women and men of the "nameless, faceless force" who instead migrated south to Florida, in "liquid movement," for the season.[73] Literary critic Martyn Bone points out that, in this respect, Hurston captured "the historical-geographical realities of *intraregional* and *transnational* patterns of black migration"[74] (emphasis in original)—both movement within the South and migration from the Caribbean to the South. These mobility patterns in the South, Bone notes, may be less familiar to us than the Great Migration, but they were no less "monumental."[75] While some criticized Hurston for overlooking, and therefore erasing, the Great Migration, historian Tiffany Patterson notes that it is easier to understand why some Black people migrated north "than to understand how they lived in the South."[76]

In the years leading up to her death, Hurston continued her work as a public anthropologist, addressing the social conditions of marginalized communities. In 1958, she wrote about Florida's migrant farm workers for what was to be a series in the *Miami Herald*. Hurston was fierce in her critique of the racist, capitalist exploitation of the men and women who performed seasonal work in Florida's citrus and vegetable fields. Most were African American, as well as Bahamian and Jamaican workers, who arrived as "alien negro laborers" under the government's Emergency Wartime Labor Program. She described them all as "the subterranean force" flowing beneath the "fabulous mansions" of wealthy, White Floridians.[77] Florida, she wrote, "was born with the gold spoon of climate on its long, stuck-out tongue." Yet Hurston pointed out that migrant farm workers made possible the $500 million agricultural industry that Florida's climate enabled. In passages still timely, she described the devastating conditions of 45,000–60,000 migrant workers suddenly made visible by a massive freeze in Florida in 1957–58: "They were stunned by hunger, cold, utter destitution. The low temperature probed out the fact that many were inadequately housed. The front pages of newspapers bloomed out with pictures of the migrant worker lined up expecting or receiving emergency rations.... The spreading circle which began with the migrant farm workers reached higher and higher until the whole state economy came down with a hard case of the weak-trembles."[78] Hurston's critique would have particular resonance decades later, as a White United States president who denigrated immigrants and African Americans regularly held court with wealthy supporters at his West Palm Beach, Florida, resort, Mar-a-Lago.

The project failed. *Herald* editor George Beebe rejected Hurston's article and canceled the proposed series. He complained that her first installment "doesn't quite jell" and that the editorial staff "couldn't quite figure what the purpose of the story was."[79] Hurston ceased work on the topic. She died two years later. The essay was among Hurston's papers set afire in a garbage bin in her yard after her death, and hastily rescued by Patrick Duval, a sheriff's deputy who was walking by. Like so many of Hurston's manuscripts, the essay went unpublished until 1991, when it was reconstructed from its charred, typewritten pages for a women's studies journal.[80] In 1960, the year Hurston died and two years after her manuscript was rejected by the *Herald*, journalist Edward R. Murrow presented the influential documentary, *Harvest of Shame*, which brought national attention to the very topic Hurston had exposed—the experiences, and exploitation, of migrant farm laborers. In the documentary, one farmer said about the workers, "We used to own our slaves; now we just rent them."[81] Hurston's unpublished migrant worker manuscript is but one example of her ethnographic stories that brought to life how places produced inner consciousness, feelings of marginality and belonging, systems of insiders and outsiders, and cultural practices of talking, thinking, and feeling.

Anthropometry, Race, Representation: One Doll's Story

In 1950, Zora Neale Hurston embarked on a collaboration to develop an African American doll. The doll would be, as Hurston put it, "anthropologically correct."[82] Jim Crow laws still enforced White supremacy. African American resistance to racial segregation and violence was ongoing. Social-science research had shown that children learned racial stereotypes, in part through play with games and dolls. An influential 1939 doll-choice study conducted by Kenneth and Mamie Clark found that even Black children preferred White dolls, suggesting how racist social hierarchies

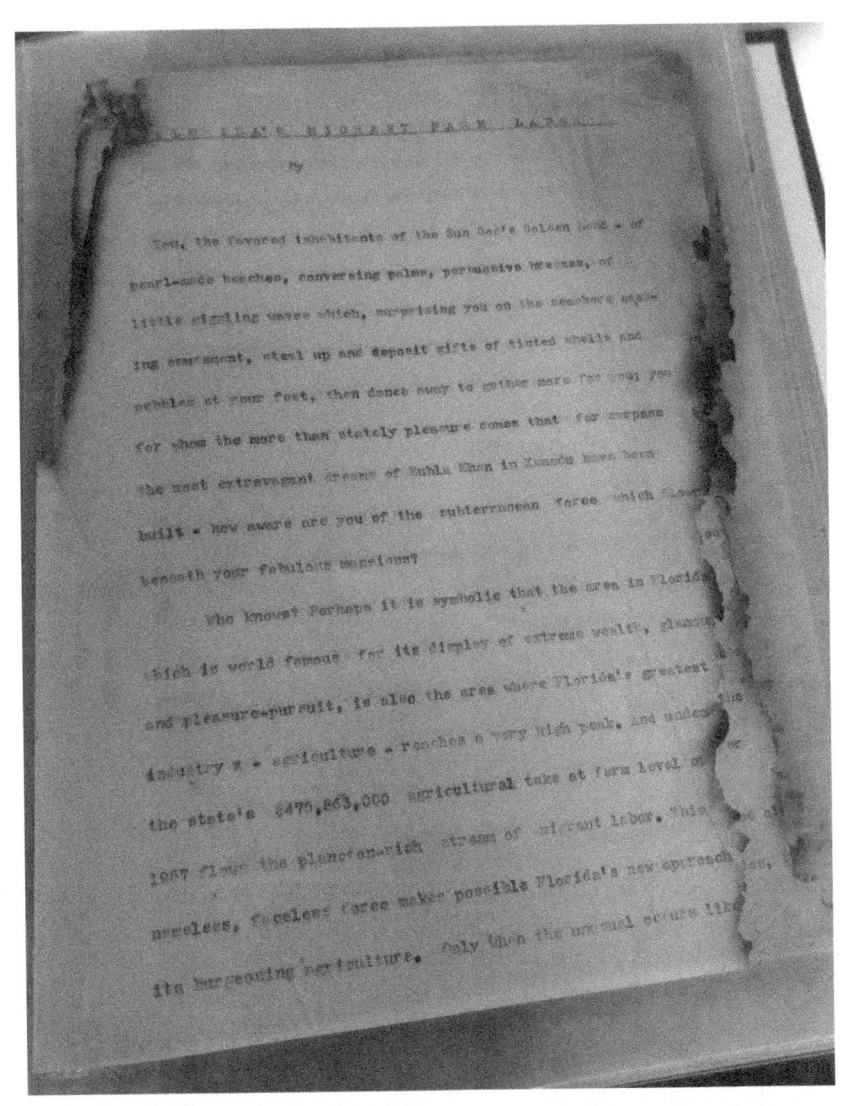

Burned, typewritten title page of Hurston's article, "Florida's Migrant Farm Labor." Courtesy of Zora Neale Hurston Papers, Special and Area Studies Collections, George A. Smathers Libraries, University of Florida, Gainesville, Florida.

infused their perceptions.[83] Hurston's project—called the Saralee Negro Doll[84]—was intended to change cultural representations of race. Its story highlights the turbulent cultural politics of knowledge about race.

The notion of an anthropologically correct doll was haunted by scientific racism—a historical belief in fixed, racialized human types—although the doll's supporters actively rejected this fiction of a singular racial body. It was a contentious era in race science. Eugenics had been discredited in the immediate aftermath of the Nazi genocide. Yet biological scientists and social scientists disagreed with each other, and among themselves, about race, differences, and, importantly, whether "race" should even be used as a category for classification. The fate of a 1950 UNESCO statement, intended to condemn racism and make public the status of scientific knowledge about race, reflected those conflicts.

Sociologists and cultural anthropologists predominated on the first UNESCO committee. Their statement—"The Race Question"—was radical in many ways. It disputed the biological facticity of race, called race "a social myth," and asserted that biological science supported "the ethic of universal brotherhood."[85] Seventeen years before the Supreme Court would strike down laws banning interracial marriage, the statement claimed that any negative effects of "race mixture" were social, not biological. It was immediately controversial, and was reissued the following year. Prominent physical anthropologists and geneticists complained that "it was chiefly sociologists who gave their opinion," and the original statement had omitted their own "authority" regarding "the biological problems of race." Their new statement reasserted the potential for biological determinism in certain areas, such as intelligence.[86] A racist cultural climate, along with these still-unresolved debates about biological versus social underpinnings of race, shadowed the doll project.

The Doll Project

A Black doll tells a cultural story of racial equality and pride. The project, pitched by her friend Sara Lee Creech, would have appealed to Hurston's passion for storytelling, African American folklore, and anthropology. Creech was a White social justice activist in Belle Glade, where Hurston had moved in spring 1950. The two became friends. Creech was familiar with the social-science research on race and children's toys, such as dolls. After noticing Black girls playing with White dolls near her house, she decided to design a doll reflective of their own lives. Hurston applauded

Creech's desire to depict what Hurston called "the beauty and character" of Black girls, writing to her, "That you have not insulted us by a grotesque caricature of Negro children, but conceived something of real Negro beauty."[87] Hurston's ethnographic and literary career was devoted to documenting and celebrating the unique differences in Black cultural life. Further, Hurston's anthropometric training probably predisposed her to look favorably on the idea of a doll boasting distinctly Black physical features.

Dolls were about to have a moment. The toy industry burgeoned after World War II, when companies applied the technology of injecting plastic into molds, allowing for mass production. The culmination of industrialized dolls would be Barbie, invented in 1959. The American engineer, Jack Ryan, who designed Raytheon's Sparrow and Hawk missiles, also developed the plastic molds used to produce Barbie. As anthropologists Jacqueline Urla and Alan Swedlund put it, the "military-weapons-designer-turned-toy-inventor" launched "Barbie and her torpedo-like breasts" into American mass consumer culture.[88] It was the height of the Cold War.

In its pre-Barbie, Jim Crow era, Creech's idea for a Black doll was radical, yet not unprecedented. There had been numerous, largely short-lived Black doll initiatives. Some challenged White supremacy while others upheld Jim Crow racism. The Negro Doll Company launched in Nashville in 1908 produced thousands of dolls before closing in 1915. "Famous Brown Dolls" were manufactured in the 1920s, and in 1919 Black nationalist Marcus Garvey founded the Negro Factories Corporation and a Black doll factory. The "dusky dark" dolls were manufactured after World War I to enhance racial pride.[89] However, many prior African American dolls were stereotypic representations, such as Mammy, Aunt Jemima, or Pickaninny dolls.[90] Early-twentieth-century toy manufacturers produced Black dolls by painting White dolls brown, and giving them stereotypic attributes. For example, P&M Doll Company introduced the Topsy doll, which featured a "black face, banjo eyes, and three little pigtails."[91] An advertisement in *House Beautiful* in the 1940s claimed, "Every little girl wants a colored 'Mammy.' Here is 'Caroline,' black as night and southern as cotton."[92] Black dolls were given names like "Darky Nurse" or worse.[93]

Creech's political acumen and social capital informed her mobilization around the doll project. She was active in women's and interracial movements, helping to found the Belle Glade Inter-Racial Council in 1948. Hurston connected Creech to her network of northern Black intellectuals, for example Mordecai Johnson, president of Howard University, and political scientist Ralph Bunche. Creech persuaded Eleanor Roosevelt, former first lady of the US, to support the doll's production. Roosevelt hosted a tea at which Creech, Hurston, sociologist Charles Johnson, and other prominent African American leaders consulted on the particulars of the doll.

What, precisely, should a Black doll look like? The doll project stumbled on this question of physical representation. How could a Black doll capture unique biological features of race without itself reinforcing racial stereotypes? Creech insisted that the doll should reflect African American children's "own attractiveness,"[94] but it became clear there was no one version of blackness. The doll, not yet even real, became the abstract embodiment of the problem of a singular racial representation. The problem became tangible when Sheila Burlingame, the artist sculpting the doll heads, asked for pictures of Black children and head measurements. Hurston, an anthropologist and sometime anthropometrist, would surely have understood that request for empirical data.

The Anthropometrist

One quirk of Zora Neale Hurston's anthropological career was her ongoing pursuit of anthropometry—the science of human body measurement. Hurston learned anthropometric methods at Barnard College, studying with Boas and Melville Herskovits. A method of physical anthropology, anthropometry was one of many techniques within eighteenth- and nineteenth-century scientific initiatives to classify race, gender, and other social differences on the basis of biology. Systematic measurement of the body would purportedly establish specific human types, and allow for comparison—allegedly without bias—of racial groups, the sexes, and various so-called degeneracies. Using calipers, anthropometers, and other tools, anthropologists measured head shapes, lips, ears, feet, middle fingers, and other body parts. An early application of the technique attempted to classify criminals in order to predict recidivism.

Franz Boas, Hurston's mentor, was one of the most ambitious of the early anthropometrists. Between 1890 and 1911, he had measured the bodies of over 27,000 native North Americans in an effort to document physical variation.[95] He created what we would now call a massive database on the physiological attributes of turn-of-the-century native peoples and immigrants. Anthropometric measurement, however, was not socially and politically innocent. Instead, it reinforced normative standards and established hierarchies of deviance. As anthropologists Urla and Swedlund put it, "women and non-Europeans did not fare well in these emerging sciences of the body."[96] Anthropometry's champions believed that their findings, such as differences in head sizes, supposedly explained variations in intelligence, criminality, sexuality, and other characteristics.

Over time, Boas changed his views on biological difference. In 1902 he defended anthropometric measurements, such as those of nose shapes, height, and cranial capacity, as objective evidence of the "great permanence of human types." A decade later, he argued that bodies, societies, and cultures are variable, fluid, and multiple. Historian Charles King calls it "one of the great shifts of opinion in the history of science."[97] By the mid 1920s, when Hurston was at Barnard, the United States had passed the highly restrictive Immigration Act of 1924, which banned Asian immigrants and imposed strict numerical quotas on immigration from Eastern and Southern European countries. New Jim Crow laws in the 1920s heightened racial segregation. Laws and policies of racial, gender, and ethnic exclusion had all been at least partially legitimized by biological determinist arguments of inferiority. And at the time, anthropometry could be, and was, deployed as a mechanism for reinforcing ideologies of White (and male) superiority.

Columbia anthropologists continued to seriously train students in anthropometric technique. In spring 1926, Hurston wrote to author Annie Nathan Meyer (who had helped her gain entrance to Barnard), "I am being trained for Anthropometry and Dr. Herskovitch [sic] is calling me at irregular intervals to do measuring." She added that Boas urged her to "learn as quickly as possible, and be quite accurate."[98] Hurston took to anthropometry with characteristic aplomb. In her first research experience, she famously measured heads of Harlem residents on the streets. Her biographers report this as a somewhat comedic episode, paired with a much-quoted quip from Langston Hughes: "Almost nobody else could stop the average Harlemite on Lenox Avenue and measure his head with a strange-looking, anthropological device and not get bawled out for the attempt, except Zora, who used to stop anyone whose head looked interesting, and measure it."[99] Hurston, biographers claim, was working with Boas to disprove biological determinist ideas of racial inferiority.

Hurston's interest in anthropometry continued after her Barnard years with Boas and Herskovits, despite recent biographers' suggestion that she held a critical view of it. In 1930, Hurston was in New Orleans, and wrote to Herskovits about ongoing anthropometric research, "Dr. Otto Klineberg and I are doing some work down here and he thinks we should do some color-top work and some lip and nose measurements. We need some tops (2) and a sliding caliper. Could you loan us a pair of calipers and send us the tops?"[100] Soon after, she asked cultural anthropologist Ruth Benedict in 1933, "I wonder if the Museum of Nat. Hist. would loan me a sliding caliper and a pair of spreading calipers too. I am working on my Negro ear placement and getting on fine. . . . If I can have the use of the head-measuring instruments, I can turn in something that Papa Franz will like I am sure."[101] She wrote to Benedict again in 1945, hoping to conduct research in Honduras on the Zambu Indians for a new book (the trip did not materialize). Again, she asked for instruments: "Where can I get hold of some instruments for anthropometry? I want to have all those necessary for measurements and see what we find."[102] Benedict, a pioneer in the culture and personality movement within anthropology, seems an unlikely source for securing anthropometric devices to measure physiological differences, but it may be that Hurston consulted her as fellow folklorist and former mentor.

The Doll

The Saralee doll project was a symbolic and political intervention into institutionalized racist representations of African Americans and Black culture. However, it required design and manufacturing specifications. Skin color was the most vexing. Color had long troubled Hurston. She explicitly addressed colorism in her writing, notably in *Dust Tracks*, where she had written, "the blackest Negro is the butt of all jokes, particularly black women."[103] Among Creech, Hurston, and the other advisors, there was disagreement about the doll's ideal skin tone, as well as anxiety about getting it wrong. One prominent educator insisted that Black parents would not buy a doll if the skin were too dark.

There was an overall sense, however, that one doll should not suggest a prototypical Black skin color. In October, 1951, Eleanor Roosevelt hosted a "color jury" reception.[104] Ultimately, Creech and her supporters opted for diversity—they should produce, and simultaneously market, a family of four African American dolls, each with a different tone and hair texture. In the meantime, they chose a "soft medium brown" color that was supposedly not too dark and not too light.[105] Later, Roosevelt wrote to Creech, "They are attractive and reproduced well with careful study of the anthropological background of the race."[106] (Ultimately, only one doll color was produced, not the proposed multihued family.)

The doll was a cultural intervention, but it was also a commodity. Although other Black doll projects had been unsuccessful, Creech and her supporters hoped it would fare differently in a different era. It was, after all, the year that UNESCO released its statement claiming universal brotherhood among races. They sought a mass manufacturer, and approached the Ideal Toy Company, which, in 1938 had produced other such dolls, including a Black version of Snow White.

Ideal Toy executives were unenthusiastic about the Saralee doll. They worried about its sales potential and took a dim view of producing a doll inspired by racial politics. However, the company's president, David Rosenstein, supported the doll (which his staff attributed to his training in sociology), and Eleanor Roosevelt lent star power. The doll's anticipated debut garnered national attention. Ideal Toy executives introduced the doll on national television shows, and print venues such as *Time*, *Newsweek*, and *Life Magazine* featured news of its impending release. News coverage repeated Hurston's phrase, "anthropologically correct," although in ways Hurston might not have appreciated. Along with a photograph of the doll, *Life Magazine* wrote that the "profile shows a large upper lip, a characteristic Negroid feature" and the "full face shows broad nose, eyes wide apart."[107] Finally, Sears, Roebuck and Company agreed to advertise the doll, and Ideal Toy put it into production. They manufactured the doll in 1951, and it went on sale in large department stores such as Gimbel's, and Jordan-Marsh. It was advertised as, "More than Just a Doll . . . an Ambassador of Good Will."[108]

In the racial politics of commodification and outsider capitalism, not all outsiders are marketable. The Saralee doll drew the ire of customers and pundits alike. Skin color was the ostensible target. Some saw her as too dark and others as too light. Some stores, such as Macy's, refused to carry the doll for fear it would attract too many African American customers.[109] Saralee sales lagged, with the New York City public schools making the largest purchases. Moreover, activism in the early civil-rights era was destabilizing the politics of racial representation. Even Kenneth Clark, whose famous doll studies had informed the 1954 Supreme Court *Brown v. Board of Education* school desegregation case, decried the notion that the Saralee doll could be "anthropologically correct."[110] Hurston, who had originally used the phrase, had also written about racial culture: "There is no *The Negro* here" (italics in original).[111] Indeed, she argued, singular racial classification was impossible. Hurston was right.

Family scholar Sabrina Thomas argues that, given her cast of celebrity supporters and advanced hype, the Saralee doll was ultimately imbued with "too much racial capital."[112] She wasn't just a doll, she was a cause, carrying the impossible burden of advancing racial pride and social transformation. It was, Thomas laments, "too much for one doll to bear."[113] Ideal

Toy stopped production in 1953, the same year author Richard Wright published his novel *The Outsider*, to mixed reviews based on its decentering of race.

Decades later, what can we make of the doll project and Hurston's ongoing engagement with anthropometric practices? It is impossible to retrospectively know Hurston's motivations and understand her intrigue with anthropometry. As a student, she contributed to Franz Boas's challenge to the fixed taxonomic race models of scientific racism. The doll project may have been a way to operationalize, literally, his view that anthropological evidence supported "a great plasticity of human types."[114] In addition, she may have planned her later anthropometric research as a way to bolster that evidence. It would have been a strategy of using tools that historically supported scientific racism in order to upend its biological determinist theories of racial inferiority. The collapse of the Negro doll project seemingly reinforced poet and writer Audre Lorde's later contention that "the master's tools will never dismantle the master's house."[115] It certainly underscores the fraught intersection of culture, biology, and social change related to differences.

A doll is a way of knowing. It tells stories about race, bodies, gender, power, and social hierarchies. Saralee was an artifact of social knowledge, similar to that era's UNESCO statement on race, Hurston's folklore collections, and anthropologists' catalogs of anthropometric measurements. It expressed particular cultural meanings of race. Saralee was entangled in midcentury arguments over biological determinism, as well as discussions about the invention, and legitimacy, of racial categories and classifications. The doll was also a cultural intervention, foundering on the tangled and brutal history of racialized bodies. If identity is fluid and multiple, if difference is social rather than biological, how can these complexities by represented? In particular, how can a tangible representation, such as a doll, capture fluid embodiment? The doll argued for racial multiplicity, but, in doing so, seemed to signify a singularity of African Americans.

Finally, the vagaries of outsider capitalism shaped what stories could be told about difference. The Saralee strategy, to produce several dolls depicting a multiplicity of color and physical features, failed. A decade after the doll's market woes, sociologist Erving Goffman's critical text, *Stigma*, identified "tribal," or racial, stigma as a form of socially produced "undesired differentness."[116] Stigma spoiled identity, Goffman argued. Stigma also spoiled the commodification of such types of differences. **(See Hyperlink 4.1**: Anthropometry of Barbie.)

Hurston's Places

Like the Chicago School sociologists, Zora Neale Hurston foregrounded the role of places in producing diverse cultures and individual selves. Hurston's stories of places deepened cultural anthropology's approach to race. She captured how different places produced different ways of inhabiting and expressing racial and cultural identities. She also showed the fluidity of places, how boundaries and border mattered, but also shifted. Likewise, insider and outsider were themselves mutable categories. As historical and social agents, places are fundamental to Zora Neale Hurston's work. This section explores just some of them.

Places of Travel

Hurston's stories captured how places shaped individuals and cultures; Hurston's life showed how places shaped her. But first she had to get there. Boats, trains, and particularly cars were vital places for her. She was peripatetic, a natural for ethnographic field research. Travel was in Hurston's creative bloodstream, whether it was her famous Southern road trip with Langston Hughes, her excursions with fellow folklorists, or her boat trips to the Caribbean. She occasionally lived on houseboats, like the *Sun Tan*, and sometimes, by necessity, lived out of her car.

When Hurston traveled during the early decades of the twentieth century, with so few paved roads, train travel was the fastest and most efficient form of travel. The railroad built modern, industrial Florida, along with its tourist destinations. The Civil War had disrupted plans for a trans-Florida railroad proposed in 1842, but by 1893 the Florida Central and Peninsular Railway linked key cities in the Panhandle, Gulf Coast, and a southwestern route. Small towns emerged along the rail lines, enabling entrepreneurs to establish the sawmills, turpentine camps, cotton mills, and phosphate mines made possible by Florida's rich natural resources. Both Black and White workers migrated to Florida to satisfy the demand for labor. Meanwhile, wealthy industrialist Henry Flagler transformed Florida's swampy, isolated east coast into a vacation destination for Northerners. He built the Florida East Coast Railway, which extended to Miami, while his Florida Overseas Railroad to Key West—a massive engineering feat—was destroyed by the Labor Day hurricane of 1935. Henry Flagler opened Florida to the rest of the US, and, as historian James Wright quips, "made it possible for the weirdness to come flowing in."[117] Trains, then, produced new types of places and new kinds of mobile people. They could be a community event, a spectacle of technological progress. Hurston described how Eatonville villagers thought themselves worldly as they gathered on Sunday afternoons "to see Number 35 whizz southward on its way to Tampa and wave at the passengers."[118]

Trains figured in Hurston's fiction. She portrayed rail travel as part of how Blacks moved around in the South (as well as their international travel from the Caribbean to the US). For example, the sharecropper John Pearson described an upcoming train trip from Alabama "Tuh Florida, man" in her novel *Jonah's Gourd Vine* (1939): "Dat's de new country openin' up. Now git me straight, Ah don't mean West Florida, Ah means de real place. Good times, good money, and no mules and cotton."[119] As historian Martyn Bone writes, Hurston's fictional narratives of workers' rail travels highlighted the historically epic migrant patterns of rural, Black workers in the South.[120] They also show how Florida could be construed as a mythical place.

Trains were also very real social places with their own racial, gender, and class-based norms and hierarchies. Historian Mia Bay notes that a dangerous color line impeding African American travel dates to the earliest days of stagecoaches and steamships.[121] Hurston herself would travel by train, yet trains in the Jim Crow South were places of White supremacy. Racist and sexist constraints limited Hurston's ability to travel for field research.

Social science field research can entail risk. One contemporary handbook on the dangers of social-science fieldwork notes, "A good number of field studies in both sociology and anthropology place even the most timid and retiring of fieldworkers in settings and situations that are potentially dangerous to their health and safety."[122] These might include, for example, the risks of accidents, disease, arrest, harassment and other types of violence, some of which lead to death. "Cultural knowledge," the handbook advises, can help minimize risk. Zora Neale Hurston was neither timid nor retiring, but she knew in her cultural bones that a virulent threat to her fieldwork in the South was Jim Crow. She wrote, "My search for knowledge of things took me into many strange places and adventures. My life was in danger several times. If I had not learned how to take care of myself in these circumstances, I could have been maimed or killed on most any day of the several years of my research work."[123] One danger Hurston faced was traveling while Black.[124]

Riding the trains posed one such fieldwork danger for Hurston. Laws imposed strict racial segregation of railroad coaches in the late nineteenth century, just as train travel was expanding in the South. Jim Crow train cars for Blacks were dirty, dimly lit, stuffy, and often simply sections of baggage or smoking cars. The "combination car," for example, partitioned one side for smokers and one side for Blacks.[125] There were no luggage racks, reducing foot space for travelers. Restrooms were small and sparse. They could be dangerous for women travelers. Black travelers actively resisted train segregation from its earliest days, with little success.[126] While federal law ostensibly outlawed racial discrimination in train accommodation when passengers paid the same fare, it was difficult for Black riders to prove inferior conditions. And the Supreme Court, in its 1896 *Plessy v. Ferguson* case, upheld the legality of Jim Crow railroad cars with so-called separate but equal accommodations. Supreme Court decisions outlawing segregated trains, buses, and dining cars came in the 1940s and '50s, after Hurston's extensive fieldwork travels. Southern states largely ignored them.[127]

Many African Americans turned to automobiles to escape from Jim Crow trains. Hurston, too, was an automobile woman. When she arrived in Jacksonville in 1927 to launch her Southern fieldwork, she and her brother agreed that she should "avoid common carriers" of Jim Crow trains.[128] She bought a car. The car was to Zora what the freight train was to many hobos: a place in itself that enabled work mobility and personal freedom. While she couldn't always afford the flashy cars she yearned for, she owned a series of used but beloved automobiles, giving them feisty nicknames. Her first car was an old Nash two-seater coupe she dubbed "Sassy Susie" (she called a later car "High Yaller"). One trip was to Eatonville: "So below Palatka I began to feel eager to be there and I kicked the little Chevrolet right along."[129] Florida had almost no paved roads in the early twentieth century. When Hurston motored through the state, much of it was wilderness. It would not have been unusual for her to see chained convicts laboring on the sides of roads.

Cars were a haven but not an escape from the Jim Crow regime of the railroad. Racism also impeded Hurston's travels by automobile. It was exceedingly dangerous for Black travelers to drive in the United States, much less navigate the often-isolated two-lane roads of the rural South. The danger was exponentially greater for a Black woman. Hurston would have encountered numerous "sundown towns," which prohibited Blacks from entering or remaining there after dark. Because Blacks encountered difficulties purchasing food, fuel, or lodging at White-owned businesses, they often traveled with their own food coolers, bedding, and gas cans. Even vending machines carried "White Customers Only" signs.[130] Hurston's early field research predated the publication of the myriad travel guides for African American motorists, such as *A Directory of Negro Hotels and Guest Houses* (1939, 1941) and *The Negro Traveler's Green Book* (1936–

1966). The *Green Book*, launched by Harlem mailman Victor Hugo Green, identified businesses throughout the US that would serve Black travelers. Without that guidance, Hurston's car sometimes became her bedroom, the woods her restroom.

Hurston's car symbolized status and freedom. It could also mark her as an outsider, impeding her research. For example, workers in the Loughman sawmill camp treated Hurston with hostility, refusing to accept her into the community. This was her first foray into the field since her unsuccessful earlier trip to Eatonville, and she quickly realized that her car and her $12.74 dress from Macy's generated suspicion. In *Mules and Men*, Hurston recounted that "I did look different and resolved to fix all that no later than the next morning."[131] She told the community that she was a bootlegger on the lam, a gambit to explain the car: "Bootleggers always have cars."[132] At that point, "Zora's car was everybody's car,"[133] and she disclosed her field research motivations once she had earned their acceptance.

Zora's Third Places

In her ethnographic focus on the rural South, Hurston wrote against both the scholarly grain and the racial politics of the era. Early sociologists were urban-centric, studying the modern city's hobohemias, taxi-dance halls, and other outsider places. In contrast, Hurston focused on the cultural lives of rural working-class and poor Southern Blacks—the group that many of her contemporary African American intellectuals considered to be "the underbelly of black life"[134]—showing how places produced culture. In so doing, she moved them from the cultural margins to the center of literary visibility and her ethnographic analysis. Moreover, her excavation of the folklore of poor, uneducated workers and formerly enslaved people defied Black intellectuals' focus on racial uplift in urban environs. As historian Tiffany Patterson suggests, Hurston "did not treat the northern metropolis as the quintessential cultural site of black expressive culture, but instead located this site in the South."[135] Her criticism of prominent Black intellectuals for ignoring rural, marginalized, Southern Black culture contributed to her own marginalization.

Hurston depicted places' complexity, and how they shaped their people. Her ethnographic stories captured the rich settings of the kind that contemporary sociologist Ray Oldenburg calls "third places,"[136] the cafés, bars, general stores, and other public hangout spots outside of home and work. They are the public spaces that foster community and get us through the day. Locations, like the state of Florida generally, and specific places within the state—turpentine and sawmill camps, churches, jook joints, a front porch in Eatonville—were not simply backdrops to human existence. They fostered collective ways of thinking, feeling, and being.

Hurston's first ethnographic field work was in Florida. Places, geographer Doreen Massey argues, are "collections of stories,"[137] and Hurston knew that her home town, Eatonville, was brimming with them. She said, "Dr. Boas asked me where I wanted to work and I said, 'Florida,' and gave, as my big reason, that Florida is a place that draws people—white people from all over the world, and Negroes from every Southern state surely and some from the North and West. So I knew that it was possible for me to get a cross section of the Negro South in the one state.... First place I aimed to stop to collect material was Eatonville, Florida."[138] Eatonville's third places produced a town of African American culture and self-determination. As she drove across the town boundary, her first stop was Joe Clarke's store, "the heart and spring of the town."[139] On Joe Clarke's store porch, women and men gathered, and Hurston collected their folktale "lying" sessions, the gossip, jokes, bragging, and arguments that comprised Black, Southern, small-town life.

Myriad third places came alive in Hurston's work. Jook joints and the Sanctified Church were two disparate but perhaps surprisingly kindred places. Jook joints were leisure places of dancing, drinking, and singing in the camps. Hurston wrote, "Polk County. After dark, the jooks."[140] She called them "Negro pleasure house[s]."[141] Meanwhile, Sanctified Churches offered their own pleasures. In both places, African Americans freely practiced traditional songs and dances. Likewise, freedom of community engagement in both places produced and reinforced rich cultural traditions. Jook joints and the Sanctified Church fostered expressive racial identities, or, as Hurston put it, produced a "revitalizing element."[142] They enabled a connection to cultural elements brought from Africa, then reenacted and reinvented in a new place.

Hurston viewed the practices of the Sanctified Church movement as both a "rebirth" and a "new era" of rural Black spirituality. She carefully differentiated the Sanctified Church from the early-twentieth-century Pentecostal revival as well as the White evangelical movement gaining political visibility. (For example, the Scopes Trial in 1925—ostensibly a conflict over the teaching of evolution in public schools—brought the antiscience beliefs of Christian fundamentalists to public attention.) Hurston called the Pentecostalists "Holy-Rollers" and claimed there were few Blacks among them. Still, ever class-conscious, she argued that the Sanctified Church was indeed a "protest," but one against assimilationist

Black congregations who adopted the staid religious rituals of Whites. The church, she showed, like the jook joints, was a place producing the exuberance of singing, dancing, and shouting.

Sacred and secular blended in both the Sanctified Church and the jook joints. They were places for cultural and individual expression through song and dance. She wrote, "All Negro-made church music is dance-possible," producing bodily possession by the gods, leading to "shouting."[143] Shouting—a rhythmic emotional response to the preacher—was part of the public culture, "a community thing."[144] Dancing in the jooks was similarly joyous and free. Hurston, who loved dancing, described them: "Polk County in the jooks. Dancing the square dance. Dancing the scroush. Dancing the belly-rub."[145] The jooks gave rise to the blues and to dances such as the Black Bottom and the Charleston that spread to places like Chicago's taxi-dance halls and black-and-tans (**see** chapter 3). Hurston's folklorist colleague Stetson Kennedy recounted how, like jazz, jooks were "a Negro contribution to Americana," with an appeal extending far beyond the Mason-Dixon Line.[146] Florida—the home of the jooks—also fomented backlash against them. Kennedy noted that the Ku Klux Klan burned a cross near a jook in Miami.[147]

Early on, Hurston recognized how Black gospel music crossed over to what she called "American music." Even as Whites and assimilationist Blacks derided rural Black spiritual traditions, these practices were "shooting new life into American music . . . the tunes from the street and church change places often."[148] Indeed, by the mid-1950s, the fusion of what the *New York Times* later called "the sacred shouts of the black church and the profane sound of the blues"[149] became embodied in Black musicians such as Little Richard and Chuck Berry, crossing over in (and appropriated by) White musicians such as Elvis Presley. When Little Richard made rock 'n' roll history in 1955 with his first hit, "Tutti Frutti," Hurston was living on Florida's east coast, writing her unfinished book on Herod the Great, whom she viewed as "a progressive rebel."[150]

The jook joint was one of Hurston's richest ethnographic places. She sprinkled the folklore she collected into her fiction, for example *Their Eyes Were Watching God*, and her essays and memoirs, *Dust Tracks on a Road*. Some of her stories spoke of the significance of places to African American laborers, in particular the Negro Mythical Places. Historian Pamela Bordelon notes that turpentiners told these tales, probably sitting on the porches of jook joints. The stories recount mythical place such as Diddy-Wah-Diddy—"a place of no work and no worry"—and Beluthahatchee. Beluthahatchee is "a land of forgiveness," a place-term used colloquially:

"When a woman throws up to her man something that happened in the past . . . , he may merely reply, 'I thought that was in Beluthahatchee.'" Stetson Kennedy later founded a writer's retreat in Florida that he named Beluthahatchee.[151]

Hurston's letters reveal her keen awareness of race and the omnipresent possibility of racist exclusion, even in her most beloved places. She wrote to a friend during an early fieldwork trip in Florida, "Flowers are gorgeous now, crackers not troubling me at all—hope they don't begin as I go farther down state."[152] Around that time, she sent a one-line postcard from St. Augustine to photographer Carl Van Vechten, featuring a large swimming pool with White bathers: "In which I did not take a dip."[153] Her anger about racism became more heated: "The iron has entered my soul. Since my god of tolerance has forsaken me, I am ready for anything to overthrow Anglo-Saxon supremacy, however desoerate [sic]. I have become what I never wished to be, a good hater."[154] Later in her life, as she tried to buy a house in a White Florida neighborhood, she wrote that the owner "must go slow about selling it to me, waiting on public reaction. . . . In what was meant to be a compliment, I have been told twice, 'You don't live like the majority of your people. You like things clean and orderly around you.'"[155]

Finally, Hurston imagined a place for the dead. Her correspondence with sociologist, artist, and activist W. E. B. Du Bois reflected poignancies of both her life and death. In June 1945, she proposed that Du Bois establish "a cemetery for the illustrious Negro dead. Something like Pere la Chaise in Paris."[156] Hurston had long-standing disagreements with Du Bois, once described him to a friend as "goateed, egotistic, wishy-washy," and privately called him "Dr. Dubious."[157] She had been obliquely critical of him in her writing on the Sanctified Church: it was, she wrote, "ridiculous to say that the spirituals are the Negro's 'sorrow songs,'" as did what she called "our latter-day pity men." This was a transparent criticism of Du Bois, who famously wrote of the "sorrow songs" of slavery.[158] There is no indication that Du Bois knew of this criticism, and her article was unpublished at the time.

Hurston thought a Negro cemetery site in the lake country of Florida would be perfect because land was cheap and the surrounding vegetation beautiful. She was keenly aware of the fragility of cultural memory and the perils of marginality: "Let no Negro celebrity, no matter what financial condition they might be in at death, lie in inconspicious forgetfulness [sic]." Such a cemetery could be a third place for African Americans, "a rallying spot that would be for all that we want to accomplish and do . . . the lack of such a tangible thing allows our people to forget, and their spirits evaporate." She offered to drive Du Bois around Florida to search for an appropriate site. Du Bois rejected her idea in a brief note, citing "practical difficulties," adding, "I regret to say I have not the enthusiasm for Florida that you have . . . in other matters more spiritual it is not so rich."[159] Hurston seems to have dropped the proposal.

It is impossible not to view Hurston's cemetery initiative in the context of her later lonely death and unmarked grave. Yet her letter to Du Bois contained a tantalizing clue about the vibrancy of her life at the time. Hurston listed her return address as "On Board the Houseboat-Cruiser SUN TAN, Daytona Beach." Indeed, she spent that summer of 1945 floating on the Halifax River in her houseboat. She was hard at work writing, and described herself as "happier than I have ever been before in my life."[160] In letters to friends, including anthropologist Ruth Benedict, she talked of going to Honduras to conduct ethnographic research for a new book. She may have anticipated that her legacy would be forgotten—it was a common enough fate for Black women—but she was still full of dreams for her life and work. Still an anthropologist.

Lost and Found; Forgotten or Erased?

In 2018, decades after Zora Neale Hurston's death, HarperCollins published her book, *Barracoon: The Story of the Last "Black Cargo."* *Barracoon*—the term for the barracks used to imprison enslaved people—was Hurston's anthropological account of her multiple interviews with Cudjo Lewis, or Oluale Kossola, the last surviving West African brought to the United States in the transatlantic slave trade. He was then living in Alabama. Her 1927 train trip from New York to Mobile launched this ethnographic and folkloric project. In interviews, Hurston captured Cudjo's life experiences from his childhood, his enslavement, and his family and community life after Emancipation. She consulted the archive of the Mobile Historical Society as well as secondary sources. *Barracoon* was Hurston's first book, completed in 1931. She worked several years to compile the manuscript, and, as in her other writing, she integrated Cudjo's vernacular speech. This use of idiom was controversial at the time, viewed by some critics as degrading. It prompted publishers, including a Knopf editor whom Hurston knew, to reject the book. The 2018 HarperCollins edition of *Barracoon* was its first time in print. It appeared 100 years after Hurston had launched her academic studies at Howard University.

Much fanfare accompanied *Barracoon*'s publication, as though an ancient treasure had been unearthed. Much of the coverage resembled that of the magazine, *Vulture*, which noted that Hurston's manuscript had "languished in a vault."[161] Yet journalist and editor Ted Genoways insisted that the so-called "lost" manuscripts of important writers such as Hurston, William Faulkner, Langston Hughes, Hart Crane, and others "are not lost—they have always been here—but they have repeatedly encountered power structures that block their publication."[162] Copyright law to protect corporate interests is one such power structure (for example, the Walt Disney Company's efforts to prevent early Mickey Mouse films from entering the public domain have resulted in copyright extensions), as well as the vagaries of the authors' literary executors. While both of these factors stalled *Barracoon*'s publication, Zora Neale Hurston also suffered the obstacles of racism, and what was at the time considered her political incorrectness. Much of her literary and ethnographic writing was unpublished during her lifetime. When historian Pamela Bordelon painstakingly excavated Hurston's unpublished Federal Writers' Project work for her dissertation research at Louisiana State University in the early 1990s, Bordelon found that the manuscripts "lie neglected in state depositories."[163] All of Hurston's published work was out of print when she died in a senior home in Fort Pierce on January 28, 1960. Bordelon collected and published Hurston's FWP work as an edited volume that appeared only in 1999, long after Hurston's so-called resurrection. As writer Alice Walker noted in a somewhat different context, "Poor Zora. An anthropologist, no less!"[164]

Zora Neale Hurston could be a case study in the erasure of scholarship and art based on intersectional biases and the marginalization of unpopular ideas. Academic erasure is not random or accidental. It is socially, politically, and economically produced. Social biases and cultural values shape which scholars get to tell the story and which ideas are erased. Hurston knew that she was a product of the intersecting influences of specific places and historical moments: "I have memories within that came out of the material that went to make me. Time and place have had their say."[165] Likewise, time and place brought about both her "disappearance" and her "recovery" as scholar and writer.

Hurston's ideas went against the grain of her intellectual and political era, and her work was marginalized. She was defiantly out of step with the racial politics of her era, the New Negro. She resisted the demands of her contemporaries to only write social-document fiction with a political agenda opposing racial oppression. She challenged the racism of White publishers and White culture overall in her article, "What White Publishers Won't Print."[166] Whites, she wrote, approach social differences with apathy or hostility: "I have been amazed by the Anglo-Saxon's lack of curiosity about the internal lives and emotions of the Negroes, and for that matter, any non-Anglo-Saxon peoples within our borders, above the class of unskilled labor." The fearful White public preferred stereotypes: "mere difference is apt to connote something malign." Hurston criticized the type of widespread minstrelsy of "the American Negro" that she herself was accused of perpetuating: "Shuffling feet and those popping, rolling eyes denote the Negro, and no characterization is genuine without this monotony." In the commercial context of White indifference, White publishers—who "are in business to make money"—would not publish unprofitable work about non-Whites (much like doll manufacturers' were unwilling to produce non-White dolls). With a critical eye, Hurston witnessed her career suffer from the absence of a market for her complex stories of a rich, fulfilling Southern Black culture.

She was a contrarian, even a marginal figure in the racial politics of the Harlem literary avant-garde. In their view, Hurston did not sufficiently engage with the critical racial politics of the times, which demanded social realism rather than romantic fiction, which is how they characterized her work. Writers such as Richard Wright, Alain Locke, and even her erstwhile friend Langston Hughes criticized her folksy representations of rural African American communities and her use of Black idiomatic speech. Wright, whose own work stressed the damaging impacts of racism and structures of White oppression, accused Hurston of employing a "minstrel technique that makes the white folks laugh."[167] In return, she penned a lacerating review of his short story collection, *Uncle Tom's Children*, calling it "a book about hatreds."[168] Hurston also challenged her critics in her 1938 essay, "Art and Such," decrying the pressure on Black writers to write only about "exploitation, terror, misery, and bitterness."[169] She emphasized Black self-determination and cultural creativity, asking, "Can the black poet sing a song to the morning?"[170] The essay was unpublished, and there is no evidence that her harshest critics ever read it.

The political cultures of race and gender had shifted by the 1970s. If Zora Neale Hurston was lost, Black feminism found her. When Alice Walker traveled to Eatonville in 1973, now famously "looking for Zora," Zora was seemingly forgotten even in her beloved hometown. When Walker asked a city-hall official if the schools taught Zora's work, the woman replied, "No, they don't. I don't think most people know anything about Zora Neale Hurston, or know about any of the great things she did." When Walker published her 1975 essay about Hurston in the newly established feminist magazine, *Ms*, it found a burgeoning and eager audience of feminists, Black Studies scholars and activists, women's studies programs, and a general literary public. Hurston's critiques of race, color, and gender had found her people in their historical and political moment. Feminist and womanist scholars around the world, as Walker put it fifteen years later, had "accomplished the resurrection of Zora Neale Hurston and her splendid work."[171] Currently all her published work is back in print, with newly discovered or recovered unpublished work intermittently appearing.

The feminist reclamation of Hurston secured her status in the literary canon, yet contemporary scholars continue to debate Hurston's place as a writer and Black public intellectual. Her political stances could be contradictory and, as literary critic Andrew Delbanco put it, never coherent: "She tended to shoot off letters to the editor or to blurt things out in interviews."[172] Carla Kaplan, who compiled Hurston's letters, described her as "famously Janus-faced," yet having an underlying logic to her thinking.[173] Some of her work, such as her last novel, *Seraph on the Suwanee*, was discomfiting even to supporters like Walker (who called it "reactionary, static, shockingly misguided and timid"[174]). Some of her positions earned her a reputation as politically conservative or reactionary, such as her opposition to the landmark Supreme Court decision *Brown v. Board of Education* prohibiting racial segregation in schools: "How much satisfaction can I get from a court order for somebody to associate with me who does not wish me near them?"[175] The woman who had grown up in a vibrant, nurturing all-Black town objected to mandated integration as insulting rather than liberating.

"Be an outcast." Alice Walker's poetic command captures Zora's defiant career. Her poem, "Be Nobody's Darling,"[176] was published in 1973—the same year Walker traveled to Eatonville to find Hurston's grave: "Let them look askance at you, and you askance reply." Never afraid to speak her mind, or change her mind, Hurston was both outsider and insider in the many places she lived and traveled. Prefiguring later poststructuralism, critical-race theory, and queer theory, she argued that categories and classifications could be multiple and mutable. Her expansive body of public anthropology—a hybrid of ethnographic books and essays, fiction, memoir, and poetry—stands as a historical record of myriad types of socially marginalized people, their vibrant cultures, and the places that shaped them.

Hurston died at the beginning of what art historian James Meyer calls "the decadal Sixties," the precise ten years starting January 1, 1960.[177] It was just days before the Greensboro sit-in, the landmark nonviolent protest staged at a North Carolina Woolworth's lunch counter. The civil rights movement had achieved victories throughout the 1950s, such as the

Civil Rights Act of 1957, and also suffered the violence of bombings, beatings, and the ongoing lynching of African Americans. During what Meyer calls "the long Sixties"—running from the end of the 1950s through the early 1970s—the country would see new movements of political activism and artistic expression, and a new generation of scholars arise. Many of these young academics saw themselves as outsiders, marginalized by race, gender, sexuality, and countercultural inclinations. Their work would later help create new intellectual and cultural space for social differences. That outsider zeitgeist produced by the art and scholarship of the many social movements of the "long sixties" enabled Hurston's rediscovery.

Hyperlink 4.1: Anthropometry of Barbie

Dolls came and went. Dolls came and stayed. A new generation of politically engaged anthropologists turned against anthropometry as being a tool that established and normalized privileged forms of difference. Some turned anthropometry against itself, using the tool subversively as a way to make visible oppressive social norms based in biological determinism. One example was the anthropometry of Barbie.

Barbie was a game changer in the doll world. Introduced in 1959 by Mattel, the teen fashion doll's popularity endures well into the twenty-first century. Although sales have waxed and waned, in 2019 Barbie sales soared 12 percent from the year before, reaching over $1.4 billion worldwide.[178] Barbie's longevity, unlike that of dolls before her, including Saralee, represents the successful commodification of dominant cultural norms based on race, class, gender, and sexualities. She is a global icon of White, American femininity. She has, therefore, long been controversial.

Barbie's success rested on her conformity to cultural ideals. Initially marketed in a historical era that saw the rise of a rebellious youth counterculture and of myriad political movements such as feminism and gay liberation, Barbie was a good girl. Marketers presented her as "affluent, well-groomed, socially conservative."[179] Barbie shopped and partied. In 1963, Barbie was sold with a diet book commanding, "Don't eat."[180] It was the year Betty Friedan published what would become a feminist classic, *The Feminine Mystique*. Nina Simone performed her famous Carnegie Hall concert. It is considered one of the defining years of the civil rights movement, with the March on Washington, the Children's Crusade, Woolworth sit-ins in Mississippi, and other historic initiatives. Tone-deaf to cultural change, Mattel produced Barbie going to the prom, skiing, and attending the theater. Although Mattel diversified Barbie's career options—a businesswoman in 1963 and astronaut in 1965—Barbie was still White. Still thin.

Conformist Barbie, in these early years, inhabited the same cultural landscape as the Beats, *Mad* magazine, Ken Kesey's novel *One Flew Over the Cuckoo's Nest*, and other forms of an emerging outsider aesthetic, which would ultimately prove to be as marketable as conformity. Barbie was the female embodiment—albeit plastic—of sociologist Erving Goffman's 1963 tongue-in-cheek critique of the fictional "one complete unblushing male in America: a young, married, white, urban, northern, heterosexual Protestant father of college education, fully employed, of good complexion, weight and height, and a recent record in sports." In other words, Goffman concluded, we are all vulnerable to stigmatization for failure to achieve dominant cultural norms, yet these idealizations "cast some kind of shadow on the encounters encountered everywhere in daily living."[181] Barbie was that shadow, her plastic perfection a constant rebuke.

Mattel slowly and awkwardly introduced racial diversity. They released a Black friend for Barbie in 1967, Colored Francie, well after the term "colored" had come to be seen as outdated and offensive, replaced by the descriptors "Black" and "African American." (Zora Neale Hurston's contemporary and critic, Richard Wright, published the book, *Black Power*, in 1954.) Colored Francie, and another Black friend, Christie, both failed in the market. In the 1980s, White Barbie acquired some ethnically diverse friends, like Kira and Miko, although the dolls' features were identical to those of White Barbie, except for yellow and brown skin tones (Mattel called its Asian doll "Oriental Barbie").

In 1991, in aggressive marketing campaigns, Mattel introduced the Shani line, an Afrocentric doll, two friends—Asha and Nichelle—and Shani's boyfriend Jamal (released in 1992). The three Shani dolls were produced with three different face molds and skin tones: dark, medium, and light. Mattel had achieved the racial diversity that Ideal Toy Company had failed to reach with the Saralee doll. Or did it?

Barbie caught the attention of anthropologists at the University of Massachusetts, Alan Swedlund and Jackie Urla. They used anthropometry to measure Barbie and compare her dimensions to those of average American women. They also examined the Shani dolls. It was, they said, "an occasion to turn the anthropometric tables from disciplining the bodies of living women to measuring the ideals by which we have come to judge ourselves and others."[182] Could the normalizing tools of anthropometry, historically used to establish hierarchical physical norms, expose and destabilize Barbie's conformity to, and perpetuation of, unrealistic and destructive norms of the female body? Among their many findings, Swedlund and Urla found that Barbie's bodily dimensions differed radically from the weight and proportions of "average" women. Walking would prove nearly impossible with those tiny feet, large breasts, prominent butt, and extreme thinness.

Having successfully marketed conformity, Mattel hit the wall trying to sell physical difference. Pundits criticized Mattel's offensive representations of Black bodies, which conflated skin color with stereotypically racialized facial features. For example, the light-skinned Shani doll had thin lips and a small nose, while the darkest doll had wide lips and nose. Despite rumors that Shani had a "Black butt," Swedlund and Urla found that her dimensions were basically the same as those of White Barbie from the neck down.[183]

Mattel suffered a 20 percent revenue dip from 2012 to 2014. In 2016, the company introduced new skin tones, hair textures, and body types: tall, petite, and curvy Barbies. After decades of unsuccessful racial diversification, now, curvy Barbie was the shocker. *Time* magazine described her as having "meat on her thighs and a protruding tummy and behind."[184] Barbie's "thin" clothes would no longer fit, a potential boon for sales, but carrying the risk of irritating parent consumers. Evelyn Mazzocco, head of the Barbie line, felt the company needed to shake things up. Still, it was a bold cultural move for Mattel, harkening back to the Saralee doll and other projects bedeviled by how to represent physical differences without reinforcing new stereotypes. Curvy Barbie had her haters; in focus groups, girls mocked her mercilessly. By 2019, research showed that only 6 percent of an ethnically diverse sample of girls aged three to ten chose curvy Barbie as their favorite, the rest complaining that she was fat.[185]

Still, Mattel persisted. By 2020, claiming to be the most diverse doll line, the company released a bald Barbie, a Barbie with a prosthetic leg, a Barbie in a wheelchair, and a Barbie with vitiligo, a skin disease. These complemented a doll line released a few months earlier, which a Mattel spokeswoman had described as "gender-neutral"[186] (activists criticize this term as offensive, instead using "gender-fluid," "nonbinary," "genderqueer," or "gender nonconforming). Outsider capitalism in the twenty-first century remains vexed by the challenges of marketing social differences. A doll's story continues.

FIVE

Asylum Stories

> The interpretive scheme of the total institution automatically begins to operate as soon as the inmate enters, the staff having the notion that entrance is *prima facie* evidence that one must be the kind of person the institution was set up to handle.[1]
>
> Erving Goffman

The bomb-sniffing black Labrador inching under our car was the perfect Goffmanian character. My cousin Tia and I had arrived at St. Elizabeths Hospital[2] in Washington, DC, on a gray March morning for a tour run by the DC Preservation League. St. Elizabeths had been the research site for sociologist Erving Goffman's ethnographic text, *Asylums*. A security guard stopped our car, requested that we get out and show our IDs, and then the frisky Lab sniffed both inside and outside while we stood uneasily in the parking lot. St. Elizabeths, like many imposing nineteenth-century asylums, had fallen into disrepair and was slated for demolition. Now, however, it was under renovation to serve as the new headquarters of the US Department of Homeland Security (DHS). Goffman, who had written about institutional surveillance, such as the frisking and searching "that penetrates the private reserve of the individual and violates the territories of his self," would no doubt have critically observed the rise of our contemporary surveillance state, of which DHS is certainly emblematic. The dog, not without its charms, exercised a clear institutional display of hierarchy and social control.

Hospital for the Insane of the Army and Navy and the District of Columbia, 1860. Courtesy of the Library of Congress.

Asylums like St. Elizabeths haunt the cultural imagination. They are unsettled places of troubled lives. Those sprawling, Gothic compounds—founded on a nineteenth-century vision of moral healing but later deteriorating into what one scholar calls "theaters of madness"[3]—feature in the nightmarish stories of numerous novels, films, and television series. Many asylums have now been demolished or repurposed, others lie abandoned on city outskirts, while some—for example, Oregon State Hospital, the setting for the film *One Flew Over the Cuckoo's Nest*—continue modified operations. These institutions were also sites for midcentury critical social-science research. Goffman's 1961 text, *Asylums: Essays on the Social Situation of Mental Patients and Other Inmates*, is one of the most influential.

Asylums exemplifies the rupture effected by mid-twentieth-century critical social theory. Goffman wrote against the grain of psychoanalysis and an increasingly dominant medical model that framed individual disturbances as mental illnesses having biological or psychiatric origins. Instead, he conjectured that mental patients were made, not born. Goffman's symbolic interactionist approach to how actions and meanings are socially produced theorized the powerful role of people's places. Moreover, he showed how places—asylums themselves—could exacerbate, and even manufacture, individual troubles, rather than heal them.

Goffman is an important bridge scholar between earlier Chicago School researchers and later postmodern theories and queer studies. Texts such as *Asylums*, Howard Becker's *Outsiders*, and Goffman's next book, *Stigma: Notes on the Management of Spoiled Identity*, were foundational for the emergent sociology of deviance.[4] Goffman, Becker, and other scholars challenged biological determinism through their clear articulation of concepts such as labeling, secondary deviance, social-control agents, moral entrepreneurs, stigma, and, emerging later, social constructionism. Their ethnographies brought to life the ways that rules, places, situations, and practices produced both normalcy and deviance.

This chapter explores both *Asylums* and asylums. These asylum stories take us inside the walls and buildings of his research site, St. Elizabeths. They examine the historical period in which Goffman conducted his research and wrote *Asylums*, a paradoxical moment in which the medicalized disciplines of psychiatry and psychology were expanding their cultural authority but were also undergoing critiques by scholars, artists, and an emergent antipsychiatry movement.

St. Elizabeths Hospital, Washington, DC, between 1909 and 1932. Courtesy of the Library of Congress.

Prehistory: Goffman and His Asylum

Asylums are material places, located in particular regions, with specific histories, norms, and practices. These bucolic campuses, originally known as "lunatic asylums" or hospitals for "the insane," were built in the United States largely during the second half of the nineteenth century. They had utopian origins. Nineteenth-century reformers viewed serene settings and specific architectural designs as themselves constituting psychiatric treatments. Advocates for the mentally ill, in particular Dorothea Dix, espoused the philosophy of "moral treatment," a vision that prioritized peaceful and natural surroundings for asylums. This approach is reflected in the "purpose-built" architecture of the design popularized by Dr. Thomas Kirkbride. The Kirkbride Plan featured long, linear corridors that ensured ample fresh air and light for the patients. This idea, "environmental determinism,"[5] suggested that places—and buildings themselves—were vital for healing madness.

The first complex built at St. Elizabeths followed the Kirkbride Plan. Originally known as the Government Asylum for the Insane Veterans of the Army and Navy and Residents of the District of Columbia, and then more simply as the US Government Hospital for the Insane, St. Elizabeths opened in 1855 as the first federally funded asylum. Dorothea Dix had identified the sweeping farmland in the Anacostia Hills as the site for St. Elizabeths, believing such a setting might promote emotional healing. Times changed. A century later, Goffman interpreted its rural isolation as an aspect of social control. Those rural settings, he thought, fostered disconnection from outside communities.

Goffman famously argued that asylums were best understood as "total institutions." Like prisons, military schools, or old-age homes, asylums stripped individual identity in a process he called the "mortification of self." He referred to patients as "inmates." He developed those arguments at St. Elizabeths, conducting his research there a century after its founding. There were approximately 7,000 patients by that time, most of them involuntarily committed.

Goffman followed in the footsteps of earlier scholars who had ventured into marginal places, such as hobohemia, taxi-dance halls, and turpentine camps. He had been a graduate student of Chicago School giants Robert Park, Ernest Burgess, and Everett Hughes, where he was influenced by the ideas of Georg Simmel, George Herbert Mead, and other social theorists. After receiving his PhD from the University of Chicago in 1953, he had an appointment at the National Institute of Mental Health, in Bethesda, Maryland (NIMH). Through that position, he secured entrée to St. Elizabeths for a year of ethnographic field research. His role of assistant athletic director allowed him inside the hospital, but he clearly pointed out that he avoided "the carrying of a key."[6] He did not operate, in other words, as the sort of social-control agent of whom he was so critical.

In *Asylums*, Goffman obscured his specific research location, an elision consistent with ethnographic practices at the time. He used the pseudonym "Central Hospital," generalizing his arguments about total institutions to sites as divergent as concentration camps, monasteries, and boarding schools. He mentioned his site location only twice, naming St. Elizabeths in his brief preface. He thanked the NIMH, his institutional sponsor, and the "fair-mindedness" of the government psychiatrists for not censoring his manuscripts. Goffman mentioned the "delicate atmosphere" of Washington, DC, by which he probably meant the political climate that might have shaped his access to fieldwork and his subsequent analysis of the hospital, a sensitive government facility. It is possible that, like earlier scholars such as Paul Cressey who balanced the moral viewpoints of his funders, Goffman may have had to navigate complicated institutional pressures.

Goffman was part of mid-twentieth-century scientific and cultural disagreements over the range of disturbances dubbed "mental illness." His was an early voice in a broader critique of biological and psychiatric approaches to problematic behavior. Other sociologists of his era studied mental hospitals, including, for example, Anselm Strauss, Alfred Stanton, and Morris Schwartz, as well as Rose Laub Coser.[7] Critics as different as Thomas Szasz, Philip Rieff, and R. D. Laing challenged what they saw as the rising cultural power of "the therapeutic society"[8] and the powerful role of institutional framing of individual behavior, selfhood, normalcy, and deviance. His work was crucial to challenges to the medicalization of everyday life, in particular biological, eugenic, psychiatric, and personality-based notions of individual mental variations and suffering. (**See Hyperlink 5.1:** Thomas Scheff.)

Medicalization and Its Challengers

The medicalization of emotional and behavioral differences had been long underway by the time Goffman conducted his field research at St. Elizabeths. In their review of this long history, sociologists Peter Conrad and Joseph Schneider argue that mental illness represents "literally the original case of medicalized deviance,"[9] a process that spanned a period of 2000 years. Medicalization swept unconventional ways of acting and being into the domain of scientific medicine. By the nineteenth century, medical experts transformed madness—a wide range of nonconforming behaviors and internal states—into the medical designation "mental illness." These new cultural authorities over mental status—biological sciences, psychiatry, and psychology—invented theoretical frameworks, vocabularies, and treatment interventions to explain, control, and eliminate mentally problematic behaviors. Medicalized frameworks supported efforts to eradicate mental deficiencies by eliminating the individuals or behaviors that were allegedly deficient. Alternatively, these individuals were removed from their social worlds.

The medicalization of suffering intensified over the decades, and asylums devolved from healing sufferers to warehousing individuals on the social margins. They became places that supported the eugenic practices of scientific racism. Compulsory sterilization, for example, entangled biological determinist ideology, eugenic interventions, and asylums. The 1927 Supreme Court decision, *Buck v. Bell*, established legal precedent for state-enforced sterilization of inmates in public institutions, based on the supposedly genetic traits of feeblemindedness, epilepsy, or imbecility. Eugenics experts in Virginia had determined that Carrie Buck, the plaintiff, was both an imbecile and promiscuous. She became the first person sterilized under Virginia's law aimed at improving genetic stock through preventing reproduction by those deemed inferior. Historians later found no evidence that Buck was intellectually inferior—she had done well in school—and determined that the pregnancy that had marked her as "promiscuous" was probably the result of rape.[10] Yet *Buck v. Bell*, which has never been overturned, legitimated the involuntary sterilization of many thousands of people. During the post–World War II Nuremberg trials, Nazi physicians cited the case in their defense of concentration-camp atrocities.[11] Asylums had veered from their utopian origins to become agents of institutionalized medicalization, eugenic practices, and other types of social control.

Although eugenics was briefly discredited after the war, psychiatry and psychology expanded their cultural authority. Clinical psychiatry refined its scientific techniques of classifying, sorting, and measuring behavioral differences, publishing the first *Diagnostic and Statistical Manual of Mental Disorders* (*DSM*) in 1952. The *DSM* attempted to create a common taxonomy and language of mental disorders, establishing 108 different diagnoses in 130 pages. Over time, the manual grew exponentially, along with the cultural expansion of psychiatry. By its most recent update in 2013, the *DSM-5* had ballooned to 991 pages and more than 350 diagnoses. *DSM* psychiatric classifications have been exported internationally, contributing to what critics call the globalization of mental illness. Increasingly controversial, the *DSM* attempts to draw clear boundaries between normal and abnormal people and behavior.

By midcentury, social scientists and political activists began to challenge labeling and institutionalization as forms of social control. On the one hand, they acknowledged that medical frameworks might reduce the stigma of behaviors previously considered sinful or illegal, facilitate access to resources and treatments, and help afflicted individuals find social networks. On the other hand, medicalization turned social problems into individual problems by locating troubles within the biology or psyche of the person. Therefore, treatment targeted the individual rather than the body politic; eugenics was an extreme example of this targeting. Moreover, medicalization reframed myriad types of differences as illness, which by its very nature is pathological. Therefore, medicalization might reduce stigma for behaviors otherwise considered sinful or bad, but it could also reinforce stigma. The medicalization of troublesome behaviors defined them as diseases, unleashing the potential for punitive measures of treatment and social control.

Instead of medical frameworks, sociologists focused on the powerful roles of labeling, situations, and places in producing dysfunction and deviants. And, as sociologist Phillip Manning notes, Goffman and other sociologists of this era defined themselves "in opposition to Freud and psychoanalysis."[12] While Goffman did believe that some mental illnesses were "organic," he focused on what he dubbed "situational improprieties."[13] In *Asylums*, he explored how an increasingly powerful psychiatric institution interpreted this behavior of "persons who seem to act oddly"[14] through the frame of pathology. Anyone's life, Goffman insisted, contained enough "denigrating facts" to provide grounds for commitment. Moreover, one's mere presence in a mental hospital could frame one as pathological. Indeed, this argument acquired dramatic empirical support a decade later in an article by psychologist David Rosenhan, "On Being Sane in Insane Places."[15]

Popularly known as the Rosenhan experiment, this study underscored the role of place—the "insane places" of mental hospitals—in determining whether individuals were normal or abnormal. A Stanford University professor of law and psychology, David Rosenhan was inspired by the growing critique of psychiatry by scholars and activists. Like Goffman, Rosenhan questioned the growth of psychiatric authority. He asked, "If sanity and insanity exist, how shall we know them?" Did mental illness reside within the individual, or was it a function of an "insane context?" Were the characteristics that produced psychiatric diagnoses internal to the patients or instead to the environmental context? Are psychiatric diagnoses themselves valid? Rosenhan designed an experiment to find out.

It was a very Goffmanian study that examined the role of place and situation in framing mental illness. Would simply showing up at a mental hospital prove that one belonged there? David Rosenhan arranged for eight "pseudopatients" to present themselves at twelve psychiatric hospitals in five states. They feigned auditory hallucinations but otherwise provided factual background information during their screening interview. All the pseudopatients were admitted and diagnosed as schizophrenic. Once in the hospital, they reported that their hallucinations had ceased, and they acted in the normal ways they typically would on the outside. Despite this, none of the psychiatric staff identified them as imposters, although some of the other patients did so. Rather, their normal behaviors and personal backgrounds were pathologized by staff to fit with the diagnosis of schizophrenia. For example, pseudopatients took field notes in their rooms. Other patients interpreted this as evidence that pseudopatients were actually undercover journalists or professors. Hospital staff, however, viewed it as pathological: "Patient engaged in writing behavior," read one nursing record. This reinforced Goffman's argument that, in a total institution, "seemingly normal conduct is seen to be merely a mask or shield for the essential sickness behind it." The pseudopatients had difficulty getting out. The average stay before discharge was nineteen days, with a range of seven to fifty-two days. When finally released, their discharge diagnosis was schizophrenia "in remission." "The normal are not detectably sane," Rosenhan concluded. Rosenhan's experiment and many other iconic psychology studies have come under twenty-first-century scrutiny for their replicability.[16] But Rosenhan and Goffman's arguments resonated with midcentury critical social scientists, who had begun to challenge psychiatric categories as fuzzy, even fictional.

Ironically, asylums were being emptied. Although the medicalization of mental illness was being amplified, Goffman, Rosenhan, and others wrote on the cusp of the deinstitutionalization movement in the United States. In later decades, as a result of deinstitutionalization, managed-care restrictions, and a faltering community mental health system, troubled individuals would have a harder time getting into mental hospitals than getting out of them.

Places, Territories, and the Difference Differences Made

Asylums relocated difference. They made it possible to move misfits, outsiders, and troubled individuals from their villages, towns, and families into new places of madness. Mental institutions became places for the social control of human differences. In the process, asylums and their practices could produce the very troubles and variations they intended to eliminate. Erving Goffman's focus on place—on the corners and territories within and outside of a brick-and-mortar asylum—was a powerful alternative to analyzing individual troubles by probing people's psyches. The focus instead was to explore the social power of their places.

How do we tell the stories of mental disturbances and institutionalization? Sociologist Jonathan Glover claims that Goffman wrote as though people had no "inner story."[17] However, in that midcentury cultural context of psychoanalytic narratives and growing psychiatric authority over stories of mental troubles and differences, *Asylums* demonstrated that there could be a different focus than on these inner stories. Goffman told stories, not about individual psychic interiors, but rather about the interiors of places.

If there were any question, Goffman's title—*Asylums: Essays on the Social Situation of Mental Patients and Other Inmates*—underscored his emphasis on places and situations that produce social and individual lives and problems. His taxonomy of total institutions included five ideal types of institutional places: those caring for "harmless" persons (such as orphanages); those caring for persons who represent a threat, albeit unintended (such as mental hospitals); those protecting communities from intentional danger (prisons, for example); those established to pursue a work task (for example, army barracks or boarding schools); and those serving as retreats from the world (such as monasteries.)

Goffman used place metaphors as a device to problematize the very idea of clear boundaries between sanity and insanity. Prefiguring anthropologist Mary Douglas's later argument that dirt is "matter out of place,"[18] Goffman described mental patients as people who had caused some sort of trouble on "the outside," having engaged in "conduct out of place in the setting." These kinds of behaviors were "situational improprieties," not biological deficiencies.

Goffman excelled at these metaphors of place, deploying them abundantly in *Asylums*. In addition to the obvious binaries of "outside" and "inside," he identified "free places," "underlives," "places of vulnerability," "damp corners," "walled-in" places, "social hothouses," "group territories," and more. His spatial metaphor, "territories of the self," reflected his focus on boundaries, public space and places, and social life. A key dynamic of his concept of total institutions was this violation of territories of the self. This included a range of mortifications whereby the individual was denied the ability to establish boundaries of selfhood. These constant intrusions taught the patient that "the self is not a fortress, but rather a small, open city."

Places operated as powerful social agents producing or constraining forms of behavior. Total institutions were sites of the collapse of boundaries between sleep, work, and play, where "all aspects of life are conducted in the same place." The social agency of buildings appeared in Goffman's analysis of everyday life within the places and spaces of asylum wards. For one, he argued that a total institution is "built right into the physical plant," such as locked cells, barbed-wire fences, and isolated settings protected by "water, forest, or moors." Buildings themselves operated as "walled-in organizations" that enforced obligations and imposed social control. This analysis belied the Kirkbride vision that architecture and design would produce healing.

Locally situational places played dramatic parts in asylums. Goffman's "free places" were scenes for taboo activities such as drinking or playing poker. These pop-up places might be constructed in woods, in far corners of the buildings, in basements, or on benches and chairs hidden in remote sections of the grounds. These places offered a certain freedom from the mortifications of the asylum. As Goffman put it, license "had a geography." He noted, "Our status is backed by the solid buildings of the world, while our sense of personal identity often resides in the cracks."

Mobility through places featured prominently in Goffman's analysis of the ward system. Again, buildings and wards held social meaning. Patients moved in and out of free places, and between desirable and less-desirable wards. Moreover, once institutionalized, individuals moved through a process of time and place that Goffman dubbed "the betrayal funnel," which stripped them of the freedom and personhood of life outside. In asylums, such a person is "gradually being transformed into a patient," in no small part through the social agency and practices of particular places.

Goffman's micro-analysis of places and interactions delivers the analytic punch of *Asylums*. His metaphoric analysis of place and practices showed, in broad generalizations, how deviance was constructed and then lived out. This underscored the role of social and interactional factors in the process of becoming deviant, representing an important approach to analyzing difference that was not based in biology. These epistemic challenges disrupted dominant medical models of mental illness.

Yet, unexplored by Goffman, asylums like St. Elizabeths were rife with larger, structural inequalities based on race, gender, and other social positions. Hierarchies were built into asylums, and reinforced by them. Social differences shaped interpretations of individual behavior, psychiatric diagnoses, and decisions about whether someone would be institutionalized and where they would be sent. Difference was emplaced. Once admitted, identity and status affected which buildings individuals were housed in and how they were treated. Difference, diagnosis, treatment, and placement were inextricable.

Definitions of sanity and insanity were historically framed by race. African Americans had been diagnosed with "drapetomania" for escaping slavery,[19] and after the Civil War were at risk of institutionalization for behavior viewed as transgressive. Likewise, the behavior of Native Americans was viewed through the prism of race and racism. Entire institutions were segregated. Early reformers such as Thomas Kirkbride reinforced institutionalized racism in the asylum movement by criticizing the "mixing up of all colors and classes" in mental hospitals.[20] A number of asylums were built solely for "insane Negroes," such as Crownsville State Hospital (originally named, until 1912, the Hospital for the Negro Insane of Maryland), Goldsboro Hospital for the Colored Insane (North Carolina), and Central State Hospital (Virginia). The Canton Asylum for Insane Indians housed indigenous people deemed insane. Like St. Elizabeths, Canton Asylum (also known as Hiawatha), which operated from 1903 to 1934, was a federally funded asylum.

The quality of facilities and treatment at asylums varied based on race.[21] At St. Elizabeths, residences were racially segregated and remained so through the 1950s, the period when Erving Goffman was there. A map from the period designates "colored" buildings for men and women. In 1929, Dr. Samuel Silk, Clinical Director of St. Elizabeths, was sent to investigate the Canton Asylum. Silk found appalling conditions, such as assaults, crippling restraints, and an absence of treatment. Significantly, he concluded that many of the patients were not, in fact, insane, but rather had clashed with White agencies or individuals and for that reason had been locked up. The Bureau of Indian Affairs shut down Canton in 1933. Many of the residents were declared sane and sent home. The rest were sent to St. Elizabeths.

Women and men could be institutionalized for transgression of gender and sexual conventions. Nonconforming behaviors as wide-ranging as depression, epilepsy, promiscuity, and sexual difference could be grounds for women's admission to mental hospitals, especially before 1900 but into the twentieth century as well. Feminist scholar Phyllis Chesler later argued that women were frequently diagnosed as mentally ill based on transgressions of gender, race, class, or sexual norms. Her pioneering book, *Women and Madness* (1972), appeared a decade after Goffman's *Asylums* was published. Likewise, both men and women were sometimes institutionalized for sexual nonconformity. This might entail having too much sex or sex with allegedly inappropriate partners.

St. Elizabeths' history shows how social class and status might also confer advantages. While most patients lived in wards that tended toward overcrowding, the wealthy Borrows family arranged for a house to be built on the hospital grounds for their daughter Sarah, who was diagnosed with premature dementia. Sarah lived in the expansive Burroughs Cottage from the time it was completed in 1881 until her death in 1917 (originally named for the family, it became known as Burroughs Cottage as a result of frequent misspellings.)

Similarly, American poet Ezra Pound's confinement at St. Elizabeths shows how artistic celebrity might shape diagnosis and treatment. Pound, who was indicted for treason in 1945 for anti–United States radio broadcasts, was committed to St. Elizabeths after being declared of "unsound mind."[22] His case illustrates disparities in institutional treatment. During his twelve years at the hospital, he received frequent visits from poets and writers such as Katherine Anne Porter, T. S. Eliot, and H. L. Mencken, holding salon-like sessions on the hospital lawn. Pound's commitment overlapped with Erving Goffman's year of field research. Did they ever meet? Writer J. J. Hill imagined that they had, in a screenplay he wrote, *And They Played Tennis in Hell*.[23] Hill wrote that he contacted Goffman's son, Tom, as well as one of Pound's frequent visitors; both sources told Hill that Pound and Goffman met at St. Elizabeths and played tennis together at least once. Regardless, it seems impossible that Goffman was unaware of the poet patient, his freedoms within the hospital, and the steady stream of famous literary visitors. Yet Goffman's analysis of total institutional life gave no hint that a patient such as Pound might have a comparatively rich experience there.

In addition, Pound's diagnosis was controversial. Although a 1945 court found him mentally unfit to stand trial, psychiatrists radically disagreed. Several psychiatrists involved in Pound's case examined him and found him to have no symptoms of mental illness. As one put it, "He definitely did not seem to be insane."[24] When discharged in 1958, St. Elizabeths superintendent Dr. Overholser said that Pound was incurably insane but that further institutionalization would serve no therapeutic purpose. Was Ezra Pound insane? This recalls David Rosenhan's question, "If sanity and insanity exist, how shall we know them?" The varied experiences of St. Elizabeths patients—from Sarah Borrow, to Ezra Pound, to Goffman's "inmates," to the Native Americans relocated there from Hiawatha—suggest how social identities, privilege, and bias shaped diagnosis and everyday life at St. Elizabeths.

Biographer Daniel Swift views Ezra Pound's release from St. Elizabeths in the context of deinstitutionalization. In 1955, when Goffman was at the asylum, it held over 7,000 patients. In 1956, 884 were released, 1,104 in 1957, and 1,076 in 1958 (one of whom was Pound). By 1959, 1,500 patients per year were discharged. As Swift notes, the hospital "was shrinking, and this is the context of Pound's release."[25] Discharge, from this perspective, wasn't about sanity or insanity. It was occasioned by historical changes in psychiatry and the impending collapse of institutionalization and asylums.

Marion Chace launched dance therapy at St. Elizabeths in 1942 and taught for several decades. In 1955, the year Erving Goffman conducted research there, the dance group produced a pageant based on the life of mental health reformer Dorothea Dix. Courtesy of St. Elizabeths Hospital Museum.

Critics charge Goffman with ignoring therapeutic developments at St. Elizabeths that might have undercut his portrait of institutional constraints and treachery. Beyond the anomalous richness of Ezra Pound's experiences there, St. Elizabeths offered farming and occupational therapy to some patients, and introduced treatment innovations such as dance therapy, art therapy, and psychodrama.[26] Patients also published internal newspapers and established ward governance. This "expressive culture"[27] is not featured in Goffman's *Asylums*. Still, historians also note that these treatment innovations would not have been widely available, and that patient dissatisfaction was not uncommon even among those who could access them. In a footnote, Goffman calculated that 100 of the total 7,000 patients at St. Elizabeths received individual psychotherapy in any one year. His resolute focus on institutional mortifications was consistent with a critical focus on social underdogs and how they are produced through practices and places.

Although the diagnosis and treatment of Goffman's inmates would have radically varied by structures such as race, class, gender, and sexuality, he did not address these disparities. As sociologist Ann Branaman notes, Goffman generally avoided debates about "the relationship between interaction and social structure," with the possible exception of social class.[28] These structural analyses of identity-based differences would come later to the social sciences. Yet, ironically, by stripping his underdogs of these social identities, by writing about them as the generic, falsely universal "he," or "a very sick guy,"[29] Goffman himself enacted the very mortifications of the self that he was critical of. His inmates were no longer different in different ways.

Goffman's Cultural Archive

In her analysis of the deep connections between early-twentieth-century Chicago urban literature and Chicago School sociology, literary critic Carla Cappetti notes that the two intellectual practices "held hands."[30] This close entanglement in storytelling about outsiders continued in midcentury, as represented by Goffman's *Asylums*. As with hobos and taxi dancers, the stories of madness and institutionalization triggered anxious attraction toward outsiders that not only captured the popular imagination but proved generative, and indeed profitable, for the culture industry.

Fear of and fascination with madness were in the air. Critical representations of asylums, insanity, and mental illness were widespread among midcentury journalists, novelists, artists, and filmmakers. The novel (1946) and film adaptation (1948), *The Snake Pit*, along with the films *Lost Weekend* (1945), *Shock Corridor* (1963), *Sunset Boulevard* (1950), and *Psycho* (1960), were prominent. Journalists and reformers published exposés of horrific conditions in mental hospitals, such as *The Shame of the States* (1948), by Albert Deutsch (which was published the same year the film *The Snake Pit* appeared). Psychiatrists and hospital staff were depicted as harsh, even evil, in novels such as Ken Kesey's *One Flew Over the Cuckoo's Nest* (1962), Sylvia Plath's *The Bell Jar* (1963), and Elliot Baker's *A Fine Madness* (1964). Sympathetic main characters, for example in *Diary of a Mad Housewife* (1966) and *Briefing for a Descent into Hell* (1971), contributed to the blurring of rigid boundaries between mental health and illness, while accounts such as actor Frances Farmer's autobiographical *Will There Really Be a Morning?* (1972) bolstered critiques of oppressive treatments such as lobotomies and electroshock therapy. Ethnographic photographer Diane Arbus shot appreciatively transgressive photographs of "freaks" (1962–1969). Documentary photographers such as Mary Ellen Mark exposed bleak conditions in mental hospitals. Photojournalism featuring patients peering out from the horrific dark regions of back-wards recalled images from the Nazi concentration camps. This milieu of cultural representation shaped Goffman's *Asylums*. (**See Hyperlink 5.2:** Ward 81.)

Ethnographic stories overlapped with artistic expression in the representation of difference and marginality. Goffman exemplified the blurring of boundaries among social research, the humanities, and popular culture, for two reasons. One, his own work was deeply literary. He wrote poetically, and perhaps partly for this reason, his work continues to find enthusiastic audiences far beyond sociology.[31] Second, Goffman used popular culture not just for inspiration, but also, crucially, as sociological evidence. Indeed, sociologist Charles Lemert noted that Goffman "composed in and around a bewildering collection of newspaper clippings, anecdotes, informal field notes, references to student papers alongside books and articles by those of presumably established repute, and such like."[32] He regularly cited fictional sources as evidence in his texts. (**See Hyperlink 5.3:** Goffman's Cultural Archive.)

Goffman's affinity for popular culture was legendary. In a recent interview, sociologist Sherri Cavan recounted how Goffman's text, *Gender Advertisements*,[33] was inspired by boxes of women's magazines that he bought at a flea market. (**See Hyperlink 5.4:** Sheri Cavan Interview.) (In her introduction to that book, writer Vivian Gornick wrote appreciatively of Goffman's work on gender advertisements, but stressed that it was feminists who influenced Goffman's choice of topic and shaped his analysis.) (**See Hyperlink 5.5:** Vivian Gornick Interview.)

In *Asylums* itself, Goffman cited thirteen novels and short stories. Occasionally he referred to a quote from a novel as a "report." He also quoted generously from memoirs, biographies, and magazine articles about prisons, concentration camps, the military, and convents. His literary sources ranged from the canonical—such as Herman Melville—to the contemporaneous. When, for example, he used the term "coming out" to describe a mental patient's entrance into the social life of the hospital, he cited James

Baldwin's *Giovanni's Room*, a novel that would later be embraced by a gay political movement. Goffman's literary archive shows how his critical analysis of mental hospitals was not only circulating in the broader culture industry, but was probably influenced by it.

The first novel Goffman cited in *Asylums* was *The Snake Pit*, the semi-autobiographical book by Mary Jane Ward (widely marketed to mainstream readers through its April 1946 selection by the Book-of-the-Month Club). Adapted into a 1948 film starring Olivia de Havilland, *The Snake Pit* described the institutionalization of a young, recently married woman writer, Virginia Cunningham. Described as hearing voices and having a "mind on vacation," Virginia was confined to Juniper Hill State Hospital, where she underwent a range of treatments from electroshock therapy, hypnotherapy, and hydrotherapy. She was released from the hospital after finally gaining self-understanding of her problems. Goffman cited the novel and not the film, but both were enormously successful; they have also been the subjects of contemporary criticism by feminist scholars for their gender bias in depicting sanity and normalcy.[34]

The Snake Pit prefigured several of Goffman's key arguments in *Asylums*. First, the novel and the film troubled the very notion of sanity. The back cover of the book noted, "It is as fascinating as a nightmare in which you, too, experience insanity, as tense and suspenseful as a mystery . . . and it points a very real moral for those of us who are presumably 'sane.'" In *The Snake Pit*, Virginia wondered, "Where will it all end? When there are more sick ones than well ones. The sick ones will lock the well ones up." Goffman, too, problematized the presumed reality of mental illness by calling his inmates "normal deviants."

Goffman's blistering critique of how institutions inflict mortifications of the self was very much consistent with this common theme in midcentury cultural production. *The Snake Pit*, while in some ways an optimistic portrayal of institutionalization, also depicted harsh nurses, degrading treatment, and coercive conditions. Virginia felt herself to be in a prison. In the film adaptation, Virginia's transfer to Ward 33, which warehoused patients in the worst condition, was depicted through scenes of chaos and terror (as Goffman noted, the "ward system" allowed for a great deal of mobility, as inmates moved in "bad as well as good directions").

Goffman used examples from this and other novels to embellish his critique of oppressive institutional bureaucracies. For example, he cited Herman Melville's *White Jacket* (1850) more than any other fictional work, a novel described as "both art and propaganda" in its indictment of abusive and cruel treatment in the Navy.[35] This theme of total institutions was also central to Ken Kesey's novel, *One Flew Over the Cuckoo's Nest*, published the year after *Asylums*, and iconic of the antipsychiatry movement. Another of his citations was the essay, "Report from the Asylum," by Carl Solomon, a poet and one of "the Beat Generation's angry young men."[36] Allen Ginsberg's famous poem, "Howl," was dedicated to Solomon, whom Ginsberg befriended in a mental hospital. Solomon's essay about his confinement at Greystone Park Psychiatric Hospital in New York State was a lacerating critique of ineffective treatments such as shock therapy and "the psychiatric ineptitude" of staff.[37] Overall, Goffman's cultural archive constituted a dystopia of asylums and psychiatry. Still, this booming cultural production about madness reflected an ongoing audience and market for the selling of outsider stories.

Deinstitutionalization and Collapse

A century after the optimistic movement for moral architecture in the treatment of mental illness, support for asylums began to collapse. By 1956, voluntary admissions to St. Elizabeths outnumbered involuntary commitments for the first time. Historian Thomas Otto suggests that new psychiatric medications either prevented institutionalization or allowed for earlier discharge.[38] The emergence of drugs such as chlorpromazine (marketed as Thorazine) is an oft-cited cause of the deinstitutionalization movement. However, this analysis assumes biological factors in mental illness, controlled by medication. Rather, a convergence of dynamics fostered the collapse of the asylum system, including synergistic challenges from critical sociology, political advocates, and popular culture.

Indeed, Thorazine did play an outsized, albeit problematic, role in the lives of patients and asylums. Synthesized in the late nineteenth century, the chemical compound failed to effectively treat the conditions on which it was tested, such as control of nausea or skin problems. The eventual discovery of its sedative effects, however, led to its rapid introduction into mental institutions. Although initially tested on only 104 patients at the end of 1953, it had been prescribed for over two million psychiatric patients a year later.[39] It was approved by the Food and Drug Administration in 1954, and along with a range of spin-off drugs, heavily marketed to practitioners in journals such as *Mental Hospitals* and the *Archives of General Psychiatry*.

Thorazine controlled behavior on the hospital wards, yet it produced what some described as a chemical lobotomy.[40] Dr. Winfred Overholser, the superintendent of St. Elizabeths at the time of its introduction there, noted that the drug "revolutionized" disturbed wards and radically improved hospital life.[41] In other words, patients were sedated into compliance. This was 1956, the year when Erving Goffman conducted his research there.

Thorazine advertisements reveal the outsized promises of its marketers. It was hailed as the solution to an improbable range of conditions such as violence, alcoholism, agitation, bursitis, stress, and more. Yet ads for the new psychotropic drugs also depicted the use of pharmaceuticals as a means to enforce pernicious racial and gender norms. Rebellious women could be soothed back to the kitchen while psychiatric medication might well control "assaultive and belligerent" African Americans.[42] Psychiatric drug advertisements of that era, now widely displayed and mocked online as though ancient artifacts, appear out of touch with the contemporaneous social change movements such as civil rights, feminism, and political challenges to psychiatric medicalization.

In the fifties and sixties, political activists in the antipsychiatry movement, the lesbian and gay movement, the feminist movement, and others criticized psychiatric labeling, enforcement of social norms, and institutionalization. The Insane Liberation Front was the first activist group, emerging in Portland, Oregon, in 1969. Others followed, including the Mental Patients Liberation Front and the Network Against Psychiatric Assault. The antipsychiatry movement challenged a politics of stigma and diagnosis that pathologized nonconformity and individual differences. Activists recounted their own experiences with institutionalization, citing critiques by Goffman, R. D. Laing, and others. Critical psychiatrist Thomas Szasz, for example, denied the reality of mental illness and saw psychiatry as a pseudoscience. Publications such as *Madness Network News*, run by former patients, disseminated antipsychiatry critiques and fostered coalitions, supporting, for example, gay protests against the American Psychiatric Association's classification of homosexuality as a psychiatric disorder.[43]

Some historians argue that despite new medications and cultural challenges to the asylum system, it was ultimately fiscal concerns that drove the deinstitutionalization movement.[44,45] Andrew Scull, for example, notes that census rates at mental hospitals had begun to decline prior to the introduction of new psychoactive drugs.[46] Maintaining such sprawling campuses was prohibitively expensive in the absence of state and federal government support. Asylums began to empty their buildings, sending patients to community mental health centers, veteran's centers, or out onto the streets. By 1978, St. Elizabeths' population had dropped to 1,200.

Goffman's ethnographic stories of deviant institutional places told different stories about the marginal people and behaviors they housed. These stories not only challenged epistemic narratives in which emotional and behavioral disturbances were classified, measured, defined as biological deficiencies, and targeted for elimination. Different stories also helped foster social-policy change concerning the treatment of sufferers. *Asylums* was cited in legal briefs and judicial decisions related to conditions at mental hospitals, and Goffman has been identified as important to the antipsychiatry and the deinstitutionalization movement.[47] In 1970, he cofounded the American Association for the Abolition of Involuntary Mental Hospitalization, which sought to abolish involuntary and abusive commitment.[48]

Conclusion

Goffman has been described as a "revered" figure, and "an outlaw theorist who came to exemplify the best of the sociological imagination."[49] His sociology has been the subject of extensive, sometimes critical, commentary. Noteworthy is the reality question—did Goffman posit mental illness as real, or "merely" as socially constructed, an invention of social-control agents? Later social constructionist and postmodern scholars would face similar criticisms that they minimized the reality of individual and social problems. Some asked whether his wife's emotional difficulties and 1964 suicide might have shifted his perspective over time.[50] However, *Asylums* has weathered criticism for theoretical oversimplification and methodological shortcomings, and still ranks as a canonical text in the social sciences and humanities.[51] By blurring supposedly clear boundaries between sanity and insanity, Goffman and other scholars challenged how medical, biological, and psychiatric determinism crept into more and more corners of daily life to frame troubles as individual rather than social problems.

More than a half-century after its publication, *Asylums* remains culturally resonant. Total institutions and institutional social control persist. Indeed, Goffman's comparison of asylums to prisons looks prescient in this age of mass incarceration. As we will see in upcoming chapters, he influenced younger sociologists, such as Laud Humphreys and Goffman's doctoral student Sherri Cavan, who continued in this tradition of telling better and different stories about difference.

Today, the east campus of St. Elizabeths still houses residential patients. The most prominent, the would-be assassin of Ronald Reagan, John Warnock Hinkley Jr., was quietly released from St. Elizabeths in September 2016. The west campus now houses the massive U.S. Department of

Homeland Security. Other asylums throughout the United States, including many of the famous Kirkbride buildings, have been closed, razed, or repurposed for housing and industry. Some now host museums charting their history, such as Oregon State Hospital.

While asylums are largely shuttered, they remain compelling settings in popular culture. Recent examples include season 3 of Ryan Murphy's *American Horror Story*, entitled "Asylum" (set in a 1964 institution for the criminally insane); Madeleine Roux's bestselling *Asylum* series (featuring archival photographs from actual asylums); the film *Unsane*, which blurs the line between sanity and insanity; and the Netflix series *Ratched*, which purportedly tells the backstory of Nurse Ratched, from *One Flew Over the Cuckoo's Nest*. The haunting attraction to, and fear of, outsiders and marginality remain powerful.

Ultimately, *Asylums* is more than an indictment of total institutions. Goffman had firmly located himself on the side of a precarious underdog. He stressed that the inevitable accumulation of denigrating facts and ordinary failures to embody social norms puts all of us on the precipice of stigma. It is no surprise that outsiders saw him as an intellectual ally. Goffman's claim that we are all vulnerable to medical labeling struck a cultural nerve. His warning that misfits and rule-breakers could be locked up and broken was a cautionary tale. In exploring the "places of vulnerability," the "underlife," and the "damp corners" of asylums, Goffman wrote dark poetry of insane places, capturing the nuanced worlds of outsiders, transgression, and marginality.

Hyperlink 5.1: Thomas Scheff

Thomas Scheff is professor emeritus in the Department of Sociology at the University of California, Santa Barbara. Erving Goffman was one of his mentors during his graduate program at the University of California, Berkeley. Scheff's first book, based on the dissertation research he discusses below, is *Being Mentally Ill: A Sociological Theory*, published in 1966. We talked in his office at UC Santa Barbara on May 14, 2014.

> Thomas Scheff (TS): I was in Berkeley, I had shifted from physics, I had three years of graduate study in physics at Berkeley but I was bored. . . . Erving Goffman was actually my advisor for my dissertation. I arranged to spend about six months at Stockton State Hospital in Stockton, California, about an hour's drive, before I went on to my first job at University of Wisconsin. So I got to the

hospital and I wandered around the admittance wards—they had a male and a female—it was a regular hospital, there was no problem. But then when I started fumbling around in the back-wards, I couldn't make out what was about. There were no doctors, no nurses, and as far as I could see, no treatment. People were sitting around all day. And I didn't know how to get a dissertation out of that. So I made an appointment with Erving and I drove back and I'm telling him about these back-wards where as far as I can tell there's nothing going on. So he let me say about three or four sentences and then he said, "Read [Edwin] Lemert." I said "What?" He said, "Read Lemert. It's a book called *Social Pathology*. There's a chapter in there about mental illness." I was a little disappointed—he gave me five minutes time. Goffman was very short with me sometimes because he knew that I didn't understand him. I was his teaching assistant for a while, and the undergraduates in the class understood him, but us TAs we didn't get it. We were in over our heads. So I went back and I could understand everything from Lemert's point of view. And that's how I got started in the sociology of deviant behavior, by writing on what I saw in the back-wards. And then I went on to some other mental hospitals. A couple of them in California, one in Wisconsin, one in England that I got to know very well. And one in Rome where they let me in the first day and that was the end, they wouldn't let me in again. But I got a glimpse of what was going on in there, and I was just as glad not to have to watch it. I wrote up the dissertation and then in Wisconsin, the legislature wanted a survey of the mental health system there and they had lots of mental hospitals. Nobody else volunteered so I did it. They gave me enough money to pay an RA. And he was very good, a social work graduate student. And we looked into the system all over Wisconsin. My RA went into some of the back-wards in other state mental hospitals which were just like California. So on the basis of this material I had gathered there, I wrote *Being Mentally Ill*.

Janice Irvine: Did you feel that it ever had policy implications?

TS: Oh yes. In the state of California there was a series of hearings about, not mental illness, but retardation. And the guy that ran them was a brilliant congressman whose name will come to me in a minute. And when they finished with retardation, they took on mental illness and somehow this guy saw my report to the Wisconsin legislature, which they had rejected; they said "It couldn't be that bad." They rejected it, they refused to believe it. But he got the report and he got me to come to the hearing. And when I started talking, that controlled the whole hearing. And they said "Well, we're gonna fix that in California. We're gonna close the state mental hospitals because we don't want them prisons masquerading as a hospital," and that's what happened. I feel like I had done some good with my work.

Hyperlink 5.2: Ward 81

Like contemporaries such as Diane Arbus, documentary photographer Mary Ellen Mark focused her artistic attention on social marginality. Raised in suburban Philadelphia, she moved to New York City in the late sixties, where she photographed antiwar demonstrations, the culture of Times Square, and people with a range of social problems such as homelessness and addiction. One reviewer of her work noted that she photographed those outside of the mainstream, focusing on the troubled fringes. She became a unit photographer, shooting production stills on movie sets such as *Alice's Restaurant* (1969) and *Catch-22* (1970).

In 1971, Mark was the still photographer on Milos Forman's *One Flew Over the Cuckoo's Nest*, filmed at Oregon State Hospital. During this period, she visited Ward 81, the women's maximum-security ward, to which she would return several years later. In 1976, Mark teamed up with social scientist Karen Folger Jacobs to photograph and interview the women on Ward 81.[52] They lived on Ward 81 for thirty-six days. By the end, both experienced the blurring of boundaries between sanity and insanity. They noted, "We felt the degeneration of our own bodies and the erosion of our self-confidence. We were horrified at the thought of what we might become after a year or two of confinement and therapy on Ward 81."[53] This description captured the essence of Erving Goffman's notion of the total institution.

The collaboration between Mary Ellen Mark and Karen Folger Jacobs was emblematic of the entanglements of artistic and ethnographic observation. This melding of art, politics, and social science in making visible the back-wards of asylums was consistent with broader critiques of the era.

Ward 81 closed in November, 1977, becoming part of a coeducational treatment ward.

Hyperlink 5.3: Goffman's Cultural Archive

Erving Goffman drew on the following literary sources as evidence in his canonical text, *Asylums: Essays on the Social Situation of Mental Patients and Other Inmates*.

Nigel Balchin, *Private Interests* (Boston: Houghton Mifflin, 1953).
James Baldwin, *Giovanni's Room* (New York: Dial, 1956).
Fyodor Dostoyevsky, *Memoirs from the House of the Dead*, trans. Jessie Coulson (London: Oxford University Press, 1956).
Sara Harris, *The Wayward Ones* (New York: New American Library, 1952).
Bernard Malamud, *The Assistant* (New York: New American Library, 1958).
Herman Melville, *White Jacket* (New York: Grove Press, n.d.) [This is how Goffman cites the book; it was originally published in 1850].
Thomas Merton, *The Seven Storey Mountain* (New York: Harcourt, Brace and Company, 1948).
John M. Murtagh and Sara Harris, *Cast the First Stone* (New York: Pocket Books, 1958).
Albert M. Ottenheimer, "Life in the Gutter," *New Yorker*, August 15, 1959.
P. R. Reid, *Escape from Colditz* (New York: Berkley Publishing Corp., 1956).
Isaac Rosenfeld, "The Party," *Kenyon Review*, Autumn 1947, pp. 572–607.
Mary Jane Ward, *The Snake Pit* (New York: New American Library, 1955).
Angus Wilson, "Saturnalia," in *The Wrong Set* (New York: William Morrow, 1950).

Hyperlink 5:4 Sherri Cavan: "Having Been Goffman's Student I Am Drawn to Voltaire's Dictum, 'To the Living We Owe Respect, to the Dead We Owe Only the Truth'"

The excerpt from this interview with Sherri Cavan, professor emerita of sociology at San Francisco State University, was recorded over the phone on November 30, 2008. Cavan was a doctoral student of Erving Goffman at the University of California, Berkeley. The interview was conducted as part of Bios Sociologicus: The Erving Goffman Archives. Dmitri Shalin transcribed the interview, after which Dr. Cavan edited the transcripts and gave her approval for posting the present version in the Erving Goffman Archives. Breaks in the conversation flow are indicated by ellipses.

> Sherri Cavan (SC): One of the ways we got along was that he liked to go to garage sales and flea markets, and I liked to go to garage sales and flea markets, so we would meet at these places sometimes. There was a wonderful flea market in Alameda, and I would run into him there. On one of his trips, he found a couple of boxes

full of women's magazines, and that was the whole basis of *Gender Advertisements*—two or three boxes of women magazines. Of course, if you have never seen a woman's magazine it looks like a foreign country. About that time Lenore Weitzman did a groundbreaking study which was presented here in San Francisco, maybe at the Society for the Study of Social Problems. Anyway, she had taken children's books and had analyzed the pictures in children's books with respect to sex roles.

That's the presentation Goffman picked up on. He had these enormous resources—big boxes of women's magazines. I am not sure, it is not easy to make something into slides, I understand it is much easier today, but in the old days you had to do photographic slides. He must have had thousands of slides made up.

Dmitri Shalin (DS): Some were published in *Gender Advertisements*.

SC: Yes, some of them were published in *Gender Advertisements*, and some of them were published just as he ripped them out, which was always amazing to me—they were willing to publish such shoddy visual images [Laughing]. I mean, some were Xeroxed. I had reservations with that book. Anyway, at that time . . . it must have been after 1965 because I was already teaching in San Francisco State. . . . The women's movement was just beginning, and there was a group of women, mainly here in the Bay Area, who had put together "Sociologists for Women and Society." Because I knew Goffman, they asked me if I could invite Goffman to make a presentation of anything at one of their meetings. He said he would do it, because he wanted to have an audience to present all of his slides, his mind-boggling, unedited slides.

The presentation was at my house. He was testy, as usual. First, he was pissed off because I couldn't make the room dark enough, which really pissed me off. I had gone to great effort to set everything up. I think, now, upon reflection, he was nervous—he was going to make a presentation about women's sex roles in front of an audience of women who knew about those matters in an intimate way. As an outsider, he would tell them things they never saw before.

[Laughter].

So he had this captive audience. I don't know, there must have been thirty women, almost all of them sociologists, PhD sociologists, not even students at that time. And he presented all of this material, talked about what he saw and he elicited discussion about what the people were seeing. That eventually became the basis for *Gender Advertisements*.

Bios Sociologicus: The Erving Goffman Archives, Dmitri N. Shalin, ed. (Las Vegas: University of Nevada–Las Vegas: CDC Publications, 2007–2017).

Hyperlink 5.5: Vivian Gornick Interview

Vivian Gornick is an author, essayist, and memoirist whose work was influential in the early feminist movement in the late 1960s. Her most recent book is *Unfinished Business: Notes of a Chronic Re-reader* (2020). She wrote the introduction to Erving Goffman's book, *Gender Advertisements*, published in 1972. On July 25, 2016, I interviewed Gornick at her New York City apartment. Below are excerpts from that conversation.

> Janice Irvine: I'll start by asking how you came to write the introduction for *Gender Advertisements*?
>
> Vivian Gornick: You know, it was interesting, he asked for me, and I was so flattered. The book was being published by Harper's I think, and Erving Goffman actually asked for me. At that point I was, like, a culture hero in the pages of the *Village Voice*, and was hot, and we were hot radical feminists on the barricades for radical feminism. And he, to his credit—we gave him his subject. He picked it up from us, and he was able to turn his peculiar point of view to our benefit, his own and ours. And you could see clearly, you would never have come up with this whole schema in his head about power arrangements in advertising if it wasn't for feminism. And he took the ball and ran. So, I was really thrilled when they approached me and said "Goffman would like you to write the Introduction."
>
> Then I had the worst problem imaginable—one of the times in my life that this has happened to me as a journalist, and it's a measure of my own insecurity, which went on for years and goes on to this day—I, to my own amazement, was intimidated by his scholarship. And you know when I found out that he himself was considered a maverick, and he was tortured by his own department for not having methodology down right, you know, I thought Jesus Christ, life is an endless schema of insecurity and not belonging. That was his thing. I often wished I would have met him, and then I thought, "No, better not to have met him, he's probably as

weird as he writes." I don't mean weird, that's not a word I usually use, but strange. I would have thought him unsociable and I don't know, I may be wrong, but anyway those are the thoughts I had. So, what happened, though, was I got intimidated by it and I couldn't find my voice. I couldn't find a way in. I kept writing this thing, and it was as if I was channeling academic prose. And the man in my life at the time read it and said, "What the hell are you doing? What are you, competing with this guy? Why are you feeling that you have to mimic his prose?" And so I really struggled to find my own voice, as they say, and to write as simply and as accurately as I could what this work meant to me.

But I was thrilled by the clear political relation between his art and our politics. And he really, he did brilliantly with it. I mean, he had so many different ways of looking at the up and the down of male and female, in advertising. It was a thrill. Every feminist I knew was just deeply gratified by the book. And I did then begin to think about what a life he had made out of looking at—I wouldn't have called it deviance, but what I would have said was, well like what's his name? Frederick Wiseman does. They look to the underside of life institutionally and politically. Not that they think it's the underside. They don't think the people that they are addressing or looking at are the underside. And that's the brilliance of the work. They are looking at the humanity in the inmates of institutions. And we had considered ourselves inmates, yes, of Western society. Inmates of the institutions. And if we hadn't seen it that way, it was like we were looking from inside the bars out at the world. And these guys saw it the same way. There's a very famous story by Chekov called "Ward Six." Supposedly—I'm sure this story's apocryphal—but supposedly Lenin, he was asked, "What work of Russian literature drove your revolution?" or you know, compelled you to it, and he said "Ward Six." "Ward Six" is the story of a doctor who lives in—the man of culture gone mad in the provinces. He's the doctor of a clinic in a provincial part of Russia, and the whole town is like something out of the French bourgeoisie of the nineteenth century, something like out of Flaubert, the incredible weirdness, the boring inanity of village life. But he runs a clinic, he runs a hospital, and in it is Ward Six, which is for the mad. And it turns out the only man in town he can talk to is the guy in Ward Six, who, he's mad but not stupid. So, the doctor holds these very intelligent conversations with this mad man, and he's full of proper bourgeois response to him. He loves talking to him, he doesn't know why, but he still thinks he's mad and he belongs where he is. And the doctor himself goes mad. And he's put into Ward Six. And the whole point of the story is, you don't understand what it's all about until you're there. Until you yourself are in the position. And that's what Lenin, of course, said about revolution. Nobody will understand how we feel until they are there. And I look upon Goffman in the same light as the doctor. But he understood, he had the emotional imagination.

SIX

Tearoom Trade

Tales of Public Sex

> Simple observation is enough to guide these participants, the researcher, and, perhaps, the police to active tearooms.[1]
>
> Laud Humphreys

By midcentury, outsiders were more culturally visible. New political movements challenged oppressive social structures, while despite conservative backlash, a youth counterculture transgressed conventionality. Subcultures of defiance flourished. The study of social outsiders was burgeoning, and graduate students influenced by new social theories of deviance explored rich ethnographic sites in that fabled era of sex, drugs, and rock-'n'-roll. However, sociologist Laud Humphreys would learn that observing these outsiders was far from simple.

Tearoom Trade: Impersonal Sex in Public Places (1970) examined sexual activity in public toilets (a practice known as "tea-rooming" in US gay slang and "cottaging" in British English; in Australia the toilets are called "beats"[2]). Laud Humphreys explored an exclusively male sexual subculture that operated outside of the normative confines of the nuclear family and, importantly, outside of cultural assumptions about homosexuality and heterosexuality. Although Humphreys used the term "homosexual encounters" in his dissertation, he changed the subtitle for the book, separating the sexual acts of the men from identity labels. The book disaggregated traditional classifications between sexual behaviors and identities, a con-

Book cover of a 1975 enlarged edition of *Tearoom Trade: Impersonal Sex in Public Places*. At this point the book had won the prestigious C. Wright Mills Award and had been the subject of intense controversy.

ceptual move that prefigured queer theory. (**See Hyperlink 6.1:** Women and the Early Gay Canon.) This critical distinction was lost on much of the mainstream, where *Tearoom Trade*, even now, is generally considered a book about homosexual men.

Heavily influenced by the ideas of Erving Goffman, *Tearoom Trade* examined complex presentations of sexual selves. The book flung open the closet doors of the tearoom, demystifying the occupants and destigmatizing their activities. It was a vivid ethnographic portrait of the marginal culture of public sex; a thick description of how place produces the social norms and interactions of the tearoom; a study of the structural locations of the men who frequent the tearoom; a critique of repressive and ineffectual sex laws; and a condemnation of sexual shame. Humphreys explored the dehumanizing operations of stigma, while putting an everyman face on the men who pursue sexual pleasure in public places, where the boundaries of outsider and insider blurred. Perhaps most strikingly, he showed how marginal sexuality is a deeply social accomplishment, rather than a biologically determined essence.

Cultural critic Michael Bronski notes that in the mid- to late sixties, the American public "was intrigued and titillated by the exposure of 'new' sex lives and the stories kept coming."[3] These new sexual stories were told by a mix of social science researchers, artists and writers, and political activists. Yet the shifting sexual culture did not save Humphreys from backlash. Of all the ethnographies discussed in this book, Humphreys's study of sex in public places provoked the most controversy about observation, and storytelling. It was perhaps sociological history's most controversial dissertation. The book triggered outrage that nearly resulted in the revocation of Humphreys's doctorate by the chancellor of Washington University. The *Washington Post* denounced Humphreys as a "sociological snooper," and his text remains a poster child of alleged ethical violations in social research. (**See Hyperlink 6.2:** Sex, Tearoom Trade, and the IRB.)

The stories Laud Humphreys told about men who sought anonymous public sex decisively broke with race science and eugenic scripts of biological determinism, degeneracy, and pathology. In an earlier era, and even throughout the sixties, both men and women could be institutionalized for nonnormative sexual behavior. Against the grain of this social control, Humphreys argued that sex, even public sex among men, is not inherently problematic. Influenced by deviance theories, he claimed it is moral entrepreneurs who have defined it as such. Moreover, Humphreys destabilized seemingly fixed biological sexual categories. *Tearoom Trade*'s pioneering, prequeer findings demonstrated that deviant places, and the public sex inside them, have a culture. A meticulous piece of research, *Tearoom Trade* answered Howard Becker's call that sociologists, who "usually take the side of the underdog," should nonetheless ensure that their research meets rigorous social scientific standards.[4] This chapter explores the different stories *Tearoom Trade* told, in the book's historical context of an unsettled sexual culture and the rise of radical sexual politics on both the left and the right.

The Social Production of Sex

Laud Humphreys began his dissertation research on the social organization of the tearoom in 1965, a time of volatile civil-rights activity and social change. A former Episcopalian minister, he was a committed progressive activist, once spending months in jail after an arrest at a draft-board demonstration. The sexual culture was shifting rapidly, but unevenly. The midsixties saw the founding of the Sex Information and Education Council of the United States, which advocated for comprehensive sex education programs for young people that would embrace sexual pleasure and refuse moralism. The more radical New York League for Sexual Freedom, also founded in 1964, demanded decriminalization of oral and anal intercourse, interracial marriage, and bestiality and called for reformation of a range of restrictive laws against censorship, public nudity, divorce, and contraception. Feminist sexual politics, the Stonewall riots of 1969, and the rise of gay liberation would effect profound upheavals in the sexual and political landscapes by the end of the decade. At the same time, a mix of secular and religious conservatives and right-wing activists coalesced politically to oppose these social changes. Diverse sexualities, increasingly popular research domains within the academy, were also targets of these new culture warriors.

Sex research became culturally visible in midcentury. Academic books by the towering figures of sexology—biologist Alfred Kinsey, physician William Masters, and his associate Virginia Johnson—became publishing-industry blockbusters. Following the success of Kinsey's two volumes on male and female sexuality, Masters and Johnson released *Human Sexual Response* in 1966.[5] Although a commercial success, the book also generated disapproval for its innovative methods of observing and measuring sexual activity in their laboratory. Kinsey, Masters and Johnson, and Laud Humphreys all faced controversy about their research. Laud Humphreys's diary shows that he met with William Masters to consult on ethics and confidentiality related to the tearoom study, and that Masters warned him to protect tearoom identities and not to trust the university chancellor.

This advice, probably based on Masters's own difficulties conducting his research, seems prescient, given the furor Humphreys later faced. The academic study of sexuality in that era was—paradoxically—vibrant, disreputable, wildly popular, and somewhat underground.

There is a voluminous literature on the long prehistory to Humphreys's tearoom research. This thumbnail sketch underscores the uneven landscape of sexual knowledge and social control practices into which Laud Humphreys ventured. Same-sex sexuality has a long discursive history, framed multifariously as sin, crime, and sickness. These frameworks overlapped historically as mechanisms of social control and condemnation. By the late nineteenth century, the medicalization of sexuality produced new classification systems, diagnostic schemas, and vocabularies that brought sex into the domain of health and illness. Medicalization, as Ian Hacking argues, was an engine for making up people. Homosexuals and heterosexuals were among these new social types.[6] After sexologists invented the terms "homosexuality" and "heterosexuality," they disagreed about their precise definitions. In particular, they debated whether homosexuality was biologically determined or socially produced. Sexual modernists such as Havelock Ellis argued that homosexuality was congenital and therefore natural, and should be decriminalized and destigmatized. Others, such as Richard von Krafft-Ebing, viewed inversion as both congenital and acquired, as well as pathological.

Scientific racism, biological and medico-psychiatric theories of sex, and a presumed immutability of sexual deviance interlocked. Sexual difference broadly construed was a key target of biologically-based eugenic practices to improve the race. For example, reproduction by those considered undesirable based on race and ethnicity, mental status, social class, and other differences was curbed through forced sterilization and birth control. Those engaging in same-sex behaviors and other sexual deviance could be readily institutionalized. The Nazi genocide of the Jews, and also lesbians, gay men, and other outsiders, was a culmination of determinist scientific theories about racial and sexual difference.

As sexologists continued to debate the biological basis of same-sex desire and behavior, sociologists and anthropologists pushed back against sexual determinism. Ethnographies showed the social influences on sexuality across cultures and over different historical periods. Noteworthy, in this brief review, are certain anthropologists who argued for the cultural relativism of sexuality. Margaret Mead, for example, framed youth sexuality as produced and constrained by cultures, roles, and norms. Anthropologist Zora Neale Hurston layered stories of the sexual worlds of Southern African Americans from her field research into her literature. In their 1951 text, *Patterns of Sexual Behavior*, anthropologists Clellan Ford and Frank Beach compiled an exhaustive text of cross-cultural sexual behavior that underscored sexual relativism and influenced later sex researchers.[7] Still, anthropologist Gayle Rubin argues that, despite this scholarship, anthropology was "oddly parochial in resisting the study of sexuality."[8] It was the Chicago School, she notes, that produced the pioneering ethnographies of sexuality.

Chicago sociologists challenged biological and psychological theories that depicted sex as dangerous and sexual deviants as societal threats. Faculty, graduate students, and undergraduates at the University of Chicago ventured into the modern city to explore urban sexual worlds. Historian Chad Heap has extensively documented this work about bars, gangs, prostitutes, hobos, dancers, homosexuality, and many more topics related to sexuality. W. I. Thomas, Robert Park, Ernest Burgess, Walter Reckless, and other prominent Chicago figures all examined sexuality in the context of the new metropolis. Graduate students Nels Anderson and Paul G. Cressey frankly took up the sex lives of hobos, and of the men and women in Chicago's taxi-dance halls. This work was entangled with antivice and social reform crusaders. Despite certain moralistic overtones, these published texts and archival papers exist today as unique historical evidence of early sexual worlds in a major US city.

Regardless of the controversies that engulfed Humphreys and his book, *Tearoom Trade* fits comfortably within this ethnographic tradition, these critical theories, and this interpretive social research into diverse social worlds. New deviance theories and symbolic interactionism enabled researchers to resist biological science, undermine discourses of fixed sexual identity, and argue that social and cultural factors were central in shaping sexuality. In 1954, sociologist Manford Kuhn wrote, "In short, the sexual motives which human beings have are derived from the social roles they play . . . physiology does not supply the motives, designate the partners, invest the objects with performed passion, nor even dictate the objectives to be achieved."[9] Studies by Albert Reiss, Maurice Leznoff and William Westley, and John Gagnon and William Simon further advanced social theories of sexuality, undermining determinist theories and the categorization of distinct homosexual and heterosexual types.[10] They reinforced biologist Alfred Kinsey's argument that everyone had the "capacity" for homosexuality: "the world is not to be divided into sheep and goats."[11] The growing social scientific view was that sexuality was far more unruly than that. (**See Hyperlink 6.3**: Albert Reiss: Queers and Peers.)

Laud Humphreys was both a pioneer and a student of these different ways of thinking about sexuality and homosexuality. He, too, wrote against the grain of biological determinism. Unique to Laud Humphreys's scholarly contribution was his empirical evidence. Like Masters and Johnson, who observed sex in the laboratory, Humphreys observed sex in the tearooms. Unlike Masters and Johnson, who observed individuals or heterosexual couples, he observed same-sex activity, making his study far more taboo. He also told ethnographic rather than medical stories. Masters and Johnson had narrated the physiological sexual body—the heart rates, blood pressures, and muscle tensions of sex. By contrast, Humphreys told stories of the social body, of the places, norms, strategies, pleasures, and disappointments of impersonal public sex. He recounted the logics, ambiguities, and complexities of the social organization of the tearooms.

Well before the fierce academic battles of the eighties over social constructionism and essentialism, Laud Humphreys challenged assumptions about fixed, congenital sexual identities. The tearoom—a restroom in which men engaged in oral sex with other men—would seemingly be the quintessential homosexual site. However, Humphreys separated the sexual acts the men engaged in from any assumption about who they were or how they identified themselves. He stressed that his book was "not a study of 'homosexuals' but of participants in homosexual acts." This argument, consistent with Alfred Kinsey's, preceded queer theory's similar theoretical contribution by decades.

Tearoom Trade depicted a kaleidoscope of sexual fluidity. It showed how sexualities, like the "self" of the symbolic interactionists, emerged in interaction. And, like the social actors on Erving Goffman's stage, individuals performed their sexual lives. The men shifted from insertor to insertee with alacrity, such "role drift" sometimes happening during a single encounter. Humphreys explained, "By 'instability' of a role, I mean its observed tendency to melt, slip, fuse, or drift into another of the standard roles. This tendency is manifested regardless of who may take up that role in the course of an encounter. The role of the 'straight' is transient. In a deviant encounter, this label is not adhesive; it does not stick to a person for an extended period of time." Myriad factors might account for such role drift.

Humphreys discussed influences such as aging, attractiveness, style, or personal preference. But he underscored that the structural pressures of risk and exposure in the tearoom made it necessary that men be able to move quickly among a variety of roles. This fluidity meant that it could not be determined who played which role until the absolute end of the sexual act—the payoff. The roles of the many actors unfolded in the interaction:

"The players (insertees and insertors) are identifiable only in the sex act; waiters—and even straights—may be transformed into players; chicken may turn out to be hustlers, toughs, straights, or participants; social control agents (nearly always in plain clothes) are generally identifiable only when disaster strikes."

Nor did physical activities of inserting or receiving have stable meaning. Humphreys noted that, consistent with "straight society," he had assumed that the insertor would be the aggressor and the insertee would be the passive actor. Yet his data undermined this notion. His observations showed that the insertee was the "aggressor," the person who initiated the act, in almost half of the sexual events. He concluded that "active" and "passive" were "systems of strategy" rather than an inherent characteristic of the players involved.

In the world of the tearoom, sexual categories and meanings were contingent and plural, not stable and singular. These empirical findings foreshadowed the arguments of poststructuralists and queer theorists by several decades. Identity was not inherent in the activity, and he stressed the diversity of his subjects: "Many men—married and unmarried, those with heterosexual identities and those whose self-image is a homosexual one—seek such impersonal sex, shunning involvement, desiring kicks without commitment." As we see later, this dynamic played out repeatedly in sex scandals on the public stage.

Public Sex in Public Parks

Tearoom Trade is a classic study of public sex in the city. Scholars have extensively explored histories of the myriad places for public sex, such as parks, restrooms, and theaters—what historian Steven Maynard calls the "sexual underground."[12] Although sometimes overlooked, *Tearoom Trade* was one of the earliest such studies. It predated, but anticipated, the "spatial turn" in its emphasis on how places produce social meanings and behaviors. An important contribution of the study was exploration of how sexual practices are constructed by, and lived out within, specific places and spaces.

In *Tearoom Trade*, Laud Humphreys told stories about marginal buildings and the men who visited and repurposed them. Like a good host, he invited us into these places, described the facilities, introduced the other guests, and indicated the proper way to behave in these settings. His research question itself, initially posed by his dissertation adviser, Lee Rainwater, centered on place—"Where does the average guy go to get a blowjob?" The question also assumed that average guys engaged in supposedly outsider sexual activity. Humphreys initially explored various locales where average men sought what he called "instant sex," such as bathhouses and movie theaters, finally settling on tearooms.

If, as Thomas Gieryn argues, place is comprised of three elements—geographical location; material form; and investment with meaning, values, norms, feelings[13]—then *Tearoom Trade* also demonstrated the mutability of such places. The "stuff" and meanings in places are not fixed but are deeply social. Places—in this case, buildings—can be reinvented, serving multiple purposes and reflecting disparate, even conflicting, norms. The public restroom exemplifies how the social meanings and functions of place are multiple and sometimes competing.

Forest Park Tearooms

Place, Humphreys argued, was crucial to the transformation of a particular restroom into a tearoom. Specific geographic locations and "physical traces" made a restroom safe for sexual activity. The most active locations were set near transportation systems, such as major highways and thoroughfares adjacent to commuting routes. The ideal tearoom sites in public parks must be set apart from buildings and recreational areas, but still be accessible. He called this the "'tearoom purlieu' (with its ancient meaning of land severed from a royal forest by perambulation)." The "getaway car" is nearby, and children, women, and "straight people" are unlikely to wander past. It would be an outsider place close enough to, and indeed converted from, insider places.

Humphreys did not disclose the specific location of the tearooms he studied. Between 1965 and 1969, he made "informal observations" of tearooms in cities such as Los Angeles, New York, Chicago, and Tulsa. But his systematic research focused on locations in one metropolitan area, which he declined to name for fear of triggering unwanted attention. We now know these tearooms were in Forest Park, St. Louis, essentially across the street from Humphreys's graduate institution, Washington University.

Many public places became sites for sexual activity in the early and mid-twentieth century. Movie theaters, bars, bathhouses, subway washrooms, and the open spaces of parks offered "privacy in public" to both men and women unable to find other settings for sex. Forest Park was one such place. Established in 1879, on over 1,200 acres west of downtown St. Louis, it was the site of the Louisiana Purchase Exposition in 1904, with

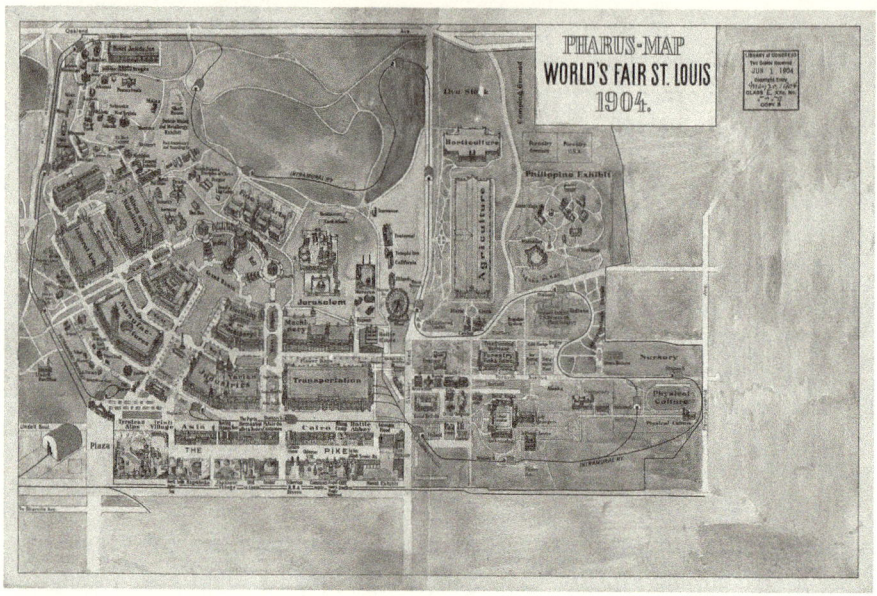

Map of the World's Fair in St. Louis, 1904, also known as the Louisiana Purchase Exposition. Forest Park was chosen as the location, and the fair significantly changed the park. Courtesy of the Library of Congress Geography and Map Division, Washington, DC.

the provision that it would be reestablished as a public park. It now houses the St. Louis Art Museum, Science Center, and Zoo. It is open year-round, filled with tourists, picnickers, museum visitors, and, at least during the mid-sixties, men seeking sex with other men.

In a charming introduction, Humphreys explained the cultural history of restrooms in public settings such as beaches and sites such as Forest Park. Public toilets, he noted, are "physical traces of modern civilization." Indeed, here is Wikipedia's 2018 family-friendly account of the purpose of public restrooms:

> Public toilets play a role in community health and individual well-being. Where toilets are available, people can enjoy outings and physical activities in their communities. By letting people get out of their cars and onto their feet, bicycles and mass transit, public toilets can contribute to improved environmental health. Mental well-being is enhanced when people are out with families and friends and know a place "to go" is available.[14]

One of the outdoor restrooms in Forest Park. Photograph by the author.

Humphreys described some of these earliest public restrooms as grand, almost "Greek temple-like structures." This grandeur waned in the Great Depression, during which time the Works Progress Administration built public restrooms in parks. This was the origin of the twelve tearooms Humphreys studied for *Tearoom Trade*. They are, he explained, "native white stone with men's and women's facilities back-to-back under one red roof. They have heavy wooden doors, usually screened from public view by a latticework partition attached to the building's exterior. In most of these doors, there is an inset of opaque French panes." Later in the book, he would tell us that one of the telltale marks of a tearoom is that the window is broken.

How to Have Sex in a Tearoom

Tearooms, Humphreys argued, differ from bars, movie theaters, and other places for public sex in that features of place produce different sexual codes and strategies. *Tearoom Trade* pioneered the argument that physical setting itself was the most significant factor in tearoom encounters, a finding that would be underscored by later historians and scholars studying the HIV epidemic.¹⁵ The text showed how spaces and buildings were transformed into sexual places by particular practices, social norms, and embodied meanings. The floor plan was crucial in producing this "living theater," such as number of urinals, location of stalls, and positionality of doors. Men effectively remodeled toilets into tearooms, places conducive to sexual activity. They did this by, for example, removing cubicle doors, cutting glory holes, penning graffiti on walls, and breaking windows for lookouts. Humphreys himself quipped that some men were more attached to the buildings than to the men with whom they had casual sex.

The buildings enabled sexual strategies for instant sex. Men approached the building strategically, after waiting in cars, to ensure the availability of encounters. They positioned themselves in stalls or at urinals in ways to signal interest and establish safety. Men "loitered" to convey willingness. Humphreys argued that dynamics and interactions within places and spaces produced sexual roles and activities among the men, not stable sexual identity. Inside the building, men produced the "interaction membrane"— Erving Goffman's term for the construction and maintenance of boundaries for social performances¹⁶—that established the boundaries for sex. The interaction membrane turned the restroom into a tearoom. It consisted of norms, strategies, and codes that communicated desire and consent. Outside of this interaction membrane was "another world" where men entered the building, relieved themselves, and left.

In the second half of the book, Humphreys once again conjured up places and metaphoric spaces in his profiles of married tearoom participants. He had discovered that most of the tearoom participants were highly conventional, married men. They were, in fact, insiders. Humphreys described these men in his chapter, "People Next Door," troubling the metaphor typically used to convey a safe, if bland, conformity. They led seemingly stable domestic lives, and Humphreys noted that they chose tearooms for "instant sex" to avoid exposure to their wives. A restroom visit on the way home from work provided men with an "instant alibi" for wives unaware of the multiple functions of these public facilities.

In other spatial metaphors, Humphreys portrayed, and then unsettled, the assumed heteronormativity of nuclear family life by describing tearoom participants barbecuing in their suburban backyards with their children playing nearby. In the section "A View from the Streets," he described a Christmas vacation he spent scouring the city streets where these men lived, looking for traces of "physical evidence" about their lives. He found material evidence of alleged normativity in swing sets, bicycles, shrines to Saint Mary, boats, and trailers in yards. Place was one important factor producing and destabilizing definitions of normalcy and deviance. Next door, these men led normal lives; in the tearooms, they became deviants.

Ultimately, *Tearoom Trade* de-moralized the tearoom by its normalizing account of a stigmatized sexual place. Humphreys argued that the tearoom posed no public threat because its social visibility required a high level of consent among its male participants. By contrast, he suggested that private sex, because of its low social visibility and lack of regulation, is the site in which most rapes and acts of incest and child abuse can occur. He noted, "It is the safeguarded, walled-in, socially invisible variety of sex we have to fear, not that which takes place in public." Once again, he upended conventional thinking by arguing that private rather than public places were most likely to foster sexual deviancy.

Finally, in a discussion of tearoom risks, Humphreys shifted emphasis from the interior places and spatial metaphors of the tearoom, and named specific locations of police regulation. Closed-circuit cameras, two-way mirrors, and radio transmitters represented an "advancing technology of police operations" that began to "invade" the tearoom. Humphreys condemned police surveillance activities in Ohio, Miami Beach, Laguna Beach, Philadelphia, and other cities. He cited the escalation in arrests in cities such as these, and condemned what he called "police lawlessness" wherein men were entrapped. Taking a counterintuitive and controversial policy position for his era, he insisted, "In order to alleviate the damaging side effects of covert homosexual activity in tearooms, ease up on it." Decades later, police still deployed these entrapment practices, sometimes sweeping up surprising figures.

Deviant Insiders: The Breastplate of Righteousness

In 2007, conservative Republican senator Larry Craig was arrested at the Minneapolis–St. Paul airport for lewd conduct in the men's restroom. The police officer, part of an undercover operation, reported that Craig, in the adjoining stall, tapped his right foot, moved his foot closer to the officer's foot, and swiped his hand under the stall divider several times. This behavior, according to the incident report, was typical of men attempting to engage in sexual behavior.

The arresting officer wrote that Craig had stated he had a wide stance when using the restroom, although a transcript of the police interrogation showed he had not. Still, pundits mockingly seized on the term, some noting that it was a drama right out of *Tearoom Trade*. The title of one article, "Wide-Stance Sociology," made the connection explicit.[17] Craig pleaded guilty to disorderly conduct and paid a fine, although when the incident later went public, he tried, unsuccessfully, to withdraw his guilty plea, saying at a press conference: "I am not gay. I never have been gay."[18] Craig did not run for re-election.

In the cultural memory of the late sixties, it is liberation movements, the sexual freedom of the counterculture, and an ethos of questioning authority that lingers. However, the country also took a swing to the right—the unsettled political climate of the sixties supported both sexual liberalism and a coalescing right-wing oppositional movement represented by Old Right groups such as the John Birch Society and Billy James Hargis's Christian Crusade. Laud Humphreys captured the collision of sexual moralism and shame among antigay conservatives that would fuel scandals such as that involving Larry Craig.

Well before the rise of the so-called pro-family movement in the mid-seventies, Humphreys exposed a pattern whereby social conservatives routinely indulged in the very sexual "improprieties" they condemned. He described the strategic defense that certain men mobilized in response to the structures of shame underpinning participation in stigmatized sexual activities. It would later become clear that this sort of shame-induced moralistic rigidity was not simply an individual strategy but was, rather, characteristic of political crusades against sexuality. Sexuality remained at the heart of right-wing cultural politics, mobilizing large constituencies on behalf of traditionally conservative family values. However, sex scandals among both secular and religious conservatives served as a counterpoint to their moral crusades.

The second phase of Humphreys's research was as methodologically innovative and culturally revealing as it was later to be controversial. He had tracked down approximately 100 of his tearoom subjects and interviewed many of them under the guise of conducting a different survey. He found that most (54 percent) were married men living with their wives. His profiles of these married tearoom participants struck a blow against the notion that the sexual universe could be neatly divided into straight and gay. Strikingly, he challenged the boundaries of normalcy and deviance. Straight men, seemingly sexual insiders, were also sexual outsiders.

Humphreys also reported a seemingly paradoxical finding—most of the men he interviewed who engaged in public sex were politically and religiously conservative. Some were members of the archconservative John Birch Society, at least one was a fundamentalist minister, and many were Roman Catholics, upset by the liberal changes wrought by Vatican II. Humphreys had developed a scale of political opinion based on four sets of social issues: economic reform, police practices, the civil-rights movement, and the war in Vietnam. Compared to his control group, the tearoom participants ranked as more conservative in each of these areas. Of the tearoom participants, sixteen ranked as conservatives, twenty-six as moderates, and a mere seven as liberals. In the control group, only four were conservatives, thirty-one were moderates, and fifteen scored as liberals. In short, men very much like Larry Craig frequented these tearooms.

Decades later, survey research by a Kinsey Institute scholar showed differences in sexual fantasies based on political affiliation. Republicans, despite espousing so-called traditional values of monogamy, heteronormativity, and missionary-style intercourse, were more likely than Democrats to fantasize about unconventional activities such as fetishism, orgies, voyeurism, and exhibitionism. Based on these findings, Kinsey researcher Justin Lehmiller concluded that "Republicans fantasized more about most of the things they aren't supposed to want than did Democrats."[19] Laud Humphreys had earlier told this story in *Tearoom Trade*.

Humphreys argued that tearoom participants varied in vulnerability to the risk of exposure. He noted that married men and men who did not have career autonomy were highly vulnerable to negative consequences if discovered in the tearooms. One might predict that these men would therefore shun tearooms because of the potentially high cost. And yet his data indicated that "tearoom behavior is not easily extinguished." Humphreys found instead that vulnerable men still frequented the tearooms, but they undertook strategies to minimize their risk of exposure. They did this, he argued, by constructing a hypermoral presentation of self to deflect suspicion. Humphreys, ever the Episcopalian minister, invoked a biblical phrase (Ephesians 6:14) to describe this strategy—"the breastplate of righteousness." This seemingly provided a "protective shield of superpropriety" that had "a particularly shiny quality, a refulgence, which tends to blind the audience to certain of his practices." It was, he concluded, the public saint/private sinner dynamic.

Secrets and shame, then, did not just destroy lives; they produced particular social and political types. Influenced by Goffman, who claimed that there was not necessarily a "real reality"[20] behind a false front, Humphreys said, "The secret offender may well believe he is more righteous than the next man—hence his shock and outrage, his disbelieving indignation, when he is discovered and discredited." Social conservatism, Humphreys argued, was "a product of the illegal roles these men play in the hidden moments of their lives." Humphreys commented that "'the Bible on the table and the flag upon the wall' may be signs of secret deviance more than of 'right thinking.'"

Subjected to harsh social condemnation and legal penalties, the tearoom participant was likely to turn his anger and hatred on himself or others in his group. "Worse yet," Humphreys argued, "he may justify himself by degrading others, displacing his hostility onto outgroups in the manner of the authoritarian personality." Indeed, right-wing religious movements of the sixties discovered that crusades against so-called perverted sexuality were effective in galvanizing supporters.[21]

The Florida Legislative Investigative Committee was an example of the type of organization that 1966 gubernatorial candidate Ronald Reagan approvingly called a "moral crusade." Established during the McCarthy era in 1956 and known as the Johns Committee after its first chairman, Charley Eugene Johns, it was charged with investigating seemingly dangerous or subversive organizations. It was vehemently anticommunist and antihomosexual, and also targeted civil-rights groups and academics. In 1964, the committee published a pamphlet that featured an explicit photograph of a man engaged in a sex act in a public restroom. The report, dubbed "the purple pamphlet," was intended to shock readers and mobilize antigay repression.[22]

Photography became one of several technologies police and moral entrepreneurs used to observe and produce evidence of sexual deviance. Yet photographic surveillance could also be subverted. After the tearoom photograph was published in the 1964 *Homosexuality and Citizenship* brochure, conservatives attacked it as pornographic. The committee quickly removed it from the report, but the photograph was reprinted and vigorously marketed by Guild Press, a publisher of homoerotic materials. Gay pulp publishing was growing by 1964, and Guild Press, established in 1962, was no doubt gleeful to find and market this photograph. The Guild advertisement pointed out that this was the only "action photo" of a glory hole scene that had ever been in print, and as historian Thomas Waugh noted, "the glory hole photo became famous."[23] The "purple pamphlet" and its widespread dissemination was an early case of how social and religious conservatives played a significant role in making visible the sexual representation that they condemned. (**See Hyperlink 6.4:** The Open Space of Glory Holes.)

Laud Humphreys began his dissertation research a year after the publication of the purple pamphlet. It was in that climate of sex panic over tearooms that he defended public sex and pleaded for policy reform to end vice-squad enforcement. Even further, based on his ethnographic evidence, he demonstrated that measures to eliminate tearoom sex were counterproductive. The removal of cubical doors to deter sex and allow police to photograph men in the stalls—the measures taken by the Johns Commission—fostered rather than eliminated tearoom encounters.

In decades to come, religious conservatives such as the Moral Majority increasingly deployed explicit sexual language and images to wage their crusades and appeal to a complicated culture of sexual anxiety and excitement. The movement that had vowed to silence public talk about sex itself became a loud voice in the sexual culture. Meanwhile, the glory hole photograph had found an enthusiastic audience among gay men.

Humphreys's stance toward his conservative tearoom participants was remarkably temperate in *Tearoom Trade*. On the one hand, there is little question that he enjoyed revealing the disparity between their public moral posturing and their clandestine sexual dalliances. For example, Humphreys questioned the men about vice squad enforcement, something with which they would have had personal involvement, given their sexual predilections. A fundamentalist minister told Humphreys that police should disregard citizens' rights and that vice squad activity should be increased, saying "This moral corruption must be stopped!" Another man said, "They should be more strict. I can think of a lot of places they ought to raid." Humphreys found that the men most vulnerable to being arrested in tearooms consistently called for heightened vice squad activity.

On the other hand, Humphreys's restraint, and even compassion, are striking in this chapter. Even when he exposed the hypocrisy of men who donned the breastplate of righteousness, he resisted the temptation to shame the men or scapegoat sex itself. Rather than calling them hypocrites, he said that conservative tearoom participants are "afraid of being liberal." He condemned structural oppression rather than individuals. *Tearoom Trade* is fascinating for its historical moment because Humphreys exposed these moral entrepreneurs while at the same time de-moralizing the tearoom with his dispassionate, ethnographic story of stigmatized sexual activity.

The Art of Public Sex

The new cultural visibility of sex probably fostered a climate in which Laud Humphreys and his sociology advisors might have reasonably expected the academy to consider a dissertation on public sex to be an acceptable research topic. A series of legal changes enabled a striking increase in the sexual content of mid-sixties mainstream media. The Supreme Court, starting in the 1930s, issued a range of decisions that relaxed legal prohibitions against printed sexually explicit material. The crucial 1957 *Roth* decision legally separated sexual explicitness and obscenity, and by 1966, the Supreme Court in the *Fanny Hill* case ruled that material must be "utterly without redeeming social value" to warrant a definition of obscenity. In the fifties and sixties, movie producers challenged the production code, formally adopted in 1927, that had banned even silhouette nudity, "profanity" (including "hell"), and scenes of childbirth.[24] These policy changes helped ease a chilling climate of self-censorship and fostered a growing media openness toward sexuality.

Sexual representation proliferated in print, on the screen, and in music. By the mid-sixties, popular music had become unabashedly sexual. One top song of 1964 was the Animals' ode to a New Orleans brothel, *House of the Rising Sun*. That year, when the Beatles first performed in the United States, thousands of adoring, screaming teenage girls created a rebellious, sexual space. Song lyrics continued their evolution toward more explicitness; the Beatles, for example, moved from "I Want to Hold Your Hand" to "Why Don't We Do It In the Road?" Likewise, the Broadway play *Hair* featured nudity and songs about masturbation and cunnilingus, while a full depiction of intercourse prompted at least part of the controversy over the Swedish film *I Am Curious (Yellow)*, which was released from customs seizure by a landmark court decision. A spate of films featured homosexuality, such as *The Fox*, *The Killing of Sister George*, and a number of independents, prompting *Women's Wear Daily* to proclaim, "Movies are Gayer Than Ever."[25]

Humphreys did not cite popular culture sources as evidence in the way that Erving Goffman did in *Asylums*. However, he conducted research amid this expansive popular sexual culture, and cited material by the gay Mexican American writer John Rechy. Recommended to Grove Press by James Baldwin, Rechy's largely autobiographical debut novel about the outsider subcultures of male hustlers and drag queens—*City of Night*—came out in 1963 and became an international bestseller.[26] Its popularity, despite negative reviews, reflected growing openness to, and fascination with, nonconformity and transgression. Like much popular culture and ethnographic research emerging in midcentury, the novel made visible, as Edmund White noted in a review, "a whole new array of characters . . . many of them for the first time in American literature."[27] It was book about marginalization and outsiders, about underground gay male life. Novels like *City of Night* facilitated the transmission of underground cultural knowledge.

City of Night was unabashedly sexual. It featured sexual places such as seedy hotel rooms, bars, and cruising areas such as parks, streets, and back alleys. Rechy wrote of "the toilets in the subways—with the pleading scrawled messages." Unlike Humphreys, who studied consensual tearoom sex (among what Rechy referred to as "the world of unpaid, mutually desiring males"), Rechy wrote about how male hustlers selling sex navigated the toilets. He cited the norms of the sexual marketplace with sociological precision: "Stand at the urinal long after youre [sic] through pissing. At the slightest indication of interest from someone in one of the cubicles, go up to him quickly before he gets any free ideas and say: 'I'll make it with you for twenty.' But go for much less if you have to." Decades later, Rechy recalled seeing a man reading the book on the subway after its initial publication, with a different jacket hiding the cover.[28]

Midcentury social (and sexual) differences were made visible by writers such as John Rechy. One particular line, repeated often, captured sexual fluidity: "No matter how many queers a guy goes with, if he goes for money, that don't make him queer. . . . It's when you start going for free, with other young guys, that you start growing wings."[29] Rechy wrote this in a 1961 short story, and sociologist Albert Reiss cited it as evidence in his "Queers and Peers" article for his argument about fluid identity. Rechy used this line again in *City of Night*, and it was later included as dialogue in the film *My Own Private Idaho*. Men were often familiar with such novels and films. Laud Humphreys pointed out that one of his respondents mentioned Rechy's later novel, *Numbers*,[30] in an interview. These new sexual stories, whether literary or ethnographic, gave voice to otherwise underground sexual subcultures.

Laud's Legacy: On Secrets and Shame

Decades have passed since the original publication of *Tearoom Trade*. The text is both revered and reviled. The same might be said about Humphreys himself. The early narratives about *Tearoom Trade* focused on ethics debates, facile generalizations about Humphreys's personal motivations and sexuality, and rumors about his altercation with a senior professor. Persistent homophobia in the academy, along with stigma attached to sexuality research, contribute to ongoing misunderstanding and misrepresentation of Humphreys's research.[31] Moreover, the condemnation of *Tearoom Trade* is undoubtedly fueled by his transgressive stories that overstepped the cultural boundaries of what could be told about men, sex, and nuclear families.

Methodology and ethics still dominate the discourse about *Tearoom Trade* in mainstream sociology. Sociology textbooks present Humphreys's research as the classic example of ethical violations, rather than exploring its ethnographic richness. Sociologist John Galliher and his colleagues found that a wide range of both introductory and methodology textbooks presented *Tearoom Trade* negatively, often exaggerating or outright misrepresenting Humphreys's research practices.[32] These critiques ignore the oversight that Humphreys's mentors provided over the project in that pre-Institutional Review Board (IRB) era. *Tearoom Trade* was published in 1970, on the cusp of what would soon become an expansive IRB "crackdown" on the social sciences, amplifying criticism of Humphreys.[33]

Moreover, criticisms of his research methods are entangled with assumptions about, or disapproval of, his sexuality. He was in a heterosexual marriage during his tearoom research. Humphreys wrote that he was able to conduct research on public sex among men by posing as "watchqueen," his term for a man who serves as lookout in the tearoom. It was, Humphreys drily noted, "a role superbly suited for sociologists." His methods section—"The Sociologist as Voyeur"—collapsed the distinction between those who observe for sexual motives and those who observe for the passionate pleasures of social research. Because he later identified as bisexual and then gay, some sociologists condemned him as a closeted gay man and assumed he was engaging in illegal sexual behavior in the tearooms.

This is unsurprising. Those who study sex have long been subject to speculation and gossip about their research motives and their own sexuality.[34] Sociologists who conducted research on sexuality during the same period as *Tearoom Trade* discussed this vulnerability to facile assumptions about the scholar's motives and methods. Sociologist Carol Warren noted that those who studied sexual "deviants" in the 1960s were the subject of gossip about their sexual preferences and assumed to be gay.[35] In 1972, sociologists Martin Weinberg and Colin Williams wrote that their colleagues "warned us of the sorry spectacle we present in mixing with social outcasts."[36] In interviews for this book, I routinely asked about *Tearoom Trade*. The interviewees were all pioneering scholars in what the discipline now calls crime, law, and deviance. The comments below exemplify this type of focus on Laud's sexuality (often mistakenly construed).

- I had no respect for Laud Humphreys. I'll tell you why. Because when he wrote the book he pretended that he wasn't gay and I mean that was just fraudulent.
- I didn't know at the time that he was gay. It would have never

occurred to me. I didn't think, you know, it wasn't the kind of question that came up for me.
- **Question**: So when that book came out, Laud was a pastor, and was married with children. Did people just assume he was gay? **Answer**: Yeah. **Q**: Because of the . . . ? **A**: Content. **Q**: And do you think that discredited the work in some peoples' eyes? **A**: Oh sure, oh gosh yes. We're talking the early '70s.

The sexuality of a researcher, real or imagined, readily complicates the reception of scholarship in this field.

While these dynamics shape the legacy of *Tearoom Trade*, some of Humphreys's contemporaries reported that he could be provocative. One incident that has achieved sociological infamy is a physical altercation between Humphreys and prominent Marxist scholar Alvin Gouldner. Gouldner, a senior professor at Washington University, had published a scathing critique of Howard Becker's call for sociologists to take the side of the underdog.[37] After a series of flyers had been posted around the sociology department mocking Gouldner, he went to Humphreys's office and physically attacked him, thinking that Laud (then a graduate student) had posted them.[38] The incident prompted a 1968 *New York Times* article, with the unusual headline: "Sociology Professor Accused of Beating Student." Humphreys's biographers explore this conflict more extensively.[39] Below, my interviewees' comments offer a glimpse into how, in retrospective memory, some contemporary sociologists (mis)remember the Humphreys-Gouldner conflict.

- Alvin Gouldner, at the University of Washington in St. Louis where Laud got his degree, confronted Humphreys in the hall and berated him over something, probably the methods of the topic, and then hit him, hit him, I don't know where, but I do know he hit him with his cane. That's the story.
- Well I wasn't there, I've only heard about it second-hand but numerous times. Basically, Laud Humphreys was a graduate student at Washington University and Alvin Gouldner said to Laud Humphreys something very nasty, and he said you're not doing sociology you're doing pornography and then they got into some discussion and the way I remember it was, Laud Humphreys took Gouldner's typewriter and threw it out the window, and Gouldner punched Humphreys in the nose. And that was the demise of the sociology department at Washington University.

- Gouldner punched him. The story was that someone was posting witty little doggerel on the department bulletin boards, making fun of Gouldner. Well, Gouldner was not somebody who would take being made fun of lightly. He had a terrible temper. So, he decided that Laud had done it. I wouldn't have put it past Laud because he did have a good sense of humor and he was smart, and he was a little smart-alecky. And Al just came in one day to his office and punched him. He was furious. He had enough of that. And then he tried to get [Laud's] degree taken away from him, which, that's just Gouldner being mean.
- When Alvin Gouldner found out what he had done [tracking down license plate numbers], Gouldner just went ballistic and in fact punched poor Laud Humphreys out. That's the only example I know in all of sociology where people came to fisticuffs over methodology.

That particular fight was not over methodology. But it is easily remembered as such because of sociology's long fight with Humphreys over his methodology.

Our sexual culture's dense affective mix of excitement, pleasure, fear, and shame may contribute to the book's mixed reception. The best ethnographies pack an emotional punch, and *Tearoom Trade* involved clever emotional dynamics of secrecy: secret sexual places, secret sexualities, secrets kept by the men in the tearooms, the secret hypocrisy of privileged heterosexual insiders, and secrets kept by the researcher. As an ethnographer, Humphreys observed tearoom participants. Like him, the reader becomes a tearoom observer. In our ethnographic imaginations, we watch men negotiate tearoom norms and enact their sexual strategies. Moreover, Humphreys draws readers into intimate contact with the tearoom participants through his later interviews with them. Like him, we know they frequent the tearooms. But in the interviews, they perform their moral outrage at sex only because they do not know that he knows their secret sex lives. By the very act of reading the book, we share the secret Humphreys keeps from the participants he interviews, and perhaps gain a voyeuristic thrill and guilty ambivalence in doing so.

Laud Humphreys had shown that one response to sexual shame was a shadowy retreat into the unyielding moralism that would prove so characteristic of the later "pro-family" movement. A different response was a progressive sexual politics to challenge stigma. Writing ethnographic stories about the ordinariness of seemingly extraordinary sex was one of his methods of doing so. Exposing secrets was another method. The book outed both a highly stigmatized sexual activity, and the hypocrisy of some men who participate but then condemn it. This endeared him to myriad scholars, political activists, and individuals vulnerable to sexual shame, as well as their allies.

Like a cult film, then, *Tearoom Trade* acquired a devoted following, underscoring the American paradox whereby we both hate and love outsiders. The book won the 1969 C. Wright Mills Award of the Society for the Study of Social Problems. It was foundational to later urban ethnographies of sexuality, difference, and place. Humphreys and his work were the subjects of a special 2004 journal issue of the *International Journal of Sociology and Social Policy*, and a recent biography.[40] Despite being misunderstood by mainstream social science as a study of homosexual men, the book has informed public-health advocates, who correctly recognized Humphreys's key finding that many men who have sex with men identify as heterosexual. *Tearoom Trade* is still in print, unlike so many other ethnographies of its era.

Conclusion

In the end, history changed the tearooms. They had withstood dogged efforts by law enforcement, park maintenance, university officials, subway police, and other social-control agents to abolish them. The men who loved and needed places on the sexual margins would always rebuild them. Over the decades, however, political activism, legal change, transformations in the sexual culture, and technological innovations eroded that need. Sexual stigma faded for some men, and an infrastructure of gay public places became less marginal. Social-networking apps such as Grindr enabled men who wanted to have sex with other men to find each other in cyberspace and then arrange a convenient physical location to meet. The need for the fixed places of tearooms diminished. If indeed the tearoom is becoming extinct, this change merely reinforces Humphreys's argument about the mutability of places and the nimble strategies of the men inside them.

Laud Humphreys's stories exemplified a sixties sociology of deviance that ventured into outsider places, troubled the very concept of deviance, and championed the underdog. He argued that the most daunting problems with sex are social control and sexual stigma. *Tearoom Trade* never succumbed to cultural panic and defensiveness about sexuality. That quality made his work transformative and transgressive. Still, *Tearoom Trade* arrived in 1970, without a mainstream knowledge infrastructure to provide an intellectual and academic context for it. As one sociologist from Humphreys's era told me, "If you were hip, you got it. It you were square, who knew what it was a study of?!" Research in the fifties and sixties on marginal sexual communities was itself marginalized. Humphreys helped bring sex into the domain of social knowledge. Both queer theory and an established sociology of sexualities were decades away.

Some stories cannot be told. They are too far ahead of their time, too culturally intolerable. Some outsiders are too far outside for different stories to render them beloved. Laud Humphreys spun his tales anyway. His ethnographic stories revealed the quotidian nature of impersonal sex among men—there were social norms to be followed in the seemingly lawless tearoom. Yet the tearoom itself defied powerful social norms that sex should be private, intimate, and heterosexual. Indeed, the last straw of cultural outrage was the exposure of the sexual secrets of heterosexual, married men.

Tearoom Trade was a cultural disturbance. Humphreys told sexual stories that were seen as threatening the idealized nuclear family and sexual normalcy, in an anxious cultural moment of a countercultural rewriting of sex and families. He wrote on this knife's-edge of cultural appreciation and fierce condemnation of sexual difference. His work posited that sex could be simultaneously transgressive and ordinary, and belied the notion that deviant sexual worlds were timeless, taboo, and unknowable.

Laud Humphreys died of lung cancer in 1988. Methodological constraints will forever disallow research like his that so intimately explores the intersectionalities of sexual lives and social worlds. Although it is about a demonized group engaged in highly stigmatized behavior, *Tearoom Trade* is ultimately a lesson in how all sexuality is a routine social accomplishment. It is about out-of-the-ordinary sex in ordinary lives. Although very much a part of its time, *Tearoom Trade* nonetheless stands alone.

Hyperlink 6.1: Women and the Early Gay Canon

Tearoom Trade was part of an emerging early literature that was dismantling identity and disentangling the concepts of sex, gender, and sexualities. In the late 1960s and early 1970s, both grassroots and academic scholars, whose publications would later be considered part of the gay canon, worked in obscurity. In March 1973, a New York City meeting of New York University faculty and graduate students soon led to the formation of the Gay Academic Union, along with other networks for LGBT scholarship, such as the Lesbian Herstory Archives.[41] By the mid-1970s, activists and scholars began producing lesbian and gay histories, as well as ethnographies and community studies. A vibrant scholarship on sexualities proliferated in the 1980s and '90s. Still, as historian John D'Emilio put it in 1990 regarding homophobia on campuses, "gay people are still swimming in a largely oppressive sea."[42] Jobs were scarce, and homophobia (along with racism and sexism) persisted in the academy.[43]

The work of two young women scholars—British sociologist Mary McIntosh and US anthropologist Esther Newton—anchor what we now recognize as that early gay canon. Their distinct histories as pioneering scholar-activists show how sexism and homophobia underpinned this vibrant era of radical politics and research. In the 1960s, when McIntosh and Newton were graduate students, women represented only 16 percent of earned doctoral degrees in the United States.[44] Like many other women scholars of the era, their work was simply invisible. Lesbian scholars suffered even deeper marginalization. McIntosh and Newton represented what would later be called "the vanished women" in the social sciences.[45] Despite having their knowledge contributions "recovered" in later decades, neither scholar fully escaped the stigma of studying outsiders.

Mary McIntosh

British sociologist Mary McIntosh was an early architect of the social-constructionist approach. Her 1968 article in *Social Problems*, "The Homosexual Role," has been recovered from that largely forgotten period of sexuality research by social scientists, and is considered canonical. Her contributions were multiple; one of them was the integration of sociological and historical analysis. When she argued that homosexuality was not an inherent individual condition but a social "role" (using the functionalist term later abandoned by sociologists), she also insisted that comparative sociology offered the analytic tools to interrogate historical changes and cross-cultural differences in how sexual categories are defined and socially organized. McIntosh went to the Human Relations Area Files, a database on cross-cultural variation, to speculate about the homosexual role in different societies. She then turned her gaze to a schematic but provocative history of how the idea of "homosexuality" developed in England. She suggested that an early form of what we might today recognize as male homosexuality emerged in London in the late seventeenth century, while also cautioning that the use of definitional terms, as well as analyses of categories and behaviors, must be historically specific. In a thirtieth-anniversary appreciation of her article, sociologist Jeffrey Weeks wrote that Mary McIntosh's historical analysis was highly influential to an early generation of historians, who explored questions about the historical invention of sexual categories, subcultures, belief systems, and languages.[46] Commonplace now, at that time McIntosh's observations constituted a radical challenge to the dominant paradigm of sexuality as a timeless and universal biological drive.

McIntosh had been a long-standing political activist. As a visiting graduate student at the University of California, Berkeley, in 1960, she was one of sixty-four people arrested at San Francisco City Hall in a student protest against investigations into alleged subversive activities convened by the controversial House Committee on Un-American Activities (HUAC). The students had been waiting outside singing civil-rights hymns when police unleashed the full force of fire hoses against them, blasting protesters down two flights of stairs. McIntosh was treated at the hospital for injuries, and her arrest made headlines in England: "London Girl is Injured in U.S. Clash."[47] After the fire hoses, she told newspapers, "Then they started using clubs. We didn't have any clubs." US Representative Edwin Willis, chair of HUAC, said, "This was probably the worst incident in the history of the committee," and HUAC never returned to San Francisco.[48] McIntosh was deported after this arrest, and continued her activism in London, including cofounding the Gay Liberation Front of the London School of Economics in 1970.

McIntosh was also one of the cofounders of the National Deviancy Conference (NDC) from 1968–1974, which created networks of scholars and activists working within the deviance framework. Women, however, were still scarce among outsider scholars. British sociologist Laurie Taylor told me, "In the first early days, Mary McIntosh was pretty well much alone. A bunch of women came along and talked and gave papers, but that was about it."[49] If women were scarce, lesbians were virtually invisible. Taylor recalled that, despite intense homophobia, McIntosh was an out lesbian in the academy in 1965, "as though it were the easiest thing in the world." Even the men of NDC, a radical academic group, found themselves shocked by her lesbianism. "I mean, I now refer to it rather glibly, but I remember we thought, here was a real live walking, talking lesbian. We'd never seen . . . we were all a bit . . . [shocked], we tried not to be. But we all now somehow make ourselves out as more liberal than we were."

Although *Tearoom Trade* was instantly controversial, in part because of a critical *Washington Post* article, McIntosh's article was largely ignored. As anthropologist Carole Vance noted, at the time of its publication, McIntosh's work "vanished like pebbles in a pond."⁵⁰ She taught at the University of Essex for twenty years, where she became the first woman department chair. Yet the university never promoted her to full professor. She left academia, worked for social service agencies, and continued her political activism. Mary McIntosh died in 2013.

Esther Newton

Published in 1972, *Mother Camp: Female Impersonators in America* ranks prominently among the so-called appreciative studies of deviance that sexuality scholars produced in the early seventies. Anthropologist Esther Newton's ethnography of the drag world, completed as her dissertation in 1968, relied heavily on the era's deviance theory and sociology of sexuality. Newton's dissertation director, anthropologist David Schneider, pointed her toward the work of Erving Goffman and Howard Becker, among others, since, as she told me, "if there was little help in anthropology, there was a great deal in the extant sociology of deviance." Given its topic—female impersonators—*Mother Camp* endures as one of the quintessential texts on gender performance; it explored impression management, staging, acts, roles, appearances, and all the intricacies of performing femininity.

Two aspects of Newton's analysis of gender performance bear comment. First, she examined gender styles within the gay world itself, well before this was openly explored. Her discussion of "butch and Nellie styles as aspects of the management of personal front, in Goffman's terms" stressed fluidity and context as she explained how lesbians and gay men managed such styles differently depending on whether they were in straight or gay situations. Second, *Mother Camp* argued that one consequence of drag was that it called into question "the 'naturalness' of the sex-role system in toto; if sex-role behavior can be achieved by the 'wrong' sex, it logically follows that it is in reality also achieved, not inherited, by the 'right' sex." Thus, several years before Goffman, Esther Newton helped denaturalize gender ("sex role," at the time) through her nuanced depiction of how it is a skillful, deliberate, and very social performance.

Several years after the publication of *Mother Camp*, Newton pointed out an enduring cultural paradox: lesbians, gay men, and other sexual/gender minorities were the targets of right-wing religious conservatives in the late-seventies culture wars, at the same time that mainstream entertainment was discovering, making visible, marketing, and profiting from drag. Gender impersonation and sexual nonconformity had been popular with smaller audiences who went slumming in the urban cabarets of the early twentieth century. By later decades, mainstream films such as *Outrageous* and cult films like *The Rocky Horror Picture Show* depicted gender nonconformity and tapped into a certain camp sensibility projected to a much wider popular audience. Newton wrote that the business world had discovered a gay market, resulting in a "cooptation of drag symbols and camp sensibility."[51] Drag and gender dissidence could be packaged and sold.

This is a persistent tension: popular culture represents marginality to the mainstream public, depicting outsiders as familiar and sympathetic figures, yet also benefiting from, and reinforcing, their strangeness. This was a critical dynamic in the drag shows Newton studied, which she noted were "offering 'sin' to Kansas Citians on their nights out," and the "freaks" are on stage, safely distant from the audience.[52] Popular culture and mass media made sexual and gender minorities more visible, resulting in both greater repression and incremental normalization. Gay and camp sensibilities became presentable, "in watered down form," for a mainstream audience, thereby changing both of them. Outsider capitalism's embrace of gender difference continued through ensuing decades—films and television shows such as *Tootsie* (1982), *The Crying Game* (1992), *Boys Don't Cry* (1999), *Pose* (2018), to name just a few. Yet political advancement and civil-rights gains were, and remain, uneven and precarious.

The political culture shaped Newton's research. Like Mary McIntosh and many early lesbian and gay scholars, Esther Newton was also politically active. She told me of her work with feminist groups: "I was a member of Upper West Side WITCH [Women's International Terrorist Conspiracy from Hell] and I went to lots of antiwar demonstrations. I was very involved in feminism and feminist activism. We went places and did interventions."[53] WITCH was one of many feminist groups burgeoning in the 1960s. Its founders identified as socialist feminists, which helped shape Newton's analysis of gender politics: "The gals that were in WITCH were very radical, and I learned a hell of a lot from them and the socialist framework they were coming from in terms of the personal and political. They viewed dominant society as the problem, not the people who were rebelling against it in one way or the other." These politics were consistent with those of deviance theorists of the era, who championed the underdog in defiance of the rule-makers of dominant society.

The stigma of both studying a marginal group and being part of a marginal group braided together to form a knot of fear and subsequent invisibility. Newton was closeted as a graduate student in the mid-sixties: "I think the biggest thing was that I myself was gay. I mean, except for two of my fellow grad students who were also gay, whom I managed to find, thank God, I never told anyone. I was very friendly with the other graduate students but they never knew, much less the faculty and so that was my big fear." Homophobia was openly and casually expressed and accepted in the academy. She continued, "I remember being at parties, I remember one in particular with this very famous anthropologist, Victor Turner. Everyone was drunk, and he made some kind of creepy dirty joke or something, to my face, about the drag queens. I don't know how much it was 'Oh she must be gay' or 'It's about sex so it's creepy and disgusting.' It was hard to disentangle all the different parts." When *Mother Camp* was published in 1972, "There were no responses. None. It was just like [the book] just dropped down a hole. The one response was by a sociologist, he was a closeted gay man. He reviewed it in an academic journal. And he just trashed it. It was like, 'These people, this is not a subculture and you know this whole framework is terrible and misleading.' I mean, he was engaged enough to trash it. For most people, most anthropologists and even sociologists, it was so left-field that it never went anywhere. There was one faculty member who took interest in it, he was in anthropology also, and he was a closeted gay man. He came up to me and said 'I read your book and I think it's really good.' That was it. No one else said anything. I think it was an embarrassment [to them]."

Activist-scholars started to recover the scholarly work of Mary McIntosh and Esther Newton in the 1990s as they began reflecting on their intellectual ancestors, writing their histories, and publishing anthologies. Both women scholars are now recognized as pioneers in that formerly forgotten period of sexuality research, and their research is frequently reprinted. In a 2018 special issue of *American Anthropology* dedicated to *Mother Camp*, anthropologist Gayle Rubin noted, "The fact that this book was not reviewed at the time is symptomatic of how marginal this kind of work actually was. The fact that it has since had such an impact is symptomatic of how much the world, and the field of anthropology, has changed. The fact that, in 2018, the trans population is such a primary target of the reactionary right is an index of how much the world described in *Mother Camp* haunts us still."[54] Yet stigma stuck to scholars like Nels Anderson, Paul Cressey, Zora Neale Hurston, Laud Humphreys, and Esther Newton. Newton told me, "You know, I never had the career that I should've had." I asked if it helped her feel better that now her work is considered part of a gay canon: "Yes, yes it has. I mean, oh, Janice, that's very complicated."

Hyperlink 6.2: Sex, *Tearoom Trade*, and the IRB

The historical context shaped Laud Humphreys's ethics trajectory. In the mid-sixties, when Humphreys conducted his study, there was no social science consensus about ethical standards. He worked closely with the eminent scholars on his dissertation committee, including Lee Rainwater, his chair. He received dissertation funding from the National Institute of Mental Health, which thoroughly vetted his proposal. Sociologist James Short, who served on that NIMH review committee, told me "The committee thought it was good research. We needed people on the inside to look at these things, not just from interview data but from participation. So, as I recall within the committee, there was no controversy whatsoever. We thought it definitely should be funded; and it was."[55] When controversy erupted, Short was contacted to testify, "but I was never asked, and as far as I know, no one else was." However, as historian Zachary Schrag notes, Humphreys became the "demon" for advocates of IRB expansion.[56]

Humphreys designed a sophisticated ethnographic study based on intensive observation and interviews. He frequented well-known tearooms around the country, but largely at Forest Park in St. Louis, near Washington University. Although many have assumed that he participated in the sex, he claimed that he was an observer ("watchqueen"), not a participant. He disclosed his research goals to only twelve trusted men, whom he interviewed at length. To acquire a broader sample, however, Humphreys copied the license-plate numbers of many men who parked outside the tearooms, and with a help of a campus police officer was able to acquire their names and addresses. A year later, he visited these men at their homes and interviewed them under the guise of a different study on social health. His files were carefully maintained for secrecy, and as controversy intensified, Humphreys gave the master list to an out-of-state colleague who burned it in his back yard.

Biomedical scandals like the Tuskegee syphilis study triggered federal momentum to protect human subjects, as represented by the congressional passage of the National Research Act in 1974. Yet demands for regulation quickly spread from medicine to the social sciences, a process of "ethical imperialism" by which regulations appropriate for one discipline (medicine) were then imposed on another (sociology).[57] In those early years of debate, regulators viewed sexuality research with suspicion. In particular, *Tearoom Trade* regularly featured in deliberations by the National Commission for the Protection of Human Subjects of Biomedical and Behavior Research, during 1977–78, as they began developing their formal recommendations.

Schrag told me, "It became a kind of shorthand for the perils of interview research, rather than something that was investigated in any depth, the way that the Commission did, say, go out to prisons to talk with prisoners about their participation in medical experimentation."[58] Humphreys was never invited to a commission meeting to discuss his research methods, nor did the commissioners specify which of his methods they considered unethical. Although other social researchers at that time had used deception, for example posing as patients at hospitals or attending Alcoholics Anonymous meetings, none of these studies other than *Tearoom Trade* were discussed by the commission. Of course, none of these studies had generated the controversy that *Tearoom Trade* did, a development not unrelated to the stigma associated with his research topic. As sociologist Earl Babbie noted, Humphreys studied not just sex, but tearoom sex between men: "Only adding the sacrifice of Christian babies could have made this more inflammatory for the great majority of Americans in 1970."[59]

Federal officials and regulators regarded sexuality, and sex as a topic of research, as dangerous. For example, in a veiled allusion to Laud Humphreys, James Shannon, who served as director of the National Institutes for Health in the sixties, told an interviewer in 1971, "It's not the scientist who puts a needle in the bloodstream who causes the trouble. It's the behavioral scientist who probes into the sex life of an insecure person who really raises hell." In later regulatory deliberations, sexuality was typically clustered with "deviance": criminal behavior, substance use, and mental illness. This came up repeatedly as officials debated to what extent the social sciences would require ethical regulation. In the late seventies, as health officials debated the level of risk posed by surveys and observation, a federal official proposed that all survey research be excluded from regulation if it did not deal with sensitive topics. Regulations in 1981 specified that social research be exempted from IRB review unless it "deals with sensitive aspects of the subject's own behavior, such as illegal conduct, drug use, sexual behavior, or use of alcohol." The assumption that sexuality is "sensitive" persists in the bureaucratic machinery of IRB operations. Even today, sociologists who study sexuality report difficulties with getting IRB approval.

The IRB regime is so culturally entrenched in the academy, and the narrative of Humphreys's ethics violations is so pervasive, that condemnation of *Tearoom Trade* is almost routine.[60] And yet, most of my interviewees did not think Humphreys had engaged in ethics violations. Some were outraged by his methods, however. In these interview excerpts, senior scholars reflect on their reactions to *Tearoom Trade* at the time of its publication.

They indicate how a matrix of anxiety, stigma, and guilt at exposing secret sexual worlds troubles any discussion of research ethics.[61]

- The world really changed when informed consent came in, so none of that stuff that any of us did, which was early ethnography, could be done. Like Laud Humphreys could never do his work [now]. And, in fact, Laud Humphreys was probably instrumental in the changing attitudes about concealed observations. Certainly one of the big issues with his work, which is ethnographically quite sound, he would get the license plate numbers of people who went into the public bathrooms and then he would go to the DMV and he would look them up. Then he would go and interview them and conceal the fact, and say "Oh, you were chosen randomly" like "Joe Schmo down the street suggested you" or whatever, never letting them know the process by which they were selected so he was able at that point to interview them.
- I liked [Humphreys's research]. It was excellent. I defended it . . . I'm not saying it was ethical, but at the same time, since nothing was done that could hurt the people, it's very hypothetical in a way, to me. I mean the things people were doing in those days, shocking undergraduates with electric shock. We were using deception. You have to put it in context. This wasn't PC times.
- I don't think that license-plate tracking is any more unethical than what many participant observers do.
- I mean it probably pushed the envelope a little, and people thought it was a little daring the way he did the research but it wasn't illegal. The complaint was, which I thought was utterly ludicrous, "Oh he wrote down their license numbers" and then he'd look them up and found out [their names], and then he went and did a health survey and he was working on this health survey for somebody during these interviews. He just took the same questionnaire and did it with them. And nobody was the wiser. And they said, "Well they could've been arrested!" I said, "You think the police don't know where those places are that Laud was doing his observing? Of course they knew." The guys who were involved in that activity knew very well that the police were watching.
- I just found the whole thing questionable from an ethical standpoint. I mean the dishonesty, I mean he was dishonest in all directions. He was dishonest with the people he was studying, he was dishonest with the publishers, and as far as I know he's dishonest

with his colleagues. One of them punched him out at one point. I just didn't have a ton of respect.
- *Tearoom Trade* came out, [and it] was greeted with either acclaim or other kinds of reactions. There was a huge dispute over the covert methods, the use of the license plates from the department of motor vehicles to then go interview. I just said, this is so good! There was controversy over the covert methods mainly. I suppose the dominant controversy would be over just studying this topic, okay? But it was done in such a thoroughly sophisticated way, I supposed, to what had come before.
- I was not incensed by the ethical issues. I'm glad we have the book and as far as I can tell nobody got hurt by the book. My view is, is that the entire IRB process is largely a moral panic. I don't think that Stanley Milgram hurt anybody and I don't think that Laud Humphreys hurt anybody. I think we are probably worrying way, way too much about the dangers and this kind of stuff. I think that if we are going to start inoculating people with syphilis, that is a human-subjects issue, but I think reasonable care was taken in those cases and so it didn't incense me then and it doesn't now.
- I thought it was neat. But I thought it was kind of a personal betrayal. And I didn't like the fact that he had infiltrated, whatever it was, I don't even remember.

Hyperlink 6.3: Albert Reiss: Queers and Peers

Sociologist Albert Reiss's article, "The Social Integration of Queers and Peers" (1961), was an important predecessor to Laud Humphreys's *Tearoom Trade*.[62] "Queers and Peers" examined the social and sexual transactions between adolescent male hustlers ("peers") and their adult male clients ("queers"), while Humphreys studied the social organization of impersonal sex among adult men in public spaces.

Reiss's article on hustling spun off from his broader research project on teenagers, social class, and illicit behavior in the mid-1950s. Reiss recounted that when he went into a high school to do this study, the principal said to him, "Look, I've got this terrible problem. My football team gathers at the field at the end of practice and these men from downtown come to pick them up in the car and take them out and pay them to have sex." Although this was before the requirement that research be approved by institutional review boards, Reiss was concerned about potential controversy among parents. He recalled that the principal "was this little guy and he's just seeing all sorts of things and he said, 'You have my permission' and I said, 'Mr. Bass (the superintendent) wouldn't approve of this. Would he?' and he said, 'I don't care what Mr. Bass approves of. I am telling you, you have my permission to do it' . . . I was interviewing them in school and we didn't have any parent consent or anything so I started it there and I just included it as my interviews in Nashville and Davidson County, Tennessee."[63]

Based on these interviews with delinquent boys and observation of sexual meeting places, "Queers and Peers" made several significant contributions to the emergent sociology of sex. First, Reiss disentangled sexual identity, sexual behavior, desires, and pleasure. He showed that, despite their routine participation in fellatio, the boys did not define themselves as either street hustlers or homosexuals. Second, his research illustrated the symbolic interactionist claim that the sexual was constituted through meaning and did not exist in the absence of such meaning. The boys' motives for fellatio were economic, not sexual. Reiss quoted the gay novelist John Rechy to make this point: "No matter how many queers a guy goes with, if he goes for money, that don't make him queer. You're still straight. It's when you start going for free, with other young guys, that you start growing wings." Moreover, the boys avoided a self-definition as homosexual by only assuming the role of fellatee not fellator, which they defined as the "queer" or female role.

Like Robert Park's pioneering research on the city,[64] Albert Reiss richly described one particular corner of an urban "moral region." He detailed the norms that governed transactions in the "common culture" of community space, showing how the role behavior of "peers," for example affective neutrality and prohibitions on specific physical acts, was essential to maintain the peer-queer social system. Echoing some of Alfred Kinsey's earlier findings on class differences in sexual behavior, Reiss stressed that the queer-peer culture was "an institutionalized aspect of the organization of lower-class delinquency oriented groups." "Queers and Peers" emphasized that sexual meaning is not inherent in particular activities or body parts. It was the first empirical, sociological study to so dramatically undermine the link between behavior and identity. Laud Humphreys extended those insights.

Hyperlink 6.4 The Open Space of Glory Holes

Architecture and desire intersect at the glory hole. Although they can vary widely in size and shape, what we might call the ideal type is a circular opening of 3–6 inches in diameter, at waist height in stalls in restrooms, saunas, adult bookstores, sex shops, and other venues of public sex. Or, as Laud Humphreys put it, at "penis height." Surprisingly, Humphreys mentioned glory holes only twice in *Tearoom Trade*, and described them as used for projecting fingers or tongue through the hole, or for peering through to the other stall. Their most common use, however, is the insertion of the penis for oral or anal sex.

The glory hole has a somewhat queer history. Although commonly associated with gay male sex, these holes in cubicle partitions date back centuries and were used by both men and women in myriad contexts. Their erotic appeal lies in their facilitation not just of anonymous sex, but of faceless sex. As Patrick O'Byrne notes, glory holes enable sex "in which the users are both exposed and hidden."[65]

Glory holes defy the intentions of the architect. They are DIY renovations by which men occupying particular buildings reshape places and spaces. Men in restrooms carve holes in metal cubicles, spaces that are open and abstract, while filled with history and intentionality. These voids invest abstract space with their own cultural norms, meanings, and practices.

Contests over norms and practices in social places are ongoing. Regulators overseeing restrooms with tearoom activity—such as park or university administrators—may often intervene in the physical settings as a way to eradicate deviant sex. They replace broken lookout windows, remove graffiti, post warning signs, and reconfigure stalls in efforts to eliminate sexual interaction. Doors may be removed or put back on, stalls may be lengthened, shortened, or removed altogether. Glory holes are a key target. One common intervention is to cover the holes with steel plates fastened onto the partitions. Sometimes, when men simply cut new holes, administrators replace the entire cubicle with steel panels in an effort to revert the open spaces of glory holes into fixed places with a sole set of cultural norms and meanings. Tearooms, however, are stubborn places, refusing banishment. Men continually repurpose the facility, writing new graffiti, breaking new lookout windows, and drilling new glory holes.

SEVEN

District for Deviants
Sherri Cavan's Hippies of the Haight

We are all outlaws in the eyes of America.[1]
Jefferson Airplane

In the contemporary imagination of the sixties, everyone went to Woodstock. Everyone smoked weed, wore tie-dyed shirts and peace symbols, lived on a commune, ate a macrobiotic diet, and enjoyed free love. Everyone, in other words, was a hippie. As more young people adopted certain hairstyles and clothing styles, hippies seemed to be everywhere; to some mainstream Americans, every young person was a hippie. In fact, hippies represented only a small but growing number of disaffected, white, middle-class youth. However, hippies are important to my narrative of deviance and marginality for three reasons: hippies embodied American paradoxes of difference; they helped change American culture; and these countercultural changes helped trigger enduring cultural battles over outsiders, social differences, and nonconformity.

Hippies, much like hobos, challenged traditional social norms that extolled a bourgeois lifestyle, a nuclear family structure, workplace productivity, consumer capitalism, and rigid gender and sexual practices. Hippies were shaped by the very cultural norms they resisted—transgressive of, yet rooted in, the dominant culture. Yet the counterculture, by its very name, lent new cultural visibility to a widespread yearning for rebellion, freedom, and nonconformity. Hippies themselves differed in how they were different. Despite the cliché of hippie free love, many hippies led heteronormative and gender-stereotypic lives. It would fall to the political activism of feminism and lesbian and gay liberation to fight for gender and sexual equality.

The hippie—a fleeting but highly visible nonconformist—was an iconic modern outsider. Cultural critic Danny Goldberg conceptualizes the hippie idea as "the internal essence of the tribal feeling."[2] I rewrite this notion. Hippies brought to life ideas about how to be a person that social theorists had extrapolated since the early twentieth century. They embraced strangeness, difference, and marginality. They did so largely from positions of social privilege in terms of race and class, yet perhaps for this very reason, their transgressions of conventionality exemplified sociological ideas that anyone could be deviant, that strangeness permeates any relationship, that we are all socially discreditable, and that outsiders become so because of restrictive social rules. They blurred the boundaries between outsider and insider. In these respects, then, the hippie idea echoed sociological ideas. None of this arose without trouble.

This flagrant, highly visible rejection of American normativity marked a turning point for American outsiders. On the one hand, hippie aesthetics and practices morphed into the mainstream, opening up cultural space for unconventionality. Nonconformity took hold among small, dissident groups in the sixties, was quickly commodified, and then spread to reshape mass culture. On the other hand, in contrast to today's nostalgia for hippies, in the sixties they were widely derided and feared. Backlash against hippies underscores our deep and enduring cultural fissures over being an outsider. Cultural divisions about conformity and difference fostered competing narratives about hippies that continue to the present.

Hippie countercultural social change is an enduring legacy of the sixties, as are the ongoing culture wars concerning them. Political conflicts over sexual values, gender, drugs, and a range of social issues all intensified in the sixties. As historian Andrew Hartman notes, the sixties "gave birth to a new America, a nation more open to new peoples, new ideas, new norms."[3] Yet these new stories met with deep ambivalence. Our contemporary cultural politics on the Left and Right bespeak intransigent tensions related to social differences and the transgression of conventionality.

Hippie transgression of normative American ideals made for sensationalist media stories. Their visibly defiant culture also made them irresistible to a generation of social scientists schooled in new ways of thinking, knowing, and storytelling about alternative cultures and social differences.

Sociologist Sherri Cavan, a student of Erving Goffman's at the University of California, Berkeley, was among them.

This chapter uses Cavan's little-known text, *Hippies of the Haight*, to explore early social knowledge about hippies as cultural outsiders in a turbulent historical moment.[4] Necessarily, I pay only brief attention to many topics covered extensively in other historical work, such as the familiar debates about political differences, drugs, and hippie music and art. Cavan's field observations provide a scaffolding for my own stories about the outsider paradoxes of hippies, and I stick to the time frame of her research. Her stories captured how hippies emerged and lived in her San Francisco district, Haight Ashbury, from the early sixties until 1968. They animate the historical moment when the United States seemed divided into stark binaries of conformity and defiance—hippies and straights. During that period, they were construed as binary social types, and Cavan capitalized the terms "Hippies" and "Straights," as do I, when recounting her work.

Before Hippies

"Hippie" is an elusive social category. We see early glimmers of something called "hippies" in 1964, which many historians consider the year that launched the infamous sixties. The Free Speech Movement, initiated that fall on the campus of the University of California, Berkeley, presaged the explosive student activism that would spread across colleges and universities throughout the world later in the decade. Music changed—the Beatles had topped the charts in the US and UK, with "Can't Buy Me Love" and other singles. The term "hippie" began appearing in a few media accounts of young rebels, and in popular culture, as in songs such as Freddy Cannon's single, "Do What the Hippies Do." Journalists, such as syndicated columnist Dorothy Kilgallen, began using "hippie," and by 1967, *San Francisco Chronicle* columnist Herb Caen popularized it through his regular columns. The term was quickly disavowed as a media construct by hippies themselves, who generally preferred "freak" or "head" (consistent with Cavan's text, I will continue to use the term "hippie"). This section offers a brief and partial context for the emergence of this ambiguous new way of being a person.

Hippie rebellion had a prehistory. American affluence, the Beat generation's repudiation of conformity, the Vietnam War escalation, the civil-rights movement's confrontations with racial bigotry, the emergence of psychoactive drugs, the invention of the birth-control pill, and more laid the groundwork for nascent countercultural changes. Demographics mattered—in 1964, seventeen-year-olds were the largest age group in the country. A year later, 41 percent of all Americans were under age twenty.[5] Adolescent and young-adult baby boomers made a defiant youth movement possible. A youth culture arose among this postwar baby boom and, by the mid-sixties, split into a counterculture.

In the years of the Cold War and McCarthyism, paradoxes of conformity and deviance were stark. On the one hand, cultural and political pressures toward conformity shaped all levels of life, from national politics to domestic life. Purges of alleged communists and homosexuals enforced conformity in the military, government service, and the private sector. Postwar affluence manifested in the "little boxes" of suburbia, along with a uniformity of White, middle-class experience captured in fictional representations such as *The Man in the Gray Flannel Suit* and critical sociological texts such as *The Organization Man*. Yet in the aftermath of World War II, many critics worried about pernicious effects of excessive conformity and the dangers of the authoritarian personality.[6] It was a familiar American tension between conformity and deviance.

While "the sixties" represented a specific cultural rupture, the entangled pleasures of sex, drugs, and rock 'n' roll also had antecedents in earlier decades. The sexual culture had been shifting since early in the century, despite *Time* magazine's 1964 cover story that proclaimed a sexual revolution in the land. The article lamented changes in sexual behavior, especially the "crisis of virginity."[7] Yet historians of sexuality have challenged the popular mythology of the sixties sexual revolution.[8] The incidence of premarital intercourse held constant from the taxi-dance-hall years of the 1920s into the 1960s.[9] The Supreme Court, starting in the '30s, issued a range of decisions that relaxed legal prohibitions against printed sexually explicit material.[10] These policy changes helped ease a chilling climate of censorship. *Playboy* commenced publication in 1953, while frank novels like *Naked Lunch* (1959), *Candy* (1958), and lesbian pulp could be found even at small-town newsstands and drugstores.[11]

Marijuana and psychedelic drugs characterized the counterculture, yet both had earlier histories. The 1933 song "Reefer Man" suggests the early familiarity of pot smoking among musicians (who often played while stoned), Black jazz culture, and a broader bohemian audience. Despite marijuana's illegality, and strict sentencing laws in the fifties, Beat-generation writers such as Jack Kerouac and Allen Ginsberg embraced cannabis and wrote while high. Cultural critic Loren Glass notes that cannabis represented a throughline linking Black, hip culture, the Beats, the counterculture, and eventually the mainstream.[12]

Psychedelics—long used in indigenous cultures around the world—found midcentury audiences prior to hippie experimentation. Based on his earlier experiences with mescaline, British writer Aldous Huxley's *The Doors of Perception* (1954) celebrated psychedelic drugs for their potential in achieving spiritual and psychological insight (the book title inspired the name for the rock group, The Doors). A 1957 article on psilocybin in *Life* magazine, "Seeking the Magic Mushroom," prefigured the impending cultural turn toward psychedelics ("A New York banker goes to Mexico's mountains to participate in the age-old rituals of Indians who chew strange growths that produce visions.")[13] In 1943, Swiss chemist Albert Hofman discovered that LSD, which he had synthesized in his laboratory, produced powerful hallucinogenic effects. The US military studied it in the 1950s for its possible uses as a weapon. From 1960 to 1962, psychologists Timothy Leary and Richard Alpert studied potential therapeutic effects in the Harvard Psilocybin Project. Drug culture was just waiting for hippies to discover it.

It was a short step from the Beats to the hippies, and writer Ken Kesey served as a bridge figure between these outsider generations. Kesey, through his "Acid Tests" conducted with the Merry Pranksters starting in 1965, distributed free LSD to thousands of young people in San Francisco's early counterculture. Kesey had his first LSD trip in 1960 as part of an experimental program launched in 1953 by the Central Intelligence Agency. Kesey had achieved fame for his 1962 outsider novel, *One Flew Over the Cuckoo's Nest*, a book *Time* magazine praised for disrupting assumptions about "the nice normalities," and issuing "a roar of protest against middlebrow society's Rules and the invisible Rulers who enforce them."[14] Kesey, who had earlier blurred the line between sanity and insanity, also helped normalize drug use.

Innovative music also drew on earlier influences. Psychedelic rock peaked between 1966 and 1969, roughly the same time Sherri Cavan was researching Haight hippies and attending concerts at venues such as the Fillmore. It evolved in tandem with psychedelic culture, incorporating instruments and sound effects to enhance the trippy effects of drugs. Psychedelic or acid rock incorporated Indian and other non-Western influences and instruments, such as the sitar (which achieved new visibility in 1967 with Ravi Shankar's blistering performance at Monterey Pop). Psychedelic rock bands freely sampled earlier forms and styles, such as soul, folk, jazz, and the music of the Beatles, Beach Boys, and other early-sixties bands. Race and gender interwove through music in complicated ways, as White musicians such as Elvis Presley, Janis Joplin, and the British rock groups Cream and the Rolling Stones appropriated the music of earlier Black musicians such as Chuck Berry, Muddy Waters, and Bessie Smith. While some critics saw White cultural theft, other saw racial boundary-crossing.[15]

Despite these continuities with earlier decades, when "the sixties" hit, they were a bit of a shock. In a documentary charting the rise of the Christian Right, a Catholic priest lamented, "I never saw the sixties coming. The early sixties were parties, and the Four Freshmen [a wholesome male vocal group], and convertibles, and picnics; everything was nice. And then, slam bam!"[16] As historian Alice Echols points out, "Although the fifties gave rise to the sixties in all sorts of unexpected ways, the fifties weren't the sixties."[17] Indeed.

The term "hippie" loosely conflated a number of disparate groups, such as student activists, weekend hippies, dropouts, drug addicts, runaways, and individuals seeking unconventional ways of living. Hippies were generally anti-authoritarian, antibourgeois, and nonconformist, with multiple splinters and ideologies. They were typically White youth, their whiteness affording them the privilege of rebelling as outsiders. While some youth of color became hippies, the rise of groups in the mid-sixties associated with racial identity politics—such as the Black Panthers, the Puerto Rican Young Lords, and the Chicano Brown Berets—offered more appealing options to many.

Hippies symbolized the rise of a larger sixties youth counterculture that emphatically rejected conventional values, what they viewed as stifling mid-twentieth-century social conformity, and the Establishment. Historian John Moretta says that hippies "first identified themselves by what they were *not*, and then engaged in a way of living that they believed would lead them down the path toward the creation of a New Age [italics in original]."[18] While very few young people committed to countercultural values, "tens of millions of Americans, young and old, watched the experimenters with dread, fascination, and envy."[19] There was both attraction and aversion.

The Knowledge Churn: Who Tells the Hippie Story?

As early hippies became visible in certain urban areas, questions about them abounded. Who were these new kinds of people? What did they believe, how did they live, in what ways could we know about them? Media, social scientists, and psychological experts all told stories about young hippies. Race science of the early twentieth century had been discredited after the Nazi genocide of World War II, and remained in the shadows during the sixties. Yet the medical profession was expanding its cultural authority over more and more areas of daily life. Individual life span was divided into stages, age—young and old—became medicalized, and "adolescence" became a way of thinking about hippies.

Although hippies were not exclusively young, this new social type was inextricable from a rising youth culture. Accordingly, a pathologizing discourse of adolescence inflected the stories told about them. Psychologist G. Stanley Hall is credited with "discovering" adolescence in the early twentieth century, with the publication of his two-volume *Adolescence*.[20] But the scientific categorization of individuals by age predates him. Throughout the nineteenth century, the biological changes associated with puberty led to adolescence being increasingly viewed as a discrete, biologically-based developmental life phase. In her queer history of adolescence, Gabrielle Owen links age-based classifications, and the consequent cultural and historical invention of adolescence, to the aggregation of other social identities in the mid- to late nineteenth century based on race, class, gender, and sexuality.[21] The adolescent came to be seen as a new type of person, one subject to the inequities of social hierarchies. Scholars and journalists framed them in negative terms as "conflicted, burdened by their ordeals, and psychologically disturbed if not ill."[22]

Adolescents became problems. Rebellion was one of them. Hall, considered the father of adolescence, claimed there were three symptoms: mood disruptions, risk-taking, and conflicts with parents, who were responsible for inculcating them with the "'true norms' of home, school, church, and state."[23] Adolescents were potentially "evil in their nature."[24] Like other social categories, such as race, class, and sexualities, adolescence operated as a form of institutional regulation, reinforcing ideals of heterosexuality, traditional gender norms, the reproductive nuclear family, consumerism, and a conventional work ethic.[25]

In Western cultures, adolescence became increasingly medicalized. Its study expanded through the work of theorists such as Sigmund Freud, Abraham Maslow, and Jean Piaget. Some attributed adolescence to the social changes of modernity, the same influences that gave rise to other forms of difference and created other outsiders. Others viewed it as biologically determined. Freud considered adolescence a pathology. Adolescent psychiatry medicalized young people and their behaviors, producing stigmatizing frames by which to understand them. Medical anthropologists Horacio Fabrega and Barbara Miller point out that this psychiatric medicalization of adolescence, "claimed as neutral and 'scientific,'" operated as a form of biopower promoting "victimization and oppression."[26] This culturally invented developmental stage of adolescence, a liminal time between childhood and adulthood, helped produce hippies and their rebellion against oppressive norms. Pathologizing tropes inflected the cultural stories told about them.

Reminiscent of hobos and the tramp scare, hippies were initially feared and reviled, and then rebranded and commodified. Mainstream media sensationalized and mocked hippies. Coverage of them focused on danger, pathologies, and newly medicalized social problems such as drug use, mental illness, sexual promiscuity, and violence. Early journalists such as Joan Didion demonized them. Her 1967 *Saturday Evening Post* signature piece—"Hippies: Slouching Toward Bethlehem"—is noteworthy because it exemplified early media stories, especially her reinforcement of the LSD panic invoked by other venues, such as *Time*. That same year, the *Atlantic* would write, "Among the hippies of San Francisco, LSD precipitated suicide and other forms of self-destructive or antisocial behavior."[27] Didion painted a dystopian portrait of social collapse, drug use, and child abuse. Critic Louis Menand recently noted that "she genuinely loathed the hippies" and saw them as "symptoms of a dangerous psychopathology."[28]

In keeping with frameworks of adolescent pathology, Didion depicted hippies as childish rebels resisting parental guidance. The hippies of the Haight were "an army of children" who were "cut loose from the web of cousins and great-aunts and family doctors and lifelong neighbors who had traditionally suggested and enforced the society's values."[29] Adults had "somehow neglected to tell these children the rules of the game." Didion condemned their violation of traditional social norms; for hippies, rejecting these norms was the point.

Youth subcultures of the sixties, in both the US and UK, were vulnerable to such pathologizing media hyperbole. Headlines like "The Hippie Cult" and "Hippie Mother Held in Slaying of Son," along with stories about free love and drug use, trafficked in the mobilization of intense affect in the service of moral politics. The 1969 film *Easy Rider*, which ends with attacks on two countercultural bikers, captured the bigotry, hostility, and physical attacks directed toward hippies. Anti-hippie billboards appeared around the country, along with store and restaurant signs such as "Hippies not served here."[30] One hippie man recently recollected, "People don't really understand this now, but at that time, in most of the country, you

Cover of *the Saturday Evening Post*, September 23, 1967, which ran writer Joan Didion's famous article, "Slouching Toward Bethlehem."

couldn't have long hair and not be in danger of being beaten up. . . . I was continually harassed, spit on, and shoved around."[31] Jefferson Airplane, the Haight Ashbury rock group that "came to epitomize the counterculture,"[32] flouted these outsider media depictions in their lyrics: "We are obscene, lawless, hideous, dangerous, dirty, violent, and young."[33]

Media distortion was the central dynamic in what sociologist Stanley Cohen called moral panics about rebellious young people. Moral panics were characterized by repressive actions such as police sweeps of countercultural urban neighborhoods like the Haight, the use of undercover agents, and routine arrests. In other words, notions of deviant youth in the sixties were socially produced, largely through medicalized frameworks inflecting inflammatory media constructions. The funeral notice for the Death of Hippie march in 1967 protested sensationalist coverage of the Haight Ashbury scene by "the media-police,"[34] who derogated hippies while simultaneously selling newspaper stories about them.

As many young people in the sixties dropped out, protested, took drugs, and experimented with transgressive ways of living, some were at universities absorbing and developing new social theories of difference and outsiders. Symbolic interactionism, deviance theories, ethnographic methods, and work by scholars such as Erving Goffman, Joseph Gusfield, and Howard Becker were on the curriculum. These young academics were often outsiders themselves, coming of intellectual age in "the disobedient generation."[35] Like hippies, sociologists were shaped by the particularities of their historical and political moment. One later reflected, "The sociologists produced during the Viet Nam War era focused on social movements, nonconformity, the politics of dissent, oppositional parties, social inequality, comparative politics, divorce, and social change."[36] American sociologists studied the youth counterculture because many were part of it during this turbulent time, and because they recognized the profound cultural shift underway. Innovative scholarship about deviance traveled across the Atlantic to influence British scholars of the National Deviancy Conference. (**See Hyperlink 7.1:** Countercultures, Moral Panics, and the National Deviancy Conference.) In both countries, whether it was smoking dope or transgressing sexual norms, many shared the new, hippie idea. Inspired by the sociological challenge to moral entrepreneurs and oppressive social systems, sociologists launched ethnographic field research to study these new outsiders. Some young sociologists considered themselves to be outsiders in the mainstream academy by their embrace of what some described as insurgent theories and methods. Some, like Sherri Cavan, were marginal women.

Sherri Cavan, a long-time resident of the Haight hippie epicenter, conducted research there between 1961 and 1968. It was the era when Didion explored the district for her *Post* article. Cavan had recently completed her dissertation under the supervision of Erving Goffman. In contrast to Didion (who later acknowledged that she had never fully succeeded in her *Post* story),[37] Sherri Cavan narrated the complicated social worlds of Haight hippies, where they developed and learned outsider knowledge and practices. Cavan saw hippies as "flesh and blood people" managing their practical daily activities in ways they understood "as proper and fitting for the time and place." She argued that hippies developed forms of cultural knowledge about being this new kind of person—a hippie—and then engaged in specific everyday hippie practices.

Sherri Cavan: Outsider Women of Sociology

Poet and writer May Sarton's novel, *The Small Room*, was published in 1961, the year Sherri Cavan started graduate school. *The Small Room* featured a small women's college in New England facing a crisis when a star pupil plagiarized a paper. The novel was noteworthy in its fictional depiction of women in academia. It boasted strong, brilliant women professors. Still, it expressed cultural anxieties about women's suitability for academic life, whether as professors or students. One of Sarton's super-star professors mused, "Teaching women is a special kind of challenge," while another asked, "Is there a life more riddled with self-doubt than that of a woman professor, I wonder?"[38] At the time the novel was published, women were quintessential outsiders in that insider place of the academy.

In *The Small Room*, an incoming professor was surprised to see how many men were on the faculty of the women's college. She need not have been—the absence of women professors was simply the norm at most universities. Women were excluded from key academic arenas—for example, Harvard University did not award degrees to Radcliffe students until 1963, or allow women access to its Lamont Library until 1967. There had been no women professors at the University of California, Los Angeles, where Cavan had received her master's degree. Sociologist Carol Warren recounted that, at the University of California, San Diego, sociology chair Joseph Gusfield declined to admit her to the graduate program because she was "too old" (she was twenty-six) and a "La Jolla housewife" (she was unmarried). She picketed outside his window with a sign reading, "Admit La Jolla Housewives" (amused, he eventually admitted her).[39]

Sociologist Sherri Cavan at her home in Haight Ashbury, standing in front of some of her sculptures, 2014. Photograph by the author.

Dynamics of exclusion and marginalization—the notorious "chilly climate"[40] for women in the academy—constructed women as outsiders, and frequently, their research topics as irrelevant. Between 1952 and 1972, the sociology department at the University of California at Berkeley awarded women only 32 of the 126 PhDs it granted. One of those was to Sherri Cavan. At twenty-three years old, Cavan had "packed books, dishes, diapers, and plants into a Volkswagen bug, strapped the baby in his car seat, and started north on Highway 1" for graduate school.[41] The department, established in 1948, would be ranked first in the nation by 1964.[42] (Governor Ronald Reagan called the university "a haven for sex deviants."[43]) From its founding until 1970, the department had no tenure-track women faculty. By the mid-1970s, women comprised 5.6 percent of the faculty at UC-Berkeley.[44] At the time, Cavan and other women graduate students considered this gender imbalance normal. Arlene Kaplan Daniels, also in the Berkeley program, later recalled about it, "We were all boys together, there was no other choice. The notion that women might have different agendas or interests or problems was unheard-of."[45]

Cavan became a student of Erving Goffman, learning ethnographic methods and participant observation. For her dissertation, she conducted research in approximately 100 San Francisco bars, including working at a skid-row bar. Gender, she discovered, worked to her advantage in research: "You know, I was just a female. It was always a kind of advantage in doing any kind of observational study because being a female you're not counted as anything, it's like being a servant. It was, in an odd way, not a disadvantage to be a female."[46] *Liquor License*, the book based on her dissertation, was published in 1966.

In 1961, her first year of graduate school, Cavan moved into a "dilapidated Victorian house" in San Francisco's Haight Ashbury district, then a working-class, ethnically diverse neighborhood.[47] As she became a social scientist, she observed her neighborhood changing. She told me, "I ended up living in the Haight Ashbury. Son of a gun, who would have believed that there were all these hippies, in my own neighborhood, and they weren't there when I moved there. I always describe it like a botanist, you look in your backyard, and here is this strange plant."[48] She collected "occasional, non-systematic" materials on the district from 1961 to 1963, and then became active in the Haight Ashbury Neighborhood Council. Her observations and documentation became more frequent, and she met "the self-identified leaders of what came to be called 'the Straight Community,'" and later "the self-identified leaders of the Hippie community."[49] Her research continued through 1968, and although she wrote that her work was not an ethnography, her field notes, informal interviews, and participant observation are all consistent with ethnographic practices.

Unlike journalists such as Joan Didion, who portrayed hippies as drug-addled threats to social order, Cavan found reasonable connections between hippie beliefs and hippie practices. Hippies were members of a community, albeit an outsider community, with normative ways of being transgressive. She recalled, "Eventually I could see that there was this enterprise that was going on, and people were making rules, and people were breaking rules, and people were watching all of this. So, I could see that [hippie] was a way of conceptualizing a social system."[50] Drug use, panhandling, macrobiotic diets, psychedelic concerts—these were all ways of being an outsider in 1967, being a hippie.

Like most women sociologists, Sherri Cavan is missing from the field's public history and its canon. Male sociologists who studied hippies garnered much more attention, such as Lewis Yablonsky, who took LSD during research for his modestly titled, *The Hippie Trip: A Firsthand Account of the Beliefs and Behaviors of Hippies in America by a Noted Sociologist* (1968). Cavan, a prolific author of books and articles, falls into what sociologist Wei Luo and his colleagues dub the "erased" category of productive women scholars who have been dropped from the discipline's history.[51] (**See Hyperlink 7.2:** An Interview with Sherri Cavan.)

How the Haight Produced Hippies

Hippies and the Haight were synonymous. San Francisco's forty-four-block Haight Ashbury District shows the importance of place in constructing outsiders and social difference. Places produce subcultures and support particular social identities and ways of living. The Haight Ashbury District both attracted young people who defined themselves as hippies, and also—through its outsider institutions, norms, and practices—produced young people as hippies. Sherri Cavan defined hippies in this historical location in time and place, as "a collectivity of identical individuals living in the Haight Ashbury District between 1966 and 1968."[52] Although hippies lived in cities and rural communes around the country, the Haight, until the end of the decade, was legendary.

Geographical location was one major factor. For one, the Haight was in California, a comparatively young state known for fostering creative communities, bohemianism, and iconoclastic lifestyles. In the early 1960s, public opinion polls ranked California first as "best state" and "ideal place to live."[53] "California Dreaming" (1965) was a widespread pastime, not just a song.

When Cavan moved to Haight Ashbury, she became an insider in what would soon become an outsider place. The prehippie Haight Ashbury was a quiet but vibrant area near Golden Gate Park and the Pacific Ocean. How you said its name was a marker of who you were. As Sherri Cavan wrote, "For the Straight residents it remained 'The Haight Ashbury.' For the media, it became 'The Hashbury.' For the Hippies, it eventually came to be called simply 'The Haight.'"[54] At the time she arrived, in 1961, it was the ideal spot for a young graduate student.

Close to several universities, Haight Ashbury was a liberal, racially mixed, middle- and working-class neighborhood, known for its striking three-story Victorian houses—what would later be called the "painted ladies." Rents were cheap—a large Victorian on Cavan's street containing six bedrooms rented for $15 a month.[55] Many Black homeowners had relocated there from the Fillmore area, which had been targeted for redevelopment. Cavan dryly noted that the established residents prided themselves on their liberalism and support for racial and economic integration.

Therefore, they "made 'not making an issue of the influx' [of Blacks] a major issue."[56] As part of neighborhood engagement, a staffer from the Student Nonviolent Coordinating Committee worked to organize poor African Americans in the area.

In addition to its liberal politics, the Haight supported a bohemian tradition. Although scores of its longtime residents were artists, writers, and actors, many more bohemians and social outsiders moved there in the early sixties as the Beat scene in North Beach collapsed. Historian John Moretta noted that the North Beach rebels brought to Haight Ashbury "anti-bourgeois bohemianism and deviance, which they kept alive long enough for the new counterculturalists to appropriate."[57] By the mid-sixties, Haight Ashbury was a mix of its long-term residents, nearby university students, and an amalgam of outsiders such as artists and bohemians from North Beach, sexual minorities, and the surge of young drop-outs who sought out the emergent countercultural space.

Moretta suggests that few predicted that Haight Ashbury would become the nation's hippie epicenter. Sherri Cavan, however, was not surprised. The older residents seem to have "forgotten," she noted, that in addition to its other demographics, Haight Ashbury had also been "a district for deviants."[58] Specifically, in the mid-sixties, Haight Ashbury featured a number of homosexual bars, and Haight Street and the nearby parks were well-known gay cruising areas. Both Haight Ashbury and its neighboring district, the Castro, attracted large numbers of gay hippies by 1967. Cavan said, "When I would remind [residents], they would typically look at me with an uncertain expression and say, 'Oh, I forgot about that.'"[59] Cavan wondered if these older residents had recognized the homosexual residents but forgotten them, or whether they failed to even notice gay residents, because homosexuality was outside their frame of reference. It could be both, she concluded.

The Haight's gay history is generally overlooked in historical accounts of hippies, but the outsider norms and values of Haight Ashbury predated the hippies. Cavan would have noticed this because she was also an insider to the gay world; her husband, who was gay (and whom she was divorcing), had facilitated her entrée into a number of San Francisco gay bars for her dissertation research. This likely attuned her to liberal Haight Ashbury's seemingly hypocritical dealings with their homosexual neighbors.

By 1965, Haight Ashbury was changing, and Cavan told a nuanced story of demographic change. The avowedly liberal ongoing residents—who became known as the "Old Community"—struggled to accommodate the influx of young, White bohemians, dubbed the "New Community." Cavan depicted a clash of worldviews and ways of living. The Haight became a deviant district for hippies because of the interplay among the arriving individual hippies, the institutions that opened to serve them, and the normative transgressions that they represented.

Deviant places like the Haight are brought into being in part by the norms and symbolism of their social institutions and commercial enterprises. Key establishments characterized the early Haight as a congenial place for outsiders: the Straight Theater, the Psychedelic Shop, and the Free Clinic. The Straight Theater, located at 1748 Haight Street, was an alternative performance space for films, concerts, plays, and other events, that operated between 1966 and 1969. The Psychedelic Shop, nearby at 1535 Haight Street, was the first head shop in the area. In addition, Cavan pointed out the establishment of the Diggers' Free Store, the Job Co-op, the Huckleberry House (for young runaways), and the Council for the Summer of Love (organized to help with the impending influx of hippies during the summer of 1967).

As an insider, Cavan knew the little-discussed backstory to the Straight Theater, an early outsider establishment. A grand vaudeville theater built in 1912, the venue became a neighborhood movie theater, but that had closed in 1963. It reopened in the summer of 1964, redecorated inside with paintings of nude men, its marquee boasting the screening of "gay films." It was, according to the local paper, the "nation's first and only homosexual movie house."[60] Cavan noted about the "self-consciously liberal" Old Community, "nothing was said either about the gay bars or the homosexuals in the area." The theater, however, was run by the mob and encountered difficulties when the owners were arrested for writing bad checks and other offenses. The *Haight Ashbury Independent* headline blared, "Gay Haight Show Closed: Owners Flee." The article noted that the owners "blew town in a new convertible with two female impersonators in the back seat."[61] The Straight Theater then became an Assembly of God church and finally closed. It reopened in 1966. Its name was probably a play on both the venue's gay history and, as Cavan put it, "a dig at the Straight residents"[62] of the Haight.

One of the Straight Theater's cofounders, Reg Williams, referred to it as a Trip Center—a place that would establish a setting for stoned people to hang out.[63] When he first passed the abandoned theater, the furnace was broken, the doors were boarded up, its heavy-gauge copper wire had been stripped, and the building was generally dilapidated. He found four partners, consulted the I Ching, and reopened as the Straight Theater in August 1967. The marquee announced, "The Haight is Straight!"

During its brief heyday, the Straight Theater hosted dance concerts by bands such as the Grateful Dead and Quicksilver Messenger Service. The new psychedelic light shows, made popular by Ken Kesey's Acid Tests, were run by artists such as Straight Lightning, and helped establish the Straight as an "environmental theater of light."[64] Always financially challenged, the Straight Theater closed in the summer of 1969.

People need places to establish communities, and in the burgeoning Haight district, stores—along with the sidewalks in front of them—emerged as hippie places. Despite hippies' critique of capitalism, as their population increased, so too did hippie shops. In January 1966, Ron and Jay Thelin opened the first head shop in Haight Ashbury. Ron Thelin was a member of the anticapitalist Diggers, and a contributor to the countercultural newspaper the *Oracle*. The store marked a "turning point" in establishing the Haight as a countercultural place.[65] The Psychedelic Shop originally sold conventional fare such as books and records, but as the hippie scene intensified they expanded to posters, incense, Indian paisley fabrics, drug paraphernalia such as Zig-Zag rolling papers, and drugs such as marijuana and LSD. It also offered a community bulletin board and sold tickets to the vitally important dance concerts recently launched at the Straight and at the Fillmore. The store served as a community center, its existence a testament to the burgeoning youth counterculture. It closed in October 1967 at the Death of Hippies march. By that time, Haight Ashbury had numerous hippie establishments selling clothing, posters, health food, jewelry, drug paraphernalia, and myriad other "psychedelic notions." Sherri Cavan, as noted later in the chapter, explored the early conflicts that emerged in the Haight between Hip Merchants and anticapitalist hippies like the Diggers, who were suspicious that Hip Merchants wanted to market "hippie" goods to chain stores.

The Haight Ashbury Free Clinic was another key institution for hippies. In Chicago, hobo physician Ben Reitman had famously provided medical care to the city's hobos. Similarly, the Free Clinic attempted to provide health services for an exploding youth population, many of whom were living on the street and had lost health insurance when they dropped out of their middle-class backgrounds. Founded by David Smith, a young physician who had been living in the district when he finished medical training, the clinic opened in June 1967 on the corner of Haight and Clayton. Other local nurses and physicians joined him to treat the hundreds of patients who daily crowded the former dental office, with conditions such as contagious diseases, drug overdoses, injuries, pregnancies, and malnourishment. Clinic staff were harassed by other (antihippie) physicians, the police, and city officials, who thought the district should be quarantined, since its residents were "infected by a socio-cultural contagion called 'hippiness.'"[66] It was always financially challenged and overwhelmed by the huge numbers of sick and desperate young people. The Haight Ashbury Free Clinic stayed open, and free, for fifty-two years, closing in 2019.

In 1967, Gray Line tour company launched a "Hippie Tour" through the Haight. Although short-lived, it was advertised as a "descent into psychedelia," selling hippies as exotic creatures living in a strange land. Decades later, when the hippie idea had become mainstream, Cavan observed, "It's funny now as you walk down the street and you hear older guys saying to younger kids, 'This is where I did this, and this is where I did that.' It has become a place that is good for the economy, lots of tourists." The Hippie Tour, like other slumming tours, created a market by exoticizing difference, strangeness, and outsider places. (**See Hyperlink 7.3:** Slumming Tours: The Spectacle of Social Difference.)

The Strange Hippie Ordinary

The rise of new social knowledge and methodologies allowed sociologists to tell these different stories about hippies. Being a hippie by definition meant being different. In a 1970 lecture, "Doing Being Ordinary," sociologist Harvey Sacks argued that ordinariness, in the sense of an "ordinary person," was not a state of being, but rather a form of work.[67] We engage in "doing being ordinary." It is a job, a preoccupation, a set of practices. Doing being ordinary, for hippies, required doing social difference. Being ordinary meant doing being strange. Strangeness and difference had cultural logics that sociologists were duly equipped to explore.

In October 1965, the hippie commune, the Family Dog, hosted "A Tribute to Dr. Strange" at Longshoreman's Hall in San Francisco. Doctor Strange himself was a Marvel Comics character who debuted in *Strange Tales No. 110* in July 1963. The comic was drawn in a surreal, hallucinogenic style that anticipated the drug-adjacent psychedelic art movement soon to emerge. On the cusp of a countercultural rise, Marvel Comics built its popularity by creating outsider superheroes like Strange, who rejected conformity. The Tribute, publicized by the now-iconic posters and handbills by psychedelic artists such as Stanley Mouse and Rick Griffin, attracted hundreds of early hippies and featured Jefferson Airplane and other rock groups. It was, one pundit observed, "something they'd been waiting for without realizing it."[68] To paraphrase Ian Hacking, by the middle of the twentieth century, a hippie became a way to be a person, and being strange was a way to be a hippie.

The Tribute marked the start of the psychedelic era, and also reflected the hippie attraction to strangeness as an aesthetic and practice. Strangeness was in the cultural atmosphere. Robert Heinlein's science-fiction novel *Stranger in a Strange Land* (1961) became a counterculture classic. In 1967, the British rock band Cream released "Strange Brew," and in the song "Strange Days," the US band the Doors sang "Strange days have found us, strange days have tracked us down."[69] A single from that album, "People Are Strange," hit number 12 on the US Hot 100 chart. Georg Simmel's stranger, the wanderer who "comes today and stays tomorrow,"[70] had come to stay in America. The strangers were America's sons and daughters.

Strangeness had cultural logics. In the way that social researchers sought to make the strange familiar, Cavan hung out in the Haight, tracking what it meant to do "everyday Hippie things." In her accounts, a strange haze colored seemingly mundane practices. Everyday hippies engaged in dressing and working (or not), being social ("rapping," walking in the park, listening to music), and "just being." "Just being" could mean a sort of meandering through the day, especially for hippies who eschewed structured workplaces (or those regularly doing drugs).

Hippies engaged in "just being," either individually or collectively, typically on the streets and in the parks. "Just being" was also a repudiation of middle-class values that celebrated constant striving and the growing expansion of the workday and workweek. Hippies, then, constructed time differently, as less linear and demanding. Cavan, who had a hippie postman, noted that "The understanding on the part of the Hippies so employed is that if the mail gets to its addressed destination, then the job has 'been done,' regardless of *when* it gets there [emphasis in original]." This rejection of conventional time norms was yet another rejection of middle-class work ethics.

Dancing was an important "everyday hippie thing." Dancing itself changed. Sociologist Frances Rust noted, "When change comes there will be new dances to mark it."[71] Hippies adopted a free-form dance style, encouraged by psychedelic music and psychedelic drugs. Gone were the structured dances of earlier generations, such as the South Side and the Shimmy, which had flourished in the taxi-dance halls of the 1920s. Indeed, the taxi-dance halls had masqueraded as dance academies established to teach such steps. The new, solitary, free-form dance established hippies as outside "the ballroom of civilization"[72] in which earlier generations danced. It was an embrace of difference, although one sociologist at the time noted (with a dubious metaphor) that structured dances were actually new in the long history of dance, and "contemporary social dancing has returned to the very beginning of the cycle—to the jungle!"[73] Cavan depicted hippie dancing through an ethnographic eye: "As understood by the members of the Hippie community, one can dance without it having to be apparent *to others* that there is some 'connection' between the movement of the dancer and the sounds of the music [italics in original]."[74] It was hippie free-style dancing.

Cavan described dancing as one potential aspect of "a happening," the term for events in which hippies were simultaneously involved in an activity within "some perceivably bounded area." In the Haight, concert halls such as the Fillmore, the Avalon, Winterland, the Longshoremen's, and the Straight Theater all hosted happenings—dances featuring rock bands, light shows, and strobe lights. In her field notes, Cavan described a dance at the Fillmore that she attended with friends, their two children, and Cavan's son, Adam, aged seven at the time (Adam told me he does not recall attending this Fillmore dance). She described the general milling about and sociability in a setting enlivened by strobe lights, black lights, and a light show that formed a psychedelic backdrop for the concert. Dancing began even before the musicians arrived—dancing "in the sense of two or three people standing in a somewhat cleared area of the floor and moving their bodies in some decisive way, unlike simply 'wandering' around." Cavan, who detected no discernible pattern, asked her friend for the names of the dances, and was told the hippies were "just dancing." Cavan mused, "I get the feeling that my request for the 'name' of the dance makes no sense to her; has no relevance to what she understands is taking place." Free-style dancing, because it defied contemporary mainstream dance styles, fostered a boundary between hippies and straights, insiders and outsiders.

Dancing was so central to Haight hippies that the owners of the Straight Theater tore out hundreds of the fixed theater chairs to create a 5,000-square-foot dance floor. Once completed, the chief of the San Francisco police denied the dancehall permit, saying, "Dance would be bad for the neighborhood." In response, and harkening back to taxi-dance-hall history, they established the Straight Theater Dance Workshop, which did not require a permit. Their first weekend of "dance classes" starred the Grateful Dead, and the "classes" highlighted improvisation. Dancing under the guise of "dance classes" continued at the Straight until it closed.[75]

Sherri Cavan's stories of ordinary hippies doing "hippie-ness" highlighted her sociological argument that the hippie was not pathological, irrational, or deviant, but rather a new social type with new social norms.

Hippie activities and hippie strangeness made sense within hippie culture. By the mid-seventies, many of the styles, behaviors, and beliefs that had made hippies seem strange had been commodified, normalized, and absorbed to become the ordinariness of mainstream culture. One such behavior was smoking pot.

Beyond Reefer Madness

In the infamous campfire scene of the 1969 counterculture film *Easy Rider*, two of the characters introduce a third, George, to marijuana. The scene captured the transgressive allure of pot smoking in that era: "Lord have mercy!" George exclaims when Billy (played by Dennis Hopper) offers him a joint. And when George asks, "How do I do it?" the scene could have been adapted from sociologist Howard Becker's iconic 1963 text, *Outsiders*. In his chapter "Becoming a Marijuana User," originally published as a journal article a decade earlier, Becker argued that the effects of marijuana are socially learned rather than physiologically induced.

Becker, who was also a professional dance musician, conducted fifty interviews, including interviews with nonmusicians. He argued that pot smokers needed to learn the technique (inhaling and holding sufficient amounts of smoke, for example). But more importantly, they needed to learn "to perceive the effects." It was not necessarily obvious to novice smokers what it would mean or feel like to be high; rather, the user needed to connect possible characteristics of marijuana use, such as hunger or feeling "something different," with their use of the drug.[76] In *Easy Rider*, George claimed his joint had gone out, and implied that he was not stoned, yet went on to spin a nutty—seemingly stoned—conspiracy theory about UFOs. Just as sociologists were doing, the film blurred the line between being straight and stoned, between normalcy and deviance.

George was played by Jack Nicholson, who forty years later admitted that the actors had smoked real pot during the filming of the scene. That would have made them part of a tiny minority; only 4 percent of Americans responded "yes" to a 1969 Gallup question about marijuana use. Indeed, the actors might have been jailed, since the Boggs Act of 1952 imposed a mandatory sentence for even first-time cannabis possession.

Marijuana had a long history among musicians, who in "reefer songs" extolled its salutary effects on auditory acuity.[77] Antimarijuana crusader Harry J. Anslinger compiled a "Marijuana and Musicians" file in the 1930s. He targeted jazz musicians, in particular African Americans, such as Billie Holiday and Charlie Parker, for alleged drug use, and used notoriously racist language in his antipot propaganda. Anslinger argued that marijuana led to criminality and insanity, and promoted the Marijuana Tax Act that passed Congress in 1937. Although the New York Academy of Medicine refuted Anslinger's claims in 1944, marijuana was still feared as a gateway drug.

Marijuana was illegal, stigmatized, and off the cultural radar screen in the early sixties. In 1965, *Newsweek* featured an article entitled, "Narcotics: Slum to Suburb," signaling growing anxiety about its crossover to White youth.[78] Its association with deviant underworlds contributed to a sense of danger and stigma. In a 1965 survey of the general public asking people to "list those things or types of persons whom you regard as deviant," homosexuals ranked first at 49 percent, followed closely by drug addicts (47 percent).[79] Law enforcement continued to target musicians, including the new hippie rock groups in the Haight. The Grateful Dead were arrested when their communal house on Page Street was raided in October 1967. FBI Director J. Edgar Hoover used drug charges as a pretense to arrest hippies, activists in the Black Panthers, and members of the New Left.

Yet pot played a crucial role in everyday hippie life. Smoking pot was transgressive and defiant, thereby enhancing its appeal to the counterculture. Drug use fostered hippie community and identity (as the term "head" for pothead signified). Sherri Cavan dedicated a chapter of her book to this "routine Hippie thing."[80] In "How to Obtain Grass in the Haight," she described the minutiae of conducting marijuana transactions. Hippies needed to know how to buy, sell, give away, and ask others for grass. They also needed to learn how to get high.

Marijuana transactions, as Sherri Cavan pointed out, were deeply cultural events, shaped by norms, shared meanings, and social networks and interactions. Her early account of pot dealing was unusual for its granularity. With the acuity (and humor) of an anthropologist's field notes about elusive island inhabitants, she described hippie lore regarding the "most satisfactory and aesthetic way" to smoke pot, for example using rolling paper versus pipes. Prerolled joints were frowned on as disallowing "stylistic flexibility." She painted portraits of hippies deliberating over marijuana pricing and quality. They worried about whether they got a good deal, or instead got scammed. Networks mattered, since the best way to obtain grass was to "know your dealer." Therefore, Cavan noted, the best way to obtain grass in the Haight required the ability to form friendships in the Haight.

Moreover, although deviants were rule-breakers by definition, sociologists recognized that deviant behavior, such as obtaining and using marijuana, had its own norms and rules. Sherri Cavan captured some of those pot norms in her Haight field observations. She noted, for example, that "Whenever grass is being smoked, it is considered proper and fitting that the joint be offered to anyone who is there. There is no requirement, however, that it be accepted; one can decline by simply saying 'no' or shaking one's head when it is offered. . . . Like eating in front of others who are not eating in the conventional community, smoking grass when others are not smoking is considered rude. The 'rudeness' in the Hippie community is allocated, not to the one who desires to engage in the activity, but to the one who has declined to engage."[81] Hippies, it turned out, did observe social proprieties, albeit those of their own making.

Howard Becker and Sherri Cavan were sociological pioneers in research on mid-twentieth-century marijuana use, influencing other young scholars to launch similar studies. One described walking through a park in New York City: "I noticed some people smoking marijuana. And I thought, 'Gee, this is interesting.' I had read Howie Becker's articles on marijuana use and I started conceiving of a study on marijuana use." In cities such as San Francisco or New York, social researchers like this one studying pot were in tune with a cultural shift: "I think a lot of the people I interview expected me to [smoke pot.] They all offered me joints while I was interviewing them. So that was kind of taken for granted anyway."[82] The culture of "reefer madness" was fading. As Sherri Cavan had observed, smoking marijuana became simply ordinary for a cohort of young people. Sociologists, some of whom were hippies, pointed out that cultural anxieties about marijuana represented a moral panic fostered by moral crusaders like Harry Anslinger.

Sixties sociologists emphasized the historical contingency of deviance. The people, places, and practices considered deviant change over time and across cultures. Pot smoking proved their point. By 1974, 445,000 people had been busted for marijuana, largely for simple possession.[83] In 1996, almost thirty years after the Summer of Love, California became the first state to legalize medical use of marijuana. Twenty years later, the state also legalized recreational marijuana use and possession of up to an ounce. By mid-2021, fifteen US states and Washington, DC, had legalized recreational marijuana, while every state except Nebraska and Idaho had passed legislation allowing some type of medical marijuana use.

Hippies Selling, Selling Hippies

In 1966, singer-songwriter Janis Joplin wrote a letter to her family back home in Texas:

> A fashion note—thought y'all would like to know what everyone looks like out here. The girls are, of course, young and beautiful looking w/long straight hair. The beatnik look, I call it, is definitely in. Pants, sandals, capes of all kinds, far-out handmade jewelry, or loose fitting dresses & sandals. The younger girls wear very tight bell-bottoms cut very low around the hips & short tops—bare midriffs. But the boys are the real peacocks. All have hair at least Beatle length & some, our manager Chet's for example as long as this [Joplin included several sketches], much longer than mine. And very ultra Mod dress—boots, always boots, tight low pants in hound's tooth check, stripes, even polka-dots! Very fancy shirts—prints, very loud, high collars, Tom Jones full sleeves. Fancy print ties, Bob Dylan caps . . .
>
> Conforming to the style to the extent of my budget, I have a new pair of very wide-wale corduroy hip-hugger pants which I wear w/ borrowed boots. Look very in. On stage, I still wear my black & gold spangly blouse w/either a black skirt & high boots or w/black Levis & sandals.[84]

The cultural politics of style burgeoned in the mid-sixties. Young people—from the hippies to the Black Panthers, to feminists and gay activists—used clothing, hairstyles, and other appearance practices to craft new body narratives and body politics of nonconformity. Sherri Cavan called that moment the "era of the 'costume,'" comprised of any outfit "from a different temporal era or a different geographical place: flowing eastern robes, uniforms that looked like those worn by Civil War officers, American Indian feathers, Victorian morning dresses, or 1930 evening gowns."[85]

Sociologist Michael Brown dubbed these hippie styles "apparel deviance" and "hair deviance," signifying tribal membership in a counterculture that defiantly rejected the uniforms of conformity.[86] It may be difficult to recognize now, but bell-bottom pants, granny dresses, buckskin fringe, mod fashions, neo-Edwardian and Victorian suits, gypsy and American Indian items, and caftans all represented a choice of strangeness over tradition. This eccentric clothing made Haight Ashbury into "a crazy quilt of living color."[87] Although a snarky *Time* magazine cover story would dub this look as "beards, beads, and bangles—conforming nonconformity,"[88] the choice of these styles over conventional fashion—at least in the early years—constructed a collective outsider identification while repudiating the bland uniformity of mainstream, middle-class appearance norms.

But where did hippies get these outsider clothes? Some knitted their own or sewed them out of bedspreads, curtains, or exotic fabrics. Embroidery produced unique flourishes on jeans or vests. Attics, vintage and surplus stores, and grandparents' trunks were also fruitful sources of retro fashion. But not everyone could make or find these outsider styles, giving rise to what some derided as "store-bought hip."[89] Others, lacking a fashion sense, found designers.

Sherri Cavan lived at 1283 Page Street, in the Haight. Down the street at 616 Page was Charles Manson, who lived there briefly in 1967 and was not yet infamous when Cavan was doing her hippie research. Musicians who became famous—Janis Joplin, Jimi Hendrix, and Jefferson Airplane—all lived a few blocks from her. Music journalist Danny Goldberg describes these artists as "key thought leaders" in the community;[90] they were also style icons, what we now call influencers, both shaping and being shaped by countercultural fashions.

Janis Joplin was the quintessential outsider, a defiant but vulnerable misfit whose transgressions of rigid cultural, gender, and sexual norms would later become more commonplace. Historian Alice Echols calls her "a breakthrough woman in American culture" who "changed the rules for all of us."[91] Still, Joplin did not immediately achieve her signature hippie flamboyance. Soon after moving to the Haight, she discarded her typical outfits of sweatshirts and jeans in favor of eclectic thrift shop purchases. She had a favorite blouse made from a recycled lace tablecloth. (Echols describes this item as "a giant doily."[92] However, designers such as Del Pitt Feldman redefined crocheting from "granny squares and doilies" to quirky garments such as the vests, minidresses, and skirts donned by counterculture figures such as Joplin, Jimi Hendrix, and Grace Slick.)[93] As Joplin got more famous, her audience may have assumed that she assembled her own edgy style, yet she had help from more fashion-savvy friends, such as Nancy Gurley, who pushed her toward the "hippie chick" look of jangly bracelets, feather boas, and velvet vests. Designer Linda Gravenites outfitted her in such clothes as a silk chiffon blouse trimmed with velvet, purple pants, and embroidery from an Art Deco opera cloak. The look helped define Joplin, the music, and the counterculture.

Paradoxically, being a hippie required both repudiating consumerism and having hip stuff. Modes of production and consumption were shifting, but consumer capitalism did not end. Core dimensions of counterculture life were quickly commodified and sold: music and art, clothing, drug paraphernalia, exotic fabrics, and more. Corporations and hippie merchants alike found a large market for nonconformity and strangeness. Outsider capitalism introduced the appeal of hippie strangeness into the mainstream.

The commercialization began early. The mass commodification of art, fashion, and especially music was simultaneously a commodification of style and of cultural difference. Its commercial success speaks to its mass appeal. A *Guardian* article described the plethora of merchandising by the Beatles as early as 1964:

> While the Beatles toured the United States, three of their singles were in the top six and their albums ranked one and two in the record-popularity charts. Beatle wigs were selling at three dollars apiece, high-school boys were combing their forelocks forward, and hairdressers were advertising Beatle cuts for women. Beatle hats, t-shirts, cookies, egg cups, ice cream, dolls, beach shirts, turtleneck pullovers, nighties, socks and iridescent blue-and-green collarless suits were on the market, and a Beatle motor scooter for children and a Beatlemobile for adults were being readied for production. "I think everyone has gone daft," says John. Adds Ringo, "Anytime you spell 'beetle' with an 'a' in it, we get the money." In 1964, Beatle-licensed products grossed $50,000,000 in America alone. As for the Beatles, their total income that year reached $14,000,000.[94]

By 1967, the Beatles had opened an Apple boutique selling clothing and jewelry (they soon closed it and gave away the inventory).[95]

In the mid-sixties, department stores dominated the retail clothing scene, with the top US department stores being Macy's, Hudson's, and Marshall Field. Such stores had represented one of the first urban spaces open to women without male accompaniment, and helped usher in White, and later Black, middle classes into new sites of retail consumption. The stores also became targets of Black Freedom–movement protests against institutionalized racism in hiring and selling practices.[96] Once a mark of cosmopolitan modernity, a sixties White counterculture seeking strangeness and authenticity derided department-store clothing as mass-produced and distinctly unhip. The boutique stores that emerged during the sixties became a factor in the decline of department stores after their peak in the late nineteenth century.

Quirky boutique fashion began in London before it appeared in the Haight. Some of these styles and clothes destabilized gender stereotypes. The clothing designer Mary Quant—the "mother of the miniskirt"—launched a boutique and clothing line for women in the early sixties that marked "women's newly fluid status, a turn away from the obligatory yokes of husband and family insisted upon during the postwar reconstruction."[97] Her short tight skirts, black stockings, high boots, and bobbed hair were a radical departure from traditional women's styles of the era. It bears remembering that even pants were taboo for women at that time. Quant recalled designing a women's suit: "When we first cut pants, instead of a skirt, with the jacket, we actually fell about laughing."[98] Likewise, designer Rudi Gernreich, infamous for designing the topless bathing suit in 1964, saw his unisex clothing as "a total statement about the equality of men and women. . . . The male is emerging from aesthetic exile as women achieve their freedom."[99] The exuberant song "My Conviction" from the 1967 play *Hair* captured this sense of the "male's emergence from his drab camouflage into the gaudy plumage which is the birthright of his sex."[100] On men, long hair alone signaled gender nonconformity. Caftans, skinny pants, and ornate vests and jackets all repudiated the proverbial gray uniformity of the 1950s.

Hip boutique owners fostered community and the new transgressive styles. For example, in 1966, well before she became famous from her electric performance at the Monterey International Pop Festival in June 1967, Janis Joplin—broke and disheveled—wandered into the shop Mnasidika. Peggy Caserta, the owner, gave Joplin a pair of Levi's that Joplin had been eyeing but could not afford. Caserta also lent musicians such as the Dead their new hip clothing for concerts and photo shoots.[101] Clothing designers such as Linda Gravenites, whose mother had taught her on a lightweight Singer sewing machine, began making custom clothing for clients. Gravenites recalled embroidering flowers on her jeans: "I'd never seen anything like them before. My jeans got stared at a whole lot. 'Turn around,' people would urge me as I walked through Golden Gate Park. . . . Two years later they were on the market."[102]

Corporations noticed the success of boutiques and outsider styles. J. C. Penney tried to order four annual collections from Mary Quant for its US chain. Quant, who thought the mass production would be "monstrous," recalled her surprise: "What we were doing here had anticipated something that was international. It was quite a shock—quite an exciting shock!"[103] By 1967, San Francisco had displaced London as the hub of countercultural style. Hippie merchants and consumers alike participated in the affluence of sixties capitalism.

It was not just clothing. Modern technologies fostered the commodification of sixties rock music. Music as a product to be bought and sold had intensified through the twentieth century, in tandem with the rapid growth of the music business. Sound recordings on physical disks improved by mid-twentieth century, becoming profitable commodities. Liquid light shows emerged and became commonplace in the mid-sixties to heighten the psychedelic power of groups such as the Doors, Jefferson Airplane, and Big Brother and the Holding Company. Together, these developments launched sixties rock concerts as epic countercultural events as well as marketing opportunities. As iconoclastic sixties musician Frank Zappa said, "The single most important development in modern music is making a business out of it."[104] Recording companies quickly capitalized on countercultural music, such as Columbia (advertising in 1968 with "But the Man can't bust our music") and CBS records, whose legendary Clive Davis signed several rock groups at Monterey.

Hippies embodied these core contradictions of both rejecting and embracing consumer capitalism. From her perch on Page Street, Sherri Cavan captured the counterculture conflict—the hippie critique of consumerism alongside the rise of so-called hip merchants. Boutiques sprung up around the Haight. Cavan noted that by the end of 1966 there were approximately thirty commercial establishments. In addition to the Straight Shop, other hip merchants launched a health food store, Far Fetched Foods; the I/Thou coffee shop; and In Gear, a hip boutique. The hippie merchants—part of the "New Community" in the Haight—sold goods such as posters, incense, jewelry, clothing and sandals, and drug-related gear. Independent craftspeople sold wares directly on the street—for example God's Eyes jewelry. However, tensions arose between the New Community and established Haight Ashbury merchants, the Old Community. Hip entrepreneurs applied for membership in the Haight Ashbury Neighborhood Merchants' Association, only to be denied because they were considered "irresponsible."[105] In response, they founded the Hip Independent Proprietors. Tensions continued between the Old and New Communities, terms that were soon replaced by the Straights and the Hippies.

Cavan's wry field observations captured a clash of worldviews. For example, the Neighborhood Council invited the Hip Merchants to a "conciliation committee" meeting, which consisted of "participants from both sides . . . airing complaints and grudges they have concerning the other side." Straights complained about hippies sitting in the doorways of stores, and about hippies having sex in public view: "It continues like this for almost twenty minutes, and then . . . the problem of whether making love in public is 'improper' also dies out."[106] Eventually, Cavan wrote, the Straights gave up, grudgingly accepted the Hippies and Hip Merchants, and even sometimes defended them against the types of police sweeps and Health Department harassment that were intensifying in the Haight.

Cavan also documented a laid-back hippie entrepreneurial ethos. She wandered the streets, visited shops, and hung out in cafés, where she found irregular work hours, shops closed during business hours, spacey (probably stoned) employees, and a relaxed attitude toward marketing. Cavan repeatedly visited a shop that was only sporadically open: "Sometimes when the shop is closed there will be a note on the door indicating when he will be back. I have encountered him at the coffee house during the hours he has posted as being 'open for business,' and mentioned that I came by the other day and he was closed; and that I came back when the note on the door said he would be back and he was still closed. He answers, to my implicit rebuke, 'That's why I have my shop on Haight Street instead of someplace else. I could probably make more money someplace else, but there would be no satisfaction in it.' He goes on to say that the reason he 'dropped out' of the Conventional society was the lack of freedom he had, that before he came to Haight Street he was 'doing the same thing I am now, only then I had to do it even when I didn't want to.'" One Hip merchant told Cavan that he only employed other hippies because working with straights "brings him down," while other hippies referred to Hip merchants as "not really being Hippies." Some Hip independent craftspeople refused to sell in hip shops because of potential "hassle" involved with the merchant.[107] Still, these complex entrepreneurial dynamics did not prevent the merchandising of hippie style.

Some hippies doggedly rejected entrepreneurialism, even by hippies. They embraced antique or old-fashioned items as partly a critique of consumerism and partly as their embrace of the strange. The "old-timey"[108] look had aesthetic appeal, while also manifesting their rejection of a materialist, acquisitive society. And so, hippie living spaces boasted outdated appliances, kitchen items, and furniture. The activist community group the Diggers perhaps most personified the critique of consumer capitalism. The Diggers had a house on Page Street near Sherri Cavan, where they gave away free items. Like their namesakes, the English Diggers, they advocated freedom from buying, selling, and private property. Their ethos was "free," whether it was through their free stores, free food services (the Oakland Black Panthers would launch their free breakfasts a few years later), free medical clinics, free crash pads, or the free parties they regularly held.

The Diggers were relentless critics of the hip merchants and the sensationalization of the Haight by the media. They staged two now-iconic marches or "happenings" in the Haight: the Death of Money march at the end of 1966, and the Death of Hippie event in October 1967, where marchers carried a coffin emblazoned with "Hippie—Son of Media." The *San Francisco Chronicle* reported that "sleepy hippies" got up early to attend their own funeral.[109] Store owner Ron Thelin reportedly said, "It must all go—a casualty of narcissism and plebian vanity. . . . [Haight Ashbury] was portioned to us by the media-police, and the tourists came to the zoo to see the captive animals, and we growled fiercely behind the bars we accepted, and now we are no longer hippies and never were."[110] A sign from his Psychedelic Shop window saying, "Be Free" (as in, be free of the hippie label) was also buried.

Long-standing corporate attraction to outsiders and rule-breaking peaked in the mid-twentieth century. Historian Thomas Frank argues that advertising became fully "hip" by 1965, well before the rise of a recognizable counterculture. Corporate advertisers, themselves beset by cultural discontent regarding fifties conformity, construed "youth culture" as a demographic, a market, and an appealing symbol of rebellion against conformist mass society. As Frank notes, "admen looked at the counterculture and saw . . . themselves."[111] And so before anyone even foresaw the Summer of Love, marketers sold a vast array of products through hip associations. Automobiles, cosmetics, hardware, even laundry detergent (Dash—"somebody had to break the rules"[112]) with the language and imagery of nonconformity, rebellion, and difference. By the apotheosis of Haight Ashbury hippie culture, around 1967–68, and even when hippies themselves were widely mocked and reviled, outsider capitalism used their music, slang, and styles to sell products. In doing so, they helped foster the migration of countercultural style to the mainstream.

Fashion signifies cultural change and the rapid cycles of rebellion and conformity. Countercultural fashion became mass produced and ubiquitous. By the early 1970s, even department stores began hawking "faux-hippie clothes."[113] Yet, as Malcolm Gladwell put it about nonconformity decades later, the "triumphant circularity of cool" is that discovering what is cool causes cool to move on.[114] Shortly before she died, Janis Joplin walked past a hip New York boutique with her friend Myra Friedman, who recalled, "Janis looked at the window, turned to me and rolled her eyes. Laughing, she complained, 'Next I'll have to start wearing tweed suits.'"[115] Joplin, an early adopter of hippie clothing styles, recognized the circularity of coolness.

Outsider capitalism appropriated and marketed hippie rebellion and lifestyles. Music, clothing, and the overall hippie aesthetic were commodified and sold to the mainstream. Yet this was part of how hippies radically transformed America. Echols points out that while sixties movements were coopted, they "transformed the country's cultural landscape in the process."[116] Hip capitalism also played a role. Sociologist Sam Binkley argues that hippie books and magazines spread hippie ideas and aesthetics into the everyday lives of middle-class Americans, fostering a modern "loosening" identity shaped by consumer and lifestyle markets.[117] Much in contemporary culture can be traced to the hippie legacy: environmental consciousness, food coops, organic and whole foods (the Diggers were known for their whole-wheat bread, a striking break from the era's presliced white Wonder Bread), and meditation and yoga (the Beatles introduced Transcendental Meditation and the Maharishi Mahesh Yogi to the West). A popular countercultural button in the late sixties had proclaimed "We Are Everywhere." Indeed, mainstream culture was tilting toward countercultural ways of being.

We Are All Hippies Now—Or Are We?

Then it was over for hippies in the Haight. By 1969, the hippie scene had moved from the Haight to Telegraph Avenue in Berkeley. Much of what we consider "the sixties" would unfold for a few more years: the breakup of the Beatles, the first Earth Day, Watergate, the shootings at Kent State and Jackson State. Janis Joplin and Jimi Hendrix died of drug overdoses within a few weeks of each other in the fall of 1970. Antiwar protests continued in the early '70s, as did the war itself. The United States invaded Cambodia. In 1973, representatives from the United States, North and South Vietnam, and the Vietcong signed the Paris Peace Accords to end the war. Sherri Cavan had concluded her research in the Haight by 1968. In 1971 she went to rural Mendocino to study hippie communes, continuing her sociological stories about the hippie idea.

The hippie as a transgressive social figure gradually vanished, absorbed into a mainstream of ersatz hippie attire, the nadir perhaps being symbolized by a pudgy Elvis in a leisure suit, shaking hands with Richard Nixon in the Oval Office in 1970. One former hippie recently recalled, "All those people who used to want to beat the hell out of me because of my long hair—now *their* hair was long!"[118] Some hippies returned to the mainstream after a rebellious period. Many young people in the Haight died of drug overdoses. Some were always only weekend hippies. Others continue their countercultural way of being, more than fifty years later. Drug use spread beyond the counterculture; by the end of the decade, 40 percent of high-school seniors reported regularly smoking pot.[119]

And yet, it wasn't over. Hippie ideas about ways of living and ways of being a person moved from the margins to the mainstream. The counterculture—outsider culture—changed dominant norms, values, and behaviors. In 1967, in his article "Why All of Us May Be Hippies Someday," sociologist Fred Davis defended hippies as a vanguard youth movement rejecting conventional middle-class values.[120] He was right, in certain respects—their rejection of conventionality became the convention.

At the same time, there was deep and abiding resistance to the cultural changes of the sixties, resulting in the polarized political conflicts that would later be dubbed culture wars. As historian Andrew Hartman noted, "The new America given life by the sixties—a more pluralistic, more secular, more feminist America—was built on the ruins of normative America."[121] The nation's political culture was changed by sixties social movements, such as civil rights, the Black Panthers, feminism, and the homophile movement, which became lesbian and gay liberation by the end of the decade. Normative America, however, preferred a culture of rules, social hierarchies and inequalities, and a culture that excluded outsiders and strangers, as evidenced in the ongoing "make America great again" slogan first used by Ronald Reagan in 1980. Sixties backlash movements attacked everything from sex education to rock music to drugs to fluoridation in the water. Social differences related to race, sexualities, immigration, and gender, braid through contemporary culture wars. Indeed, not everyone went to Woodstock. And hostility toward the cultural changes associated with that era persist.

Alice Echols suggests that one defining aspect of the generation that came of age in the sixties was its determination to defy the conformist straits of earlier generations, and to "live outside the parameters of reasonable behavior."[122] Hippies were young people defying conventional norms in a culture where youth (and their so-called unreasonableness) is medicalized. Medical and psychiatric discourses framed ways of thinking and feeling about hippies as psychologically aberrant, dangers to themselves and others, or as merely going through a phase. The new social knowledge of difference represented by scholars such as Sherri Cavan ruptured those sorts of pathologizing stories about young nonconformists.

Universities both embraced and resisted the change of new ideas. Many young scholar-activists were influenced by this new scholarship of difference, particularly concepts such as labeling and stigma. They recognized themselves as marginalized outsiders and found that the literature spoke to them personally and politically. Anthropologist Gayle Rubin recalls, "The sociology of deviance literature was the most progressive approach I could find, and it completely changed how I felt."[123] Howard Becker had called on sociologists to take the side of the underdog. Yet Cavan told me that some sociologists at her graduate institution, U.C. Berkeley, an epicenter of sixties protest, disapproved of student activism, and "they didn't take a political position because they thought it would infringe on their quote 'objectivity.'"[124] Despite this, Cavan remembered, "In the sixties, [deviance studies] was emerging as a field. All of that stuff was so exciting because it really changed the paradigm that people had. Before they said, you know, it was literally that to break a rule was to be pathological." The modern deviance framework provided legitimation for their research on marginalized subcultures.

The hippie was a symbol of change and transgression. The Haight, as historian Charles Perry put it, was not just a bunch of young people hanging out and getting stoned; rather, the vision, the hippie idea, was serious and utopian: "It was heroic."[125] Perhaps the heroism of the hippie was the courage, the optimism, to challenge conformity in a deeply conformist era. They embodied the outrageous idea that it was possible to be different, if only for the weekend.

Hyperlink 7.1: Countercultures, Moral Panics, and the National Deviancy Conference

Modern deviance concepts from the US, in particular labeling theory, traveled to young sociologists in the UK, who put a Marxist and anarchist spin on them. They held a series of National Deviancy Conferences (NDC) from 1968 to 1974, which created networks of scholars and activists all working within the modern deviance framework. The NDC, as one scholar said, "was really important in British sociology in general, because it was the only space really in Britain where there was quite a strong interactionist-type of focus." The first National Deviancy Conference was held in York, in 1968. The central founding figures were young sociologists, Laurie Taylor, Stanley Cohen, Mary McIntosh, Ian Taylor, Jock Young, Kit Carson, and David Downes. They organized thirteen conferences, ending in 1974, and published edited volumes of presented papers. Many of them went on to distinguished academic careers.

One enduring example of this movement to build new forms of social

Life Magazine cover depiction of the new youth communes as a transgression of the conventional norms of the United States. July 18, 1969.

knowledge is Stan Cohen's concept of moral panics, based on his dissertation at the London School of Economics on the battles between the Mods and Rockers. In the spring of 1964, British youth subcultures fought each other in southern beach towns such as Clacton and Brighton. Those battles between the Mods and the Rockers featured angry crowds, aggressive police reactions, and hyperbolic press attention condemning the youth as "vermin" and "louts." This vitriolic media coverage prefigured later sensationalist media depictions of hippies.

Cohen's 1972 book, *Folk Devils and Moral Panics*, depicted the Mods and Rockers as "new social types," constructed by media discourse into "folk devils."[126] In his first sentence, Cohen made a broad claim: "Societies appear to be subject, every now and then, to periods of moral panic." A vivid analytic term, the moral panic had a natural history, progressing through several stages. First, a group, person, or issue emerges to become defined as a social threat, a folk devil. The media frame this "threat" in a simplistic, stereotypical way, fueling intense public concern. Then, moral entrepreneurs devise coping mechanisms and solutions. Finally, the perceived threat diminishes and the panic recedes.

And indeed, moral panics, and the strong feelings they provoke, are transient, as were the Mods and Rockers themselves. Cohen noted in his preface that the book was already out of date when published in 1972, and that readers probably wondered, "Who . . . *were* the Mods and Rockers?" Indeed, like most subcultures, they resist easy characterization, but Mods were fashion-forward, bohemian, scooter riders while Rockers wore leather jackets and rode motorcycles. One British sociologist described Mods as having "introvert, narcissistic and homosexual undertones" while Rockers were "characterized by an aggressive masculinity."[127] No matter, there would be other moral panics after the Mods and Rockers.

The National Deviancy Conference, along with scholars in the US, studied a range of marginal social figures. Notably, they viewed social difference as a fluid process that was shaped by culture, situations, politics, and history. Concepts such as Stan Cohen's moral panics—"a sixties fusion of labeling theory, cultural politics, and critical sociology"—helped transform British criminology and, along with deviance studies in the US, shifted sociology from focusing on outsiders to studying the processes by which individuals are constructed as marginal and deviant.

Their ideas and their impact are enduring, but the NDC was not. It ended in 1974. As cofounder Laurie Taylor told me, "People wanted to go their own ways. There was a split between the Marxists and the others. We had done about thirteen or fourteen conferences, we were tired. So we decided to put the money—we had an accumulation of money, about three hundred quid, we put it on a horse, and the horse lost. Which I think was a nice way to end the whole thing."

Below are excerpts from interviews I conducted in 2012–15 with British sociologists connected to the NDC. Laurie Taylor, who became professor of sociology at the University of York and currently hosts the BBC Radio series, *Thinking Allowed*, was one of the NDC cofounders. Stevi Jackson and Victoria Greenwood were graduate students who attended the conferences. Sociologist Ken Plummer (now emeritus professor of sociology at the University of Essex) gave three papers at the NDC conferences. They reflect on two topics: how the politics and sixties counterculture shaped their scholarship, and male domination of the NDC.

Biography, Politics, and Research

The iconic, motorcycle-riding sociologist C. Wright Mills inspired many young academics who took seriously his argument that the sociological imagination required analysis of individuals in their broader social context. Biography and history intersect. NDC founders and participants described how during those political times, young sociologists engaged in allegedly deviant behavior sought alternate theoretical frameworks to analyze this behavior. They studied themselves, as young people engaging in transgressive cultural activities in a rapidly changing social and political context. UK scholars describe integrating Marxist and anarchist politics into deviance concepts, even when such politics were debated or disavowed by US scholars.

> LAURIE TAYLOR: Really, these were political times. And here were people engaged in various forms of subcultural behaviors whether it was smoking dope or various sorts of queer behavior or whatever. At the same time, they were looking around for sociology to provide some understanding of this deviant behavior, as with sexual behavior, because people who were engaging in homosexual behavior weren't prepared to describe themselves as criminals any more than people who were smoking pot while doing a bit of acid were prepared to think of themselves as criminals. So there was a biographical as well as an intellectual element. Biography and scholarship came together.
>
> There was a British criminological conference at which a number of dissatisfied people who met in pubs began to talk and said

"Look, we're underrepresented here. These people don't take us seriously." So we then decided to form an alternative group [which organized the National Deviancy Conference].

When we held these conferences in York in the late sixties going through the early seventies, the people who turned up were often as much recognizable by their aberrant lifestyles as by their commitment to a new form of sociology of deviance. And they often were, really in a way, speaking from their own biographical experience. So when Jock Young wrote a book about drug takers and spoke about the nature of drug taking, he wanted to point out the ways in which this culture was totally misrepresented in the press. He was writing from his own experience, Jock was. When Dick Hebdige came along and wrote one of the most brilliant books that came out of this, on subculture and the meaning of style, he was a Mod. Dick Hebdige dressed as a Mod, he looked like a Mod. In the bar, Dick Hebdige wouldn't be drinking pints of bitter with Ian Taylor, he would be giving people pills. When Ken Plummer came along and wanted to talk about being gay, Ken Plummer was gay. When Mary Mcintosh wanted to come along and talk about the homosexual role, Mary was homosexual. There was the biography, the lifestyles, the ways in which people in the sixties were having experimental lifestyles and they wanted to find some sort of either theoretical justification or ethnographic parallels with what we were doing.

People began referring to us in slightly reverent terms. The NDC was being described as a major sociological movement. We all felt embarrassed because we all knew we'd been taking a lot of dope and dropping a bit of acid . . . and generally misbehaving ourselves, as well as giving papers. We knew we were somewhat less than serious at times. You can't understand the NDC without understanding that biographical impetus.

And of course, what we were interested in was taking the most outrageous form of deviant behavior, not exactly normalizing it, but making sense of it, seeing it in context, seeing it as a subculture. Some of the people who attacked the NDC said we weren't so much appreciating, we're celebrating [deviance.] Of course it was political, it was very political at the time. The politics, the politics was Marxism, really.

STEVI JACKSON: [The NDC] was just considered the really cool place to be. It was where something different and exciting was happening in sociology in the late '60s and early '70s. In the British context, it was one of the few places where you were actually exposed to some sort of criticism of a very top-down sociology that didn't leave much space for human experience or agency. At that time it was quite radical, it was quite political. But I think it was seen by a lot of those in mainstream sociology as not being properly critical.

VICTORIA GREENWOOD: Oh, it was absolutely intellectually exciting. We all thought, we were all on a project. It was exciting to be engaged and we liked being on the wild side and we were very, very critical of any form of traditional criminology. Anyone who mentioned a criminal statistic as a fixed entity, we said, "This is a joke. They need to understand that crime statistics are made up and how they're made up, don't these people understand sociology?" So it was very much, "We are sociologists, you criminologists before, you were doctors, you were mathematicians, you were economists, you were all deeply straight, but we're cool and you know, we come from different politics and we see the world differently and the world is different. And we're gonna show you that we're right." People were doing interesting projects, there was no question.

KEN PLUMMER: They were all just radical. Radical, radical, radical, no matter what it was it had to be radical. But which version of radical would be very hard to pin down precisely. For example, I knew Stan Cohen wasn't a Marxist, but I thought Jock Young was. And Ian Taylor certainly was, and Laurie Taylor wasn't any of those things but rather more like a showbiz personality. And indeed, he had been in the theater before he turned to sociology. All these people went on to become professors of sociology very quickly, by the way.

Politics was much more lightweight in America than it was here. I mean obviously, we got deviance theory from America, it was people like Howard Becker, early 1960s, in the moment where not just *Outsiders*, but *The Other Side* was published and it brought together a number of different people . . . I've always been perplexed by this—because even Howard Becker I was left with a puzzle about, "Well he must be radical, but he doesn't sound it." And all the others were a bit like that, Erich Goode, [I thought] "Well, you do this sort of stuff but you don't seem to be very political about any of it." The National Deviancy Conference was political through and through. I mean, all kinds of politics, anarchism was pretty strong.

A lot of sociology is personal life written large, their preoccupations in their personal life get pushed into the academic world of academic theory and so forth. Howie Becker is one is the most manifest because he was using marijuana and was a dance-band musician in the late '40s and early '50s. Erving Goffman's wife was in a mental institution, Jock Young was a marijuana smoker and all the rest of it. Stan Cohen, well, in a sense he's spent most of his academic life looking at institutionalized marginal people. It just goes on and on, really. People studying alcohol who had drinking problems. There's a long history of it.

Women (or Not) in the NDC

Women were social outsiders in politics, certainly in the New Left and in the academy. Gendered dynamics manifested in the National Deviancy Conference as well. As Laurie Taylor notes below, the founders of the NDC were all men except for Mary McIntosh. Sociologist Ken Plummer, who attended as a young sociologist, told me, "The women's movement really starts in the late '60s, roughly the same time as the National Deviancy Conference. So by about the 1970s, it's filtering into the National Deviancy Conference, though I can't remember, quite honestly, a huge feminist input at that point." Additionally, in both the UK and the US, there were very few women professors in the '60s, although young women were entering graduate school in larger numbers by then. They encountered both sexism and vibrant intellectual environments. In addition to Laurie Taylor (below), Stevi Jackson, who went on to a position as professor of women's studies at the University of York, and Victoria Greenwood, who left sociology to become a lawyer—both graduate students at the time—recently reflected on their experiences of sexism and male domination at the NDC.

> LAURIE TAYLOR: The original members of the committee were myself, Paul Walton, Stan Cohen, David Downes, Paul Rock, Mary McIntosh. I mean the male-female imbalance reflected the times. There were later people who became associated with it like Angela McRobbie, but in the first early days, Mary McIntosh was pretty well much alone.
>
> STEVI JACKSON: There was probably still sexism in the NDC. Quite a lot of the guys saw women as fair game. And women were a minority, and they were mostly grad students. But there was not

homophobia amongst the NDC lot, because there were quite a few gay men there. Obviously Ken Plummer was one of them, Jeffrey Weeks, Mike Brake, Don Milligan. Quite a lot of gay men. Again, they were all fairly young gay men at that time. They were very definitely out in that context. I think they felt it a comfortable context to be in. I didn't find the sociology of deviance any more sexist than any other branch of sociology. In fact, somewhat less so, I would say.

VICTORIA GREENWOOD: That was 1971. My memory is of a lot of drinking, a lot of guys, I mean for women you were constantly fending them off. I can remember the place, I can remember the hall, I can remember the atmosphere, it was a lot of late-night sitting around talking and at work they had these kind of units, maybe five rooms and a common area and so the people would end up in one of those communal areas and there'd be a lot of drink and chat and there was a lot of discussion on politics, crime, and deviance. A lot of politics. I remember it was tiring for me, the first one, I was sort of intimidated. I mean I was young. Jock Young was nine years older than me, Laurie Taylor, I mean all of these guys were a lot older, and for me it was a new kind of arena.

When I joined the NDC nobody talked about anything to do with women. There was very little information and there were a lot of stereotypes out there. So I started to do papers on women in crime.

It was very sexist. They picked up whoever they wanted. I don't think it was any different from any other conference at the time except there was a kind of element of, "We're cool." But you know there was quite a lot of sex and drugs and rock and roll that's for sure. There was often a band playing, there was certainly a jukebox. I can remember an evening of people sitting around smoking dope, I can remember who it was but they will remain nameless.

The women's movement gained political momentum and visibility in many Western countries in the late '60s, eventually challenging male domination and effecting broader, and ongoing, social change. The National Deviancy Conference was a microcosm of other social and political spaces of the '60s, in which women occupied subordinate status while also contributing to intellectually and politically vibrant movements. Historian Alice Echols makes a similar point about the male-dominated Left movement, which "despite its considerable sexism, provided much of the intellectual foundation and cultural orientation for the women's liberation movement."[128] The blend of politics and theory proved a potent mix for women mobilizing against gender and sexual inequalities and developing their own political theories.

Mary McIntosh and Stanley Cohen both died in 2013. In a website remembrance, sociologist Ken Plummer, who had been part of the NDC along with McIntosh and Cohen, wrote about them, "They were both inspirational; both pioneers in their works for rights and better worlds; both serious intellectuals; and both very dear people."[129] In July 2013, I had contacted NDC cofounder Jock Young for an interview. He was then at City University of New York, and immediately agreed to talk with me, although then dropped out of touch. On August 9, I received the following email from him, explaining his silence, while I was on an Amtrak train headed to New York City: "I'm not being difficult it is just that I have laryngitis and my voice keeps disappearing!!!!" He offered me two short windows of opportunity for an interview, neither of which I could make. Jock Young died three months later, on November 16, of anaplastic thyroid cancer, a rare and aggressive disease. A number of former NDC colleagues attended a memorial service for him, including Victoria Greenwood.

Hyperlink 7.2: An Interview with Sherri Cavan

I first interviewed Sherri Cavan about her career over the phone in 2013. We had an almost immediate follow-up phone call, wanting to complete what had felt to both of us like a dangling conversation. In 2014, when the American Sociological Association held its annual meeting in San Francisco, I visited Sherri at her striking Victorian home on Page Street in the Haight. She showed me her artwork, graciously gave me one of her sculptures, and then we shared a dinner filled with academic stories and gossip. Below is a brief interview excerpt where she talked about being Erving Goffman's student and launching her research on hippies. Sherri Cavan died in February 2016. Her son, Adam, noted that her dog and cat were by her side.

> Sherri Cavan (SC): One of the classes that I was taking with Erving Goffman, I guess one of the first ones, was based on his work that was later published as *Behavior in Public Places*. And we were allowed to choose a research topic. My ex-husband at that time was involved in a little theater group and through this little theater group he knew a lot of people in the bar scene down in North

Beach in San Francisco. And there was one bar which was really kind of interesting. It was a gay bar. At that time, there were half a dozen gay bars in the whole city, maybe a few more than that, and nobody knew about them, or if they did it was not widely known. But this was a strange kind of bar. It would frequently get a lot of tourists. There was this interesting dynamic of interaction between the regulars, who were all gay, who claimed the bar as their home territory, and the tourists who had heard about this place and would come to see what they could see. Because I knew the people who were in the bar scene who owned bars and who were gay at that time, I had the opportunity to spend a lot of time there. So that was the first paper that I wrote, which was for Goffman, which was called "Interaction in Home Territories." It had to do with the dynamics of interactions between these two groups. It was interesting in a lot of ways to me, first because it was really a public space, so here we had a superimposed definition, a claim being made by a group who was discreditable if not discredited. It was fascinating and I wrote apparently a good-enough paper to impress Mr. Goffman.

Janice Irvine (JI): So that was a different approach. A lot of people in the '60s and even the '70s and '80s would have looked at the gay aspect of it, you know as the "nuts, sluts, and perverts" notion but you took a really different approach. Why do you think that is?

SC: That's an interesting question. I think it was because I was studying with Goffman at that time. And he really was concerned with the organization of social groups. I didn't approach it from that pathology framework that I had been introduced to at UCLA. At that time, Goffman was questioning the whole psychiatric establishment and all of those issues just kind of normalized it, really normalized this activity in the sociological sense. In the end I was not interested in the gayness, I was not interested in the deviant quality of those establishments as I was in the fact that they and many other social groups claimed these public establishments as their own and treated them as home territory. To me, a gay bar is a home territory, or a working-class Irish bar, a bar where newspaper people went, they were all in the same category. So again, I didn't see that I was studying deviant behavior.

JI: How was your research topic received at Berkeley? What did people think about it?

SC: Well we had to fill out a form that went to the dean of graduate studies. It was part of filing, when you filed to go advance on your doctorate. I did describe my study of how people were behaving in public drinking places. In those days, you couldn't even say "bar," you couldn't print the word "bar."

JI: Why?

SC: They were just things that you couldn't say. You couldn't use the word "bar," like you could use "bar and grill" but you couldn't have a sign outside of your establishment saying, "bar." A part of Prohibition was still kind of hanging over it. So anyway, I described it as a public drinking place and that I was going to use these observational methods. So I got called into the graduate dean's office and he explained to me in no uncertain terms that I had to be very careful that I did not do anything that brought the name of the university to the attention of the community and in any way besmirched the University of California at Berkeley.

JI: Oh my God!

SC: Now this was, I don't know maybe about six weeks before the Free Speech movement [laughs].

JI: It's interesting that he wasn't worried about you, he was worried about the university.

SC: That's right. And when I went to talk to Goffman he gave me the same spiel. Well, he was even worse, but he said "Now don't do anything that would get you in trouble and if you do, don't call me" [laughs].

JI: So tell me about the *Hippies of the Haight* project. You were living in the Haight?

SC: Right. Out of nowhere, essentially, these young people started congregating. The Beat scene in North Beach at that time was beginning to close down and the rents in North Beach were beginning to increase, so a lot of people who were Beats migrated to the Haight Ashbury, so there was already a kind of bohemian ethos in the neighborhood. It was also a working-class neighborhood and it was very politically and self-consciously progressive. So, the hippies were able to get a foothold established in the neighborhood because the neighborhood didn't feel that they had a right to exclude them. The scene began to emerge at the time and it was known as *the* place and young people from all over the world—I know people from England and Germany, and places like that coming. And I'll tell you that they're still coming [laughs].

JI: It must have been really intense then.

SC: Well it was, because it was so brand new. So brand new. And the other thing that was brand new was the music. It energized and vitalized the whole scene. The Doors had a house. Jimmy Hendrix had a house just the next block up. I'm not lying, he had a house up on Central one block up. Jefferson Airplane was over on Fulton Street. Janis Joplin was around the corner. They have these little guidebooks now that have all these addresses and people go and see them. The address that they don't have is like a few doors down from Janis Joplin was where Charlie Manson lived. He's not in the guidebooks [laughs].

JI: What made you think it would be interesting to study them?

SC: Well, because they were there. They were dressed outrageously, prototypically Janis Joplin. With feathers, and beads, and scarves and things from their grandmother's chest, and odd things, and making all this wonderful music and they had this very free lifestyle, and I was working then, and so I was, I guess in a way, a little bit envious of the total freedom that they apparently had. But more than anything it was because they were there.

JI: So, you hung out with them?

SC: I hung out in all of the public places because I already had all this experience of the bar studies, so the first places that I went to were public places like the park, like coffeehouses and shops. I got to know a lot of the shopkeepers on Haight Street. I got to know a lot of people in the Haight. At that time I think I rented the room in the basement to a couple who were early hippies. I rented the room to them because I needed the money and they took over my whole basement so all I had to do [for research] was go in the basement [laughs]. It was kind of a loose community. People who were dressed in anything that looked not strictly conventional were assigned to this category "hippie." I didn't think of myself as a hippie because I had a job [laughs].

JI: You didn't think of yourself as a hippie?

SC: Not then, but I've come to realize, yes [laughs]. I didn't think of myself as a hippie because I'm the kind of person who's really averse to any kind of label. But I have to say, so were they.

Hyperlink 7.3: Slumming Tours: The Spectacle of Social Difference

The bus chugged down an already-bustling Haight Street. It was April 1967, and Haight Ashbury was approaching what would be called the Summer of

Love. Gray Line tour company launched its first "Hippie Tour" through the neighborhood. It was advertised as a "descent into psychedelia," and, in a nod to the neighborhood's strangeness to mainstream Americans, "the only foreign tour" within the United States. Most of the tourists riding the bus, according to the *San Francisco Chronicle*, were from the Midwest and "had never seen a live hippie."[130] *Chronicle* photographer Art Frisch went on that first ride. His photos captured observers from both inside and outside the bus, as the straights and hippies gawked at each other. These tours figured in a long history of slumming—privileged Americans venturing into deviant urban places to stare at residents who were different from them by race, class, ethnicity, sexuality, and even hipness.

Urban tourism dates to the mid-nineteenth century, as prosperous Americans ventured into strange new spaces of the modern city. Urban sketches about places such as New York, Chicago, and San Francisco appeared in newspapers before their later publication as hefty travel books. These sketches advised readers how to find and negotiate "moral regions" of the city, titillating them with imagined anxious pleasures.[131] These mid-century moral tourists, however, were largely motivated by the desire to reform such places.

Slumming as a cultural practice of commercialized leisure came later. The extension of railroads and later the popularity of the automobile facilitated leisure travel. By the late nineteenth and early twentieth century, affluent White urban tourists actively explored neighborhoods marked by social differences. They wandered through immigrant spaces such as Chinatown as well as African American neighborhoods. In nighttime slumming, they frequented saloons and dance halls such as the black-and-tans, which were refuges of racial and sexual intermingling.

Social marginality and difference became a commodity to be bought and sold. Outsider capitalism facilitated exploration of these places. Tour companies, railroad trips, guidebook authors, and publishers all promoted and profited from urban tourism. Resentment and anger sometimes prompted resistance by residents. Yet outsider entrepreneurialism was not only practiced by mainstream businesses like Gray Line tours. Some residents found a way to profit from outside observers by establishing businesses providing lodging and selling souvenirs or local food and drink. Slums and other marginal places became not simply spectacles, but spectacles generating profit, and they changed in the process. Observation changed the observed.

Slumming tours were popular in the early Chicago of hobohemia and taxi-dance halls, although they were not always billed as such.

Social researchers set out to observe institutions and neighborhoods of the modern city. Perhaps most well-known, among sociologists at least, are the tours led by University of Chicago professor Robert Park, who considered the city a laboratory and regularly took students on what one called a "tour of exploration."[132] Depending on the topic, the tours covered the city's hotels, flophouses, dance halls, skyscrapers, and more. Park considered these explorations essential for social-science research. Archival research was important, he said, "but one more thing is needful: first-hand observation."[133] This was the task of ethnography, which sought to capture and represent the secrets, strangeness, and differences constituting the modern city. For some students, such as those who joked about studying the alcoholic drinks in neighborhood bars, the line blurred between slumming for research and slumming for pleasure.

Hobo physician Ben Reitman, an associate of Chicago sociologists, led similar slumming tours, although he was far more entrepreneurial. Reitman developed for-profit tours of Chicago's slums, vice districts, and marginal places. He advertised his "sociological clinic and tour" to Chicago's underworld on handbills describing himself as "Social Pathologist Ben Reitman." His customers included researchers, social reformers, students, and society women. He wrote in one letter, "Next week I take a group of Gary, Indiana society women on a sociological tour."[134] This particular group requested to see "some of the really 'slummy' places." Reitman promised them "many a thrill," including dinner with "a few underworld characters—prostitutes, gangsters, and beggars."[135] The representative for this women's group emphasized that they wanted to see the "worst" of the city so that they might work harder at reform.

Reitman led these tours for many years in the 1930s and '40s. He conducted a tour for members of the American Sociological Association. He led physicians (whom he referred to as "syphilis tourists") on "syphilis slumming tours" where they visited an abortionist, a pornographer, and various con men before moving on to a bar for female impersonators and other allegedly seamy establishments.[136] These tours could last up to six hours, and like many city tours today, tourists could reserve a spot and be picked up in their hotel lobby.

Reitman led tours for the University of Chicago, often for sociology courses such as Urban Problems. As it turned out, his vice tours seemed to entail his own vices. He was fired in 1940. The university president ordered him barred from campus after declaring him "a bad man and unfit" because one of his tours had "ended tragically for one of the girls." Reitman admitted the assault (at the time dubbed a seduction), saying "I make no denial. Everything said about me may be true, or worse."[137]

Meanwhile, many affluent, White Chicago residents went slumming, making no pretense of doing so for research or reform. They went to observe and they went for fun. Historian Chad Heap examined different "slumming vogues" from the late nineteenth century until approximately 1940: the search for "bohemian *thrillage*," the Negro vogue, and the pansy and lesbian craze.[138] These different waves of slumming represented the excursions of well-to-do Whites into marginal places inhabited by residents stigmatized by factors such as race, ethnicity, class, sexuality, and artistic temperament. Slummers went to saloons, dance halls, brothels, and other commercial establishments in these marginalized districts, in search of social outsiders. And some went for the experience of being transient outsiders themselves.

Undeniably, slumming practices made social differences visible to a broad public. Yet there were disparate consequences to this visibility. On the one hand, these practices represented an exoticization of difference that could render slummers "largely complicit" in reinforcing racial, sexual, and class inequalities.[139] They were typically White, affluent heterosexuals with the privilege to move into, and more importantly, out of, marginal places. Yet slumming also prompted racial, sexual, and class mixing. Historian Catherine Cocks suggests that urban tourism facilitated a growing cosmopolitanism and a modern appreciation of cultural difference, while residents found they could profit from the commodification of immigrant neighborhoods.[140] Urban guidebooks regaled affluent readers with the shopping opportunities in ethnic bazaars and markets. This cultural mixing played an important role in a gradual reconfiguration of social norms and knowledge about difference.[141] Slumming reified hierarchical social categories; it also exposed deep desires for otherness, nonconformity, and social transgression. Slumming, especially with its *frisson* of danger, epitomized the American attraction to, yet fear of, social outsiders.

Decades later, back on Haight Street, the Hippie Tour proved fleeting. Gray Line discontinued the tours after they were widely derided by journalists, pundits, and residents. Regardless, tourists still wandered the streets, and Sherri Cavan recounted the generally derisive hippie reaction: "The 'tourists' have been heavy on the street for the past few weeks and their presence has been a constant topic of conversation in the community in general. Ted tells me that the 'tourists bring everybody down; they think the Haight is a zoo. They look at us like animals, not individuals. They're all uptight and they're trying to contaminate us too.'"[142] Tourists were conformists, according to the hippies, who sometimes created street spectacles aimed at embarrassing observers.

More than fifty years after the Summer of Love, tourists can still re-experience it through Flower Power Walking Tours, a Magic Bus Experience, and myriad other Haight Ashbury tours.[143] Nostalgia, nonconformity, and the thrill of difference remain a potent commercial mix.

EIGHT

Conclusion

> The capacity to live with difference is . . . the coming question of the twenty-first century.[1]
>
> Stuart Hall

Time passed, as it does. The profound social changes wrought by time, or what sociologist C. Wright Mills called the "historical push and shove" of changing societies, is at the center of the sociological imagination—analysis of the intersection between individual lives and the historical moment.[2] Time takes us places. And with enough time, and luck, we arrive at what poet and writer May Sarton called the "foreign country" of old age, "with an unknown language to the young, and even to the middle-aged." It is a foreign place where we are all, at least initially, strangers. Sarton reflected, "I wish now that I had found out more about it."[3]

This book winds through several central themes: the production of new social knowledge about modern outsiders and strangers, written against the grain of scientific-racist paradigms; the enduring American paradox regarding normalcy and difference, conformity and nonconformity; and the role of deviant places in producing cultural worlds and individual selves. The last ethnography we discuss, *Number Our Days*, anthropologist Barbara Myerhoff's 1978 study of elderly Eastern European Jews at a senior center in Venice Beach, California,[4] brings us full circle to sociologist Georg Simmel's strangers. In his 1908 essay, "The Sociological Significance of the Stranger," European Jews who were traders typified his

Barbara Myerhoff with members of the Israel Levin Senior Center. Courtesy of USC Libraries, University of Southern California.

idea of the stranger.[5] Strangers, Simmel said, were not the wanderers who come today and go tomorrow, but those who come today and stay tomorrow. Initially strange, they become part of the group. Strangeness, then, is fluid. It is a form of interaction, not a fixed identity or ineluctable way of being. In what the *Los Angeles Times* called her "study of impoverished Jews struggling to preserve their heritage in the foreign, unfriendly environment of Venice," Myerhoff painted a portrait of the complicated social worlds of those real-life strangers, and how they fared in their later years.

Myerhoff's ethnography of the Israel Levin Center (called the Aliyah Senior Center in her book) vividly depicted the everyday lives, triumphs, struggles, political battles, and deaths of Jewish immigrants who had reinvented themselves in a new place. Basha, Shmuel, Faegl, and the other senior-center members were lively flesh-and-blood characters, yet they also bring to life our themes of marginal people in deviant places. Most were born in the shtetls of Russia and Eastern Europe into a rich Yiddish culture that came under attack by the late nineteenth and early twentieth century. Pogroms, economic and legal persecutions, and modernizing forces that drew their young people away from traditional customs prompted Jewish emigration by the hundreds of thousands among those who had the means for mobility. The center's members were among the population of

2.5 million Jews residing in the United States between 1881 and the enactment of the restrictive Johnson-Reed Immigration Act of 1924, which had been fueled by eugenicist arguments that "profound and inborn racial differences" produced biological inferiority.[6] The law limited the emigration of European Jews to approximately 41,000 annually, a decrease with fatal consequences during the Nazi genocide.

Center members had come to the United States, where they were outsiders and strangers by dint of national origin, ethnicity, and religion. They would escape the Holocaust of Hitler's Europe, but not a vicious anti-Semitism fueled by the intersecting mix of race science and a mainstream eugenics movement in the United States. They would encounter, in the late nineteenth and early twentieth centuries, anti-Semitism entangled with the Ku Klux Klan, Jim Crow culture, and other nativist forces. A widespread and mainstream adoption of race science's ideologies of immutable Jewish traits such as "craftiness, cunning, money-lust" reinforced longstanding pernicious stereotypes of Jews as dangerous, parasitic, subhuman, and evil.[7] No surprise, then, as Myerhoff recounted, that center members created "an entire, though miniature, society" in which they turned to each other for social, emotional, and political engagement.[8]

The Israel Levin Center was a struggling institution perched on the boardwalk of Venice Beach. In the early 1970s, when Myerhoff did her research, the neighborhood was filled by day with a colorful cast of characters such as surfers, hippies, families, bicyclists, and artists, while at night it saw muggings, rapes, and harassment. The broader area had long been a magnet for Eastern European Jewish immigrants who staked out their territory to socialize and play chess or mah-jongg on benches and picnic tables. Some peddled socialist periodicals on the boardwalk, or collected petition signatures or money for political causes. They were a disparate group ideologically, but Yiddish culture made these strangers familiar to each other. By the late 1950s in Venice Beach, urban development of what Myerhoff called this "Yiddish ghetto" displaced as many as 6,000 senior citizens, sent rents skyrocketing, and destroyed many of the synagogues, kosher butcher shops, and delicatessens. Distraught senior residents, alongside their "awareness of approaching individual death,"[9] foresaw cultural doom as well.

Myerhoff said of center members, "Previously, in Eastern Europe, they had been marginal people, even pariahs, as they were now."[10] In time, they also became outsiders by dint of advanced old age. The center became their refuge. Many members lived alone, some were estranged from families, and most struggled financially. Yet this very experience of isolation and marginality generated a subculture. They built new social worlds and places. The members reproduced Yiddish culture in the center—particular ways of being and talking—and conversely found themselves renewed inside these cultural dynamics. Places begat social worlds and cultures.

Benches, six or so outside on the boardwalk, fostered community engagement. Although they were public benches, center members occupied them as their home territory. One member, Basha, said, "Always there are people to talk to on the benches." They gathered there to debate, gossip, problem-solve, argue, or grieve. Sitting on a bench outside the center prior to her first visit, Myerhoff herself had pondered whether and how to conduct her research (she subsequently studied them for four years). Benches were, as she put it, "like a village plaza."[11] What happened outside on the benches anchored center culture.

Politics divided them, but also held them together. They would argue bitterly in the dining room, at center talks, and on the benches, about Zionism, internationalism, communism—everything. Raucous fights were the norm. Many of them sent money to and worked on behalf of the young nation of Israel. Others had been in the internationalist union movement. And center members, who had typically been politically engaged their entire lives, also mobilized more locally for their own causes. They competed for space in a neighborhood increasingly beset by tourists, bicyclists, and roller-skaters. One morning, a skater struck and killed eighty-six-year-old resident Anna Belsky as she left the Center. Center members took to the streets in protest after the skater reportedly said, "She got in my way." They marched down the boardwalk behind an empty coffin, carrying placards saying, "Life Not Death in Venice," and, in a rejoinder to their opponents' slogan—"K.O.S.—Keep Our Skaters,"—they replied, "K.O.S.—Kill Our Seniors."[12] Aging itself became part of their politics.

Life at the Senior Center garnered a wider audience. Myerhoff collaborated with filmmaker Lynne Littman to document its vibrant and contentious Yiddish cultural world. The documentary, *Number Our Days*, won a documentary short subject Academy Award in 1977. The center, which had long struggled financially, became, as Myerhoff put it, "a tourist attraction."[13] Donations poured in, along with heartfelt letters containing lengthy life histories by aging immigrants. The center shifted a bit from the margins; old people might be cool! And yet, its elderly members still confronted problems of housing, health, and financial exigency.

Political activists change the historical trajectory of outsiders. By the middle of the twentieth century, political advocacy by and for older adults emerged alongside mobilization by women, sexual minorities, dis-

K.O.S. Protest. Courtesy of USC Libraries, University of Southern California.

ability groups, and other social outsiders. Medicare, federal health insurance for those over sixty-five, was passed in 1965, while age discrimination in employment was prohibited in 1967. In 1970, Maggie Kuhn brought together like-minded older women to organize intergenerational activists. Originally called the Consultation of Older and Younger Adults for Social Change, it acquired the catchier nickname, the Gray Panthers, in 1972. The organization continues to mobilize for peace, healthcare, and campaign reform, and to challenge ageism, racism, and sexism. In the way that Sherri Cavan's ethnography of hippies spotlighted the rise of a youth counterculture, Myerhoff captured a culture of old age on the cusp of broader social change.

Throughout the twentieth century, outsider art also brought visibility and social change to marginal social worlds. Perhaps surprisingly, popular culture found old age. For example, the award-winning television series, *The Golden Girls*, launched in 1985, featured four older women sharing a home in Miami. The show broke ground on several levels. It defied the cultural invisibility of older women with its all-women cast, including an eighty-year-old character, Sophia. Friendship, rather than stereotypical cattiness (although there was some of that, too), bonded them as they reinvented the meaning of family. Three of the characters were immigrants or daughters of immigrants, and episodes showed them dealing with myriad dynamics of social class and gender. The show tackled then-controversial topics such as homosexuality and sexual harassment. They were all single women, widowed or divorced, confronting and reveling in the new world of old age. The show won critical acclaim over seven seasons.

The story of old age told by *The Golden Girls*, and by writers such as Myerhoff and May Sarton, emphasized that aging is a culture as much as it is a biological experience. Those who reach old age will grapple like strangers with new cultural rules and ways of being in that foreign country. Georg Simmel said as much in his insights about the stranger in 1908. Later sociologists discouraged the view that social difference was simply a biological characteristic of a small minority. For example, sociologists John Gagnon and William Simon wrote, "The deviant is really not a stranger ... we are all potential deviants."[14] These new theoretical frameworks, as we have seen, embraced marginality and the fluidity of difference, and encouraged a universalizing notion that we are all strangers, all potentially deviant. Deviance was produced by breaking the rules of moral entrepreneurs, and its meaning could change over time and across cultures. Indeed, deviance was just one letter away from defiance.

This is a book about ideas, as expressed through stories, whether told by scholars, political activists, or popular culture. The histories recounted in these chapters traveled forward through the ensuing decades. These themes—specifically, social differences and ways to know about them, power and inequalities, and social conflict over who matters—echo through the ensuing decades. Ideas changed and evolved. By the time of Myerhoff's research, the social science of difference was shifting.

Number Our Days appeared in the early years of anthropology's local turn. Myerhoff, a middle-aged scholar, lamented how contemporary culture cut younger individuals off from old people. She noted that, unlike anthropologists who studied exotic tribes and would therefore never truly inhabit their cultural mindset, "I would be a little old Jewish lady one day; thus, it was essential for me to learn what that condition was like, in all its particulars." To cultivate this ethnographic imagination, she deployed strategies to understand the physical limitations of the elderly center members. She wore stiff garden gloves during the day, went without her eyeglasses, plugged her ears, and wore heavy boots for long periods. She caught glimpses of the members' daily bodily challenges and their pluck in overcoming them. She wrote, "I *see* old people now in a new way, as part of me, not 'they'" [emphasis in original].[15] Still, she worried that she was engaged in a "personal quest" rather than anthropology, finally concluding, "I never fully resolved the question."[16]

As some anthropologists like Myerhoff began studying their own local cultures, the sociology of deviance came under critical scrutiny. A number of factors contributed to this. For one, scholars questioned its conceptual rigor, relevance, and politics. As early as 1972, sociologist Alexander Liazos accused the field of theoretical impoverishment and ideological bias.[17] Critics accused modern deviance scholars of voyeurism, and sociologist Alvin Gouldner famously mocked them for penning "essays on quaintness."[18] In addition, sociological knowledge production, political mobilization, and popular culture all helped make diverse social worlds visible, fostering social change and controversies about difference. This in turn helped to erode the category of deviance within sociology. Some scholars and activists expressed discomfort with its name, despite recognizing the literature's radical critiques of essentialism and race science. Sociologists declared the death of deviance, and then its "resurrection," in contentious journal exchanges.[19]

By the late 1970s, "deviance" largely turned into "difference," and studies of difference fractured into now-institutionalized identity studies: critical race/ethnic studies, women's and gender studies, sexuality studies, and disability studies. These identity-based studies of difference rose to prominence, seeming to offer more sophisticated theoretical and methodological advances than the allegedly obsolete and irrelevant deviance framework. The congenial American market for French interpretive theory,[20] such as that of Michel Foucault and Jacques Derrida, no doubt bolstered a view that deviance concepts were old-fashioned. Paradoxically, deviance studies had been both radically transformative while also coming to be historically overshadowed and itself a bit stigmatized.

Political activists both utilized deviance studies and contributed to its alleged obsolescence. By the early 1990s, "queerness" arose out of HIV/AIDS activism. The concept of "queer" is not simply another term for individual sexual identity. Although "queer" resists definition, it operates as a critique of normativity, and as an epistemology that challenges fixed categories of identities broadly, not just those of sexuality and gender. Queer was political, and as a concept it quickly spread in the academy. The so-called queer turn in the social sciences prompted a rethinking of reified social categories, meanings, and definitions of the self. Early and midcentury sociologists and anthropologists had pioneered many of these new ideas about difference—strangers, outsiders, marginality, deviance—that spoke to a twentieth-century zeitgeist of otherness.[21]

Deviance studies anticipated the radical intellectual challenges of queer studies by half a century. Like the earlier sociology of deviance, queer studies embraces nonidentitarian approaches to the self and difference, including anti-essentialism, and a focus on multiplicity, hybridity, marginality, mutability, performances, surfaces, situations, and place and space. Outsiders inhabit the margins as a result of stigma and the regulatory strategies of moral entrepreneurs. Seemingly stable categories blur, such as normalcy and deviance. Queer critics of essentialism called for new conceptual and methodological approaches that capture the ambiguities and instabilities of social categories.[22] Both subfields took names—deviance, queer—that reference marginal social types. Both subfields faced controversy and stigma because of these names, although both fundamentally challenged and redefined the dominant pejorative meanings of these terms. Like queerness, deviance was an analytic category that resisted categorization; it was paradoxical and ambiguous, carrying with it the possibility, but not inevitability, of normalization. Indeed, before queer, there was deviance. Yet queer became cool in the academy, while deviance became suspect.

Meanwhile, biological determinism made a comeback. Scientific racism in the post–World War II era had been both morally discredited and scientifically debunked after the eugenic massacres by the Nazis. Theories of a biological basis to differences by race, gender, class, and sexuality, as well as intelligence and other attributes and behaviors, had been thoroughly challenged. However, some scholars repackaged these ideas in the early- to mid-seventies in the form of sociobiology.

Sociobiology posited a biological model of human nature, and a biological basis to culture and human behavior, in particular sexuality, gender, reproduction, and parenting. Harvard biologist Edward O. Wilson popularized the term and its ideas in *Sociobiology: The New Synthesis*. Wilson intended to establish the discipline of sociology as a branch of evolutionary biology, a goal met with skeptical reactions among sociologists. The progressive group, Science for the People, condemned sociobiology as a new incarnation of biological determinism.[23] They argued that sociobiological theorists misused genetic concepts and data, asserted falsehoods about social groups, and ignored countervailing evidence: "In order to make their case, determinists construct a selective picture of human history, ethnography, and social relations." Some of Wilson's sociological reviewers praised the book's attempt at dialogue between biologists and sociologists, but critics decried the work as flawed, disappointing, nonrigorous, biased, and "sexist," while worrying that sociobiology would be "used to justify racism."[24] He was accused of racism, misogyny, and complicity with Nazi-style eugenics due to his arguments that some individuals are genetically superior to others. His Harvard colleague Stephen Jay Gould called sociobiology "speculative storytelling,"[25] and insisted that "cultural evolution" was more significant to human behavior and difference than Darwinian selection for genetic influence. Demonstrators poured a pitcher of water over his head at an academic conference. This opposition reflected the politics of stories, and the high stakes for outsiders in what kinds of stories get told about difference, and who gets to tell them.

Tensions abound in this book, continuing to the present. An American paradox of difference persists—a historical romance with, and repulsion toward, those who are different. These chapters have explored different types of differences, in particular, ways of living outside of conventional norms in a modern century, as inflected by differences such as race, gender, class, age, and more. Increasingly, the answer to Robert Lindner's question posed in the introduction to this book—"Must You Conform?"—has become, no. And also, yes. Norms governing individual and social life, in particular regarding gender, sexuality, and families, have markedly destabilized from the early twentieth century alongside persistent social pressures to adhere to them.

An outsider capitalism gradually developed, helping effect these normative shifts as it unevenly marketed both social differences and conformity. As we saw in chapter 7, consumer culture honed outsider marketing rhetoric in the countercultural sixties. Cool-hunting consultants emerged by the early 1990s to identify nascent outlier trends that could then be mass produced and sold to aspiring nonconformists.[26] Apple, Inc., exemplified the conflation of outsider identity with outsider products in their "Think Different" commercial in 1997: "Here's to the crazy ones. The misfits. The rebels. The troublemakers. The round pegs in the square holes. The ones who see things differently. They're not fond of rules . . . they change things. They push the human race forward. And while some may see them as the crazy ones, we see genius."[27] Strikingly, the romantic outsiders celebrated in this ad harken back to the likes of the hobos, mental patients, taxi dancers, immigrants, men in tearooms, and hippies whose stories we found in these pages. They were outsiders who broke the rules, but they were also punished by law, institutionalization, violence, and stigma.

While nonconformity seems popular (everyone is doing it!), outsider merchants conversely market conformity. The conformity market succeeds because, as social research suggests, individuals generally choose conformity out of fear of social rejection.[28] As bioethics philosopher Carl Elliott notes, the popularity of new medical and cosmetic enhancement technologies bespeaks a widespread yearning to fit in.[29] Political scientist Jennie Ikuta points out the discontinuity between rhetoric and practice: "In light of research indicating that most Americans are not actually nonconformists—and that they are actively hostile to those who refuse to conform—many have doubled down on the rhetorical commitment to nonconformity as an ideal."[30] These chapters explored the new kinds of outsiders made possible by modernity. While some of them became culturally attractive, an anxious hostility toward nonconformists and strangers persists. We love and hate them.

There is a darker side to our cultural ambivalence toward conformity and difference. I focus here on two developments salient to twenty-first-century approaches to difference: those related to social knowledge, and to politics. For one, biological theories about individual variation gained new audiences. A century after the publication of the first sociological text we examined in this book—*The Hobo*—new biological and genetic sciences spin narratives that essentialize difference. Second, an emotional politics of anger, suspicion, and intolerance of difference has intensified, with an embrace of re-emergent essentialist narratives.

The twenty-first century has seen a resurgence of biological determinism. As science scholar Banu Subramaniam notes, the history of science "is like playing whack-a-mole. Each time a claim of biological determinism has been dismantled, another one rises up."[31] Since the 1990s, the rise of genetic science, with new technologies such as DNA analysis and ancestry testing, harkens back to earlier scientific practices, such as cranial measurements and scientific epistemologies that posit biological differences as inherent in groups and individual identities.[32] Human variation is once again explained as biological difference, and medicalization of social difference has intensified, fueled by the pharmaceutical industry. While some researchers attempt to forge a middle-ground between biological and environmental arguments, such as controversial psychologist Kathryn Paige Harden's emphasis on genetic influences on life outcomes and character traits, the pernicious legacy of eugenics haunts their work.[33]

Many scholars hotly contest these biological explanations. For example, sociologist Dorothy Roberts said of Harden's research, "There's just no way that genetic testing is going to lead to a restructuring of society in a just way in the future—we have a hundred years of evidence for what happens when social outcomes are attributed to genetic differences, and it is always to stigmatize, control, and punish the people predicted to have socially devalued traits."[34] Yet as contemporary genetic science promotes new biological understandings of populations and individuals, some political activists have adopted a "biologically inflected strategic essentialism" in advocating for goals such as same-sex marriage.[35] Eugenics was based on the idea that people are born, not made. The new popularity of genetic ancestry testing and "born this way" arguments shows some enduring scientific and public appeal of biological conceptions of the self and human differences.

Ideas matter. History justifies contemporary concern about the rising popularity of biological determinism. The knowledge produced by race science supported ways of thinking and feeling that pathologized difference, reinforcing social inequality. The rhetoric of normalcy and deviance, justified by race science, has led to eugenic practices and the mass extermination of individuals and groups deemed inferior and deviant. Biological determinist narratives supported the myriad structures of exclusion and cultural systems of oppression we encountered in these chapters, such as Jim Crow laws, restrictive immigration quotas, the exclusion of women from work and public places, and antigay policing. This vocabulary of difference—depravity, degeneracy, inferiority, pathology—supported aversive feelings such as fear, anxiety, anger, hatred, and disgust toward human variation. There are reasons, after all, that essentialist race science earned the designation, scientific racism.

Social differences—ways of knowing, thinking, writing, and feeling about them—reside at the center of American social, cultural, and political life. Social scientists have insisted that, while we may all be outsiders, strangers, and different, we are not always outsiders, strangers, and different in the same way. The ethnographies in this book captured the complex worlds of outsiders—the hobos, taxi-dancers, immigrants, jook-joint dancers, hippies. But, although all were outsiders, they had differing levels of social privilege. Historian Heather Cox Richardson argues that such inequality is a tension at the heart of American democracy: "That central paradox—that freedom depended on racial, gender, and class inequality—shaped American history as the cultural, religious, and social patterns of the new nation grew around it."[36] Many of these underlying social inequalities have persisted and even worsened—for example, income inequality, homelessness, unemployment, racism, and the "new Jim Crow" of mass incarceration, failures in mental health treatment, and more. Cultural fears and hostility toward some types of difference pervade entrenched structural problems.

Knowledge and politics are inextricable. Social differences underpin much of the polarization known as the "culture wars" or our "cold civil war."[37] The term "culture wars" refers to a bruising set of conflicts about values and lifestyles launched by secular and religious conservatives in the eighties, although battles over inclusion and exclusion are long-standing. Many of these battles concern social differences such as race, immigration, gender, and sexualities. In these types of culture wars, ways of thinking about difference entwine with ways of feeling about them. Ideas, emotions, politics, and policies intertwine in what scholars Jennifer Harding and E. Deirdre Pribram call "embodied discourse." They note that emotions drive cultural politics through "their capacity to circulate meanings, to transmit social relations and to constitute subjectivity."[38] Equality and democracy are at stake in these ways of knowing and arguing about social differences. As Richardson observed, "Once you have replaced the principle of equality with the idea that humans are unequal, you have granted your approval to the idea of rulers and servants. At that point, all you can do is to hope that no one in power decides that you belong in one of the lesser groups."[39] Different ways of knowing about marginal people in deviant places have shaped who counts, who is included, and how we measure social worth and equality.

Division even shows up in discussions about whether we are divided. Scholars disagree about the existence of culture wars and polarization. Popular books such as *Why We're Polarized* currently sit on library shelves alongside those of contemporary culture-war denialists.[40] One such denialist, sociologist Irene Thomson, asks, "Why does it matter whether there is or is not a culture war? A society experiencing a culture war would face grave difficulties."[41] Indeed. Culture wars inflict casualties.

Decades into the twenty-first century, political conflicts over social differences, outsiders, strangers, and whose lives matter burn fiercely. The contemporary Republican party continues to stoke long-standing divisions over immigration, race, religion, and gender. Young trans people are the current folk devils in the type of scapegoating that sociologist Stan Cohen decades ago dubbed moral panic. Republican-sponsored voter suppression initiatives presage a frightening return to Jim Crow. Terms such as "authoritarianism," "demagoguery," and "fascism" entered mainstream political conversation. Historians have warned that the United States is drifting toward fascist politics with its hierarchical discourses of us versus them, friends versus enemies, insiders versus outsiders, and the demonization of certain individual and group differences.[42] Public intellectual Masha Gessen advocates for a national "storytelling project," harkening back to the Works Progress Administration initiatives of the 1930s, because, in surviving democratic threats, the "countries that do best are countries that have a story, a story that promises a sense of belonging."[43] Such a project would necessitate better stories of human differences. Yet the arc of the political universe seemed to bend toward polarization.

Culture clashes have escalated from an agenda to change laws and policies to actual civil unrest, violence, and urban warfare on the streets and in government centers. The US State Department has warned that White nationalism is "on the rise and spreading geographically," targeting racial and religious minorities, LGBTQ people, and "other perceived enemies."[44] White supremacists launched armed insurgencies on the national capitol and in some state capitols. Black Americans are nearly three times more likely to die from police violence than White Americans.[45] Grim heights have been reached in murder rates of transgender and gender nonbinary people, in particular Black and Latina trans women.[46] Harkening back to early race science, contemporary White supremacists invoke debunked methods such as craniometry to support biological determinist ideologies of racial inferiority, calling it a "repressed" field of study.[47] Whack-a-mole, indeed.

This book posits that stories are powerful, knowledge is political, and ideas shape history by how they bring into being policies, culture, communities, and individual lives. The rise of a new social knowledge of difference, with cultural rather than biological stories about outsiders, strangers, and deviance, helped confound—but did not end—categories and meanings of difference that fostered social exclusion and vilification. Ideas play a powerful role in the furious energies of cultural politics, as evidenced by what pundits have identified as the war on colleges and universities.[48] Recalling J. Edgar Hoover's FBI surveillance of midcentury sociologists, many conservatives again view knowledge and critical thinking as dangerous, and therefore support attempts to defund, delegitimize, and dismantle higher education. One study found that 80 percent of "core conservatives" were anticollege, ranking it as worse for the country than labor unions or Islam.[49] Republican lawmakers targeted critical race pedagogy at public schools and universities as "a grave threat" to America, deploying false and inflammatory rhetoric in strategies similar to earlier twentieth-century attacks on the teaching of evolution and comprehensive sex education.[50]

Things change. In 2018, forty years after the publication of *Number Our Days*, I went to Venice Beach to visit the Israel Levin Senior Center. It was gone. All that was left was a skeletal structure with its iconic murals and a few remaining benches out front, strewn with trash. In 2017 the California Coastal Commission had approved a project "redeveloping an underused senior facility on the Venice boardwalk" into a modern three-story complex that "reimagines the center" as a place to intermingle both old and young Jews—a "Jewish community center for the 21st century."[51] Basha, Faegl, and the others might have felt ambivalent about such renovation to their marginal place on the boardwalk. They had resisted the earlier razing and redevelopment of their beloved neighborhood in the 1950s. Basha had described it then as "a second Holocaust. It destroyed our shtetl life all over again," and she protested with a sign that said, "Let my people stay."[52]

Unexpectedly, Barbara Myerhoff's next project again entangled her personal story with ethnographic research on cultural difference. She launched a study of Orthodox Jews in Los Angeles, a thriving yet insular community she described as "not ordinary . . . it's not weird but it's certainly not what you expect to find all around you."[53] That new project took a sudden turn when she was diagnosed with lung cancer. The subsequent ethnographic documentary, *In Her Own Time: The Final Fieldwork of Barbara Myerhoff*, told stories about the rituals, beliefs, and cultural practices of Orthodox Jews through the prism of Myerhoff's illness, an exploration shadowed by the indeterminacy of her immediate future.

Barbara Myerhoff died at the age of 49, two weeks after filming. She never became an old Jewish lady. In *Number Our Days*, Myerhoff had invoked *Homo narrans*—humankind as storyteller—to argue that culture is produced not by biology, but by the stories we tell about ourselves. Her tales of outsiders, marginality, and strangers turned the spotlight on the margins. Myerhoff, like the other scholars featured in this book, made difference the beginning, not the end of the story. By asking different questions, troubling tidy answers, and opening cultural space for new ways of thinking, knowing, and feeling, their work endures.

Notes

Preface

1. Joan Didion, *The White Album* (New York: Simon & Schuster, 1979), 1.
2. "Fuss Over English Egghead," *Life Magazine*, October 1, 1956, 73.
3. Lena Dunham, "The Enduring Spell of *The Outsiders*," *New York Times Style Magazine*, September 9, 2018, 90.
4. See Colin Wilson, *The Outsider* (New York: Penguin Random House LLC, 1956); S. E. Hinton, *The Outsiders* (New York: Penguin, 1967); Howard S. Becker, *Outsiders: Studies in the Sociology of Deviance* (New York: Free Press, 1963); Richard Wright, *The Outsider* (New York: Harper & Brothers, 1953).
5. Sarah Relyea, "The Vanguard of Modernity: Richard Wright's *The Outsider*," *Texas Studies in Literature and Language* 48, no. 3 (2006): 188.
6. Carla Cappetti, *Writing Chicago: Modernism, Ethnography, and the Novel* (New York: Columbia University Press, 1993), 32.
7. Roger Salerno, *Sociology Noir* (Jefferson, NC: McFarland & Company, 2007).
8. Frederick Gross, *Diane Arbus's 1960s* (Minneapolis: University of Minnesota Press, 2012).
9. C. Wright Mills, *The Sociological Imagination* (New York: Oxford University Press, 1959).
10. See *Ruptures: Anthropologies of Discontinuities in Times of Turmoil*, eds. Martin Holbraad, Bruce Kapferer, and Julia F. Sauma (Chicago: University of Chicago Press, 2020).
11. Scott Frickel and Neil Gross, "A General Theory of Scientific/Intellectual Movements," *American Sociological Review* 70, no. 2 (April 2005): 204–32.
12. Raymond Williams, *Marxism and Literature* (New York: Oxford University Press, 1977): 132.
13. Dian Georgis, *The Better Story: Queer Affects from the Middle East* (Albany: State University of New York Press, 2014).

14. Kathy Davis, personal communication, January 26, 2021.
15. Charles King, *Gods of the Upper Air: How a Circle of Renegade Anthropologists Reinvented Race, Sex, and Gender in the Twentieth Century* (New York: Doubleday, 2019), 7–10.
16. Esther Newton, interview with author, December 1, 2014.
17. Clifford Geertz, *The Interpretation of Cultures: Selected Essays* (New York: Basic Books, 1973).
18. John D'Emilio, "Capitalism and Gay Identity," in *Powers of Desire: The Politics of Sexuality*, eds. Ann Snitow, Christine Stansell, and Sharon Thompson (New York: Monthly Review Press, 1983), 102.
19. Patricia Adler and Peter Adler, "Tales from the Field: Reflections on Four Decades of Ethnography," *Qualitative Sociology Review* VIII, Issue 1 (2012): 26.
20. I deploy this term differently than Willis's notion of "sensuousness" or Atkinson's focus on textuality and authenticity. See Paul Willis, *The Ethnographic Imagination* (Cambridge, UK: Polity, 2000); and Paul Atkinson, *The Ethnographic Imagination: Textual Constructions of Reality* (New York: Routledge, 2012).
21. Carol J. Greenhouse and Davydd J. Greenwood, "Introduction: The Ethnography of Democracy and Difference," in *Democracy and Ethnography: Constructing Identities in Multicultural Liberal States* (Albany: State University of New York Press, 1998), 14.
22. Howard Becker, *Outsiders: Studies in the Sociology of Deviance* (New York: Free Press, 1963), 79.
23. Georgis, *Better Story*, 26.
24. Jason Stanley, *How Fascism Works: The Politics of Us and Them* (New York: Random House, 2018), xxi.
25. Stanley, *How Fascism Works*.

Chapter 1

1. Robert Lindner, *Must You Conform?* (New York: Rinehart & Company, 1956).
2. Anna Creadick, *Perfectly Average: The Pursuit of Normality in Postwar America* (Amherst: University of Massachusetts Press, 2010).
3. Burgess, Ernest Watson, Papers, Addenda [Box 289, Folder 7]. Hanna Holborn Gray Special Collections Research Center, University of Chicago Library.
4. Edwin Lemert, *Social Pathology: A Systematic Approach to the Theory of Sociopathic Behavior* (New York: McGraw-Hill Book Company, 1951), 21.
5. Eve Kosofsky Sedgwick, *Epistemology of the Closet* (Berkeley: University of California Press, 1990), 22.
6. David N. Livingstone, *Putting Science in Its Place: Geographies of Scientific Knowledge* (Chicago: University of Chicago Press, 2003), 12.
7. Michel Foucault, *Abnormal: Lectures at the College De France, 1974–1975* (New York: Picador, 1999), 323.
8. Steven Smith, *Modernity and Its Discontents* (New Haven: Yale University Press, 2018), ix.
9. Charles Taylor, *Modern Social Imaginaries* (Durham: Duke University Press, 2004).

10. Christine Stansell, *American Moderns: Bohemian New York and the Creation of a New Century* (New York: Henry Holt & Co., 2000), 3.

11. John D'Emilio, "Capitalism and Gay Identity," in *Powers of Desire: The Politics of Sexuality*, eds. Ann Snitow, Christine Stansell, and Sharon Thompson (New York: Monthly Review Press, 1983), 102.

12. Thomas Frank, *The Conquest of Cool: Business Culture, Counterculture, and the Rise of Hip Consumerism* (Chicago: University of Chicago Press, 1997), 20, 26.

13. Ian Hacking, "Making Up People," *London Review of Books* 28 (August 17, 2006), https://www.lrb.co.uk/the-paper/v28/n16/ian-hacking/making-up-people

14. See Peter Conrad and Joseph Schneider, *Deviance and Medicalization: From Badness to Sickness* (Philadelphia: Temple University Press, 1992).

15. Aldon Morris, *The Scholar Denied: W. E. B. Du Bois and the Birth of Modern Sociology* (Berkeley: University of California Press, 2015).

16. John Jackson and Nadine Weidman, *Race, Racism, and Science* (New Brunswick: Rutgers University Press, 2006).

17. Jacqueline Urla and Jennifer Terry, "Introduction: Mapping Embodied Deviance," in *Deviant Bodies*, eds. Jacqueline Urla and Jennifer Terry (Bloomington: Indiana University Press, 1995), 1.

18. Banu Subramaniam, *Ghost Stories for Darwin: The Science of Variation and the Politics of Diversity* (Urbana: University of Illinois Press, 2014).

19. Isabel Wilkerson, *Caste: The Origins of Our Discontents* (New York: Random House, 2020).

20. Wilkerson, *Caste*, 171.

21. Nikolas Rose, *Governing the Soul* (London: Free Association Books, 1999), vii.

22. Ramya M. Rajagopalan, Alondra Nelson, and Joan H. Fujimura, "Race and Science in the Twenty-First Century," in *The Handbook of Science and Technology Studies*, 4th ed., eds. Ulrike Felt, Rayvon Fouche, Clark Miller, and Laurel Smith-Doerr (Cambridge, MA: MIT Press, 2017), 351.

23. See Daniel Okrent, *The Guarded Gate* (New York: Scribner, 2019); Stefan Kuhl, *The Nazi Connection: Eugenics, American Racism, and German National Socialism* (New York: Oxford University Press, 1994).

24. Tracy Teslow, *Constructing Race: The Science of Bodies and Cultures in American Anthropology* (Cambridge: Cambridge University Press, 2014).

25. See, for example, Aldon Morris, *Scholar Denied*; Mary Jo Deegan, "Goffman on Gender, Sexism, and Feminism," *Symbolic Interaction* 37 (2014): 71–86; Zine Magubane, "Common Skies and Divided Horizons? Sociology, Race, and Postcolonial Studies," *Political Power and Social Theory* 24 (January 2013): 81–116; and Michael Warner, *The Trouble with Normal* (New York: Free Press, 1999). Although psychologists have disagreed about their role in promulgating racial intelligence tests that lent alleged scientific legitimacy to racist doctrines and policies such as the 1924 Quota Law, the discipline clearly claimed that biological traits influenced intelligence and so-called degeneracy.

26. Teslow, *Constructing Race*, 11.

27. Joanne Meyerowitz, "'How Common Culture Shapes the Separate Lives': Sexuality, Race, and Mid-Twentieth-Century Social Constructionist Thought," *Journal of American History* (2010): 1057–84.

28. Neil McLaughlin, "Origin Myths in the Social Sciences: Fromm, the Frankfurt School, and the Emergence of Critical Theory," *Canadian Journal of Sociology* 24, no. 1 (Winter 1999): 109–39.

29. Barbara Lal, "Black and Blue in Chicago," *British Journal of Sociology* 38, no. 4 (1987): 546–66.

30. W. I. Thomas, *The Unadjusted Girl* (New York: Little, Brown and Company, 1923), 1.

31. Robert E. Park and Ernest W. Burgess, *Introduction to the Science of Sociology* (Chicago: University of Chicago Press, 1921).

32. Robert E. Park and Ernest W. Burgess, *The City: Suggestions for Investigation of Human Behavior in the Urban Environment* (Chicago: University of Chicago Press, 1925), 1.

33. Georg Simmel, "The Sociological Significance of the 'Stranger,'" *Soziologie* (1908), 685–91; published in the US in Robert E. Park and Ernest W. Burgess, *Introduction to the Science of Sociology* (Chicago: University of Chicago Press, 1921), 322–27.

34. Ralph Leck, *Georg Simmel and Avant-Garde Sociology* (Washington, D.C.: Rowman & Littlefield Publishers/Humanity Books, 2000).

35. Nedim Karakayali, "The Uses of the Stranger," *Sociological Theory* 24, no. 4 (2006): 312-30.

36. Robert Park, "Human Migration and the Marginal Man," *American Journal of Sociology* XXXIII, no. 6 (May 1928): 881–93.

37. Matthew Yeager, *Frank Tannenbaum: The Making of a Convict Criminologist* (New York: Routledge, 2016).

38. Frank Tannenbaum, *Crime and Community* (Boston: Ginn and Company, 1938), 20.

39. Everett Hughes, "Social Change and Status Protest: An Essay on the Marginal Man," *Phylon* 10, no. 1 (1949): 58–65.

40. Helen Mayer Hacker, "Women as a Minority Group," *Social Forces* 30, no. 1 (1951): 60–69.

41. For one recent overview, see Lucy Jackson, Catherine Harris, and Gill Valentine, "Rethinking Concepts of the Strange and the Stranger," *Social & Cultural Geography* 18, no. 1 (2017): 1–15.

42. Lemert, *Social Pathology: A Systematic Approach to the Theory of Sociopathic Behavior* (New York: McGraw-Hill Book Company, 1951).

43. Lemert, *Social Pathology*, 3.

44. Lemert, *Social Pathology*, 19.

45. Lemert, *Social Pathology*, 19.

46. Howard Becker, *Outsiders: Studies in the Sociology of Deviance* (New York: Free Press, 1963); Erving Goffman, *Stigma: Notes on the Management of Spoiled Identity* (New York: Penguin Pelican, 1968).

47. Howard Becker, interview with author, May 13, 2013.

48. Becker, *Outsiders*, 8.

49. Edward Sagarin, ed., *The Other Minorities: Nonethnic Collectivities Conceptualized as Minority Groups* (New York: John Wiley & Sons, 1971).

50. Anthony Harris, interview with author, December 13, 2013.

51. Becker, *Outsiders*, 181.
52. Peter Conrad, interview with author, August 19, 2013.
53. Mark Solovey and Hamilton Cravens, eds., *Cold War Social Science: Knowledge Production, Liberal Democracy, and Human Nature* (New York: Palgrave MacMillan, 2012).
54. Stanley Milgram, *Obedience to Authority: An Experimental View* (London: Tavistock, 1974).
55. See Erich Fromm, *Escape from Freedom* (New York: Holt, Rinehart, and Winston, 1941); Theodor Adorno, Else Frenkel-Brunswik, Daniel Levinson, and Nevitt Sanford, *The Authoritarian Personality*, Vol. I (New York: Harper & Brothers, 1950); David Riesman, Nathan Glazer, and Reuel Denney, *The Lonely Crowd: A Study of the Changing American Character* (New Haven: Yale University Press, 1950); C. Wright Mills, *The Sociological Imagination* (New York: Oxford University Press, 1959); William H. Whyte, *The Organization Man* (New York: Simon & Schuster, 1956).
56. Becker, *Outsiders*, 197.
57. Donna Haraway, "Situated Knowledges: The Science Question in Feminism as a Site of Discourse on the Privilege of Partial Perspective," *Feminist Studies* 14, no. 3 (1988): 575–99.
58. Howard Becker, "Whose Side Are We On?" *Social Problems* 14, no. 3 (1967): 239–47. See also Alvin Gouldner, "The Sociologist as Partisan: Sociology and the Welfare State," *American Sociologist* 3, no. 2 (May 1968): 103–16. Alvin Gouldner (who appears in chapter 6 for having assaulted graduate student Laud Humphreys) criticized Howard Becker and other deviance scholars for being "liberal" rather than "radical" in their defense of the "underdog." He suggested a tendency by deviants to accept the role of "passive victims." (History ultimately proved Gouldner wrong, as political movements of alleged deviants rose up to challenge power and systems of oppression addressed by sociological research.)
59. Jack Douglas, *Observations of Deviance* (New York: Random House, 1970), 5.
60. Mike Keen, *Stalking the Sociological Imagination: J. Edgar Hoover's FBI Surveillance of American Sociology* (Piscataway, NJ: Transaction Publishers, 2003).
61. Gayle Rubin, "Studying Sexual Subcultures: Excavating the Ethnography of Gay Communities in Urban North America," in *Out in Theory: The Emergence of Lesbian and Gay Anthropology*, eds. Ellen Lewin and William Leap (Urbana: University of Illinois Press, 2002), 21.
62. Barbara Myerhoff, *Number Our Days* (New York: Simon & Schuster, 1978), 18.
63. See James Clifford, "Anthropology and/as Travel," *Etnofoor* 9, no. 2 (1996): 5–15. Clifford Geertz quoted Clifford's phrase, not very flatteringly, in an article of the same name: Clifford Geertz, "Deep Hanging Out," *New York Review of Books* 45, no. 16 (1998): 69–72.
64. Jack Douglas, *Observations of Deviance* (New York: Random House, 1970), 4.
65. Philip Manning, *Freud & American Sociology* (Malden, MA: Polity Press, 2005), xi.
66. Tim Cresswell, *In Place/Out of Place: Geography, Ideology, and Transgression* (Minneapolis: University of Minnesota Press, 1996), 27.

67. Robert Park and Ernest Burgess, *The City: Suggestions for Investigation of Human Behavior in the Urban Environment* (Chicago: University of Chicago Press, 1925), 3.

68. Shulamit Reinharz, "The Chicago School of Sociology and the Founding of the Brandeis University Graduate Program in Sociology: A Case Study in Cultural Diffusion," in *A Second Chicago School?*, ed. Gary Alan Fine (Chicago: University of Chicago Press, 1995), 273–93.

69. Shulamit Reinharz, "The Chicago School," 292.

70. Sarah Pink, "An Urban Tour: The Sensory Sociality of Ethnographic Place-Making," *Ethnography* 9, no. 2 (2008): 175–96.

71. Burgess, Ernest Watson, Papers [Box 130, Folder 7]. Hanna Holborn Gray Special Collections Research Center, University of Chicago Library.

72. Laud Humphreys, *Tearoom Trade: Impersonal Sex in Public Places* (Chicago: Aldine Publishing Company, 1970).

73. Thomas Gieryn, "A Space for Place in Sociology," *Annual Review of Sociology* 26 (2000): 463–96; John Logan, "Making a Place for Space: Spatial Thinking in Social Science," *Annual Review of Sociology* 38 (2012): 507–24.

74. Tim Cresswell, *Place: A Short Introduction* (Oxford: Blackwell, 2004).

75. Gieryn, "Space for Place," 466. In addition, meanings vary temporally. As cultural geographers Johnston and Longhurst note, "it matters that bodies occupy particular positions marked in time and space." As such, it matters that the people and bodies that ethnographers study occupy positions at specific times and places. See Lynda Johnston and Robyn Longhurst, *Space, Place, and Sex: Geographies of Sexualities* (New York: Rowman & Littlefield Publishers, 2010), 2.

76. "The Places We Tell Our Stories," Moth Radio Hour, https://themoth.org/radio-hour/the-places-we-tell-our-stories, accessed December 1, 2018.

77. Livingstone, *Putting Science in Its Place*, 18.

78. Joyce Davidson, Liz Bondi, and Mick Smith, *Emotional Geographies* (Aldershot, UK: Ashgate, 2005).

79. Allan Pred, "Place as Historically-Contingent Process," *Annals of the Association of American Geographers* 74 (1984): 279–97.

80. Doreen Massey, *Space, Place, and Gender* (Minneapolis: University of Minnesota Press, 1994). Also see Brett Christophers, Rebecca Lave, Jamie Peck, and Marion Werner, eds., *The Doreen Massey Reader* (Newcastle upon Tyne: Agenda Publishing, 2018).

81. Cresswell, *Place*.

82. William Whyte, "How Do Buildings Mean? Some Issues of Interpretation in the History of Architecture," *History and Theory* 45 (2006): 153–77.

83. Whyte, "How Do Buildings Mean?"

84. Ray Oldenburg, *The Great Good Place: Cafés, Coffee Shops, Community Centers, Beauty Parlors, General Stores, Bars, Hangouts and How They Get You Through the Day* (New York: Paragon House, 1989).

85. Keen, *Stalking Sociologists*, 7.

Chapter 2

1. Jeff MacGregor, "The Last of the Great American Hobos," *Smithsonian Magazine*, May 2019, https://www.smithsonianmag.com/arts-culture/last-great-american-hobos-180971913/

2. Todd DePastino, *Citizen Hobo: How a Century of Homelessness Shaped America* (Chicago: University of Chicago Press, 2003).

3. Jack London, *The Road* (New York: Macmillan, 1907).

4. See DePastino, *Citizen Hobo*, xx.

5. Quoted in Frank O. Beck, *Hobohemia* (Rindge, NH: Richard R. Smith Publisher, 1956), 74.

6. DePastino, *Citizen Hobo*.

7. Nels Anderson, *The Hobo: The Sociology of the Homeless Man* (Chicago: University of Chicago Press, 1923), 95.

8. An interview with Todd DePastino, https://www.press.uchicago.edu/Misc/Chicago/143783in.html, accessed July 29, 2019.

9. A-No. 1, *Adventures of a Female Tramp* (A-No. 1 Publishing Co., 1st ed., 1914).

10. Interview with Todd DePastino.

11. Nels Anderson, *The American Hobo: An Autobiography* (Boston: Brill Publishers, 1975), xii; Anderson, *The Hobo*, xi.

12. See, for example, Pauline V. Young, *Scientific Social Surveys and Research* (New York: Prentice-Hall, 1951); Robert Prus, *Symbolic Interaction and Ethnographic Research: Intersubjectivity and the Study of Human Lived Experience* (Albany: State University of New York Press, 1996); Tim Cresswell, *The Tramp in America* (London: Reaktion Books, 2001); and Roger Salerno, *Sociology Noir: Studies at the University of Chicago in Loneliness, Marginality and Deviance, 1915–1935* (Jefferson, NC: McFarland & Company, 2007).

13. Martin Bulmer, *The Chicago School of Sociology: Institutionalization, Diversity, and the Rise of Sociological Research* (Chicago: University of Chicago Press, 1984).

14. Anderson, *American Hobo*, 169.

15. Rolf Lindner, "Nels Anderson and the Chicago School of Urban Sociology," in *The Chicago School Diaspora: Epistemology and Substance*, eds. Jacqueline Low and Gary Bowden (Montreal: McGill–Queen's University Press, 2013), 171.

16. Anderson, *The Hobo*, xi.

17. Anderson, *American Hobo*, 163.

18. Anderson, *American Hobo*, xiii.

19. Anderson, *American Hobo*, 169.

20. John Jackson and Nadine Weidman, *Race, Racism, and Science* (New Brunswick, NJ: Rutgers University Press, 2006).

21. Banu Subramaniam, *Ghost Stories for Darwin: The Science of Variation and the Politics of Diversity* (Urbana: University of Illinois Press, 2014).

22. Jeffrey Brown, "Situating The Hobo," in *The Chicago School Diaspora*, 289.

23. See Cresswell, *The Tramp in America*, for this excellent history.

24. Anderson, *The Hobo*, xviii.

25. Anderson, *The Hobo*, xvii.

26. Anderson, *The Hobo*, xvii.

27. Everett C. Hughes, *Men and Their Work* (Glencoe, IL: Free Press, 1958).

28. Anderson, *American Hobo*, 48.

29. London, *The Road*.

30. Glen H. Mullin, "Riding the Roads," in *On the Fly!: Hobo Literature & Songs, 1879–1941*, ed. Iain Mcintyre (Oakland: PM Press, 2018), 190.

31. Anderson, *American Hobo*, 62.

32. Dean Stiff, *The Milk and Honey Route: A Handbook for Hobos* (New York: Vanguard Press, 1931).

33. Anderson, *The Hobo*, v.

34. Anderson, *American Hobo*, xii.

35. Anderson, *American Hobo*, 168.

36. Stiff, 15.

37. Anderson, *The Hobo*, 137.

38. J. J. McCook, "A Tramp Census and Its Revelations," *The Forum* 15, August, 1893, 753–66; Ben Reitman, *Sisters of the Road: The Autobiography of Boxcar Bertha* (Oakland: AK/Nabat Books, 2002), 13.

39. Clifford Maxwell, "Lady Vagabonds," *Scribners Magazine*, March 1929, 289.

40. Cresswell, *The Tramp in America*.

41. Nan Cinnater, "Hoboes," in *Lesbian Histories and Cultures*, ed. Bonnie Zimmerman (New York: Garland Publishing, 2000), 372–73.

42. Lynn Weiner, "Sisters of the Road: Women Transients and Tramps," in *Walking to Work: Tramps in America, 1790–1935*, ed. Eric Monkkonen (Lincoln: University of Nebraska Press, 1984).

43. Thomas Minehan, *Boy and Girl Tramps of America* (New York: Farrar and Rinehart, 1934).

44. Michael Uys and Lexy Lovell, *Riding the Rails*, Out of the Blue Productions, WGBH Educational Foundation, PBS series, American Experience, 1997.

45. Ian Hacking, "Making Up People," *London Review of Books* 28 (August 17, 2006), https://www.lrb.co.uk/the-paper/v28/n16/ian-hacking/making-up-people

46. Quoted in Cresswell, *The Tramp in America*, 100.

47. Weiner, "Sister of the Road."

48. Walter Reckless, "Why Women Become Hoboes," *American Mercury*, February 1934, 175–80.

49. Reckless, "Why Women Become Hoboes."

50. Anderson, *The Hobo*, 142.

51. Siobhan Somerville, *Queering the Color Line: Race and the Invention of Homosexuality in American Culture* (Durham: Duke University Press, 2000), 10.

52. See Chad Heap's excellent discussion of this history in the exhibition catalog: Chad Heap, *Homosexuality in the City: A Century of Research at the University of Chicago* (Chicago: University of Chicago Library, 2000).

53. Chad Heap, "The City as a Sexual Laboratory: The Queer Heritage of the Chicago School," *Qualitative Sociology* 26, no. 4 (2003): 460.

54. Chad Heap, "The City as a Sexual Laboratory."

55. Jonathan Ned Katz, *The Invention of Heterosexuality* (New York: Dutton, 1995), 92.

56. Anderson, *The Hobo*, 142.

57. Anderson, *The Hobo*, 141.

58. Anderson, *The Hobo*, 144.

59. Paul Robinson, *The Modernization of Sex* (New York: HarperColophon Books, 1976).

60. Havelock Ellis, *Studies in the Psychology of Sex*, Vol. 2, *Sexual Inversion* (The University Press, Limited, 1900).

61. Anderson, *The Hobo*, 144.

62. Regina Kunzel, *Criminal Intimacy: Prison and the Uneven History of Modern American Sexuality* (Chicago: University of Chicago Press, 2008).

63. Anderson, *The Hobo*, 103.

64. See Nicholas Klein, "Hobo Lingo," *American Speech* 1, no. 12 (1926): 650–53.

65. See DePastino, *Citizen Hobo*, 88; Mcintyre, "Big Rock Candy Mountain," and https://en.wikipedia.org/wiki/Big_Rock_Candy_Mountain#Other_renditions, accessed August 5, 2019.

66. Anderson, *The Hobo*, 147.

67. Robinson, *Modernization of Sex*, 11.

68. Anderson, *The Hobo*, 149.

69. Anderson, *The American Hobo*, 172.

70. Anderson, *The Hobo*, 12.

71. Donald Miller, *City of the Century: The Epic of Chicago and the Making of America* (New York: Simon & Schuster, 1996).

72. Robert E. Park, "Editor's Preface," in Anderson, *The Hobo*, xxv.

73. Susan Phillips, "Notes from the Margins: Graffiti, Community, and Environment in Los Angeles," *Journal of the West* 48, no. 2 (2009): 35–42.

74. DePastino, interview.

75. Frank O. Beck, Hobohemia (Rindge, NH: Richard R. Smith Publisher, 1956), 13.

76. Anderson, *The Hobo*, xvi.

77. Anderson, *The Hobo*, 5.

78. DePastino, *Citizen Hobo*.

79. See DePastino for more on race and hobohemia.

80. Anderson, *The Hobo*, 4.

81. DePastino, *Citizen Hobo*, 78.

82. Anderson, *The Hobo*, 19.

83. Anderson, *The Hobo*, 18.

84. London, *The Road*, http://www.online-literature.com/london/the-road/4/

85. Mike Schafer with Mike McBride, *Freight Train Cars* (Osceola, WI: MBI Publishing Company, 1999), 46.

86. Jack London, *Boxcar Politics: The Hobo in U.S. Culture and Literature, 1869–1956* (Amherst: University of Massachusetts Press, 2014), 5.

87. London, *The Road*, 6.

88. Cresswell, *The Tramp in America*.

89. Cresswell, *The Tramp in America*, 9.

90. Cresswell, *The Tramp in America*, 9.

91. See DePastino, *Citizen Hobo*, and Cresswell, *The Tramp in America*, for this discussion of early tramp entertainment.

92. See MacGregor for a comment on contemporary university students dressing as hobos.

93. DePastino, *Citizen Hobo*, 157.

94. DePastino, *Citizen Hobo*, 153.

95. DePastino, *Citizen Hobo*, 152.

96. Charlie Chaplin, quoted in Charles Maland, *Chaplin and American Culture* (Princeton: Princeton University Press, 1989), 6.

97. Norman Rockwell, *Norman Rockwell: My Adventures as an Illustrator*, as told to Thomas Rockwell (Garden City, NY: Doubleday, 1960).

98. Richard Halpern, *Norman Rockwell: The Underside of Innocence* (Chicago: University of Chicago Press, 2006), 23.

99. Quoted in DePastino, *Citizen Hobo*, 110.

100. Anderson, *The Hobo*, 200.

101. Quoted in DePastino, *Citizen Hobo*, 104.

102. DePastino, *Citizen Hobo*, 96.

103. See DePastino, *Citizen Hobo*, for elaboration of this argument, chapter 4.

104. Anderson, *American Hobo*, ix.

105. *Riding the Rails*.

106. Mekado Murphy (producer), *New York Times*, December 5, 2014, "Anatomy of a Scene."

107. Josh Mack, *The Hobo Handbook: A Field Guide to Living by Your Own Rules* (Avon, MA: Adams Media, 2011), xxi.

108. Ian Hacking, "Making Up People," *London Review of Books* 28, no. 16 (August 17, 2006).

109. Roger Salerno, *Sociology Noir: Studies at the University of Chicago in Loneliness, Marginality and Deviance, 1915–1935* (Jefferson, NC: McFarland & Company, 2007).

110. Nels Anderson, "A Stranger at the Gate: Reflections on the Chicago School of Sociology," *Urban Life* 11, no. 4 (1983): 396–406.

111. Anderson, *American Hobo*, 171.

112. Anderson, *The Hobo*, xii.

113. Anderson, *The American Hobo*, 170.

114. Anderson, *The American Hobo*, 173.

115. Anderson, *The American Hobo*, 173.

116. Richard Kirby and Jay Corzine, "The Contagion of Stigma: Fieldwork Among Deviants," *Qualitative Sociology* 4, no. 1 (1981): 3–20.

117. Kathy Davis and Janice Irvine, "Introduction," in *Silences, Neglected Feelings, and Blind-spots in Research Practices*, eds. Kathy Davis and Janice Irvine (London: Routledge, 2022).

118. Anderson, *The Hobo*, xxi.

119. Ben Reitman, *Sister of the Road: The Autobiography of Boxcar Bertha* (Oakland: AK/Nabat Books, 2002). See Amazon.com for the advertising copy, https://www.amazon.com/Sister-Road-Autobiography-Boxcar-Reitman/dp/1902593030

120. Lisa St. Aubin de Teran, ed., *Indiscreet Journeys: Stories of Women on the Road* (London: Virago Press, 1989); Mary Morris and Larry O'Connor, eds., *Maiden Voyages: Writings of Women Travelers* (New York: Vintage Books, 1993); Mari Jo Buhle, *Women and the American Left: A Guide to Sources* (Boston: G. K. Hall, 1983), 92.

121. Barry Pateman, "Afterword," in Reitman, *Sister of the Road*, 201.

122. Salerno, *Sociology Noir*.

123. For a discussion of Chicago sociology and early-twentieth-century literature, see Carla Cappetti, *Writing Chicago: Modernism, Ethnography, and the Novel* (New York: Columbia University Press, 1993).

124. Martha Lynn Reis, "Hidden Histories: Ben Reitman and the 'Outcast'

Women Behind *Sister of the Road: The Autobiography of Boxcar Bertha*," PhD diss., University of Minnesota (September 2000), 70.

125. Reis, "Hidden Histories," 58.
126. Reis, "Hidden Histories," 104.
127. Reitman, *Sister of the Road*, 106.
128. Reis, "Hidden Histories," 266.
129. See Jonathan Ned Katz, *The Daring Times and Dangerous Life of Eve Adams* (Chicago: Chicago Review Press, 2021).
130. Reis, "Hidden Histories," 265.
131. Reis, "Hidden Histories."
132. Anderson, *American Hobo*, 165.
133. London, *The Road*. All quotes in this paragraph are from the chapter "Pictures."
134. Cyd Cipolla, Kristina Gupta, David Rubin, and Angela Willey, eds., *Queer Feminist Science Studies: A Reader* (Seattle: University of Washington Press, 2017), 19.
135. Susan Phillips, "Notes from the Margins," 42.
136. A-No. 1, *Adventures of a Female Tramp*.
137. Susan Phillips, *The City Beneath: A Century of Los Angeles Graffiti* (New Haven: Yale University Press, 2019), 28.
138. All quotes in this paragraph from A-No. 1, *Adventures of a Female Tramp*.
139. Susan Phillips, *The City Beneath*, 23.
140. Danny Lewis, "After a Century, An Anthropologist Picked Up the Trail of the 'Hobo King,'" Smithsonian.com, June 6, 2016, https://www.smithsonianmag.com/smart-news/after-century-anthropologist-picked-trail-original-hobo-king-180959313/, accessed July 30, 2019.
141. Susan Phillips, *The City Beneath*, 22.
142. Susan Phillips, *The City Beneath*, 29.

Chapter 3

1. Paul Goalby Cressey, *The Taxi-Dance Hall: A Sociological Study in Commercialized Recreation & City Life* (Chicago: University of Chicago Press, 1932), 33.
2. Salerno, *Sociology Noir*.
3. William Tuttle Jr., *Race Riot: Chicago in the Red Summer of 1919* (New York: Atheneum, 1970).
4. Joanne J. Meyerowitz, *Women Adrift: Independent Wage-Earners in Chicago, 1880–1930* (Chicago: University of Chicago Press, 1988).
5. Meyerowitz, *Women Adrift*, xv.
6. Meyerowitz, *Women Adrift*, xv.
7. For discussion of these agencies and groups, particularly in relation to Chicago, see Meyerowitz, *Women Adrift*; Chad Heap, *Slumming: Sexual and Racial Encounters in American Nightlife, 1885–1940* (Chicago: University of Chicago Press, 2009); Kevin Mumford, *Interzones: Black/White Sex Districts in Chicago and New York in the Early Twentieth Century* (New York: Columbia University Press, 1997); and Derek Vaillant, *Sounds of Reform: Progressivism & Music in Chicago, 1873–1935* (Chapel Hill: University of North Carolina Press, 2003). See also James A. Morone, *Hellfire Nation: The Politics of Sin in American History* (New Haven: Yale University Press, 2003).

8. Carole S. Vance, *Pleasure and Danger: Exploring Female Sexuality* (Boston: Routledge & Kegan Paul, 1984). See also Ellen Carol DuBois and Linda Gordon, "Seeking Ecstasy on the Battlefield: Danger and Pleasure in Nineteenth-Century Feminist Sexual Thought," in *Pleasure and Danger*, ed. Carole S. Vance, 31–49. For discussion of early-twentieth-century Chicago and the JPA, see Chad Heap, *Slumming*.

9. Heap, *Slumming*, 64.

10. Meyerwitz, *Women Adrift*, 64.

11. Quoted in Salerno, *Sociology Noir*, 121.

12. Quoted in Salerno, *Sociology Noir*, 68.

13. Derek Vaillant, *Sounds of Reform*.

14. Quoted in Vaillant, *Sounds of Reform*, 206.

15. Heap, *Slumming*, 52.

16. Daniel Okrent, *The Guarded Gate: Bigotry, Eugenics, and the Law That Kept Two Generations of Jews, Italians, and Other European Immigrants Out of America* (New York: Scribner, 2019), 343.

17. Rhacel Salazar Parreñas, "'White Trash' Meets the 'Little Brown Monkeys': The Taxi Dance Hall as a Site of Interracial and Gender Alliances between White Working Class Women and Filipino Immigrant Men in the 1920s and '30s," *Amerasia Journal* 24 (1998): 115–34.

18. Burgess, Ernest, Papers [Box 130, Folder 7]. Hanna Holborn Gray Special Collections Research Center, University of Chicago Library; Paul Goalby Cressey, "A Study of Gaelic Park," 84.

19. Martin Bulmer, *The Chicago School of Sociology: Institutionalization, Diversity, and the Rise of Sociological Research* (Chicago: University of Chicago Press, 1984), 105.

20. Burgess, Ernest, Papers [Box 130, Folder 5]. Hanna Holborn Gray Special Collections Research Center, University of Chicago Library. "Summary of Work Done on Research Project during Winter Quarter," Student—Paul G. Cressey. Angela Fritz argues that the women were in Lawndale for mandatory venereal disease testing. Angela Fritz, "The Women Who Danced for a Living: Exploring Taxi Dancers' Childhood in Chicago's Polish American Communities, 1920–1926," *Journal of the History of Sexuality* 23, no. 2 (2014): 247–72.

21. Salerno, *Sociology Noir*, 128.

22. Salerno, *Sociology Noir*, 128.

23. See Martin Bulmer, "The Methodology of The Taxi-Dance Hall," *Urban Life* 12, no. 1 (1983): 95–120; Albert Reiss, "Systematic Observation of Natural Social Phenomena," in *Sociological Methodology*, Herbert Costner(San Francisco: Jossey-Bass, 1970), 3–33; Jennifer Platt, *A History of Sociological Research Methods in America, 1920–1960* (Cambridge: Cambridge University Press, 1996).

24. Material in this paragraph from Platt, *A History of Sociological Research Methods* (Cambridge: Cambridge University Press, 1996). Quote, 263.

25. Cressey, *Taxi-Dance Hall*, 31.

26. Cressey, *Taxi-Dance Hall*, 287.

27. Ernest Burgess, "Introduction," in Cressey, *Taxi-Dance Hall*, xv.

28. Sandy Isenstadt, *Electric Light: An Architectural History* (Cambridge: MIT Press, 2018).

29. Isenstadt, *Electric Light*, 1.

30. Emily Thompson, *The Soundscape of Modernity: Architectural Acoustics and the Culture of Listening in America, 1900–1933* (Cambridge: MIT Press, 2002), 2.

31. Meyerowitz, *Women Adrift*, xvi.

32. Christian Wolmar, *The Great Railroad Revolution: The History of Trains in America* (New York: PublicAffairs, 2012).

33. Christine Stansell, *American Moderns: Bohemian New York and the Creation of a New Century* (New York: Henry Holt and Company, 2000), 7.

34. John D'Emilio and Estelle Freedman, *Intimate Matters: A History of Sexuality in America* (New York: Harper & Row Publishers, 1988).

35. D'Emlio and Freedman, *Intimate Matters*.

36. Joanne Meyerowitz, "Sexual Geography and Sexual Economy," *Gender & History* 2, no. 3 (1990): 274–96.

37. Meyerowitz, "Sexual Geography," 289.

38. Quotations throughout this section are from Cressey, *Taxi-Dance Hall*.

39. Mumford, *Interzones*.

40. Quoted in Randy McBee, *Dance Hall Days: Intimacy and Leisure among Working-Class Immigrants in the United States* (New York: New York University Press, 2000), 90.

41. McBee, *Dance Hall Days*, 89.

42. Parreñas, "'White Trash' Meets the 'Little Brown Monkeys,'" 126.

43. McBee, *Dance Hall Days*.

44. Quotes in this paragraph are from Cressey, *Taxi-Dance Hall*.

45. David Riesman, Nathan Glazer, and Reuel Denney, *The Lonely Crowd* (New Haven: Yale University Press, 1950); Robert Putnam, *Bowling Alone: The Collapse and Revival of American Community* (New York: Simon & Schuster, 2000).

46. *Chicago Daily Times*, May 4, 1932. University of Chicago Press Records 1892–1965 [Box 135, Folder 1]. Hanna Holborn Gray Special Collections Research Center, University of Chicago Library.

47. Paul Goalby Cressey.

48. W. E. Burghardt Du Bois, *The Georgia Negro: A Social Study* (1900). http://hdl.loc.gov/loc.pnp/ppmsca.33863

49. Whitney Battle-Baptiste and Britt Rusert, "Introduction," in *W. E. B. Du Bois's Data Portraits: Visualizing Black America*, eds. Whitney Battle-Baptiste and Britt Rusert (New York: Princeton Architectural Press, 2018), 11.

50. Residents of Hull-House, *Hull-House Maps and Papers: A Presentation of Nationalities and Wages in a Congested District of Chicago, Together with Comments and Essays on Problems Growing Out of the Social Conditions* (Urbana: University of Illinois Press, 2007 [originally 1895]). Quote from "Introduction," by Rima Lunin Schultz, 30.

51. Kathyrn Kish Sklar, "Hull House Maps and Papers: Social Science as Women's Work in the 1890s," in *Gender and American Social Science*, ed. Helene Silverberg (Princeton: Princeton University Press, 1998), 146.

52. Mary Jo Deegan, *Jane Addams and the Men of the Chicago School, 1892–1918* (New Brunswick, Transaction Publishers, 1988), 55.

53. Robert Park and Ernest Burgess, *The City* (Chicago: University of Chicago Press, 1925).

54. Cressey, *Taxi-Dance Hall*, 56, 58.
55. See Meyerowitz, *Women Adrift*; and Fritz, "The Women Who Danced for a Living."
56. Fritz, "The Women Who Danced for a Living."
57. Quotations in this section are from chapter IV, "The Family and Social Backgrounds of the Taxi-Dancer," and chapter VI, "The Patron: Who He Is, Why He Comes," in Cressey, *Taxi-Dance Hall*.
58. Quoted in McBee, *Dance Hall Days*, 58.
59. Martin Booe, "Taxi Dancers: It's No Longer 10 Cents a Dance, But Lonely Men Can Still Hire Partners by the Minute in Dim Downtown Clubs," *Los Angeles Times*, July 15, 1990, http://articles.latimes.com/1990-07-15/magazine/tm-549_1_taxi-dance-hall
60. W. I. Thomas, "The Professor's Views," *Chicago Daily Tribune*, April 22, 1918, 15–16.
61. Janice M. Irvine, "Is Sexuality Research 'Dirty Work?': Institutionalized Stigma in the Production of Sexual Knowledge," *Sexualities* 17, no. 5–6 (2014): 632–56. See this volume for a discussion of this question by a number of international scholars. See also Feona Attwood and I. Q. Hunter, "Not Safe for Work? Researching and Writing the Sexually Explicit," *Sexualities* 12, no. 5 (2009): 547–57.
62. Erving Goffman, *Stigma: Notes on the Management of Spoiled Identity* (New York: Simon &Schuster, 1963.)
63. Paul Cressey, unpublished letter, August 11, 1931. University of Chicago Press Records 1892–1965 [Box 134, Folder 7]. Hanna Holborn Gray Special Collections Research Center, University of Chicago Library.
64. I am grateful for Chad Heap's rigorous research on this topic: Chad Heap, "The City as a Sexual Laboratory: The Queer Heritage of the Chicago School."
65. Paul Cressey, "The Closed Dance Hall in Chicago," MA thesis, University of Chicago (1929), 127.
66. Paul Cressey, unpublished letter, August 17, 1931. University of Chicago Press Records 1892–1965 [Box 134, Folder 7]. Hanna Holborn Gray Special Collections Research Center, University of Chicago Library.
67. Rollin D. Hemens, unpublished letter, April 9, 1931. University of Chicago Press Records 1892–1965 [Box 134, Folder 7]. Hanna Holborn Gray Special Collections Research Center, University of Chicago Library.
68. G. J. Laing, unpublished letter, May 7, 1931. University of Chicago Press Records 1892–1965 [Box 134, Folder 7]. Hanna Holborn Gray Special Collections Research Center, University of Chicago Library.
69. Paul Cressey, unpublished letter, June 22, 1932. University of Chicago Press Records 1892–1965 [Box 134, Folder 7]. Hanna Holborn Gray Special Collections Research Center, University of Chicago Library.
70. Cressey, unpublished letter, June 22, 1932.
71. Cressey, unpublished letter, June 22, 1932.
72. G. J. Laing, unpublished letter, July 7, 1932. University of Chicago Press Records 1892–1965 [Box 134, Folder 7]. Hanna Holborn Gray Special Collections Research Center, University of Chicago Library.
73. Garth Jowett, Ian Jarvie, and Kathryn Fuller, *Children and the Movies: Media Influence and the Payne Fund Controversy* (Cambridge: Cambridge University Press, 1996), p. 84.

74. Jowett, Jarvie, and Fuller, *Children and the Movies*, 85.
75. Quoted in Angela Fritz, "'I Was a Sociological Stranger': Ethnographic Fieldwork and Undercover Performance in the Publication of The Taxi-Dance Hall, 1925–1932," *Gender & History* 30, no. 1 (March 2018): 146.
76. Fritz, "'I Was a Sociological Stranger,'" 146.
77. See, for example, Meyerowitz, *Women Adrift*, and in particular, Fritz, "I Was a Sociological Stranger."
78. "Look in the Mirror," *Chicago Daily Times*, June 1, 1932. University of Chicago Press Records 1892–1965 [Box 135, Folder 1]. Hanna Holborn Gray Special Collections Research Center, University of Chicago Library.
79. "Why They Must Dance," *Chicago Daily Times*, May 20, 1932. University of Chicago Press Records 1892–1965 [Box 135, Folder 1]. Hanna Holborn Gray Special Collections Research Center, University of Chicago Library.
80. "It's Either Dance or Starve," *Chicago Daily Times*, May 24, 1932. University of Chicago Press Records 1892–1965 [Box 135, Folder 1]. Hanna Holborn Gray Special Collections Research Center, University of Chicago Library.
81. "Up To Each Girl," *Chicago Daily Times*, May 26, 1932. University of Chicago Press Records 1892–1965 [Box 135, Folder 1]. Hanna Holborn Gray Special Collections Research Center, University of Chicago Library.
82. Fritz, "'I Was a Sociological Stranger,'" 148.
83. "Up To Each Girl," University of Chicago Press Records 1892–1965 [Box 135, Folder 1]. Hanna Holborn Gray Special Collections Research Center, University of Chicago Library.
84. Winifred Raushenbush, *Book Review Digest*, September, 1932. University of Chicago Press Records 1892–1965 [Box 135, Folder 1]. Hanna Holborn Gray Special Collections Research Center, University of Chicago Library.
85. Evelyn Buchan Crook, "Book Review," *American Journal of Sociology* 40, no. 1 (July 1934): 33.
86. Martin Bulmer, "The Methodology of The Taxi-Dance Hall," *Urban Life* 12, no. 1 (1983): 95–120; Steven Dubin, "The Moral Continuum of Deviancy Research: Chicago Sociologists and the Dance Hall," *Urban Life* 12, no. 1 (1983): 75–94.
87. Joanne Meyerowitz, "Sexual Geography." Based on my reading of *The Taxi-Dance Hall*, Meyerowitz overstates her argument about this text, since Cressey does discuss family conflicts, as well as the taxi dancer's vulnerability to what we would today call sexual coercion or harassment.
88. Meyerowitz, "Sexual Georgraph," 62.
89. Fritz, "'I Was a Sociological Stranger.'"
90. Mumford, *Interzones*.
91. Vaillant, 220.
92. Vaillant, 221.
93. There is an extensive literature on the race and gender politics of the Chicago School, and a productive, ongoing conversation about racism, colonialism, and the founding of sociology. For example, University of Chicago sociologists in the early twentieth century actively engaged in the marginalization of scholars such as W. E. B. Du Bois. Anthropologist Zora Neal Hurston was similarly erased as a scholar (chapter 4).
94. Salerno, *Sociology Noir*, 127.

95. Meyerowitz, "Sexual Geography."

96. Lorenz Hart and Richard Rodgers, "Ten Cents a Dance," Warner/Chappell Music, 1930.

97. Meyerowitz, *Women Adrift*, 128.

98. Cynthia J. Miller, "A Heart of Gold: Charlie and the Dance Hall Girls," in *Refocusing Chaplin*, eds. Lawrence Howe, James E. Caron and Benjamin Click (Lanham, MC: Scarecrow Press, 2013): 45–60.

99. Charles Chaplin, producer, writer, and director, *The Gold Rush*, United Artists, June 26, 1925.

100. Susan Stryker, *Queer Pulp: Perverted Passions from the Golden Age of the Paperback* (San Francisco: Chronicle Books, 2001), 5.

101. Eve Linkletter, *Taxi Dancers* (Fresno: Fabian Books Publication, 1958).

102. Meyerowitz, *Women Adrift*, 40.

103. Christine Fletcher, *Ten Cents a Dance* (New York: Bloomsbury, 2008); Michelle Cox, *A Girl Like You: A Henrietta and Inspector Howard Novel* (Berkeley: She Writes Press, 2016).

104. Eve Linkletter, *The Gay Ones* (Fresno: Fabian Books Publication, 1958).

105. Ernest W. Burgess Collection [Box 130, Folder 7]. Hanna Holborn Gray Special Collections Research Center, University of Chicago Library. Paul Goalby Cressey, "A Study of Gaelic Park," 84.

106. Chad Heap, "The City as a Sexual Laboratory: The Queer Heritage of the Chicago School," *Qualitative Sociology* 26, no. 4 (2003): 471.

107. Richard Dellamora, *Radclyffe Hall: A Life in the Writing* (Philadelphia: University of Pennsylvania Press, 2011).

108. Leslie Taylor, "'I Made Up My Mind to Get It': The American Trial of *The Well of Loneliness*, New York City, 1928–29," *Journal of the History of Sexuality* 10, no. 2 (2010): 250–86.

109. Heap, *Slumming*, 2.

110. Heap, *Slumming*, 82.

111. Heap, *Slumming*, 83.

112. Paul Cressey, "The Closed Dance Hall in Chicago," MA thesis, University of Chicago (1929), 128–29.

Chapter 4

1. Zora Neale Hurston, *Dust Tracks on a Road: An Autobiography* (London: Hutchinson & Company, 1942), 91.

2. Zora Neale Hurston, "How It Feels to Be Colored Me," *The World Tomorrow*, May 1928.

3. Damien Cave, "In a Town Apart, the Pride and Trials of Black Life," *New York Times*, September 28, 2008.

4. Alice Walker, "In Search of Zora Neale Hurston," *Ms*, March 1975, 74–79, 84–89.

5. Poncie Rutsch, "Novelist Zora Neale Hurston Was a Cultural Anthropologist First," *The Pulse*, WHYY/PBS/NPR, March 17, 2017, https://whyy.org/segments/novelist-zora-neale-hurston-was-a-cultural-anthropologist-first/

6. Tiffany Ruby Patterson, *Zora Neale Hurston and a History of Southern Life* (Philadelphia: Temple University Press, 2005), 10.

7. Lori Jirousek, "Ethnics and Ethnographers: Zora Neale Hurston and Anzia Yezierska," *Journal of Modern Literature* 29, no. 2 (2006): 19.
8. Patterson, *Zora Neale Hurston*, 6.
9. Zora Neale Hurston, "What White Publishers Won't Print," *Negro Digest*, April 1950.
10. Helen A. Robbins, "The Ethnography of Zora Neale Hurston: A Postmodern Writer Before Her Time," *Arizona Anthropologist* 7 (1991).
11. Saidiya Hartman, *Wayward Lives, Beautiful Experiments: Intimate Histories of Riotous Black Girls, Troublesome Women, and Queer Radicals* (New York: W. W. Norton & Company, 2019), xv.
12. Valerie Boyd, *Wrapped in Rainbows: The Life of Zora Neale Hurston* (New York: Scribner, 2003), 101.
13. Letter from Zora Neale Hurston to Constance Sheen, January 5, 1926. In *Zora Neale Hurston: A Life in Letters*, collected and edited by Carla Kaplan (New York: Doubleday, 2002), 75.
14. David Levering Lewis, *When Harlem Was in Vogue* (New York: Penguin Books, 1979), 103, 108.
15. Hurston, *Mules and Men*, in *Zora Neale Hurston: Folklore, Memoirs, and Other Writings*, ed. Cheryl A. Wall (New York: The Library of America Series, 1995), 1.
16. Hurston, *Mules and Men*, in Wall, *Hurston*, 10.
17. Hurston, *Mules and Men*.
18. Hurston, *Mules and Men*, in Wall, *Hurston*, 9.
19. Boyd, *Wrapped in Rainbows*, 165.
20. Letter from Zora Neale Hurston to Walter and Gladys White, July/August 1932. In *Zora Neale Hurston: A Life in Letters*, 209.
21. Irma McClaurin, "Zora Neale Hurston: Enigma, Heterodox, and Progenitor of Black Studies," *Fire!!! The Multimedia Journal of Black Studies* 1, no. 1 (2012): 49–67.
22. Hurston, *Dust Tracks on a Road*.
23. Robert E. Hemenway, *Zora Neale Hurston: A Literary Biography* (Urbana: University of Illinois Press, 1977).
24. Joanne Meyerowitz, "'How Common Culture Shapes the Separate Lives': Sexuality, Race, and Mid-Twentieth-Century Social Constructionist Thought," *Journal of American History* 96, no. 4 (2010): 1057–84.
25. Charles King, *Gods of the Upper Air: How a Circle of Renegade Anthropologists Reinvented Race, Sex, And Gender in the Twentieth Century* (New York: Doubleday, 2019).
26. King, *Gods of the Upper Air*, 204.
27. Patterson, *Zora Neale Hurston*, 10.
28. Zora Neale Hurston, "Race Cannot Become Great Until It Recognizes Its Talent," *Washington Tribune*, December 29, 1934.
29. Zora Neale Hurston, "My People! My People!" in Wall, *Hurston*, 733.
30. Pamela Bordelon, ed., *Go Gator and Muddy the Water: Writings by Zora Neale Hurston from the Federal Writers' Project* (New York: W. W. Norton & Company, 1999), 36.
31. Hemenway, *Zora Neale Hurston*, see p. 251.
32. Quoted in *The Florida Negro: A Federal Writers' Project Legacy*, ed. Gary McDonogh (Jackson: University Press of Mississippi, 1993), xiv.

33. Nick Taylor, *American-Made: The Enduring Legacy of the WPA, When FDR Put the Nation to Work* (New York: Bantam Books, 2008), 312.

34. Cathy Salustri, *Backroads of Paradise: A Journey to Rediscover Old Florida* (Gainesville: University Press of Florida, 2016), 4.

35. *Florida: A Guide to the Southernmost State*, Compiled and Written by the Federal Writers' Project of the Work Projects Administration for the State of Florida (New York: Oxford University Press, 1939), n.p.

36. *Guide to the Southernmost State*, 348.

37. *Guide to the Southernmost State*, 3.

38. Cathy Salustri, personal conversation with author, July 11, 2020.

39. See Bordelon, *Go Gator*.

40. Pamela Bordelon, "*The Federal Writers' Project's Mirror to America*: The Florida Reflection," (1991). LSU Historical Dissertations and Theses, https://digitalcommons.lsu.edu/gradschool_disstheses/5168

41. Bordelon, *Go Gator*.

42. McDonogh, *The Florida Negro*.

43. Bordelon, *Go Gator*, 35.

44. Bordelon, *Go Gator*, 25.

45. Bordelon, *Go Gator*, 26.

46. *Guide to the Southernmost State*, 362.

47. Zora Neale Hurston, "Goldsborough," in Bordelon, *Go Gator*, 127.

48. Bordelon, *Go Gator*, 126.

49. *Florida: A Guide to the Southernmost State*, 457.

50. Patterson, *Zora Neale Hurston*, 87.

51. Letter from Zora Neale Hurston to Douglas Gilbert, February 4, 1943. In *Zora Neale Hurston: A Life in Letters*, 476.

52. Bordelon, *Go Gator*, 190.

53. Neal Conan, host, "StoryCorps and Stetson Kennedy," National Public Radio, Talk of the Nation, May 23, 2005.

54. See Patterson, *Zora Neale Hurston*, chapter 3, for discussion of Florida's turpentine industry.

55. Quoted in Jeffrey Drobney, "Where Palm and Pine are Blowing: Convict Labor in the North Florida Turpentine Industry, 1877–1923," *Florida Historical Quarterly* 72, no. 4 (1994): 416.

56. See Drobney; also Jerrell Shofner, "Forced Labor in the Florida Forests 1880–1950," *Journal of Forest History* 25, no. 1 (January 1981): 14–25.

57. Hurston, *Mules and Men*, in *Zora Neale Hurston: Folklore, Memoirs, & Other Writings*, ed. Cheryl A. Wall (New York: Library of America, Penguin Random House, 1995), 61.

58. Patterson, *Zora Neale Hurston*, 129.

59. Boyd, 169.

60. Hurston, *Mules and Men*, in Wall, *Hurston*, 2.

61. Hurston, *Mules and Men*, in Wall, *Hurston*, 150.

62. Patterson, *Zora Neale Hurston*, 134.

63. Bordelon, *Go Gator*, 39.

64. Quoted in Kaplan, *Zora Neale Hurston*, 181.

65. Quoted in Bordelon, *Go Gator*, 40.

66. Zora Neale Hurston, "Dust Tracks on a Road," in *Hurston: Folklore, Memoirs, & Other Writings*, edited by Cheryl A. Wall (New York: Library of America, Penguin Random House, 1995), 690–91.
67. Zora Neale Hurston, "Turpentine," now published in Bordelon, 129–30.
68. Zora Neale Hurston, "Turpentine."
69. Stetson Kennedy, *Palmetto Country: A Classic Florida Book* (Cocoa, FL: The Florida Historical Society Press, 1989), 278. Author copyright, 1942, Stetson Kennedy.
70. Kennedy, 277.
71. Valerie Boyd, *Wrapped in Rainbows: The Life of Zora Neale Hurston* (New York: Scribner, 2003), 323.
72. Zora Neale Hurston, "Dust Tracks on a Road," 690.
73. Zora Neale Hurston, "Florida's Migrant Farm Labor," *Frontiers: A Journal of Women Studies* 12, no. 1 (1991), 199–200.
74. Martyn Bone, *Where the New World Is: Literature about the U.S. South at Global Scales* (Atlanta: University of Georgia Press, 2018), 31.
75. Bone, *Where the New World Is*, 34.
76. Patterson, *Zora Neale Hurston*, 21.
77. Hurston, "Florida's Migrant Farm Labor," 199.
78. Hurston, "Florida's Migrant Farm Labor," 199–200.
79. Letter from George Beebe to Doug Silver, July 9, 1958. Zora Neale Hurston Papers, George A. Smathers Libraries, University of Florida Digital Collections, https://ufdc.ufl.edu/AA00009755/00011
80. Hurston, "Florida's Migrant Farm Labor," 199–203.
81. Fred W. Friendly, director, *Harvest of Shame*, CBS, November 25, 1960.
82. Quoted in Kaplan, *Zora Neale Hurston*, 598.
83. Kenneth Clark and Mamie Clark, "The Development of Consciousness of Self and the Emergence of Racial Identification in Negro Preschool Children," *Journal of Social Psychology* 10, no. 4 (1939): 591–99.
84. The doll was named after Sara Lee Creech, although Saralee was one word. See https://blackdollcollecting.blogspot.com/2018/02/ideals-saralee-negro-doll-1951-1953.html
85. "The Race Question," UNESCO and Its Programme, 1950, 8–9.
86. Tracy Teslow, *Constructing Race: The Science of Bodies and Cultures in American Anthropology* (New York: Cambridge University Press, 2014).
87. Letter from Zora Neale Hurston to Sara Lee Creech, June 29, 1950. In Kaplan, *Zora Neale Hurston*, 598.
88. Jacqueline Urla and Alan Swedlund, "The Anthropometry of Barbie," in *Deviant Bodies*, eds. Jennifer Terry and Jacqueline Urla (Bloomington: Indiana University Press, 1995), 279–80.
89. Sabrina Lynette Thomas, "Sara Lee: The Rise and Fall of the Ultimate Negro Doll," *Transforming Anthropology* 15, no. 1 (April 2007): 38–49.
90. Gordon Patterson, "Color Matters: The Creation of the Saralee Doll," *Florida Historical Quarterly* 73, no. 2 (1994): 147–65.
91. Patterson, "Color Matters," 151.
92. Thomas, "Sara Lee," 38.
93. Madison Peterson Starr, "The Fabric Behind the Doll—The Performance

of the Black Doll in Early 20th Century America," senior thesis, Trinity College, Hartford, CT (2016), http://digitalrepository.trincoll.edu/theses/606

94. Patterson, "Color Matters," 152.

95. See Richard L. Jantz, "The Anthropometric Legacy of Franz Boas," *Economics and Human Biology* 1 (2003): 277–84.

96. Urla and Swedlund, 287.

97. King, *Gods of the Upper Air*, 78.

98. Letter from Zora Neale Hurston to Annie Nathan Meyer, spring 1926. In Kaplan, *Zora Neale Hurston*, 82–83.

99. Quoted in Boyd, *Wrapped in Rainbows*, 114.

100. Letter from Zora Neale Hurston to Melville Herskovits, January 24, 1930. In Kaplan, *Zora Neale Hurston*, 185–86.

101. Letter from Zora Neale Hurston to Ruth Benedict, December 4, 1933. In Kaplan, *Zora Neale Hurston*, 283–84.

102. Letter from Zora Neale Hurston to Ruth Benedict, June 19, 1945. In Kaplan, *Zora Neale Hurston*, 522.

103. Zora Neale Hurston, "Dust Tracks on a Road," in Wall, *Hurston*, 725.

104. Thomas, "Sara Lee," 42.

105. Thomas, "Sara Lee," 42.

106. Emily Temple, "How Zora Neale Hurston Helped Create the First Realistic Black Baby Doll," Literary Hub, January 7, 2019, https://lithub.com/how-zora-neale-hurston-helped-create-the-first-realistic-black-baby-doll/

107. Quoted in Thomas, "Sara Lee," 42.

108. https://blackdollcollecting.blogspot.com/2018/02/ideals-saralee-negro-doll-1951-1953.html

109. Thomas, "Sara Lee."

110. See Thomas, "Sara Lee."

111. Zora Neale Hurston, "My People! My People!" in Wall, *Hurston*, 733.

112. Thomas, "Sara Lee," 46.

113. Thomas, "Sara Lee," 47.

114. Franz Boas, *Changes in Bodily Forms of Descendants of Immigrants* (New York: Columbia University Press, 1912), 5.

115. Audre Lorde, "The Master's Tools Will Never Dismantle the Master's House," in *This Bridge Called My Back: Writings by Radical Women of Color*, eds. Cherríe Moraga and Gloria Anzaldúa (New York: Kitchen Table Press, 1983), 94–101.

116. Erving Goffman, *Stigma: Notes on the Management of Spoiled Identity* (New York: Simon and Schuster, 1963).

117. James Wright, *A Florida State of Mind: An Unnatural History of Our Weirdest State* (New York: St. Martin's Press, 2019), 19.

118. Zora Neale Hurston, "The Eatonville Anthology," in Wall, *Hurston*, 815.

119. Zora Neale Hurston, *Jonah's Gourd Vine*, in Wall, *Hurston*, 88.

120. Martyn Bone, *Where the New World Is*.

121. Mia Bay, *Traveling Black: A Story of Race and Resistance* (Cambridge: Belknap Press of Harvard University Press, 2021).

122. Raymond Lee, *Dangerous Fieldwork* (Thousand Oaks, CA: Sage Publications, 1995), vii.

123. Hurston, "Dust Tracks on a Road," in Wall, *Hurston*, 689.
124. Bay, *Traveling Black*.
125. Kenneth Mack, "Law, Society, Identity, and the Making of the Jim Crow South: Travel and Segregation on Tennessee Railroads, 1875–1905," *Law & Social Inquiry* 24 (1999): 377–409.
126. See Bay, *Traveling Black*.
127. Stetson Kennedy, *Jim Crow Guide to the U.S.A.* (London: Lawrence & Wishart, 1959).
128. Letter from Zora Neale Hurston to Lawrence Jordan, postmarked February 18, 1927. In Kaplan, *Zora Neale Hurston*, 90.
129. Hurston, *Mules and Men*, in Wall, *Hurston*, 10.
130. Candacy Taylor, *Overground Railroad: The Green Book and the Roots of Black Travel in America* (New York: Abrams Press, 2020), 14.
131. Hurston *Mules and Men*, in Wall, *Hurston*, 63.
132. Hurston, *Mules and Men*, in Wall, *Hurston*, 66.
133. Boyd, *Wrapped in Rainbows*, 164.
134. Tiffany Patterson, *Zora Neale Hurston*, 8.
135. Tiffany Patterson, *Zora Neale Hurston*, 10.
136. Ray Oldenburg, *The Great Good Place: Cafés, Coffee Shops, Community Centers, Beauty Parlors, General Stores, Bars, Hangouts and How They Get You Through the Day* (New York: Paragon House, 1989).
137. Doreen Massey, *For Space* (Thousand Oaks, CA: Sage Publications, 2005), 130.
138. *Mules and Men*, 9.
139. Hurston, "Dust Tracks," in Wall, *Hurston*, 599.
140. Zora Neale Hurston, "Dust Tracks," in Wall, *Hurston*, 692.
141. Zora Neale Hurston, *The Sanctified Church* (New York: Marlowe & Company, 1981), 62.
142. Hurston, *Sanctified Church*, 105.
143. Hurston, *Sanctified Church*, 103–4.
144. Hurston, *Sanctified Church*, 91.
145. Hurston, "Dust Tracks on a Road," in Wall, *Hurston*, 693.
146. Kennedy, *Palmetto Country*, 190.
147. Kennedy, *Palmetto Country*, 189.
148. Hurston, *Sanctified Church*, 98.
149. Tim Weiner, "An Electrifying Link from R&B to Rock 'n' Roll," *New York Times*, Sunday, May 10, 2020, 1.
150. Letter from Zora Neale Hurston to William Bradford Huie, May 14, 1954. In Kaplan, *Zora Neale Hurston*, 710.
151. Quotes in this paragraph from Pamela Bordelon, *Go Gator*, 106–11.
152. Letter from Zora Neale Hurston to Lawrence Jordan, March 24, 1927. In Kaplan, *Zora Neale Hurston*, 94.
153. Letter from Zora Neale Hurston to Carl Van Vechten, March 28, 1927. In Kaplan, *Zora Neale Hurston*, 96.
154. Letter from Zora Neale Hurston to Claude Barnett, February 4, 1943. In Kaplan, *Zora Neale Hurston*, 475.

155. Letter from Zora Neale Hurston to Jean Parker Waterbury, July 9, 1951. In Kaplan, *Zora Neale Hurston*, 663.

156. Letter from Zora Neale Hurston to W. E. B. DuBois, June 11, 1945. All quotes from Hurston in this paragraph are from this letter.

157. Letter from Zora Neale Hurston to Maxeda Von Hesse, April 7, 1951. In Kaplan, *Zora Neale Hurston*, 652. See also Boyd, *Wrapped in Rainbows*, 436.

158. Zora Neale Hurston, *Sanctified Church*, 104. W. E. B. DuBois, *The Souls of Black Folks* (Chicago: A. C. McClurg & Co., 1903).

159. Letter from W. E. B. DuBois to Zora Neale Hurston, July 11, 1945.

160. Quoted in Boyd, *Wrapped in Rainbows*, 374.

161. Quoted in Ted Genoways, "How Copyright Law Hides Work Like Zora Neale Hurston's New Book from the Public," *Washington Post*, May 7, 2018.

162. Genoways, "How Copyright Law Hides Work."

163. Bordelon, "The Federal Writers' Project's Mirror to America," viii. Some of these archives include George A. Smathers Libraries, University of Florida (including the papers burned in her yard after her death, salvaged by the passing deputy); the Florida Historical Society Library; Beinecke Collection, Yale University; Florida Bureau of Folklife, Tallahassee; the National Archives, Washington, DC; the Folklore Division of the Library of Congress. Some of her correspondence resides in the collections of other writers and scholars, such as the Alain Locke Papers, Moorland-Spingarn Research Center, Howard University; and the Dorothy West Papers, Special Collections, Boston University Library.

164. Alice Walker, "Foreword," in *Barracoon: The Story of the Last "Black Cargo"* (New York: HarperCollins, 2018), x.

165. Hurston, *Dust Tracks on a Road*, in Wall, *Hurston*, 1.

166. Zora Neale Hurston, "What White Publishers Won't Print," *Negro Digest*, April 1950. All quotes in this paragraph are from this article.

167. Richard Wright, "Between Laughter and Tears," *The New Masses*, October 5, 1937: 22–23.

168. Zora Neale Hurston, "Stories of Conflict," *Saturday Review*, April 2, 1938, 32.

169. Claudia Roth Pierpont, "A Society of One: Zora Neale Hurston, American Contrarian," *New Yorker*, February 10, 1997, https://www.newyorker.com/magazine/1997/02/17/a-society-of-one

170. Zora Neale Hurston, "Art and Such," published in Bordelon, *Go Gator*, 139–45.

171. Alice Walker, "Anything We Love Can Be Saved: The Resurrection of Zora Neale Hurston and Her Work," in *Reflections from Zora! Celebrating 25 Years of the Zora Neale Hurston Festival of the Arts and Humanities*, created by the Florida Historical Society in conjunction with the Association to Preserve the Eatonville Community (Cocoa, Fl: Florida Historical Society Press, 2014), 15.

172. Andrew Delbanco, "The Political Incorrectness of Zora Neale Hurston," *Journal of Blacks in Higher Education* 18 (Winter 1997–1998): 106.

173. Kaplan, *Zora Neale Hurston*, 13.

174. Pierpont, "A Society of One."

175. Letter from Zora Neale Hurston to the *Orlando Sentinel*, August 11, 1955. In Kaplan, *Zora Neale Hurston*, 738.

176. Alice Walker, "Be Nobody's Darling," in *Revolutionary Petunias: Poetry* (Boston: Mariner Books, 1973).

177. James Meyer, *The Art of Return: The Sixties & Contemporary Culture* (Chicago: University of Chicago Press, 2019), 33.

178. Annabelle Timsit, "Barbie is Back to Being a Billion-Dollar Brand," *Quartz*, February 9, 2019, https://qz.com/1546252/barbie-is-back-to-being-a-billion-dollar-brand/

179. Quoted in Urla and Swedlund, "The Anthropometry of Barbie," 280.

180. Eliana Dockterman, "Barbie's Got a New Body," *Time* magazine, January 27, 2016.

181. Erving Goffman, *Stigma: Notes on the Management of Spoiled Identity* (New York: Simon and Schuster, 1963).

182. Urla and Swedlund, "The Anthropometry of Barbie," 293.

183. For this analysis of Shani, see Elizabeth Chin, "Ethnically Correct Dolls: Toying with the Race Industry," *American Anthropologist* 101, no. 2 (1999): 305–21.

184. Dockterman, "Barbie's Got a New Body."

185. Renee Engeln, "Why Young Girls Reject the New 'Curvy' Barbie," *Psychology Today*, June 28, 2019, https://www.psychologytoday.com/us/blog/beauty-sick/201906/why-young-girls-reject-the-new-curvy-barbie

186. Maya Salam, "Mattel, Maker of Barbie, Debuts Gender-Neutral Dolls," *New York Times*, September 25, 2019, https://www.nytimes.com/2019/09/25/arts/mattel-gender-neutral-dolls.html

Chapter 5

1. Erving Goffman, *Asylums: Essays on the Social Situation of Mental Patients and Other Inmates* (New York: Anchor Books, 1961), 84. All quotations from Goffman are from *Asylums* unless otherwise indicated.

2. The historically correct name of St. Elizabeths omits the apostrophe.

3. Benjamin Reiss, *Theaters of Madness: Insane Asylums & Nineteenth-Century American Culture* (Chicago: University of Chicago Press, 2008).

4. Howard Becker, *Outsiders: Studies in the Sociology of Deviance* (New York: Free Press, 1963); Erving Goffman, *Stigma: Notes on the Management of Spoiled Identity* (New York: Touchstone Press, 1986).

5. Carla Yanni, *The Architecture of Madness* (Minneapolis: University of Minnesota Press, 2007).

6. Goffman, *Asylums*, ix.

7. See Peter Conrad and Joseph Schneider, *Deviance and Medicalization: From Badness to Sickness* (Philadelphia: Temple University Press, 1992), for a longer review of this literature.

8. Philip Rieff, *The Triumph of the Therapeutic* (New York: Harper & Row, 1966).

9. Conrad and Schneider, *Deviance and Medicalization*, 38.

10. Paul Lombardo, *Three Generations, No Imbecile: Eugenics, the Supreme Court, and Buck v. Bell* (Baltimore: Johns Hopkins University Press, 2008).

11. Harry Bruinius, *Better for All the World: The Secret History of Forced Sterilization and America's Quest for Racial Purity* (New York: Vintage Books, 2007).

12. Philip Manning, *Freud and American Sociology* (Malden, MA: Polity Press, 2005): x.

13. See Manning for a discussion of this alleged distinction.

14. Alfred Stanton and Morris Schwartz, *The Mental Hospital: A Study of Psychiatric Participation in Psychiatric Illness and Treatment* (New York: Basic Books, 1954); Rose Laub Coser, *Life in the Ward* (East Lansing: Michigan State University Press, 1962); Thomas Szasz, *The Myth of Mental Illness* (New York: Harper, 1961); R. D. Laing, *The Divided Self: An Existential Study in Sanity and Madness* (New York: Penguin, 1965).

15. David L. Rosenhan, "On Being Sane in Insane Places," *Science* 179, no. 4070 (January 1973): 250–58. Quotes in this section are from this article.

16. See Susannah Cahalan, *The Great Pretender: The Undercover Mission that Changed Our Understanding of Madness* (New York: Grand Central Publishing, 2019); Gina Perry, *Behind the Shock Machine: The Untold Story of the Notorious Milgram Psychology Experiments* (Royal Oak, MI: Scribe, 2012); John Bohannon, "Many Psychology Papers Fail Replication Test," *Science* 349, no. 6251 (August 2015): 910–11.

17. Jonathan Glover, *I: The Philosophy and Psychology of Personal Identity* (London: Allen Lane, Penguin Press, 1988).

18. Mary Douglas, *Purity and Danger* (New York: Routledge, 1966).

19. Samuel Cartwright, "Report on the Diseases and Physical Peculiarities of the Negro Race," *New Orleans Medical and Surgical Journal* (May 1851): 691–715.

20. Vanessa Jackson, "Separate and Unequal: The Legacy of Racially Segregated Psychiatric Hospitals, A Cultural Competence Training Tool," http://www.healingcircles.org/uploads/2/1/4/8/2148953/sauweb.pdf

21. Martin Summers, *Madness in the City of Magnificent Intentions: A History of Race and Mental Illness in the Nation's Capital* (New York: Oxford University Press, 2019).

22. Daniel Swift, *The Bughouse: The Poetry, Politics, and Madness of Ezra Pound* (New York: Farrar, Straus and Girous, 2017).

23. JJ Hill, "And They Played Tennis in Hell: A Screenplay," thesis project, Simon Fraser University, Fall 2012.

24. Swift, *Bughouse*, 10.

25. Swift, *Bughouse*, 249.

26. Thomas Otto, *St. Elizabeths Hospital—A History*, DC Preservation League (May 2013), https://dcpreservation-wpengine.netdna-ssl.com/wp-content/uploads/2013/05/0-COMPLETE-St.-Elizabeths-Hospital-A-History.pdf; Matthew Gambino, "Erving Goffman's Asylums and Institutional Culture in the Mid-twentieth-century United States," *Harvard Review of Psychiatry* 21, no. 1 (2013): 52–57.

27. Matthew Gambino, "Erving Goffman's Asylums."

28. Ann Branaman, "Erving Goffman," in *Profiles in Contemporary Social Theory*, eds. Anthony Elliott and Bryan Turner (Thousand Oaks, CA: Sage Publications, 2001), 98.

29. Erving Goffman, "The Insanity of Place," *Psychiatry* 32, no. 4 (1969): 32.

30. Carla Cappetti, *Writing Chicago: Modernism, Ethnography, and the Novel* (New York: Columbia University Press, 1993), 32.

31. See, for example, Heather Love, "Doing Being Deviant," *Differences* 26 (2015): 74–95.
32. Charles Lemert, "'Goffman,'" in *The Goffman Reader*, eds. Charles Lemert and Ann Branaman (Malden, MA: Blackwell Publishers, 1997).
33. Erving Goffman, *Gender Advertisements* (New York: Harper Colophon Books, 1976).
34. Leslie Fishbein, "The Snake Pit (1948): The Sexist Nature of Sanity," in *Hollywood As Historian*, ed. Peter C. Rollins (Lexington: University of Kentucky Press, 1983).
35. William Plomer, "Introduction," *White Jacket*, by Herman Melville (London: John Lehmann, 1952).
36. Gene Feldman and Max Gartenberg, eds., *The Beat Generation and the Angry Young Men* (New York: Dell Publishing, 1958).
37. Carl Solomon, "Report from the Asylum," in *The Beat Generation and the Angry Young Men*, 178.
38. Otto, *St. Elizabeths Hospital*, 271.
39. Andrew Scull, *Madness: A Very Short Introduction* (New York: Oxford University Press, 2011).
40. Scull, *Madness*, 106.
41. Grob, *The Mad Among Us*, 230.
42. Jonathan Metzl, *Prozac on the Couch: Prescribing Gender in the Era of Wonder Drugs* (Durham: Duke University Press, 2003).
43. David Rissmiller and Joshua Rissmiller, "Evolution of the Antipsychiatry Movement into Mental Health Consumerism," *Psychiatric Services* 57 (June 2006), https://pubmed.ncbi.nlm.nih.gov/16754765/
44. Edwin Schur, *The Politics of Deviance* (New York: Prentice-Hall, 1979).
45. Benjamin Reiss, *Theaters of Madness: Insane Asylums & Nineteenth-Century American Culture* (Chicago: University of Chicago Press, 2008).
46. Scull, *Madness*.
47. Scull, *Madness*; Grob, *The Mad Among Us*.
48. See Javier Trevino, *Goffman's Legacy* (Lanham, MD: Rowman & Littlefield Publishers, 2003).
49. See https://en.wikipedia.org/wiki/Erving_Goffman
50. See, for example, Dmitri Shalin, "Goffman on Mental Illness and 'The Insanity of Place' Revisited," *Symbolic Interaction* 37, no. 1 (2014): 122–44. Also, Shalin curates Bios Sociologicus: The Erving Goffman Archives, which contains numerous interviews and essays raising these questions, https://digitalscholarship.unlv.edu/goffman_archives/
51. For a brief but thorough review essay, see Branaman, "Erving Goffman."
52. Photographs by Mary Ellen Mark and Text by Karen Folger Jacobs with an Introduction by Milos Forman. New York: Simon and Schuster, 1979.
53. Photographs by Mary Ellen Mark and Text by Karen Folger Jacobs with an Introduction by Milos Forman. New York: Simon and Schuster, 1979.

Chapter 6

1. Laud Humphreys, *Tearoom Trade: Impersonal Sex in Public Places* (Chicago: Aldine Publishing Company, 1970). Quotations throughout this chapter are from the main text.

2. All text in quotation marks in this discussion are from the text *Tearoom Trade*, unless otherwise specified.

3. Michael Bronski, *Culture Clash: The Making of a Gay Sensibility* (Boston: South End Press, 1984).

4. Howard Becker, "Whose Side Are We On?" *Social Problems* 14, no. 3 (1967): 244.

5. See Alfred Kinsey, Wardell Pomeroy, and Clyde Martin, *Sexual Behavior in the Human Male* (Philadelphia: W. B. Saunders Co., 1948); Alfred Kinsey, Wardell Pomeroy, Clyde Martin, and Paul Gebhard, *Sexual Behavior in the Human Female* (Philadelphia: W. B. Saunders Co., 1953); William Masters and Virginia Johnson, *Human Sexual Response* (Boston: Little, Brown & Co., 1966).

6. Ian Hacking, "Making Up People," *London Review of Books* 28, no. 16–17 (August 2006), https://www.lrb.co.uk/the-paper/v28/n16/ian-hacking/making-up-people

7. Clellan S. Ford and Frank A. Beach, *Patterns of Sexual Behavior* (New York: Harper & Brothers, 1951).

8. Gayle Rubin, "Studying Sexual Subcultures," in *Out in Theory: The Emergence of Lesbian and Gay Anthropology*, eds. Ellen Lewin and William Leap (Urbana: University of Illinois Press, 2002), 18.

9. Manford Kuhn, "Kinsey's View on Human Behavior," *Social Problems* 1, no. 4 (April 1954): 123.

10. Albert Reiss, "The Social Integration of Queers and Peers," *Social Problems* 9, no. 2 (Autumn 1961): 102–20; Maurice Leznoff and William Westley, "The Homosexual Community," in *Sexual Deviance*, eds. John Gagnon and William Simon (New York: Harper and Row, 1967), 184–96.

11. Kinsey, *Human Male*, 639.

12. Steven Maynard, "Through a Hole in the Lavatory Wall," *Journal of the History of Sexuality* 5, no. 2 (1994): 207–42.

13. Thomas Gieryn, "A Space for Place in Sociology," *Annual Review of Sociology*, 2000.

14. https://en.wikipedia.org/wiki/Public_toilet, accessed November 4, 2018.

15. Juliet Richters, "Through a Hole in the Wall: Setting and Interaction in Sex-on-Premises Venues," *Sexualities* 10, no. 3 (2007): 275–97.

16. Erving Goffman, *The Presentation of Self in Everyday Life* (New York: Doubleday Anchor Books, 1959).

17. Scott McLemee, "Wide-Stance Sociology," *Inside Higher Ed*, September 12, 2007, https://www.insidehighered.com/views/2007/09/12/wide-stance-sociology

18. "Sen. Larry Craig: 'I am not gay,'" MPRNews, Boise, Idaho, August 28, 2007, https://www.mprnews.org/story/2007/08/28/craig

19. Justin Lehmiller, *Tell Me What You Want: The Science of Sexual Desire and How It Can Help You Improve Your Sex Life* (New York: Da Capo Press, 2018).

20. Goffman, *Presentation of Self*.

21. Janice M. Irvine, *Talk About Sex: The Battles Over Sex Education in the United States* (Berkeley: University of California Press, 2002).

22. *Homosexuality and Citizenship in Florida: A Report of the Florida Legislative Investigation Committee*, Tallahassee, Florida, January 1964.

23. Thomas Waugh, *Hard to Imagine: Gay Male Eroticism in Photography and*

Film from Their Beginnings to Stonewall (New York: Columbia University Press, 1996).

24. James Skinner, *The Cross and the Cinema: The Legion of Decency and the National Catholic Office for Motion Pictures, 1933–1970* (Westport, CT: Praeger, 1993). See also Charles Lyons, "The Paradox of Protest," in *Movie Censorship and American Culture*, ed. Francis G. Couvares (Washington, DC: Smithsonian Institution Press, 1996), 277–318.

25. See Janice M. Irvine, *Disorders of Desire: Sex and Gender in Modern American Sexology* (Philadelphia: Temple University Press, 1990).

26. John Rechy, *City of Night* (New York: Grove Press, 1963). Subsequent quotes from pp. 42, 43, 51.

27. Edmund White, "The Making of John Rechy," *New York Review*, April 3, 2008.

28. Charles Casillo, "Fifty Years of Rechy's 'City of Night,'" *Los Angeles Review of Books*, October 13, 2013.

29. John Rechy, "A Quarter Ahead," *Evergreen Review*, July–August 1961, 18.

30. John Rechy, *Numbers* (New York: Grove Press, 1967).

31. Janice M. Irvine, "Is Sexuality Research Dirty Work?" *Sexualities* 17, no. 5/6 (2014): 632–56.

32. John Galliher, Wayne Brekhus, and David Keys, *Laud Humphreys: Prophet of Homosexuality and Sociology* (Madison: University of Wisconsin Press, 2004.)

33. Janice M. Irvine, "Can't Ask, Can't Tell: How Institutional Review Boards Keep Sex in the Closet," *Contexts*, Spring 2012.

34. Janice M. Irvine, "The Sex Lives of Sex Researchers," *Contexts*, Fall 2014.

35. Carol Warren, "Sex and Gender in the 1970s," *Qualitative Sociology* 26, no. 4 (2003): 499–514.

36. Martin Weinberg and Colin Williams, *Male Homosexuals: Their Problems and Adaptations* (New York: Oxford University Press, 1974).

37. Alvin Gouldner, "The Sociologist as Partisan: Sociology and the Welfare State," *American Sociologist* 3, no. 2 (May 1968): 103–16.

38. John Galliher, Wayne Brekhus, and David Keys, *Laud Humphreys: Prophet of Homosexuality and Sociology* (Madison: University of Wisconsin Press, 2004).

39. Galliher, Brekhus, and Keys, *Laud Humphreys*.

40. Steven Schact, ed., "Special Issue on Laud Humphreys," *International Journal of Sociology and Social Policy* 24, no. 3/4/5 (2004); John Galliher, Wayne Brekhus, and David Keys, *Laud Humphreys: Prophet of Homosexuality and Sociology* (Madison: University of Wisconsin Press, 2004).

41. John D'Emilio, "Not a Simple Matter: Gay History and Gay Historians," *Journal of American History* 76, no. 2 (1989): 435–42; Lara Leigh Kelland, *Clio's Foot Soldiers: Twentieth-Century U.S. Social Movements and Collective Memory* (Amherst: University of Massachusetts Press, 2018).

42. John D'Emilio, "The Campus Environment for Gay and Lesbian Life," *Academe* (January–February 1990): 17.

43. D'Emilio, "Not a Simple Matter"; Lisa Duggan, "The Discipline Problem: Queer Theory Meets Lesbian and Gay History," *GLQ: A Journal of Lesbian and Gay Studies* 2, no. 3 (1995).

44. Wei Luo, Julia Adams, and Hannah Brueckner, "The Ladies Vanish? Ameri-

can Sociology and the Genealogy of Its Missing Women on Wikipedia," *Comparative Sociology* 17, (2018): 519–56.

45. Luo, Adams, and Brueckner,, "Ladies Vanish?"

46. Jeffrey Weeks, "The 'Homosexual Role' After 30 Years: An Appreciation of the Work of Mary McIntosh," *Sexualities* 1, no. 2 (1998): 93–107.

47. BUP, "London Girl is Injured in U.S. Clash," *Standard*, May 14, 1960.

48. Seth Rosenfeld, *Subversives: The FBI's War on Student Radicals, and Reagan's Rise to Power* (New York: Farrar, Straus and Giroux, 2012), 87.

49. Laurie Taylor, interview with Janice Irvine, June 14, 2013.

50. Carole S. Vance, "Anthropology Rediscovers Sexuality: A Theoretical Comment," *Social Science & Medicine* 33 (1991): 875–84.

51. Esther Newton, "Preface to the Phoenix Edition," in *Mother Camp: Female Impersonators in America* (Chicago: University of Chicago Press, Phoenix edition, 1979), xii.

52. Newton, *Mother Camp*, 113, 118.

53. Esther Newton, interview with author, December 1, 2014. Subsequent quotes from Newton are from this interview.

54. Gayle Rubin, "Esther Newton Made Me a Gay Anthropologist," *American Anthropologist*, November 19, 2018.

55. James Short, interview with author, Dec. 5, 2013.

56. Zachary Schrag, *Ethical Imperialism: Institutional Review Boards and the Social Sciences, 1965–2009* (Baltimore: Johns Hopkins University Press, 2010).

57. Schrag, *Ethical Imperialism*.

58. Schrag, conversation with author.

59. Earl Babbie, "Laud Humphreys and Research Ethics," *International Journal of Sociology and Public Policy* 24, no. 3/4/5 (2004): 12–19.

60. Heather Love, "Queer Method and the Postwar History of Sexuality Studies," https://www.youtube.com/watch?v=Azlvbenijis. Note how Love sets up Humphreys's methods as a laugh line by mock-warning, "Don't try this at home."

61. Interview excerpts in this chapter from Robert Faulkner, University of Massachusetts (emeritus); Joel Best, University of Delaware; Martin Weinberg, Indiana University (emeritus); Sherri Cavan, San Francisco State University (emerita); Roland Chilton, University of Massachusetts (emeritus); James Short, Washington State University; Anthony Harris, University of Massachusetts (emeritus); Peter Conrad, Brandeis University (emeritus); Howard Becker, Northwestern University (emeritus); Esther Newton, University of Michigan (emerita).

62. Albert Reiss, "Queers and Peers."

63. Interview with Albert Reiss, American Society of Criminology, interviewed by Lawrence Sherman, November 1995.

64. Robert E. Park and Ernest Burgess, *The City: Suggestions for Investigation of Human Behavior in the Urban Environment* (Chicago: University of Chicago Press, 1925).

65. Dave Holmes, Patrick O'Byrne, and Stuart Murray, "Faceless Sex: Glory Holes and Sexual Assemblages," https://www.academia.edu/497201/Faceless_sex_glory_holes_and_sexual_assemblages, accessed December 25, 2018.

Chapter 7

1. Paul Kantner, "We Can Be Together," recorded at Wally Heider Studios, San Francisco, October 1969 release date.
2. Danny Goldberg, *In Search of the Lost Chord: 1967 and the Hippie Idea* (Brooklyn, Akashic Books, 2017): 16.
3. Andrew Hartman, *A War for the Soul of America* (Chicago: University of Chicago Press, 2019), 2.
4. Sherri Cavan, *Hippies of the Haight* (St. Louis: New Critics Press, 1972).
5. David Farber, *The Age of Great Dreams: America in the 1960s* (New York: Hill and Wang, 1994), 57.
6. Theodor Adorno, Else Frenkel-Brunswik, Daniel Levinson, and Nevitt Sanford, *The Authoritarian Personality*, Vol. I (New York: Harper & Brothers, 1950).
7. "Morals: The Second Sexual Revolution," *Time*, January 24, 1964.
8. See, for example, Susan J. Douglas, *Where the Girls Are: Growing Up Female with the Mass Media* (New York: Times Books, 1994); D'Emilio and Freedman, *Intimate Matters*; and Todd Gitlin, *The Sixties: Years of Hope, Days of Rage* (New York: Bantam Books, 1987).
9. John D'Emilio and Estelle Freedman, *Intimate Matters*, 256.
10. D'Emilio and Freedman, *Intimate Matters*.
11. Lillian Faderman, *Odd Girls and Twilight Lovers* (New York: Penguin, 1992).
12. Loren Glass, "The Mighty Mezz, Marijuana, and the Beat Generation," *Los Angeles Review of Books*, May 7, 2015, https://lareviewofbooks.org/article/the-mighty-mezz-marijuana-and-the-beat-generation/
13. R. Gordon Wasson, "Seeking the Magic Mushroom," *Life* 49, no. 19 (May 13, 1957), 100–2, 109–20.
14. "Life in a Loony Bin," *Time*, February 16, 1962, 90.
15. There is a vast literature on this topic. For an early critique, see Margo Jefferson, "Ripping Off Black Music," *Harper's Magazine*, January, 1973. See also Jack Hamilton, *Just Around Midnight: Rock and Roll and the Racial Imagination* (Cambridge: Harvard University Press, 2016).
16. Brad Lichtenstein (director) and Cal Skaggs (producer), *With God on Our Side: The Rise of the Religious Right in America, 1950–1994*, Lumiere Productions, September 27, 1996 (premiere date).
17. Alice Echols, *Shaky Ground: The '60s and Its Aftershocks* (New York: Columbia University Press, 2002), 60.
18. John Anthony Moretta, *The Hippies: A 1960s History* (Jefferson, NC: McFarland & Company, 2017), 6.
19. David Farber, *The Age of Great Dreams: America in the 1960s* (New York: Hill and Wang, 1994), 169.
20. G. Stanley Hall, *Adolescence: Its Psychology and Its Relations to Physiology, Anthropology, Sociology, Sex, Crime, Religion and Education* (New York: D. Appleton & Co., 1904).
21. Gabrielle Owen, *A Queer History of Adolescence* (Athens: University of Georgia Press, 2020).

22. Horacio Fabrega and Barbara Miller, "Toward a More Comprehensive Medical Anthropology: The Case of Adolescent Psychopathology," *Medical Anthropology Quarterly* 9, no. 4 (1995): 433.

23. Quoted in Owen, *A Queer History*, 57.

24. Hall, *Adolescence*.

25. See Owen, *A Queer History*.

26. Fabrega and Miller, "Toward a More Comprehensive Medical Anthropology," 450.

27. Mark Harris, "The Flowering of the Hippies," *The Atlantic*, September, 1967.

28. Louis Menand, "Out of Bethlehem," *New Yorker*, August 24, 2015, https://www.newyorker.com/magazine/2015/08/24/out-of-bethlehem

29. Joan Didion, "Hippies: Slouching Toward Bethlehem," *Saturday Evening Post*, no. 19 (September 23, 1967), 94.

30. Michael Brown, "The Condemnation and Persecution of Hippies," *Trans-Action* 6, no. 10 (September 1969): 33–46.

31. Jennie Rothenberg Gritz, "The Death of the Hippies," *The Atlantic*, July 8, 2015.

32. Toby Manning, "Kantnerculture: Tribute to Paul Kantner," *Red Wedge*, April 11, 2016, http://www.redwedgemagazine.com/online-issue/tribute-paul-kantner

33. Paul Kantner, "We Can Be Together," recorded at Wally Heider Studios, San Francisco, October 1969 release date.

34. Quote from Psychedelic Shop owner Ron Thelin. Bill Van Niekerken, "'Death of the Hippies': Haight-Ashbury's 1967 Funeral for Counterculture," *San Francisco Chronicle*, October 3, 2017, https://www.sfchronicle.com/thetake/article/Death-of-the-Hippies-Haight-Ashbury-s-12245473.php

35. *The Disobedient Generation: Social Theorists in the Sixties*, eds. Alan Sica and Stephen Turner (Chicago: University of Chicago Press, 2005).

36. Karen Schweers Cook, "Sociology of Power and Justice," in *The Disobedient Generation*, 127.

37. Menand, "Out of Bethlehem."

38. Quotes from May Sarton, *A Small Room* (New York: W. W. Norton & Company, 1961), 29, 247.

39. Carol A. B. Warren, "Sex and Gender in the 1970s," *Qualitative Sociology* 26, no. 4 (Winter 2003): 499–514.

40. Bernice Sandler, "The Chilly Climate Revisited: Chilly for Women Faculty, Administrators, and Graduate Students," Washington, DC: Association of American Colleges, 1986.

41. Sherri Cavan, "Becoming an Ethnographer," in *Gender and the Academic Experience: Berkeley Women Sociologists*, eds. Kathryn Orlans and Ruth Wallace (Lincoln: University of Nebraska Press, 1994), 62.

42. Kathryn Orlans and Ruth Wallace, eds., *Gender and the Academic Experience: Berkeley Women Sociologists* (Lincoln: University of Nebraska Press, 1994.)

43. Hartman, *War for the Soul of America*, 3.

44. Louis Menand, "Integration by Parts," *The New Yorker*, January 20, 2020, 62–68.

45. Arlene Kaplan Daniels, "When We Were All Boys Together: Graduate School in the Fifties and Beyond," in Orlans and Wallace, eds., *Gender and the Academic Experience*, 30.
46. Sherri Cavan, interview with author, August, 2013.
47. Cavan, "Becoming," 68.
48. Sherri Cavan, interview with author, August, 2013.
49. Sherri Cavan, *Hippies of the Haight* (St. Louis: New Critics Press, 1972), 32.
50. Sherri Cavan, interview with author, August 2013.
51. Luo, Adams, and Brueckner, "The Ladies Vanish?," 519–56.
52. Cavan, *Hippies*, 42.
53. David Farber, *The Age of Great Dreams: America in the 1960s* (New York: Hill and Wang, 1994), 53.
54. Cavan, *Hippies*, 53.
55. Robert Cottrell, *Sex, Drugs, and Rock 'n' Roll: The Rise of America's 1960s Counterculture* (New York: Rowman & Littlefield, 2015), 139.
56. Cavan, *Hippies*, 44.
57. John Anthony Moretta, *The Hippies: A 1960s History* (Jefferson, NC, 2017), 32.
58. Cavan, *Hippies*, 45.
59. Cavan, *Hippies*, 45.
60. "Gay Haight Show Closed: Owners Flee," *Haight Ashbury Independent*, August 20, 1964.
61. "Gay Haight Show Closed."
62. Cavan, *Hippies*, 55.
63. Reg E. Williams, *The Straight on the Haight*, 2006: http://www.thestraight.com/book.html
64. Williams, *The Straight on the Haight*.
65. Goldberg, *In Search of the Lost Chord*, 25.
66. John Anthony Moretta, *The Hippies*, 174.
67. Harvey Sacks, "On Doing 'Being Ordinary,'" in *Structures in Social Action*, eds., J. Maxwell Atkinson and John Heritage (Cambridge: Cambridge University Press, 1984), 413–40.
68. Charles Perry, *The Haight Ashbury: A History* (New York: Random House, 1984), 29.
69. The Doors, "Strange Days," produced by Paul Rothchild, Elektra Records, September 25, 1967.
70. *Georg Simmel on Individuality and Social Forms*, edited by Donald Levine (Chicago: University of Chicago Press, 1971), 143.
71. Frances Rust, *Dance in Society* (London: Routledge & Kegan Paul Limited, 1969), 16.
72. Rust, *Dance in Society*, 119.
73. Rust, *Dance in Society*, 119.
74. Quotes in this dancing section from Cavan, *Hippies*, 101–6.
75. Dance at the Straight Theater from https://www.thestraight.com/dance.html
76. Howard S. Becker, *Outsiders: Studies in the Sociology of Deviance* (New York: Free Press, 1963), 50.

77. Larry "Ratso" Sloman, *Reefer Madness: A History of Marijuana* (New York: St. Martin's Griffin, 1979), 126.

78. Jacquin Sanders and Pat Reilly, "Narcotics: Slum to Suburb," *Newsweek*, February 22, 1965.

79. J. L. Simmons, "Public Stereotypes of Deviants," *Social Problems* 13, no. 2 (1965): 223–32.

80. Cavan, *Hippies*, 113.

81. Cavan, *Hippies*, 138.

82. Erich Goode, interview with author, August 10, 2013.

83. David Farber, *The Age of Great Dreams: America in the 1960s* (New York: Hill and Wang, 1994), 177.

84. Janis Joplin to the Joplin family, August 13, 1966. Quoted in Holly George-Warren, *Janis: Her Life and Music* (New York: Simon & Schuster, 2019), 152.

85. Cavan, *Hippies*, 50.

86. Michael Brown, "The Condemnation and Persecution of Hippies," *Trans-Action* (September 1969): 44.

87. Linda Gravenites, quoted in Joel Lobenthal, *Radical Rags: Fashions of the Sixties* (New York: Abbeville Press Publishers, 1990), 114.

88. Quoted in Goldberg, *Lost Chord*, 122.

89. Lobenthal, *Radical Rags*, 114.

90. Goldberg, *Lost Chord*, 33.

91. Alice Echols, *Scars of Sweet Paradise: The Life and Times of Janis Joplin* (New York: Metropolitan Books, 1999), 305, 311.

92. Alice Echols, *Scars*, 135.

93. Rachel Feldman, "Del Pitt Feldman, 90, Designer Who Made Crocheting Hip," *New York Times*, February 2, 2020, 26.

94. Al Aronowitz, "Beatlemania in 1964," *The Guardian*, January 29, 2014, https://www.theguardian.com/music/2014/jan/29/the-beatles

95. Lobenthal, *Radical Rags*, 207.

96. Traci Parker, *Department Stores and the Black Freedom Movement* (Durham: University of North Carolina Press, 2019).

97. Lobenthal, *Radical Rags*, 13.

98. Lobenthal, *Radical Rags*, 17.

99. Lobenthal, *Radical Rags*, 139.

100. Jonathan Kramer, "My Conviction," from *Hair: The American Tribal Love-Rock Musical*, off-Broadway debut October 17, 1967.

101. Echols, *Scars*.

102. Lobenthal, *Radical Rags*, 112.

103. Lobenthal, *Radical Rags*, 14.

104. Florindo Volpacchio, "The Mother of All Interviews: Frank Zappa on Music and Society," *Telos* 24, no. 1 (1991): 124–36.

105. Cavan, *Hippies*, 48.

106. Cavan, *Hippies*, 51–52.

107. All quotes in this paragraph are from Cavan, *Hippies*, 86–89.

108. Echols, *Shaky Ground*, 22.

109. Michael Grieg, "Death of the Hippies," *San Francisco Chronicle*, October 7, 1967.

110. Bill Van Nierkerken, "'Death of the Hippies': Haight Ashbury's 1967 Funeral for Counterculture," *San Francisco Chronicle*, October 3, 2017, https://www.sfchronicle.com/thetake/article/Death-of-the-Hippies-Haight-Ashbury-s-12245473.php

111. Thomas Frank, *The Conquest of Cool: Business Culture, Counterculture, and the Rise of Hip Consumerism* (Chicago: University of Chicago Press, 1997), 121.

112. Frank, *Conquest of Cool*, 134.

113. Echols, *Scars*, 287.

114. Malcolm Gladwell, "The Coolhunt," *New Yorker*, March 10, 1997.

115. Lobenthal, *Radical Rags*, 215.

116. Echols, *Shaky Ground*, 187.

117. Sam Binkley, *Getting Loose: Lifestyle Consumption in the 1970s* (Durham, NC: Duke University Press, 2007).

118. Perry, *The Haight Ashbury*, 275.

119. Jennie Rothenberg Gritz, "The Death of the Hippies," *The Atlantic*, July 8, 2015.

120. Farber, *The Age of Great Dreams*, 189.

121. Echols, *Shaky Ground*, 48.

122. Fred Davis, "Why All of Us May Be Hippies Someday," *Trans-Action* 5, no. 2 (1967): 10–18.

123. Sherri Cavan, interview with author, August 2013.

124. Gayle Rubin, interview with author, September 2, 2013.

125. Hartman, *War for the Soul of America*.

126. All quotes on moral panic are from Stanley Cohen, *Folk Devils and Moral Panics: The Creation of the Mods and Rockers* (London: MacGibbon & Kee, 1973).

127. Rust, *Dance in Society*, 116.

128. Echols, *Shaky Ground*, 77.

129. Ken Plummer, "World Critical Humanism and Intimate Citizenship," https://kenplummer.com/2013/01/08/inspiration-and-in-memoriam-mary-mcintosh/, accessed July 23, 2020.

130. Peter Hartlaub, "Haight Street in 1967, As Seen from a Tour Bus Full of Squares," https://blog.sfgate.com/thebigevent/2015/04/16/haight-street-in-1967-as-seen-from-a-tour-bus-full-of-squares/, accessed October 14, 2019.

131. Catherine Cocks, *Doing the Town: The Rise of Urban Tourism in the United States, 1850–1915* (Berkeley: University of California Press, 2001), 22.

132. Quoted in Martin Bulmer, *The Chicago School of Sociology* (Chicago: University of Chicago Press, 1984), 97.

133. Quoted in Bulmer, *The Chicago School*, 97.

134. Martha Lynn Reis, "Hidden Histories: Ben Reitman and the 'Outcast' Women Behind *Sister of the Road: The Autobiography of Boxcar Bertha*," PhD diss., University of Minnesota (September 2000), 303.

135. Reis, "Hidden Histories," 307.

136. Roger Bruns, *The Damndest Radical: The Life and World of Ben Reitman, Chicago's Celebrated Social Reformer, Hobo King, and Whorehouse Physician* (Urbana: University of Illinois Press, 1987), 279.

137. Reis, "Hidden Histories," 297.

138. Chad Heap, *Slumming: Sexual and Racial Encounters in American Nightlife, 1885–1940* (Chicago: University of Chicago Press, 2009).
139. Heap, *Slumming*, 11.
140. Cocks, *Doing the Town*.
141. Chad Heap, *Slumming*.
142. Cavan, *Hippies*, 74.
143. See, for example, https://www.sftravel.com/article/experience-summer-love-history-these-7-walking-tours, accessed October 14, 2019.

Chapter 8

1. Stuart Hall, quoted in Lucy Jackson, Catherine Harris, and Gill Valentine, "Rethinking Concepts of the Strange and the Stranger," *Social & Cultural Geography* 18, no. 1 (2017): 1.
2. C. Wright Mills, *The Sociological Imagination* (New York: Oxford University Press, 1959), 6.
3. May Sarton, *As We Are Now* (New York: Norton & Company, 1973), 17.
4. Barbara Myerhoff, *Number Our Days* (New York: E. P. Dutton, 1978).
5. Georg Simmel, "The Sociological Significance of the 'Stranger,'" *Soziologie* (1908), 685–91. Published in the US in Robert E. Park and Ernest W. Burgess, *Introduction to the Science of Sociology* (Chicago: University of Chicago Press, 1921), 322–27.
6. H. F. Osborn, "Can We Save America?" unpublished, quoted in Daniel Okrent, *The Guarded Gate* (New York: Scribner, 2019), 3.
7. Talia Lavin, *Culture Warlords: My Journey into the Dark Web of White Supremacy* (New York: Hachette Books, 2020), 28.
8. Myerhoff, *Number*, 8.
9. Myerhoff, *Number*, 2.
10. Myerhoff, *Number*, 9.
11. Myerhoff, *Number*, 2, 5.
12. Myerhoff, *Number*, 275.
13. Myerhoff, *Number*, 274.
14. John Gagnon and William Simon (eds.), "Preface," in *Sexual Deviance* (New York: Harper & Row, 1967), vii.
15. Myerhoff, *Number*, 19.
16. Myerhoff, 12.
17. Alexander Liazos, "The Poverty of the Sociology of Deviance," *Social Problems* 20, no. 1 (1972): 103–20.
18. Alvin Gouldner, "The Sociologist as Partisan," *American Sociologist* 3, no. 2 (1968): 106.
19. Colin Sumner, *The Sociology of Deviance: An Obituary* (New York: Continuum, 1994); Erich Goode, "Does the Death of the Sociology of Deviance Claim Make Sense?" *American Sociologist* 33, no. 3 (2002): 107–18; Michael Dellwing, Joseph Kotarba, and Nathan Pino, *The Death and Resurrection of Deviance* (New York: Palgrave Macmillan, 2014).
20. Michele Lamont, "How to Become a Dominant French Philosopher: The Case of Jacques Derrida," *American Journal of Sociology* 93, no. 3 (1987): 584–622.
21. For more of this history and analysis, see Stephen Epstein, "A Queer

Encounter," *Sociological Theory* 12, no. 2 (1994): 188–202; and Arlene Stein and Ken Plummer, "I Can't Even Think Straight: Queer Theory and the Missing Sexual Revolution in Sociology," *Sociological Theory* 12, no. 2 (1994): 178–87. For a different view of this history from a humanities scholar, see Heather Love, "Doing Being Deviant: Deviance Studies, Description, and the Queer Ordinary," *Differences* 26, no. 1 (2015): 74–95.

22. Mary Wyer, Mary Barbercheck, Donna Cookmeyer, Hatice Orun Ozturk, and Marta Wayne, "Introduction," in *Women, Science, and Technology*, eds. Mary Wyer, Mary Barbercheck, Donna Cookmeyer, Hatice Orun Ozturk, and Marta Wayne (New York: Routledge, 2014), xix–3.

23. Richard C. Lewontin, "Sociobiology: Another Biological Determinism," *International Journal of Health Services* 10, no. 3 (1980): 347–63.

24. Devra Kleiman, "*Sociobiology: The New Synthesis*, by Edward O. Wilson," *Signs* 3, no. 2 (1977): 494–95.

25. Stephen Jay Gould, "Sociobiology: The Art of Storytelling," *New Scientist*, (November 16, 1978): 531.

26. See Thomas Frank, *The Conquest of Cool: Business Culture, Counterculture, and the Rise of Hip Consumerism* (Chicago: University of Chicago Press, 1997).

27. Quoted in Jennie C. Ikuta, *Contesting Conformity: Democracy and the Paradox of Political Belonging* (New York: Oxford University Press, 2020), 5.

28. See Jennie Ikuta for a review of this literature.

29. Carl Elliott, *Better Than Well: American Medicine Meets the American Dream* (New York: W. W. Norton & Co., 2003).

30. Ikuta, *Contesting Conformity*, 3.

31. Banu Subramaniam, *Ghost Stories for Darwin: The Science of Variation and the Politics of Diversity* (Urbana: University of Illinois Press, 2014), 23.

32. See Subramaniam, *Ghost Stories*. See also Dorothy Roberts, *Fetal Invention: How Science, Politics, and Big Business Re-create Race in the Twenty-first Century* (New York: New Press, 2012); and Nadia Abu El-Haf, *Facts on the Ground: Archaeological Practice and Territorial Self-Fashioning in Israeli Society* (Chicago: University of Chicago Press, 2002).

33. Kathryn Paige Harden, *Genetic Lottery: Why DNA Matters for Social Equality* (Princeton, Princeton University Press, 2021).

34. Gideon Lewis-Kraus, "Force of Nature," *The New Yorker*, September 13, 2021, 57.

35. Patrick Grzanka, "Queer Survey Research and the Ontological Dimensions of Heterosexism," *WSQ: Women's Studies Quarterly* 44, no. 3/4 (Fall/Winter 2016): 131–49.

36. Heather Cox Richardson, *How the South Won the Civil War* (New York: Oxford University Press, 2020), xv–xvi.

37. Zack Budryk, "Princeton Professor: 'We are in a Cold Civil War,'" *The Hill*, August 4, 2019, https://thehill.com/homenews/sunday-talk-shows/456111-princeton-professor-we-are-in-a-cold-civil-war

38. Jennifer Harding and E. Deidre Pribram, "Introduction: The Case for a Cultural Emotion Studies," in *Emotions: A Cultural Studies Reader*, eds. Jennifer Harding and E. Deidre Pribram (New York: Routledge, 2009), 18.

39. Heather Cox Richardson, "Letters from an American" (newsletter), January 5, 2021.
40. Ezra Klein, *Why We're Polarized* (New York: Simon & Schuster, 2020).
41. Irene Taviss Thomson, *Culture Wars and Enduring American Dilemmas* (Ann Arbor: University of Michigan Press, 2010), 12.
42. Jason Stanley, *How Fascism Works: The Politics of Us and Them* (New York: Random House, 2018).
43. Masha Gessen, "Our Democracy," on "You and Me Both" podcast, host Hillary Clinton, with Masha Gessen and Rashad Robinson, March 16, 2021.
44. Carlie Porterfield, "White Supremacist Terrorism 'On the Rise and Spreading,'" *Forbes*, July 4, 2020, https://www.forbes.com/sites/carlieporterfield/2020/06/25/white-supremacist-terrorism-on-the-rise-and-spreading/?sh=3621b1ff5a0f
45. See "Black Americans 2.5x More Likely than Whites to be Killed by Police," Statista, June 2, 2020. https://www.statista.com/chart/21872/map-of-police-violence-against-black-americans/
46. "Murders of Transgender People in 2020 Surpasses Total for Last Year in Just Seven Months," National Center for Transgender Equality, August 7, 2020, https://transequality.org/blog/murders-of-transgender-people-in-2020-surpasses-total-for-last-year-in-just-seven-months
47. Lavin, *Culture Warlords*, 23.
48. Henry Giroux, *Neoliberalism's War on Higher Education* (Chicago: Haymarket Books, 2013).
49. "GOP-Leaning Groups Differ on the Impact of Colleges, Democratic-Leaning Groups are Divided Over Churches," Pew Research Center, October 23, 2017, https://www.pewresearch.org/politics/2017/10/24/4-governments-role-and-performance-views-of-national-institutions-expertise/4-2-2/
50. Michelle Goldberg, "The Campaign to Cancel Wokeness: How the Right Is Trying to Censor Critical Race Theory," *New York Times*, February 26, 2021, https://www.nytimes.com/2021/02/26/opinion/speech-racism-academia.html. See also Janice M. Irvine, *Talk About Sex: The Battles Over Sex Education in the United States* (Berkeley: University of California Press, 2002).
51. Eitan Arom, "Innovative Jewish Center Moves Forward on the Venice Boardwalk," *Jewish Journal*, March 15, 2017, https://jewishjournal.com/culture/50_plus/216625/innovative-jewish-center-moves-forward-venice-boardwalk/
52. Myerhoff, *Number*, 7.
53. *In Her Own Time: The Final Fieldwork of Barbara Myerhoff*. Film. Directed by Lynne Littman. Santa Monica: Direct Cinema Limited, 1985.

Index

A–No. 1 (Leon Ray Livingston), 30, 37, 64–66
academic erasure, 84, 117, 134–135, 217
acid, 208, 220, 239–240
Addams, Jane, 74, 84
adolescence, 201, 207, 210–211
Adventures of a Female Tramp (A–No. 1), 37
Adventures of a Scholar Tramp (Mullin), 35
African American(s), 3, 5, 15, 17, 48, 53, 75, 81, 84, 93, 102–105, 108–109, 111–112, 117–118, 120–122, 124–126, 128–133, 136, 138–139, 151, 159, 174, 211–218, 224, 248
Algren, Nelson, xxv, 60
ambient places, 22–23, 81
American Sociological Association, 14, 25, 244, 249
anarchism, 60, 236, 239, 241
Anderson, Nels, 15, 17, 26–28, 30, 32–37, 39–46, 48–49, 51–58, 60, 62, 64, 73, 76, 84, 91, 95, 174, 197
Anslinger, Harry J., 224–226
anthropology, xxvii, xxix, xxxi–xxxiii, 7–8, 13, 16–17, 102, 104–105, 107–108, 110, 118, 120–124, 126, 128, 134–135, 137, 138–139, 150, 173–174, 193–195, 197, 211, 225, 236, 252, 257–258

anthropometry, 40, 105, 118, 121–124, 126, 138–139
antipsychiatry movement, 13, 143, 158–160
antiwar activism, 163, 196, 234
Arbus, Diane, xxv, 156, 163
art therapy, 20, 154
Autry Museum, 65–66
Aycock and Lindsay turpentine camp, 115–116

Baldwin, James, 157, 164, 186
Barbie, 121, 126, 138–140
Barnard College, 102, 105, 122–123
Barracoon: The Story of the Last "Black Cargo" (Hurston), 134–135
Beatles, 186, 206, 209, 229, 234
Beats, 37, 139, 158, 207–208, 218, 246
Becker, Howard, xxiii, xxxiv, 11–13, 143, 195, 213, 224, 226, 236, 241–242
Being Mentally Ill (Scheff), 161–162
Benedict, Ruth, xxix, 105, 123–124, 134
Berkeley, California, 60, 161, 164, 206, 215, 234, 236, 245–246
Berry, Chuck, 132, 209
"Big Rock Candy Mountain" (song), 43, 53
Big Sweet, 114, 117
Binford, Jessica F., 74, 84, 86, 90

biological determinism, xxv, xxx, xxxiii, 2, 5–10, 12, 15–16, 23, 34, 36, 39, 58, 71, 75, 83, 94, 104, 108, 120, 122–123, 126, 138, 143, 146–147, 150–151, 160, 171, 173–175, 194, 210, 254, 257, 259, 261–262, 264–265
biomedicine, xxxi, 5, 12–13, 198
birth control, 60, 173, 207
black-and-tan clubs/cabarets, 16, 40, 59, 81, 132, 248
Black dolls (Saralee), 118, 120–122, 124–126, 136, 138–140
Black Panthers, 209, 225, 227, 232, 235
Boas, Franz, xxix, 7, 17, 105, 107–108, 122–123, 131
Bohemians, xxiv, 4, 33, 40, 61, 71, 78, 97, 207, 217–218, 238, 246, 250
Bordelon, Pamela, 111–113, 115–116, 132, 135
Bowen, Louise DeKoven, 74–75
Boxcar Bertha, 37, 50, 59–63
Boyd, Valerie, 107, 117
breastplate of righteousness, 181, 183, 185
Brown v. Board of Education, 12, 137
Burgess, Ernest, 2, 8, 16, 18, 25, 32–33, 41, 73, 75–77, 86, 145, 174

cannabis, 207–208, 224
capitalism, xxiv, xxvii, xxxii, 1, 4–5, 26–27, 29, 45, 50, 52, 54, 57, 67, 84, 91, 125–126, 140, 204, 220, 229, 231–234, 248, 260. *See also* outsider capitalism
Cavan, Sherri xxxi, 15, 17, 156, 160, 164, 206, 208, 213–223, 225–228, 231–232, 234–236, 244, 250, 256
Cappetti, Carla, xxiv, 155
Caribbean, 117, 127–128
caste, xxv, 6
Chaplin, Charlie, 51–52, 54, 59, 95
Chicago, Illinois, xxiv, xxvi, 17, 32–33, 40, 45–48, 52–53, 59–60, 64, 71–74, 77–79, 81–88, 91–92, 95, 97–100, 155, 177, 220, 248, 250
Chicago, University of (Chicago School), xxv–xxvi, xxxi, xxxv–xxxvi, 2, 7–9, 16–18, 25, 32–35, 40–41, 45–47, 55–56, 59–60, 71, 73, 75–77, 84–85, 87, 89–90, 92, 94, 97–98, 103, 127, 143, 145, 155, 174, 249
Chicago Daily Times, 84, 91
Chicago Tribune, 50, 87
City of Night (Rechy), 186–187
civil rights, 13, 125, 137–138, 159, 172, 183–184, 194, 206, 235
Civil War, American, 26, 73, 113, 127, 151, 227, 262
Clark, Kenneth and Mamie, 118, 125
classification, 5–6, 8, 12, 16, 40, 55, 120, 125–126, 137, 147, 159, 169, 173, 210
Cohen, Stanley, 50, 213, 235–236, 238, 241–242, 244, 263
Cold War, xxiii, 12, 121, 207
Columbia University, 102, 105, 123
communists, xxiii, 12, 54, 109, 207, 255
concentration camps, 145, 147, 156
conformity, xxiii, xxvii, 1–2, 5, 8, 11–12, 19, 24, 54, 96, 138–140, 180, 205–207, 209, 221, 227–228, 233, 235–236, 252, 260–261
conventionality, xxiii, xxx, xxxiii–xxxiv, 6, 27, 36, 38, 42, 44, 51, 83, 93–95, 98, 169, 180–181, 205, 209–210, 220, 222, 226, 228, 232, 235, 237, 247, 260
copyright laws, xxxvi, 43, 135
counterculture, 15, 37, 46, 138, 169, 182, 192, 204–205, 207–209, 211, 213, 218, 220–222, 224–225, 227–229, 231, 233–236, 239, 256, 260
Cream (rock group), 209, 222
Creech, Sara Lee, 120–122, 124
Cressey, Paul Goalby, 15, 17, 62, 70–71, 73–78, 80–100, 146, 174, 197
Cresswell, Tim, 16, 20
Crime and Community (Tannebaum), 9
criminals, 2, 9–11, 38, 40, 42, 50, 59, 122–123, 161, 172–173, 199, 225, 238–239, 241
criminology, 10, 238, 241
critical race theory and studies, xxxiii, 93, 137, 258, 264
culture industry, 155, 157
culture wars, xxviii, xxx, xxxiv, 195, 205, 235, 261–264

dance therapy, 20, 154
Darwinism, 25, 260

deinstitutionalization, 149, 153, 158–160
delinquents, xxiv, 7, 10, 34, 202
D'Emilio, John, xxxii, 4, 193
Democrats, 183
DePastino, Todd, 30, 46, 48, 51
depressions (economic), 30–31, 34, 37–38, 53–54, 109, 179
determinism, xxx, xxxiii, 6–8, 12, 36, 39, 94, 108, 120, 126, 138, 143, 160, 171, 173, 175, 259, 261–262
deviance studies, xxvii–xxxviii, xxx, 2–3, 11, 19–20, 24–25, 236, 238, 258–259
Didion, Joan, xxiii, 211–212, 214, 216
Diggers, 219–220, 232–233
dirty work, 35, 87–88
Dix, Dorothea, 144–145, 154
Doors, the (rock group), 208, 222, 231, 247
Doors of Perception, The (Huxley), 208
Douglas, Jack, 13, 16
Downes, David, 236, 242
drag world, 186, 195–197, 230
drug use, 199, 208, 211, 216, 225, 235
Du Bois, W. E. B., 7, 23–24, 34, 84, 104, 108, 133–134
Dust Tracks on a Road (Hurston), 117, 124, 132

Eastern Europeans, xxvi, 48, 53, 85, 95, 252–254
Easy Rider (film), 211, 224
Eatonville, Florida, xxiv, xxxv, 102–103, 105, 107, 111–113, 128–131, 136–137
Echols, Alice, 209, 228, 234–235, 243
Ellis, Havelock, 40, 42–44, 98, 173
erased scholars, 84, 134–135, 217
essentialism, xxvii–xxviii, xxxiii–xxxiv, 5, 7–8, 15, 23, 34–36, 39–40, 44, 73, 89, 93, 149, 175, 258–259, 261–262
ethnography, xxv–xxix, xxxi–xxxv, 2–3, 5, 7, 11, 13, 15–17, 19–22, 24, 32, 39, 61, 76, 93–94, 102–105, 107–108, 111, 114–115, 117–118, 121, 127, 130–132, 134–135, 137, 141, 143, 145, 156, 159, 163, 169, 171, 173–175, 185–188, 190–193, 195, 198, 200, 213, 215–216, 223, 240, 249, 252–253, 256–257, 259, 262, 265
eugenics, xxv, 6–7, 34, 40, 55, 71, 75, 108, 120, 146–147, 171, 173, 254, 259–262
Eureka Dancing Academy, 81, 86, 89

Farrell, James T., xxv, 60
fascism, xxxvii, 263
Federal Bureau of Investigation (FBI), 13–14, 24–25, 74, 225, 264
Federal Writers' Project (FWP), 107, 109–111, 113–117, 135
female impersonators, 195–196, 219, 249
Filipinos, 71, 80, 82, 85, 88–89, 95, 101
Fillmore, 208, 217, 220, 223
Florida, University of, xxxv–xxxvi, 106, 110, 119
Florida: A Guide to the Southernmost State, 110–113, 117
Forest Park, St. Louis, Missouri, 17, 20, 177–179, 198
Fort Pierce, Florida, xxxv, 102–103, 135
Foucault, Michel, 3, 258
Frank, Thomas, 4, 233
freaks, xxv, 156, 196, 206
free love, 61, 204–205, 211
freight trains, 16, 29, 32, 35–36, 38, 49, 50, 54, 129
Freud, Sigmund, 148, 210
Fromm, Erich, 8, 12, 108

Gagnon, John, 174, 257
gangsters, 78, 90, 249
gay canon, 109, 171, 192–193, 197
Gender Advertisements (Goffman), 156, 165–166
genetics, 34, 120, 147, 259–262
Gieryn, Thomas, 18, 177
Ginsberg, Allen, 158, 207
Giovanni's Room (Baldwin), 157, 164
glory holes, 22, 180, 184, 202–203
Goffman, Erving, xxxi, 11, 15–16, 20–21, 24–25, 88, 126, 139, 141, 149, 152–154, 159, 161–164, 166, 171, 175, 180, 186, 195, 206, 213–215, 242, 244
Golden Girls, The (television show), 256–257
Goldman, Emma, 60–61
Gornick, Vivian, 156, 166
Gouldner, Alvin, 189–190, 258

graffiti, 26, 45, 48, 66–67, 203
Grateful Dead (rock group), 220, 223, 225, 230
Gravenites, Linda, 228, 230
Great Migration, 48, 53, 117
Greenwood, Victoria, 239, 242, 244

Hacking, Ian, 5, 38, 55, 173, 221
Haight Ashbury, xxvi, 16–17, 204, 206, 208, 211, 213–223, 225–226, 228, 230–234, 236, 244, 246–247, 250–251; Free Clinic, 219–221
Harlem, 123, 130, 136; Harlem Renaissance, xxiii, 102, 105
Heap, Chad, 41, 89, 98, 174, 250
Hendrix, Jimi, 228, 234
Herskovits, Melville, 105, 122–123
heteronormativity, 36, 71, 180, 183, 205
heterosexuality, xxxii, 4, 27, 40–44, 80, 82, 95, 98, 139, 169, 173–176, 188, 190–192, 210, 250
Hinton, S. E., xxiii–xxiv
Hippies of the Haight (Cavan), 204, 206, 246
"Hippie Tour" (Gray Line tour company), 221, 248, 250
Hirschfeld, Magnus, 40, 88
Hobo College, 30, 52, 59
Hobo Convention, xxxv, 26
hobohemia, 17, 32–33, 37, 39, 43–46, 48, 52–53, 56–57, 59, 130, 145, 248
hobo women, 29, 34, 37–39, 44, 48, 55, 59, 61
Holocaust, 12, 254, 265
homophobia, 61, 187, 193–194, 197, 243
homosexuality, 7, 9, 40–44, 56, 61, 88, 99, 159, 169, 171, 173–176, 181, 184, 186, 191, 193, 202, 207, 218–219, 225, 238–240, 257
Hoover, J. Edgar, 13, 24–25, 225, 264
Howard University, 105–106, 121, 134
Hughes, Everett, 10, 17, 35, 88, 145
Hughes, Langston, 123, 127, 135–136
Hull House, 7, 34, 74–75, 84, 100
Human Sexual Response (Masters and Johnson), 172
Humphreys, Laud, xxxi, xxxv, 15, 17, 19–20, 22, 160, 169, 171–192, 197–203

Hurston, Zora Neale, xxvi, xxix, xxxi, xxxv, 15, 17, 102–132, 173, 197
hustlers, 7, 11, 101, 176, 186–187, 201–202

imagination: anthropological, 104–105; emotional, 168; ethnographic, xxxii–xxxiii, 257; sociological, xxvii, 160, 239, 252
immigrant(s), xxvi, xxxi, xxxiv, xxxvii, 3, 5, 7, 8, 10, 15, 46, 48, 53, 71, 73–75, 77, 80, 82–87, 95, 119, 122–123, 248, 250, 253–255, 257, 260, 262
incarceration, 34, 160, 262
Industrial Workers of the World (IWW) (Wobblies), 10, 53–54
inmates, xxxi, 141, 143, 145, 147, 150, 153, 155, 157, 164, 167
insanity, 144–145, 148, 150, 152–153, 155, 157, 159–161, 163, 208, 225
institutionalization, 6, 34, 40, 147, 149, 151–153, 155, 157–159, 171, 173, 202, 242, 260
institutional review boards (IRBs), 93, 171, 188, 198–199, 201
interaction membrane 22, 180
interracial relationships, 81, 89, 120–121, 172
Israel Levin Center, Venice Beach, California, 253–254

Jackson, Stevi, 239, 242
Jazz, 71, 75, 132, 207–208, 224
Jefferson Airplane, 204, 213, 221, 228, 231, 247
Jews, xxvi, xxxi, xxxiv, 7, 9–10, 15, 173, 252–254, 257, 265
Jim Crow, 6, 103, 105, 112–113, 115, 118, 121, 123, 128–129, 254, 262–263
Johnson, Virginia, 172, 175
Johnson–Reed Immigration Act of 1924, 6, 254
Jonah's Gourd Vine (Hurston), 107, 128
jook joints, 16, 117, 131–132, 262
Joplin, Janis, 209, 227–230, 233–234, 247
jungles, 36, 39, 45, 49, 52, 54, 81
Juvenile Protection Association (JPA), 44, 56, 73–75, 77, 82–84, 91

Kennedy, Stetson, 106, 111, 113, 115–116, 132–133
Kesey, Ken, 139, 208
King, Charles, xxix, 108, 123
Kinsey, Alfred, 172, 183
Kirkbride, Thomas, 144–145, 151–152, 161
Ku Klux Klan, 116, 132, 254

labeling/labeling theory, xxxiv, 10–13, 23, 143, 147–148, 159, 161, 169, 236, 238
lady lovers, 60, 101
Laing, R. D., 146, 159
Lawndale Hospital, 60, 76
Lemert, Edwin, 2, 10–11, 156, 162
lesbians, xxxvi, 12–13, 38, 44, 59, 61–62, 78, 97–99, 101, 159, 173, 192–196, 205, 207, 235, 250
Life Magazine, 125, 208, 237
Lindner, Robert, 1, 4, 260
Linkletter, Eve, 96–97
Lippincott, J. B., 60, 107
Little Tramp (Chaplin), 51–52, 54, 59
Livingstone, David, 3, 19
lobotomies, 156, 158
London, England, 50, 193–194, 230; School of Economics xxxvi, 194, 238
London, Jack, 29, 35–36, 43, 48–49, 62, 64
loneliness, 51, 71, 83–84, 87, 94, 97–99
Los Angeles, California, 26, 57, 63–64, 66, 68, 87, 97, 177, 214, 253, 265
LSD, 208, 211, 216, 220
lynching, 42, 108, 138

Mad magazine, xxv, 139
madness, 143, 145–146, 149, 152, 155–156, 158–159, 167–168, 224, 226
making up people, 5, 55, 173
mapping, 71, 84–85, 110
marginality, xxiii–xxvi, xxviii–xxxv, 4, 7–11, 13, 15–17, 22–23, 25, 27, 32, 34, 55–56, 59, 63, 69, 71, 75, 81–82, 87–88, 91–92, 94–96, 98, 103, 117–118, 130, 133, 135–138, 145, 156, 160–161, 163, 171, 176, 186, 191–193, 196–197, 204–205, 213, 215, 236, 238, 242, 248–250, 253–259, 263, 265

marijuana, xxiv, 207, 220, 224–226, 242
Mark, Mary Ellen, 156, 163
Marxism, 189, 236, 238–241
Masters, William, 172, 175
Mattel, 138–140
McCarthyism, xxiii, 12, 24, 184, 207
McIntosh, Mary, 193–197, 236, 244
Mead, Margaret, xxix, 108, 173
media, 1, 50, 53, 63, 66–67, 109, 186, 196, 205–206, 210–211, 213, 217, 233, 238
medicalization, xxxi, 5, 40, 143, 146–149, 159, 173, 210–211, 213, 261
Melville, Herman, 156–157, 164
mental hospitals, 20, 24, 146, 148–150, 152, 155–160, 163
mental illness, 10, 143, 146–149, 151, 153, 155, 157–160, 162, 199, 211
mental patients, xxvi, xxxi, 11, 15, 143, 150, 156, 159, 260
Meyerowitz, Joanne, 8, 74, 80, 92, 94–96
Miami, Florida, 103, 117, 127, 132, 181, 256
Miami Herald, 117–118
migratory workers, 30, 32, 53
Milgram, Stanley, 12, 201
Mills, C. Wright, xxvii, xxxiii, 12, 170, 191, 239, 252
misfits, xxxiii, 60, 84, 94, 98, 116, 149, 161, 228, 260
Mod (fashion style), 227, 240
modernity, xxvi–xxviii, 1, 3–5, 8–9, 16, 29, 38, 51, 57, 78, 84, 210, 229, 261
Modern Times (film), 54, 59
monikers/monicas, 50, 64–66
Monterey International Pop Festival, 208, 230–231
moral entrepreneurs, 11, 23, 50, 143, 171, 184–185, 213, 238, 257, 259
moral panic (Cohen), 50, 201, 213, 226, 236, 238, 263
mortification, 20, 145, 150–151, 155, 157
Mother Camp (Newton), 195, 197
Mules and Men (Hurston), 107, 111, 130
music, xxiii–xxiv, 50–53, 70, 75, 78, 94, 109, 132, 186, 206–209, 222–225, 228–231, 233–235, 242, 247

Myerhoff, Barbara, xxxi, 15–16, 252–258, 265

National Deviancy Conference (NDC), 194, 213, 236, 238–244
National Institute of Mental Health (NIMH), 145, 198
Nazis, 7, 12, 120, 147, 156, 173, 210, 254, 259
negroes, 10, 84, 104–105, 107–108, 110–112, 116–117, 120–121, 124–126, 129, 131–133, 135–136, 152, 250
New Deal, 74, 108
Newsweek 125,225
Newton, Esther, xxxi, 193, 195–197
New York City, New York, xxxvi, 10, 105, 125, 163, 166, 192, 226, 244
New York Times, 67, 98, 103, 132, 189
nonconformity, xxv, xxviii, xxxiv, 1–2, 4, 8, 27, 51, 54–55, 71, 98, 140, 146, 152, 159, 186, 195–196, 204–205, 209, 213, 227–230, 233, 235, 250–252, 260–261
nuclear families, xxx, xxxii–xxxiii, 4, 27, 36, 39, 44, 54, 169, 180, 187, 192, 204, 210
Number Our Days (documentary film), xxxi, 252, 255, 257, 264–265
"nuts, sluts, and perverts," 11, 13, 245

Ocoee, Florida, 112–113
Oldenburg, Ray, 22, 130
One Flew Over the Cuckoo's Nest (Kesey), 139, 143, 155, 158, 161, 163, 208
Outcast Narratives (Reitman), 60
outsiders: outsider capitalism xxiv, xxvii, xxxii, 4–5, 54, 125–126, 140, 229, 233–234, 248, 260; *Outsiders* (Becker), xxiii, 11–12, 143; *The Outsider* (Colin Wilson), xxiii; *The Outsider* (Richard Wright), xxiii, 126; *The Outsiders* (Lena Dunham), xxiii; *The Outsiders* (S.E. Hinton), xxiii

Park, Robert, 8–10, 16, 18, 23, 33, 41, 45, 76, 105, 108, 145, 174, 249
participant observation, 32, 76, 200, 216
pathology, xxv, 2, 8, 10–11, 13, 26–27, 34–36, 40, 50–51, 67, 148–149, 159, 162, 171, 173, 210–211, 223, 235–236, 245, 262
Patterson, Tiffany, 114–115, 117, 130
Phillips, Susan, 46, 48, 63–66, 68
Plummer, Ken, 239–240, 242–244
Polarization, xxxvii, 235, 262–264
Polk County, Florida, 103, 107, 111, 114, 116–117, 131–132
popular culture, xxiv–xxv, 26–27, 37, 50, 54–55, 60, 70, 80, 93–95, 97, 156, 158, 161, 186, 196, 206, 256–258
positivism, xxv, 8, 12, 24
post-modernism, 143, 160
poststructuralism, xxviii, 9, 137, 176
pot, 207, 224–226, 235, 239
Pound, Ezra, 153–154
Presley, Elvis, 132, 209, 234
prisons, 43, 60, 113, 145, 150, 156–157, 160, 163, 199
Prohibition, 59, 71–72, 246
promiscuity, 6, 44, 74, 100–101, 147, 152, 211
prostitution, 10–11, 24, 39, 41–42, 44, 48, 56, 60, 74, 96, 100–101, 174, 249
psychedelics, 207–208, 216, 219–223, 231, 233, 248
Psychedelic Shop, 219–220, 233
psychiatry, 1, 5, 10–11, 13, 23, 55, 108, 143–151, 153, 155, 158–160, 173, 184, 210–211, 235, 245
psychology, 5, 10, 12, 39, 143, 146–149, 174, 208, 210, 235
public restrooms, 17, 22, 81–82, 129, 176–181, 184, 187, 202–203
public sex, xxvi, xxx–xxxi, 16, 169, 171, 175–176, 179, 182, 184–185, 188, 203

queerness, xxviii, xxix, xxxiii, 2, 9, 36–37, 59, 63, 93, 97, 99, 137, 143, 171, 175–176, 192, 210, 258–259
"Queers and Peers, The Social Integration of" (Reiss), 174, 187, 201–202

race science, xxv, xxvii–xxviii, xxxi–xxxii, xxxiv, 2–3, 6–8, 12, 15, 27, 34, 58, 71, 77, 84, 108, 120, 171, 210, 254, 258, 262, 264
racial identities, 99, 131, 209
railroads, 29–30, 33–35, 37–38, 45–46,

48–50, 64, 67, 73, 78, 109, 127–129, 248, 259
Rainwater, Lee, 176, 198
Reagan, Ronald, 160, 184, 215, 235
Rechy, John, 186–187, 202
Reckless, Walter, 39, 174
reefer, 207, 224–226
Reis, Martha Lynn, 61–62
Reiss, Albert, 174, 187, 201–202
Reitman, Ben, 32, 37, 41, 52–53, 56, 59–62, 220, 249
Richardson, Heather Cox 262–263
Riesman, David, 12, 83
right-wing activism, 172, 182, 184, 195
Roosevelt, Eleanor, 121–122, 124–125
Rosenhan, David, 148–149
rule-makers, xxxiv, 15, 23, 196

Salerno, Roger, xxv, 60, 76, 94
Sanctified Church, 16, 131–133
San Francisco, California, 65, 164–165, 194, 206, 208, 211, 216, 218, 221, 223, 226, 230, 244–245, 248
San Francisco Chronicle, 206, 233, 248
Sarton, May, 214, 252, 257
Saturday Evening Post, 52, 107, 211–212, 214
Scheff, Thomas, 146, 161–163
scientific racism, xxv–xxvi, 3, 5–8, 39–40, 73, 94, 104, 108, 120, 122, 126, 147, 173, 252, 259, 262
scientific sexism, 39–40, 173
sexology, 40, 42–43, 98, 172–173
sex research, 40, 88, 90, 172, 187, 193, 197–8
sexual culture, 40, 43, 71, 80, 87, 171–172, 185–186, 191, 207
sexual identity, 174–175, 180, 202, 258
sexual pleasure, 39, 80, 87, 96, 171–172
sexual politics, 172, 190
Shimmy (dance), 88, 101, 222
Simmel, Georg, 7, 9–10, 23, 29, 145, 222, 252–253, 257
Sister of the Road: The Autobiography of Boxcar Bertha, 59, 61–63
slumming/slumming tours, 80, 98–99, 196, 221, 247–250
Small Room, The (Sarton), 214
Smith, Bessie, 114, 209

Smith, Chris, 72
Snake Pit, The (Ward, also a film), 155, 157, 164
social agents, 19, 127, 145, 150
social constructionism, 9, 39, 143, 160, 175, 193
social control, 24, 141, 143, 145, 147–149, 151, 160, 171, 173, 176, 191
socialists, 196, 254
social knowledge, xxv–xxxii, 3, 5, 12, 16, 23, 33, 71, 126, 192, 206, 221, 235, 252, 261, 264
social margins xxiv, xxxiv, 4, 13, 23, 71, 75, 147, 163, 248
social networks, 5, 147, 225
Social Pathology (Lemert), 10, 162
social reform, xxxii, 27, 37, 40–43, 50–51, 71, 73–74, 87, 91, 174, 249
societal reaction, 10, 23
sociobiology, 259–260
"sociology noir," xxv, 56, 60
Souls of Black Folk, The (Du Bois), 24
South Side (dance), 82, 222
spatial metaphors, 17, 22–23, 77, 84, 150, 176, 180–181
St. Elizabeths Hospital, xxx, 20–21, 141, 143–146, 151–155, 158–160
sterilization, 34, 147, 173
Stigma: Notes on the Management of Spoiled Identity (Goffman), 11, 24, 126, 143
stigmatization, xix–xx, xxiv–xxvi, xxx, xxviii, xxxi–xxxii, xxxv, 11, 13, 20, 23–24, 31, 35, 40, 55–56, 58, 73, 87–91, 95, 143, 147–148, 159, 161, 171, 181–182, 185, 187, 190–192, 196–197, 199–200, 211, 225, 236, 250, 258–265
St. Louis, Missouri, xxxv, 17, 19–20, 177–178, 189, 199
stoned, 207, 219, 224, 232, 236
Straight Theater, 219–220, 223
strange, stranger(s), strangeness xxv–xxviii, xxxi–xxxv, 2, 4, 7–10, 15, 23, 29, 56, 83–84, 96, 103, 105, 167, 205, 221–222, 224, 227, 229, 232, 235, 245, 248–249, 252–254, 257–258, 261
subcultures, 4, 13, 16, 29–30, 59, 169, 186–187, 194, 197, 211, 217, 236, 238, 240, 255

Summer of Love, 219, 226, 233, 251
Supreme Court, 120, 125, 129, 137, 147, 186, 207
surveillance, 13, 24, 74, 141, 181, 184, 264
Swedlund, Alan, 121–122, 139–140
symbolic interactionism, 13, 143, 174–175, 202, 213
syphilis, 50, 198, 201, 249
Szasz, Thomas, 146, 159

Tannenbaum, Frank, 9–10
Taxi-Dance Hall, The (Cressey), xxxi, 71, 73, 77, 83, 85–89, 91–94
Taylor, Ian, 236, 240–241
Taylor, Laurie, 194, 236, 238–239, 241–243
tearooms, xxxv–xxvi, 16–17, 19–20, 22, 169–203
Tearoom Trade (Humphreys), 17, 20, 169–172, 174–177, 179, 181–183, 185, 187–192, 194, 198–199, 201, 203
"Ten Cents a Dance" (song by Etting, movie, novel by Fletcher), 89, 95, 97
territories of the self, 22, 141, 150
Their Eyes Were Watching God (Hurston), 107, 111–112, 132
Thelin, Ron and Jay, 220, 233
third places, 22, 130–131, 133
Thomas, W.I., 8, 41, 87, 174
Thorazine (chlorpromazine), 158–159
Time magazine, 140, 207–208, 211, 228
tramps, 26, 29–31, 34–35, 37–38, 42–44, 49–52, 54, 58–59, 64, 73, 95, 211
transgressions, xxx, 3–4, 20–22, 38, 51, 54–55, 75, 81, 95–97, 103, 151–152, 156, 161, 169, 186–187, 191–192, 204–205, 213, 216, 219, 224–225, 230, 234, 236–237, 239, 250
turpentine, 103, 110, 114–117, 127, 131–132, 145
Tuskegee, 9, 198

Un-American Activities, House Committee on (HUAC), 109, 194
undercover observation, 149, 181, 213

underdogs, 13, 58, 155, 161, 172, 189, 191, 196, 236
UNESCO, 120, 124, 126
Unfinished Business: Notes of a Chronic Re-reader (Gornick), 166
urban tourism, 248, 250
Urla, Jacqueline, 6, 121–122, 139–140

venereal disease, 41–42, 60
Venice Beach senior center, xxvi, 16, 23, 252–255, 264
vice, 17, 41, 56, 74, 185, 249
Victorians, 75, 216–217, 227, 224
Vietnam War, 183, 206, 213, 234
von Krafft-Ebing, Richard, 40, 42, 98, 173

Walker, Alice, 102, 110, 135–137
Wandering Women (Reitman), 60
Ward, Mary Jane, 157, 164
"Ward Six" (Chekov), 167–168
Warren, Carol, 188, 214
Washington, DC, xxx, 20, 113, 138, 141–142, 144–146, 226
Washington Post, 171, 194
Washington University, 17, 20, 171, 177, 189, 198
Weeks, Jeffrey, 194, 243
Well of Loneliness, The (Hall), 83, 97–99
West, American, 30, 65–67
White supremacy, 71, 118, 121, 128, 133, 264
"Whose Side Are We On?" (Becker), 12
Wilson, Colin, xxiii–xxiv
women adrift, 73, 77, 85, 94–95
Women and Madness (Chesler), 152
Woodstock, 204, 235
Works Progress Administration (WPA), 109–110, 112–113, 116, 179, 263
World War II, 1, 121, 147, 207, 210, 259
Wright, Richard, xxiii, xxv, 60, 108–109, 126, 136, 139

Yiddish culture, 253–255
Young, Jock, 240–244